The Rise and Fall of *Rock* Radio

by RICHARD NEER

For Vicky

Foreword

ALL I REMEMBER is waking up one morning in 1967 and the whole world had changed.

I'd love to paint you a sky-opening Voice from the Heavens melodramatic picture of it, but the truth is, I can't remember it. And put that smirk away because I wouldn't start smokin' dope until the cops busted me for being the only long-haired freak in town and planted marijuana in my cigarette pack and that was still a year away.

Let's back up a bit.

Things were going along alright. In 1964, AM radio was the only radio and there was nothing wrong with that. With the cold dread of high school ahead of me and puberty kickin' my ass from behind, radio was the only thing making any sense to me.

What helped a lot was the Beatles and the Rolling Stones having a new hit single every three months and the Kinks, Animals, Byrds, and Dave

Clark Five keeping up with them. Throw in seven or eight classic Motown acts and a few legendary James Browns, Curtis Mayfields, Arethas, and a Sam and Dave or two and, well you get the idea. It was the beginning of nine or so glorious years when the best music being made was also the most commercial. We had stumbled into a renaissance and I, a pimply, horny thirteen-year-old struggling to press the strings down on my grandfather's old acoustic guitar, had turned the magic dial on my little transistor radio and found God.

So things weren't bad.

And then it happened.

Was it a friend who suggested it? An advertisement somewhere? A predestined, primordial, physical compunction? I wish I could remember it for you. Anyway, for whatever reason, and I swear it seemed like it happened all across the country at the same moment, a whole generation of American kids noticed a never-used switch on our radios and flicked it from AM to FM.

And the world changed in a Paulie Walnuts snap of the fingers.

Alright maybe it wasn't as dramatic back then as it obviously is now. I mean the new art form of rock had quietly arrived in 1965 with Bob Dylan, the Beatles, and the Rolling Stones all influencing each other and forever changing pop music into a means of personal expression. Nobody noticed until *Sgt. Pepper,* but it was there. So maybe it was a smooth transition rather than the cultural explosion we can so clearly see in retrospect.

What that crazy kid Dylan would introduce to the Beatles and Stones was consciousness. When the reality-based personal and cultural themes of folk and blues music (Dylan) got mixed together with the accessibility of pop melody, pop structure, and rampant pubescent sexuality (Beatles) and shaken not stirred by streetwise cynical attitude and the dirty long-haired rebellion of rock guitars (Stones) you got consciousness flowing into mainstream media for the first time ever.

And FM would quickly become that mainstream media.

The difference between AM and FM was dramatic, obvious from day one.

FM was quieter, even though the music was often louder. Peaceful, while it spoke of revolution. Slower, while we evolved at an inconceivably rapid pace.

It was important. Just as the new rock music had transcended the pop

LIBRARY OF CONGRESS CATALOGING-IN-PUBLICATION DATA

Neer, Richard.
    FM : the rise and fall of rock radio / Richard Neer.
        p.   cm.
    ISBN 0-679-46295-3
    1. Neer, Richard.   2. Disc jockeys—New York (State)—New
York—Biography.   3. Rock music—History and criticism.
    4. WNEW (Radio station : New York, N.Y.)—Anecdotes.   I. Title.
    ML429.N44 A3   2001
    791.44'028'092—dc21   2001033251
    [B]

Villard Books website address: www.villard.com

Printed in the United States of America on acid-free paper

9   8   7   6   5   4   3   2

FIRST EDITION

Book design by Judith Stagnitto Abbate/Abbate Design

VILLARD | NEW YORK

music of the past's sole purpose to entertain and had become important and culturally essential and influential.

The DJs on AM radio were great. They represented the exuberance and exultation of the times. It was a 1950s sensibility that celebrated a then-brand-new form of pop music called rock and roll and a historically new paradigm where teenagers were separated from their parents and given a social distinction of their own for the first time in history.

The FM DJs were very different and would represent the sixties birth of consciousness. There were textures and tones to their voices that we'd never heard on radio before. They had distinct personalities, they seemed younger—certainly hipper, they were relaxed and took their time, and they communicated a sensibility that was both intimate and intellectual without condescension.

Rock music had become my religion. Radio my church. And these DJs my priests, rabbis, and gurus. They would preach from the gospel of Dylan, Lennon and McCartney, Jagger and Richards, the Book of Townshend, the Song of the Byrds, and the Acts of Davies. The New Testament would include Procol Harum, Them, Traffic, Cream, the Jeff Beck Group, Buffalo Springfield, Jefferson Airplane, Jimi Hendrix, and Led Zeppelin. After *Sgt. Pepper* it was the Exodus of singles and the Revelations of albums. And we listened and listened and listened and learned.

102.7 WNEW was our local Temple of Solomon and somehow radio stations just like it were popping up in every major city simultaneously like a planned invasion from outer space. And with them a new generation of DJs, our generation, speaking to us. Personally. Understanding as only we understood. Inspiring us, motivating us, conjuring up images and stimulating the senses as only radio can do when it is in the hands of the righteous.

And then it was over.

The Renaissance would end with either the Who's "Won't Get Fooled Again" in 1971 or the Stones' *Exile on Main Street* in 1972, take your pick. Righteous Rock Radio would continue on a bit longer, struggling valiantly into the eighties, and die quietly in the nineties like a spent stick of incense.

In its place, anybody twenty-one years old or younger inherited a wasteland of corporate conservatism tightly controlling lifeless depersonalized deregionalized homogenized DJs spewing out depersonalized deregionalized homogenized playlists or adolescent talk reflecting the toxic digital apolitical robotic culture they think we've become.

Do I seem upset?

Oh, there's a few small candles in the stygian darkness. A Bill Kelly on FMU, an Arnie Pritchett on NYU, a Vin Scelsa on FUV. But they are kept far away from the mainstream where their disease that is called passion won't infect the masses.

How could this happen? you might reasonably ask. You mean like "acceptable" levels of pollution or arsenic in our water? Good question.

Video killed the radio star. Did it also kill radio?

Well . . . yeah, but it had a lot of help. I'm as curious as you are.

As luck would have it, I happened to have a good friend who was there. Let's read his book.

Little Steven
4:30 A.M., April 2, 2001
radio off

ACKNOWLEDGMENTS

IN ADDITION TO being main actors in creating the phenomenon of progressive radio, the following people were vital contributors in telling this story, submitting to hours of questions, reliving good times, and having the courage to recount the tough ones:

From WNEW-FM—Scott Muni, Bill "Rosko" Mercer, Dave Herman, Jonathan Schwartz, John Zacherle, Dennis Elsas, Tony Pigg, Marty Martinez, Vicky Callahan, Peter Larkin, Vin Scelsa, Ken Dashow, Jim Monaghan, and Dan Neer.

Terry Malia from Mel Karmazin's office. Charles Laquidara and Marc Parenteau, once of WBCN. Charlie Kendall of Click Radio. Ted Utz of SFX. Jo Maeder of many stations. Mark Chernoff at WFAN. Bonnie Simmons, once of KSAN. Michael Harrison of *Talkers* magazine. Bruce Morrow, a radio legend who gave freely of his time and advice. Lee Abrams and Dave Logan of XM. The Museum of Television and Radio. Kid Leo and Jim DelBalzo of Sony Records. Steve Friedman of CBS. Steven "Silvio" Van Zandt for constant inspiration.

To my father for introducing me to radio and my mother for her many sacrifices along the way.

I'm greatly indebted to my editor, Bruce Tracy, and all the folks at Villard—Katie Zug, Janet Wygal, and Diane Frost—who guided me through the process.

Special thanks to David Black, who convinced me that there was a story to be told and had faith in my ability to tell it.

Contents

FM

The Promise

I LAY AWAKE for a sunrise that never broke through the clouds. I hadn't slept much the night before. Most of the weekend I had been awake, preparing for today—the most important day of my life—all twenty-one years of it.

Not every day you think is going to be pivotal toward your future turns out that way. How often do life-changing days happen with no warning, no chance to prepare? An anonymous driver swerves into your lane. An unknown IRS agent decides that you are the one to be audited. The results of a PSA test come in. Or on the plus side—the lottery calls your number. A major headhunter hears from an old college chum that you are the perfect candidate to head a large corporation. The dot-com stock you buy early is unexpectedly acquired by Microsoft.

But this Monday morning in March of 1971, I was sure that in a few hours the course of my life and that of my best friend would be changed. Michael Harrison and I lived in a small apartment above a bakery in Oceanside, Long Island, and had shared many adventures together. For the past two years, he and I had put in sixteen-hour days at WLIR-FM, a small suburban radio station. We'd slept at the station more nights than we cared to remember, sometimes because we were working late, sometimes because we had no place to live. We'd missed meals, desperately trying to make it until the next paycheck with only change in our pockets. We'd often devote hours to meticulous strategy planning, designed to convince our boss at WLIR that we merited an extra twenty-five cents per hour.

We made these sacrifices for one ultimate goal: to get a job at WNEW-FM—real *New York* radio, with studios in Manhattan, where the stars of every type of showbiz lived and played. And now *this* day could be the payoff for those months of deprivation, or it could sentence us to a longer term of penance before we could deserve another shot at nirvana.

In 1971, the absolute coolest place to work in radio was WNEW-FM. The disc jockeys had total freedom to play whatever records they chose. They could say what they wanted, whenever they wanted. They didn't need to put on ballsy radio voices; they spoke like real people, with regional accents or immature timbres. Some were intelligent, others sexy or funny. They brought themselves to the airwaves unvarnished—what you heard was what they were.

They made comfortable salaries, although not the megabucks of AM radio superstars. They came from different places, different experiences. Some were veterans of the Top Forty wars who'd tired of the battle, some were freshly out of college and idealistically striving to reinvent a medium that had grown old and irrelevant. A couple were entertainers from other fields who had sought to be actors or poets, but found a haven in a darkened studio behind a microphone. Some were handsome, some had been cursed with faces made for radio. But collectively, they formed a dream team that the cognoscenti acknowledged as the industry's pinnacle. And due to a unique set of circumstances, Harrison and I had talked ourselves into believing that we were ready to join their ranks.

We'd had two opportunities over the past year, but they'd proven ephemeral. There was our unsuccessful attempt to get to WNEW-FM through a side entrance by beseeching Metromedia Group president George Duncan for a job at one of the company's out-of-town outlets.

Duncan presided over several stations, in places like Philadelphia, Los Angeles, and San Francisco, as well as New York. We figured if we could impress the company at one of its far outposts, we might earn a ticket back to WNEW-FM within a reasonable period of time. But we'd blown the interview with Duncan.

At the time, John Lennon had released a song called "Working Class Hero." It was a bitter, self-deprecating view of his life and the whole idea of being known as an ex-Beatle. It contains the line, "You're still fucking peasants as far as I can see." Many underground stations were playing it. Some bleeped out the offending lyric, some reversed the word, and a few played it uncensored.

The FCC was not happy with progressive radio: Richard Nixon was constantly vilified and its strident antiwar political bent chafed the administration. As we now know, the president didn't hesitate to punish his enemies with whatever means were at his disposal. The FCC issued warnings that licenses could be at stake if lyric content was deemed objectionable—either obscene or condoning illicit activity, mainly drug use. In fear of governmental discipline, George Duncan had banned innocuous songs like Brewer and Shipley's "One Toke over the Line," or the Grateful Dead's "Uncle John's Band" (containing the phrase "Goddamn, well I declare"). Though he could be profane himself, he didn't want anything to endanger the Metromedia broadcast empire.

But we weren't aware of this conservative approach and when Duncan casually brought up "Working Class Hero," asking how we were handling it at WLIR-FM, I blurted out, "We're playing it uncut. Our audience deserves to hear an artist like John Lennon as he intends to be heard. And the song's message is far from obscene."

The interview continued for a few minutes thereafter, but my impulsive answer troubled me the rest of the way. Duncan graciously said that changes were always happening at Metromedia, so that even though nothing was available now, he'd consider us in the future. Several months had passed and we hadn't heard anything, so we assumed we were out of the running.

We'd also interviewed at CBS, another company that controlled radio stations, although none so desirable as Metromedia's stable of progressive stations. CBS held on to vestiges of conventional AM radio: a more upbeat, insincere style with music that was programmed by one director; the individual jocks holding no sway over what they played. Our strategy was to take over one of their less profitable stations and build it up to the point that Metromedia would have to take notice and hire us away.

Those attempts had proven fruitless; we were seen as too independent to work within the buttoned-down CBS corporate structure. Harrison and I were beginning to lose faith, feeling condemned to work in radio's hinterlands forever, never tasting the sweet freedom that WNEW-FM offered. But the preceding Friday night, we heard Rosko, the station's star attraction, resign on the air. Bill "Rosko" Mercer was a fixture on nighttime radio in New York, a spiritual black man who read poetry and spoke eloquently against the war with words and music. At that moment, however, we put the cultural significance of his resignation aside and concentrated on what it meant to us: There was an opening at WNEW-FM! As we listened to subsequent shifts, it became apparent to us that no successor was imminent.

So Michael and I spent the entire weekend at the WLIR studios in Hempstead, Long Island, honing audition tapes and crafting résumés for an all-out assault on New York. We planned to camp out on program director Scott Muni's doorstep at 230 Park Avenue in Manhattan by seven that Monday morning. From there, we'd improvise our way in to plead our case. Muni is another broadcasting legend, who had worked at both WMCA and WABC, New York radio's Top Forty giants, before alighting at WNEW-FM. He had a deep gravelly voice, and knew the Beatles personally (as well as every other top musician of the day). We feared that he'd laugh at our hubris and throw us out on our ears, but we were naïvely determined to try.

Since our interview with George Duncan, we realized that if we were to err, it had to be on the side of conservatism. To that end, we dressed in business suits (the only ones we had, accepted in payment for an in-store appearance). Any question about "Working Class Hero" would be answered noncommittally, if at all.

By that morning, Michael and I were fully prepared to be told that Mr. Muni had a full day scheduled: a morning meeting with Robert Plant, lunch with Eric Clapton, and dinner with Joe Cocker. But we hoped that if we were there when he first arrived, he might take pity and squeeze us in during his morning coffee. So we drove in early through the Queens-Midtown Tunnel, parked at a ridiculously expensive garage near Grand Central Station, and walked two blocks to the New York General Building, which housed WNEW-FM's studios. There was no problem with building security: We simply walked past the guard as if we belonged and casually pressed the elevator button. But when we reached a door on the thirteenth floor that was embossed with the familiar green logo "WNEW-FM, 102.7, The New Groove," it was firmly bolted and there appeared to be no doorbell. We knocked, but no one answered. I searched around the corridors for another entrance but found none, so we sat on the terrazzo floor and waited, nervously rehearsing our rap, trying to anticipate any eventuality.

Two hours later, at around nine, an extremely attractive young woman passed us and inserted a key into the lock. "Excuse us, miss, I'm Richard Neer, this is Mike Harrison. We're from WLIR and we're here to see Scott Muni."

The expected response came. "Did you have an appointment?"

"Not exactly but—"

"No problem. Why don't you wait in here instead of in the hall. He'll probably be in within the hour."

Our jaws dropped as we followed her into the offices. We had rehearsed a response to the appointment question, but she had made it unnecessary. In fact, all our carefully planned material proved useless that day. As it turned out, she was one of two secretary/receptionists that the station employed. One worked solely for the general manager, Varner Paulsen, and our new best friend worked for program director Muni, answered the phones, and greeted visitors. In addition to being exceptionally attractive, she had an effervescent personality and spent the next hour chatting with us, interrupted only by the occasional phone call. She was younger than we were, and she gave us lots of unsolicited tidbits about the staff, to our shock and delight.

We hadn't planned on this briefing, but we didn't mind listening to her stories, thinking they might come in useful during our interview with Muni. She told us of her boyfriend, with whom she was having trouble at the time. He was a musician and traveled a lot. He lived in Los Angeles and only could see her once a year when his band came to town, but they talked on the phone. And oh yes, he was married—didn't love his wife but they had a child and he didn't want to leave her. *The oldest line in the book.* I wondered why this gorgeous, intelligent woman would waste her time on a married man three thousand miles away who was obviously using her whenever his band came to New York. It seemed pretty clear to us that he probably had someone like her in several other cities, but that was something she needed to realize for herself. She swore her love for him and pledged to remain faithful. What a waste! And what a cad he was if my suspicions were true. After hearing her story, I never could listen to a Beach Boys song with Mike Love on vocals the same way.

By the time Muni arrived, we'd swapped enough stories with her to feel like old friends, and I'm sure she lobbied for us to be granted an audience with her boss. He came in wearing a brown corduroy jacket over a short-sleeve madras shirt with the requisite faded blue jeans and cowboy boots. A saddlebag briefcase stuffed with albums and unopened mail was slung casually over his shoulder. "Scottso," as he was known in his AM radio days, was a ruggedly handsome man, an ex-Marine with military swagger and confidence. His hero and role model was John Wayne, not exactly a popular choice given the antiwar sentiment of 1971. Muni's bearing was similar to Wayne's, even if his five-foot-ten stature did not quite reach that of the film legend. His hair was short and black, with long sideburns just beginning to gray—his only concession to hipness.

"Come in, dudes," he beckoned, after a whispered exchange with his secretary. We spent the next two hours in his office enduring the strangest job interview ever conducted. It felt as if we were interviewing him: He regaled us with tales as if we'd known him for years. We had told him that we'd caught Rosko's last show and that we had heard some college kid from New Jersey on the overnight show, filling in. That was the plan, he told us. Jonathan Schwartz, a talented writer and raconteur, was starting as Rosko's permanent replacement that evening, and Alison Steele, a sexy former television performer, would temporarily be doing Schwartz's old 10 A.M. to 2 P.M. shift. There were no openings until they decided on whether the Nightbird (as Steele called herself) would fly during the day.

We were intimidated by Muni's reputation, but he was very kind and spoke gently with us. His disjointed phrasing was interrupted by long pauses, as if he were taking a private journey in his mind before returning to Earth. At one point, he seemed distracted while intently scanning his mail. Then he yelled excitedly for the secretary to come in.

"I've found a goodie. Check this out." He pointed to an envelope and she smiled knowingly.

"I think you're right, Scott. Let me get you some boiling water. I think we can save that one."

Harrison and I were dumbfounded when we realized that Muni was perusing the mail for uncancelled stamps, steaming them off for reuse. To us, that was like discovering that Warren Buffet clipped coupons. We laughed as he proudly displayed a container holding dozens of stamps, all neatly extracted from fan letters and junk mail.

We were able to glean that the recently departed Rosko had not been very well liked at the station. Everyone thought him to be unnecessarily confrontational and more than a trifle rude, a man who created arguments for the sheer pleasure of embarrassing his colleagues. That appraisal seemed at odds with the sensitive poet we knew from the airwaves.

Muni often would talk about someone, only referencing them by nickname, as if we knew everyone he did. So we got juicy gossip but couldn't tell if the subject was a rock star or someone in the mail room. There would be lulls in the conversation during which we'd be tempted to interject something about ourselves, because we weren't sure that Muni knew who *we* were either. After an hour, we sensed that extending the interview further would be counterproductive, but Scottso always had another story and we couldn't break off without appearing rude.

Our biggest surprise came when a rotund black man wearing large glasses and an orange leisure suit walked into the room. Was this Rosko?

"Hello, Tammy." Muni sneered, not bothering to introduce us.

"And who are these two gorgeous young boys, you old bug-eyed mother humper?"

This was obviously not Rosko.

"Shut up, you black faggot. What are you in here for, did your mother forget to wipe your bottom this morning?"

"You leave my mother out of this, you aging, gravel-throated bag of horseshit."

"Why don't you go back to your cave, you African Queen? Leave this new meat alone. They probably don't like your queer old black bubble ass anyway."

This badinage went on for five minutes, each insult topping the next until "Tammy" turned up his nose and left the room. Muni rebounded as if nothing had happened.

"Tammy," he chuckled to himself. He acted as if such dialogue was routine office chatter, and didn't even look up to see our reaction. We'd never witnessed such an exchange, even in the movies, and we had no idea what to make of it. Was Scott Muni a racist? Was he gay?

We later found out that "Tammy" was in fact Tom Tracy, a longtime producer, who worked on the Giants games on WNEW-AM and produced the taped weekend shows and the public service programming for WNEW-FM. He and Muni were the closest of friends, each having grown up in the South with many similar experiences, albeit from a different sexual orientation. They delighted in razzing each other with the most graphically obscene language imaginable. I actually laundered the preceding exchange, because it was too crude even for me to recount.

In our stunned silence after the "Tammy" encounter, it seemed like a natural time to close out the interview.

"Well, Mr. Muni, we've taken up enough of your time. Thanks for seeing us. We brought some tapes and résumés."

"Don't need 'em. Leave 'em with the girl on the way out if you want to." It sure sounded as if we were being blown off. "We'll be in touch."

Just then, Alison Steele burst into the room. "Boys, how are you?" She gave us both extravagant hugs and kisses on the lips. "Scott, I hope you're treating my friends well. These are the nicest boys ever. Got to get back on the air. 'Bye."

With that, the whirlwind departed the room, sucking all the air out of it with her. We'd known Steele casually for a few months, having invited her out to WLIR for an on-air interview and then having lunch with her in the city, ostensibly seeking career advice. But we hardly expected such a ringing endorsement. We were breathless as we smiled lamely at Muni and left his office. He never called us back.

After a week, we called him. Couldn't take the call, our secretary friend coldly informed us. *We'll get back to you.*

Another week passed. Again no call. Again we called him.

"Sorry, he's in a meeting. Leave your number." No acknowledgment of our shared intimacies.

At that point, we were thinking of going public with the Beach Boys story, but our thoughts of vengeance soon subsided into a sad acceptance of the fact that we hadn't measured up to New York standards, whatever they were. Were we not ready for prime time? Had someone else gotten the job? But as we listened to the station, we heard a college radio guy on overnight. We knew we were better than he was. And Alison was definitely a creature of the night. Her sensual style seemed merely an annoying distraction during the lunch hour. They *couldn't* be happy with this lineup.

One more call, a week later. We decided that this was it—if there was no response to this one, we were flogging a dead horse and it was time to move on to greener pastures. Trouble was, our pastures all seemed a wintry gray. No leads, no hope.

This time our secretary friend seemed in a better mood. "Let me see if he's in." She put us on hold, displaying a coyness on the phone that belied her frankness in person. Had she unburdened herself too much during our visit and was now too embarrassed to be friendly?

"He says 'Can you come in tomorrow morning at ten?' "

Michael was too excited to play the game of pretending to check his book. "We'll see you at ten," he said, hanging up before she could change her mind.

"Wooooooo!!!" we yelped in unison. "We're not dead yet." And you thought Monty Python invented that line.

The next morning, we had another shapeless session with Muni, punctuated by another visit from Tammy. We were prepared for him this time, even extending a hand and introducing ourselves to save Scott the embarrassment of having to remember our names. After Tammy left, we heard more about Muni's radio philosophy, but were able to respond with precious little of our own. When we started to, he'd interrupt with another story and we grew frustrated by our inability to plead our case. As noon rolled around and the interview faded, it seemed obvious he wasn't interested in us. Was he using the sessions to pick our brains about WLIR? That might have made sense if he allowed us a word edgewise. We noticed our audition tapes and résumés laying exactly where he'd placed them after our last visit, untouched. Clearly, we hadn't made much of an impression. Even Alison was too busy to come in and say hello.

But as we were leaving, Muni glanced at his calendar. "Our GM is away today. Could you guys come in Thursday? I'd like you to meet him."

A radio GM, or general manager, is the boss of all bosses at the local level. He presides over the sales manager and program director, and in most cases, his word on new hires is the final one. Michael gulped down his surprise at this bit of unexpected good news. "Sure, Mr. Muni. By the way, would you like another tape? Anything in particular you'd like us to bring?"

"No, Fats, we have a guy out on the Island. If I need a tape, he can get it."

Since Michael and I each weighed no more than 170 pounds, the word "Fats" didn't offend. This is one of Muni's quirks: If he likes you, he calls you Fats. And his friends call him Fats. I got the feeling that he employed it like Babe Ruth used the moniker "Kid," or "Keeyid," as he pronounced it. Since both men were known to many more people than they could be expected to keep track of, it saved them from having to remember all those names. It had the added bonus of sounding like a term of endearment.

He had similar nicknames for other things that the FCC demanded be kept off the radio by their more commonly used colloquialisms. He called the sex act "hooky-dooky," an expression he picked up from a Turkish friend at Atlantic Records. He often used the term on the air to the befuddlement of many of the artists he was interviewing. He referred to male genitalia as "the little guy." Frequently, after a particularly lighthearted lunch, he'd begin his program with a status report: "The little guy's good today." Whenever a particularly attractive female would pass or make a provocative remark, his comment would be: "The little guy moved." After a while, everyone in the office understood his code words and found them amusing. But he never took the time to initiate strangers to his lingo, and they came away shaking their heads at what they perceived as this odd man. By this point in our interview process, I had given up trying to figure the method in Muni's madness.

Two days later, we were back in the office to meet general manager Varner Paulsen. The staff called him the "Viking," but never to his face. He had the cold appearance and demeanor of a German U-boat commander, with thinning reddish blond hair swept across his forehead, icy blue eyes, and a weatherbeaten complexion. His diction was very precise, in fact everything he did was precise. As he curtly shook my hand, I half-expected him to click his heels.

He spent only a few minutes with us, firing off a couple of general questions, almost as if he just wanted to hear the sound of our voices and how we put our words together. He bid us a formal farewell, sizing us up critically as he departed. I literally shivered as he left the room. Muni had another appointment and hustled us out of the office.

On the drive back to Long Island, we were more puzzled than ever. I felt like a prospective groom meeting the bride's family for the first time. Michael couldn't read Paulsen, either. We didn't hear from anyone at the station for another week and our spirits sagged again. Was this what the vetting process was like everywhere?

Finally, the following Tuesday morning the phone rang at our apartment above the bakery. It was Muni's secretary, asking if we could come in the next day. We'd persevered through too many unfulfilling visits with these people to get overly excited, but we didn't think they'd make us journey all the way to Manhattan to tell us of our rejection in person. When we arrived, Muni was strangely quiet, telling us that Paulsen was on the phone and that as soon as he was finished, he wanted to see us in his office.

Excited anticipation inspired crazy speculation. We weren't working there, so he couldn't fire us. Was it a setup, engineered by our boss at WLIR to test our loyalty? Was this some sort of government sting and we were about to be incarcerated for God knows what? Playing "Working Class Hero" unedited?

Muni had told us that although Varner was a tough guy, he didn't lack a sense of humor. He'd once received a rambling twelve-page diatribe filled with obscenities from a job applicant that finally asked for a position in the final two paragraphs. After reading it carefully and making notations, he sent it back to Scott with the inscription, "Hey, SM. This guy sniffs bicycle seats. VP."

Paulsen looked solemn as he motioned to two leather chairs in front of his large desk. Muni stood behind us, lurking in the background.

"Am I correct in assuming that you two come as a package?" the Viking intoned somberly.

We had hoped that this moment wouldn't come, but it was like being in the foxhole alongside a buddy with a shell coming in. If it *had* to hit one of you . . .

Michael recited a line we had spent hours discussing. "We prefer to work together, but neither one of us would stand in the way of the other's opportunity."

"Well, our problem is this: We don't have two full-time openings on the air. That's why we've been so circumspect." I'd have to look that one up later.

He cleared his throat. "So here's what we can offer. We have a morning show. We have a part-time weekend opening, amounting to two shifts weekly. And we'd couple that with the music director's position. We'd feel comfortable offering either job to either of you, but we thought that since you seem to be more into the music side of things, you, Richard, would like the MD job with the weekend shifts. And that Michael would be suited for mornings. Now the money isn't equal, I warn you. But I'll discuss that with each of you privately, if you wish. Or together, if you don't have a problem with it."

We looked at each other. At WLIR, we'd both made the same amount. But I wasn't about to be jealous if Harrison made more, and I hoped he felt the same. "I've got no problem discussing it now," I said. Michael nodded his assent.

"We are a little embarrassed here. I don't know what you're making now and when you hear our offer, you might not want the job. FM money isn't like it is on the other side of the dial. Revenues aren't, either. But it's not negotiable. You'll find I don't start low and bid myself up. I make a fair offer, take it or leave it."

Oh, no. Finally, a chance for a job at WNEW-FM and we might lose money on the deal? It was costing us a lot for tolls and parking to get into the city from Long Island. Even in 1971, parking could run over sixty dollars a week. But even for less money, the chance to work there was irresistible.

Paulsen saw the fear flash across our faces. "The music gig plus weekends pays $350 a week. The morning show $425. You boys talk it over and let us know. Scott, can I see you for a moment?" he said, leaving the room to give us privacy.

There was little time to reflect on the inequities the offer presented. Although the seventy-five-dollar pay differential was substantial then, $350 a week was more than I'd ever hoped to make in my first big radio job. Five shows in the morning might be preferable to two programs on weekends but in 1971, mornings were the least important shift on FM radio. The music director's position was prestigious and filled with fringe benefits, although I was unaware of how extravagant they could be at this level. Rather than coldly evaluate who was coming out ahead in this deal, I was so happy that we'd both have the opportunity to continue to work together at the station of our dreams that the call was a no-brainer.

"Are you okay with this?" Michael asked me.

"Are you kidding? We got it made. Let's go for it."

We tried to act professionally and not too giddy as we told Paulsen of our decision to accept. He shook our hands firmly and smiled, genuinely happy for us. We might have wondered how far down on the list we were and if others had turned down the same offer, but at that moment, we were too elated to be anything but completely overjoyed. We ran to the studio to share the good news with Alison, and she congratulated us.

"I knew you guys had it all along," she said.

"It would have been nice if you'd told us," I answered.

. . .

IN THE EIGHTIES, Wall Street was where the action was. The nineties saw the rise of computers—software and the World Wide Web. At various times in the last decades of the past millennium, the glamour profession might have been professional athlete, politician, actor, rock star, TV talk show host. But I'm convinced that at the beginning of the seventies, there was no greater glory than being a disc jockey at WNEW-FM.

At the beginning of the twenty-first century, the very idea seems laughable. Today, in terms of financial position and cultural respect, disc jockeys are on the lower deck of a sinking ship. They are generally paid modest salaries in relation to other entertainers, and are deemed as replaceable as bald tires. At the first sight of ratings trouble, they are abandoned by their corporate superiors for the next flavor of the month. Instead of creating culture, they mimic it. One radio savant recently opined that in every other phase of entertainment, a presentation is greeted with, "That's been done before, got anything original?" In radio, it's "Where has this succeeded before?" Uniqueness is now career poison, as in real estate, where the word "quaint" once meant charming but is now a code word for "hopelessly outdated."

In the early seventies, though, I couldn't think of a more exhilarating profession. Imagine having a job that paid you handsomely for toiling but four hours a day. You got to meet every rock star in creation, usually while dining for free at sumptuous restaurants. You had primo tickets to every major concert or sporting event, paid for by others. Celebrities in all walks of life were *your* fans: Politicians curried your favor and athletes were thrilled to be in your presence. You got to work side by side with radio veterans that you grew up idolizing. Every new music release was shipped to your home address, free of charge. And if your conscience allowed, you could have a personal cadre of record promotion men slavishly devoted to your every whim.

In your daily four hours, *you* were the show. The music was entirely of your own selection. You never had to play anything you didn't love. If your mood was quiet and contemplative, you could play long sets of Joni Mitchell or Gordon Lightfoot. If you were ready to party, the entire Rolling Stones collection was at your fingertips. If you didn't like the limits of the world's largest music library, you were free to bring in tunes from your personal cache. Or if you had something to get off your chest, you could vent for as long as you liked. An amusing story? Fire away. Take phone calls. Play Monty Python routines. It truly was a license to thrill.

And the ratings didn't matter because we barely knew what they were. When the quarterly Arbitron reports were issued, we occasionally got a memo suggesting we play more familiar music. The word "familiar" was never defined, leaving it to our wide-ranging and subjective opinions—from playing the Beatles once an hour to merely avoiding the fifth-best track on the Lothar and the Hand People album. Management philosophy seemed to be simple: Hire good people and leave them alone. We had two- or three-year contracts, at yearly increases of 20 percent. Life was good.

And then there were the other fringe benefits. Whereas it would be presumptuous to suggest that any individual had the power to make or break an artist's career, one disc jockey could champion a favored per-former and dramatically increase his or her record sales. There were almost a dozen major record labels plus a host of minor ones, each repre-sented by two or three promotion men with credit cards. Competition for a DJ's ear could be fierce. Legally, the inducements were simple: a lavish dinner or lunch, a show, a few drinks. Company policy set a limit on the value of personal gifts, but each Christmas, there was fine wine in wooden crates, buttery leather jackets, luggage . . . whatever was hip that year. That was usually enough to get a record at least *some* attention.

Illegal inducements were readily available—drugs, prostitutes, you name it. As music director, I had the power to add a record to the studio li-brary, which would hugely increase its airplay. I suggested individual tracks for the jocks, and if my judgment was sound, I could help push singles up the charts. My first day in the library at WNEW-FM saw a steady stream of visitors from the labels setting up lunch dates. One younger guy hung in the background until the others had left, and then surreptitiously closed the heavy steel door to the music library. From under his trench coat, he extracted a bulky package wrapped in brown craft paper and clumsily tied with cotton twine. As he unveiled his prize, I recoiled physically at the sight of a lump of marijuana large enough to intoxicate several counties. Was this guy a cop, setting me up? As I chased him away, he sheepishly apologized for not knowing that I didn't use the stuff and maybe I should keep it anyway, for friends, or perhaps to sell.

I was appalled. Was this the way it worked? You get to your dream job and you find it's as corrupt as the business world we sixties kids were rebelling against? Luckily, word got around quickly and I was never offered drugs again. But there were women who worked for record companies who were seemingly very available. Most of us flattered ourselves that it was our boyish charm or unique take on the world that made us attractive to these women. Indeed, I never uncovered any outright prostitution, and maybe in those heady times sex was just easier, before AIDS and our renewed faith in the sanctity of vows. Or maybe some Machiavellian promoter hoped that pillow talk would help get some spins.

So, as Alison Steele used to say, "Come, fly with me." We'll go back to an era when radio mattered. When it was so revered that the appellation "DJ" seemed inadequate—we looked to be called "air personalities," or as Jonathan Schwartz facetiously referred to himself—"jocque du disques." The voices made love to you. When the normal world shut down, you hung on to every word for inspiration, revelation, even redemption. Or maybe you just needed a friend to help you through the night. You could hear poetry and politics and amazing new music that not only entertained but enlightened.

And the music seemed created just for this type of radio. There were no time restrictions: If the Rolling Stones needed seven minutes to elicit "Sympathy for the Devil," so be it. It was not necessary to prune Ray Manzarek's organ solo from "Light My Fire" to make the Doors anthem suitable for airplay. Murray the K could debut "Whiter Shade of Pale" by Procol Harum without fear that an angry program director would come crashing through the door to rip it from the turntable.

It was all so honest, before the end of our collective innocence. Top Forty jocks screamed and yelled and sounded mightier than God on millions of transistor radios. But on FM radio it was all spun out for *only* you. On a golden web by a master weaver driven by fifty thousand magical watts of crystal clear power . . . before the days of trashy, hedonistic dumbspeak and disposable three-minute ditties . . . in the days where rock lived at many addresses in many cities.

Who Are You?

I STUMBLED INTO free-form radio simply because I didn't know any better.

My father had a lifelong interest in radio. As early as I can remember, he had tape machines and microphones in whatever home we occupied in Syracuse, New York; Lynchburg, Virginia; or northern New Jersey. He formed a radio drama group with several of his college friends called the "Four Bell Playhouse." Initially, they used classic literature that they adapted for radio, but eventually began to write original scripts. Most of these never made it to the airwaves, but the quality of production and acting was quite good. The nights of watching them polish their scripts, invent sound effects, and alter their voices attempting to sound like a big-budget extravaganza must have rubbed off on me. I have boyhood memories of listening to *A Christmas Carol,* starring Ronald Colman as

Scrooge, on a six-record set of clay 78s. Working with yellow legal pads and an old Smith-Corona typewriter, I copied it word for word and organized the family around my father's Voice of Music tape recorder to create our own version of the Dickens classic. It was great fun, and the prospect of doing this for a living became very appealing.

But as I grew up, radio drama began to vanish from the airwaves. On our long car trips from Virginia to Syracuse to visit relatives, we were no longer entertained by *Gunsmoke* or NBC's *Monitor.* The rides became squabbles over which station we'd listen to. We kids were bored by the music our parents enjoyed. The elders thought WABC was noise, but its signal could be heard throughout the entire journey if we drove by night. In any case, when I graduated high school in 1966 and began attending Adelphi University on Long Island, my career interest was more oriented toward acting than radio.

I'd never seen a real radio station until then, so when some of my freshman classes were held in an old Quonset hut that also housed the campus station, I was intrigued. There was a battered half-glass door with rattling blinds on one side and the faded gold-leaf inscription WALI-AM 620 facing the corridor. I assumed that radio stations were housed in stone palaces with spacious, elegant studios guarded by ferocious Hessians who would shoot anyone who dared to trespass. Even at a campus level, there must be hundreds of applicants for every position, willing to perform almost any menial task to be near the center of the action. Weeks passed before I summoned up the courage to knock on the door, curious to see what the grand stage was really like.

I tapped meekly on the glass, fearful that too loud a knock might be heard on the air and cause me to be expelled from school. It was early evening and I imagined the station to be buzzing with workers, preparing the night's programming. No answer, so I tapped a little harder, still wary of disturbing someone's art. I could vaguely make out dim fluorescent lighting through the blinds, so I knew someone must be there. But the ON AIR beacon, a translucent plastic square with embossed red letters, was not lighted next to the entry. I was about to walk off dejectedly when the door swung open, revealing a slender young man with a crew cut and prominent Adam's apple, dressed in a loose-fitting madras shirt. I was nearly bowled over by the smell of stale tobacco smoke and the odor of something electrical burning.

"Hi, I'm John Schmidt. What can I do for you?" He smiled, revealing crooked teeth.

"Uh, I go to school here and I was interested in touring, ah, well, taking a look at the station," I stammered.

"Not much to see. Come on in. I was just doing some soldering. Feel free to look around."

I was dumbfounded. Before me was an untidy little room measuring no more than twelve by fifteen feet. Leaky jalousie windows encrusted with grime comprised one wall; another was entirely made up of chipped gunmetal-gray floor-to-ceiling filing cabinets. A worn Formica-topped desk, littered with papers and folders, was against the wall nearest me. But what immediately drew my attention was the studio, behind a soundproof window. The entrance was a creaky-looking white plywood door, featuring another ON AIR beacon above it. This too was extinguished, and the studio area beyond the glass was illuminated only by Schmidt's work lights.

"Excuse me, uh, sir," I muttered. I wasn't trying to be obsequious, but I've always had a regrettable tendency not to pay attention to people's names when they are introduced to me. "Aren't you on the air now?"

"Call me John," he said, again flashing a crooked smile. "Naw, the guy who should be on the air didn't show up and the next one doesn't come on until nine. I'm just doing some maintenance till he gets here."

"Oh, I see. Would it be possible for me to look at the studio?"

"Suit yourself. I've got work to do." He retreated behind the plywood door and I gingerly followed. I wanted to make some insightful comment about the equipment but most of it was strange to me. The air studio was tiny. It couldn't have been more than ten by ten, smaller even than my bedroom at home. Celotex ceiling tile covered the entire space in a primitive attempt at soundproofing. The Gates audio console was bigger and more complex looking than anything my father had at home; it reminded me of an airplane cockpit, with knobs and buttons that I could never hope to fathom. Two turntables with heavy brushed-aluminum tonearms counterbalanced with stainless steel weights were on one side of the console, and two strange-looking devices that resembled eight-track tape players were opposite. Rack mounted behind the broadcast position stood two Ampex tape decks . . . at least those I recognized. But surrounding them were all sorts of curious gauges and VU meters, and a panel of perforations with black cords dangling from them. There were green and red blinking lights above a clipboard with some sort of algebra written on it. Next to the studio was a small glass-encased booth, with an old RCA ribbon microphone hanging from a boom. My dad had several of these. Everything was dusty and reeked of age, as if it had been salvaged from German bunkers after the Second World War.

"You interested in working here?" Schmidt said from beneath the console, where he was soldering some circuits together.

"Well, uh, sure, but I don't really know much about radio." I kicked myself. Some way to get a job. But I hadn't come in looking for a job, had I?

"There're applications in that rack just outside the control-room door. Why don't you fill one out? They're always looking for people." He went back to his soldering, still chattering away.

I retraced my steps through the dim corridor and spotted a Lucite rack with some papers mounted to the wall. Name, address, major, and campus mailbox number were about the extent of the information required on the application. So I filled one out and placed it on the desk before going back into the room to thank Schmidt. The big clock on the wall read seven-thirty.

Five hours later I was out of there. Not only did the nine o'clock host fail to show, but the ten-thirty man didn't materialize either. Sign-*off* was at midnight—but the station had yet to sign *on*.

I was trapped like a fly in a spiderweb. Little did I realize that John Schmidt spent many lonely nights at the studio. He proceeded to tell me all about WALI in more detail than I cared to know. He talked about the general manager and how he worked at a real station somewhere on the Island. The program director was a student who was elected by the staff weeks before but hadn't a clue. The chief announcer—what was that? I found out all sorts of gossipy things about people I hadn't met, and perhaps never would meet. Schmidt shared confidences with me about the inner workings of the station.

I was fascinated for a while, but I was getting tired and had studying to do. He asked if I would mind running out to fetch him some coffee before the campus cafeteria closed, and I obliged. I figured that when I returned I'd keep my coat on and then gracefully bid him good night. No way. He chewed my ear off for hours, until he ran out of steam shortly after midnight. I later found out that I wasn't alone in hearing these rambling monologues. An engineer's life can be a solitary existence, especially when you're the only one a station employs. You're on call day and night if any of the jury-rigged equipment fails. He welcomed someone to talk to—*anyone*. Most veteran staffers had perfected their escape routes, or resorted to rudeness to make their move. But I didn't want to offend him for fear of blowing my chances.

I was hooked. I wanted to try this radio thing, and it seemed that I might be able to squeeze in the door if I made a good impression on chief engineer Schmidt.

Before I left, I ascertained the correct person to speak with about a try-out and Schmidt told me to come by the next night. I already was looking for excuses to avoid a repetition of the endless chatter, but I told him I'd try to make it. It took me another week to follow through. I figured that maybe Monday nights were slow around WALI, and that next time I might catch someone in authority who could teach me the basics of announcing.

This time the place was fairly active. All the hosts had shown up, and the station manager was actually there. He was a student and his position was unpaid as opposed to the *general* manager, who worked full-time at a commercial FM station and, like the chief engineer, was given a small stipend for supervising WALI. The station manager was an overweight, rumpled man, but had great pipes and was doing the hourly newscasts that evening.

"So, you filled out an application?" he asked as I introduced myself.

"Yes, sir, I stopped by last week and left it right here on this table."

He rummaged around for it, amid half-filled cups of cold coffee and greasy paper from fast-food burgers. He only searched the first few layers of debris, so it well could have been buried beneath the clutter. "Don't see it. Why don't you fill out another one?"

I agreed, although I was pessimistic that the new one would receive any more attention than the first. I had no credits to recommend me, so I was strictly at their mercy.

"Drama major, eh?" he said perusing my latest application. "Know anything about sports?"

I only happened to live for sports, but by the way he sneered as he uttered the word "sports," I sensed a certain contempt, so I bridled my enthusiasm. "Sure."

"Well, our sports guy is a no-show tonight. He's not much good anyway. Think you can prepare three minutes of sports by nine? UPI wire is down the hall. It's just basically rip and read."

"Sure." My voice cracked a little and I hoped the adolescent squeak wouldn't disqualify me. I had a decent baritone, devoid of regionalisms, but I certainly couldn't match the polished tones of the man across the desk. And what did "rip and read" mean exactly? To ask would only demonstrate my ignorance, so I hoped to learn on the fly.

"Great. Follow me," he said, leading me outside the offices down a wide hallway toward a small closet, mere steps away from where I took earth science. "Here's our newsroom."

He pointed to the claustrophobic little room, probably a converted janitorial closet. It was barely wide enough to squeeze past the clattering UPI machine, which was banging out the day's top stories. "Here's the switch for UPI. Remember to turn it off when you hit your mic key. And don't forget to flip it back on again as soon as you're finished so that we don't miss anything. What do you want us to call you on the air?"

This was a big decision. I hadn't considered any flashy radio names. I wasn't prepared to be thrust onto the air, but I didn't want to risk losing my big shot. "Uh, I don't know. Richard Neer's my name. I guess that'll be good."

"Dick Neer, great. When I say, Here's Dick Neer with sports, you start talking. See ya."

With that he left, the objection still forming in my mouth. I hated the name Dick and had always quickly disabused anyone I cared about of the notion of using it. It conjured up Dick Nixon, Tricky Dick, and hundreds of ribald puns I didn't want to be associated with. But now here I was, stuck with it. Once it was used on the radio, it became official. But rather than chase down the corpulent station manager and express my distaste, I figured I'd better practice this sports report, now due in ten minutes.

With the UPI machine's racket destroying my concentration, I selected a few stories that were tacked up on a pegboard above it and tried to read them aloud. Finally, I threw the "off" switch on the ticker a few minutes before nine. How would they know anyway? As long as I turned it back on promptly when I was finished. As the newscast began, I placed the hard plastic headphones over my ears. Oh God. The station manager, who had such a booming professional voice, sounded small and tinny in the headphones. What would I sound like? Was it too late to run away, screaming that I just couldn't do this? Would my career be over forever if I did?

"And that's the WALI news at nine, now with sports here's Dick Neer—"

Silence.

I was saying, "Thank you John, here's what's happening in sports," but I wasn't hearing anything in the headphones. Was that how it worked? You heard others but not yourself? I kept reading, thinking that if I *was* on the air and stopped that I'd sound foolish. After what seemed like an eternity but was really only twenty seconds, I saw a madras-sleeved arm out of the corner of my eye. It reached across and pushed the mic key, and suddenly, I could hear myself. I actually thought I sounded okay, and my confidence grew as I continued. I read the remainder of the stories plus the formatted out-cue taped to the paper stand. My voice did sound higher than I thought it did in real life, and I had a nasal, flat *A* sound that must have been left over from my upstate New York childhood. I got up and practically floated back toward the main offices before I realized I'd forgotten to turn the teletype back on.

As I walked through the door, the station manager was furious. "Where were you? You made me look stupid. I throw it to you and you're not there. What the hell happened?"

So I wasn't really on the air in the beginning. I looked mournfully at Schmidt, without whom I would never have been on at all. I didn't remember if the station manager had told me to throw the mic switch or just assumed that I'd know something so elementary. I thought that some engineer controlled everything. I was ruined already before I'd even started.

But Schmidt spoke up. "Sorry boss," he said, "but that damn mic switch was sticking again. The kid thought it was on but I had to jiggle it to make proper contact."

"Well damn it, have it fixed before the next sports report. Can't you get anything right, Schmidt? Embarrass the poor guy on his first show with your incompetence. Actually, Dick, once you got going, you sounded pretty good. Are you busy at eleven? That's our final sports wrap of the night."

Schmidt had just performed the most courageous act I'd ever seen in person. He winked at me as we walked out of the office to grab a cup of coffee and said, "Don't let that guy bug you. He yells at everybody."

That's how I learned radio—by doing it. I did sports for a couple of weeks and then a DJ position opened up. The elusive chief announcer was supposed to meet me before I went on and explain the guidelines, but he never arrived because he had a hot date that night. So I just went on and winged it, playing whatever I liked from the albums contained in the office filing cabinets. It was an eclectic mix, some light jazz, folk, rock, whatever they had. I started trying to imitate the Top Forty patter of the jocks I grew up listening to, but the style seemed unnatural to me. So as the show progressed, I toned it down, finding a comfortable level of conversation. My dorm roommate, George Yulis, stopped by to wish me well, and I invited him to join me. We talked as we did off the air, about girls, music, comedy, clothes, whatever we found relevant. We got absolutely no feedback from management about the show; we assumed they hadn't listened. So we did it the same way the following week, and continued unsupervised throughout the semester. We didn't call it free form at the time: We didn't call it anything. We played album cuts, singles, comedy bits, whatever we felt like. I'm sure hundreds of other college kids were inventing their own kind of radio concurrently. The baby boomers were getting their first taste of a new kind of radio that spoke to them directly. It certainly wasn't the hyped-up, commercialized pap we grew up with on the AM dial. Some FM stations were even attempting to duplicate this largely college phenomenon for profit.

In 1966, free-form radio was in its infancy on commercial airwaves. To understand what led to it becoming a dominant form of radio just a few years later, one must understand what came before.

Rock and Roll High School

I T W A S A L L about fun, fun, fun till your daddy takes the T-bird away, or at least that's what we thought growing up.

As the Beach Boys reverberated on low-fidelity AM radios in the early sixties, no one expected much more from the box. Most of the popular music of the early sixties was exceedingly forgettable. Recording artists rarely possessed much talent. The songs were written by others, often nine-to-fivers in New York's Brill Building. Cigar-chomping promoters and managers discovered kids with pretty faces and molded them into stars, steering them toward the right songs, hiring tutors to improve their presentations, and arranging airplay or guest shots on influential television shows. The teen idols of the day were often as disposable as their music.

Those who endured did possess something special. Maybe it was the intelligence to foresee the inevitable decline in looks or the cruel whimsy of fad, and lay a foundation for a more substantial career. Perhaps it was a gut instinct for survival and an entrepreneurial ability to sense the next big thing. Or maybe it was truly a God-given gift, the ability to interpret a song and make it one's own, translating a three-minute escape into an emotional experience fans could relate to. In a very few cases, it was the skill to express those sentiments without the middleman, giving birth to the singer-songwriter.

No matter what form it took, the music needed a forum to be heard and to be sold and radio provided that. When Martin Block began playing recordings in the thirties under the moniker *The Make-Believe Ballroom* on WNEW-AM, it opened a new era for the medium and the music. Previously, live entertainment ruled. Radio stations had house bands, or traveled to remote locations to bring the stars of the time into your living room. The ballroom was real: Audiences paid to be serenaded by Glenn Miller or Tommy Dorsey. The announcer's role was simply to present the artist, usually in sonorous tones, reading from prepared text. The script, enhanced by the imagination, served to transport the listener to the site, painting a "word picture" of an actual event. Block simply took it one step further: The event itself was imaginary, the ballroom existing only in his mind and in those of his audience. Instead of costly live remotes, one could just play records, and fill in the blanks with sound effects and lively banter. It was cost effective for the radio station, and ultimately beneficial to musicians, having to create the performance only once to gain national exposure, night and day.

With the coming of rock and roll, the basic formula was unchanged but stylistically light-years away. *How* music was presented became important, since the actual recorded content was the same. One couldn't sign a band to play exclusively for one station or even one network—the material was there for all to play. Executives like Rick Sklar were charged with taking the same records that the guy across town had and convincing people that it was cooler to hear them on his station.

Sklar came to be known as the man who embodied all that was good and bad in Top Forty radio, as the new genre was soon named (because it was based on the forty top-selling records). Born and raised in New York City with a love for radio, Sklar responded to an ad in a trade publication and found himself working locally as a gofer at WINS. The station had just brought in the legendary Alan Freed, "King of the Moondogs," from Cleveland to host a nightly rock and roll show. Some have given Freed credit for inventing the very term "rock and roll," although that is in dispute. Sklar's work ethic and promotional creativity saw him rise quickly to the post of assistant program director at WINS, sharing an office and ambitions with Freed. His résumé included a stop at WMGM, but he made his name at New York's WABC, where he started as community affairs director in 1961 before becoming the program director in late 1963.

Sklar quickly learned three basic tenets that would sustain him throughout his lengthy broadcast career. First, he learned the value of promotion. Today it is common for radio stations to flood the television airwaves with commercials, heavily produced and/or featuring expensive celebrity endorsements. Sklar had no such budget available to him. In fact, the rise of television caused many to believe that radio was dying and not worth investing in. After all, why just listen when you can watch and listen simultaneously? So Rick Sklar had to come up with innovative ways to promote his product without spending a lot of money.

Second, his association with Alan Freed instructed him that a short playlist works better than a lengthy one. Although called Top Forty, the playlist was pared to fewer than twenty songs throughout much of his career. At one point, Sklar's research told him that the audience didn't want to hear anything more than three years old. Overnight, to the jocks' chagrin, oldies disappeared. But even with a longer list, emphasis was always put on the seven or eight most popular songs. Rotations and clocks were designed to ensure that at peak listening times, the record would always be played, to the point where the number one record might be aired every forty minutes. Repetition, the bane of all who work in radio, was seen as a key to keeping an audience. An old saw goes, "Just when your jocks are getting sick of a record, the audience is just discovering it."

The third cornerstone to Sklar's success was to hire interesting personalities and give them some creative license. Like a football coach, a programmer must sketch out a framework of inviolate rules that apply to everyone, but allow room within the system for individual expression. Thus, when Sklar took over at WABC, Bruce Morrow was allowed to screech and bellow at night, while Dan Ingram delighted his afternoon audiences with racy double entendres and self-parody. Scott Muni was the music guru who respected artistry and lionized those who created the songs that were the mainstay of his early evening soirée. Diversity was encouraged as long as one executed Sklar's mechanics flawlessly.

WABC's success was largely a product of Sklar's design, but sometimes plain old luck entered into the picture. As with any product, "ease of use" is something the consumer expects, and only notices in its absence. If a product isn't simply and logically laid out, people gravitate toward one that is. In radio, this translates to dial position and signal strength, something a programmer can't easily control. At 770, WABC enjoyed an easy-to-remember frequency and call letters. Along with the network engineers' foresight in choosing an antenna height and location, the low dial position resulted in a strong signal that could easily be heard throughout the metropolitan area. Its reach was so powerful that longtime afternoon jock Dan Ingram once accurately quipped, "We're only the fourteenth-highest-rated station . . . in Pittsburgh." To add to the natural edge WABC had, Sklar believed in boosting the compression and equalization on the station to maximize the sound. They also used a slight echo when the DJs were on microphone to give them a more powerful presence.

Above and beyond having a great signal, a radio station needs to provide tangible reasons to tune to it over another. Why should I listen to WABC over WMCA or WINS? Sklar and his contemporaries had to gain an understanding of how the consumer mind works, especially the fickle minds of teenagers. Of necessity, it began with music. Clever promotions and entertaining disc jockeys aside, music comprises two thirds of the broadcast day. The selection of songs has to be right. Originally, this was the most important role of the disc jockey.

In the early days of rock radio on the AM band, broadcast companies were confounded by the new music. They didn't understand the appeal of what was commonly refered to as "race music." But the numbers didn't lie—the music was selling to teenagers with disposable income and those same teens were glued to the radio, often on distant stations when local ones didn't serve their needs. As a boy in Lynchburg, Virginia, I listened to the powerful signal of WABC booming in at night, and revered Scott Muni and Dan Ingram from four hundred miles away. It didn't take long for every market to realize the economic windfall to be reaped by playing rock and roll on the radio. So they followed an age-old pattern: Find a successful disc jockey in a small market and pay him more to work in your bigger market. Listen to him, analyze the reasons for his success and either nurture him to greater heights or replace him with a cheaper model when you've replicated his act or he leaves of his own volition for a better job.

True originals might be copied but not duplicated. Just as many singers tried to be Elvis Presley, Alan Freed and Wolfman Jack were models for aspiring DJs. But the package was more than just the sound of their voices, or the quality of their humor. Much of it was not in the larynx, but in the ears. They knew a hit record upon first listen. One jock was even nicknamed "the man with the 45 rpm ears." They understood what their audience wanted because they, unlike their corporate superiors, actually loved the music. They listened to it at home, in the car, in the office. They took pride in being the first to expose an artist that would go on to achieve greatness. They went to clubs to hear new bands. They gave struggling local acts spots on their live extravaganzas. Therefore, their selections weren't based on what the audience said they wanted through research, but by what their guts told them to be right. They were trendsetters and taste *makers* as opposed to followers. Whereas much of today's punditry is based on polls, these pioneers knew on a visceral level what was great and what was fraudulent.

But with any sector where big money can be made, it follows the path of least resistance. Rather than earning success the old-fashioned way, by producing compelling records that couldn't be ignored, record companies tried to cut corners by corrupting influential disc jockeys. This evolved into what came to be known as "payola," a form of bribery that eventually destroyed freedom of choice on AM radio.

The theory was simple. More radio exposure = more sales. More sales = more airplay. The cycle repeats exponentially. Offering bribes to play music was nothing new. According to the Rock and Roll Hall of Fame, folk songwriters in the 1850s were paying to have their songs performed in concerts to increase sales of sheet music. It was a common practice of Gilbert and Sullivan to subsidize live performances of their work to ensure greater exposure. It got to be so accepted as the way business was done that record execs actually wrote checks to disc jockeys and kept records of their payments. When some states started passing laws against payola, checks gave way to cash.

Veteran promoters will regale you with stories of the evenings when they'd retreat to the studio of their favorite DJ—smoking cigars, playing cards, drinking beer, and swapping tales. Every so often, one of them would approach the jock with an ensleeved 45 rpm single.

"Maybe you'd like to play this one next. I think you'll like it."

Discreetly tucked into the sleeve was a crisp C note. One promoter tells of a new single that he got played five times in one three-hour show with a big New York personality. It cost him five hundred dollars. The next day the record sold ten thousand copies, for which he received a large bonus.

Some jocks thought that cash payments were a little too crass, not to mention a bit obvious. Word could get around, so payola became more subtle. "Cleans" is music biz terminology for shrink-wrapped, salable albums that could be quickly and easily redeemed for cash at a local record store. Services could be provided—trips, women, booze, whatever one's particular preference happened to be.

The most ingeniously devious path lay in royalties. Listing a prominent jock's mother on a songwriting credit might result in a royalty of a penny per copy. A million seller could be quite a payoff. If questioned, a record exec could say that he was a friend of the lady's and that she had contributed a line or two that was better than the original.

The most widespread excuse given for payola was that everyone did it—it was accepted practice. However, the detail that gives the lie to that pretext is the secrecy in which most transactions were conducted, and the lengths to which most conspirators went to cover their tracks. If there is absolutely nothing wrong with an act, why hide it? And from whom?

All along, the music had enemies who thought that rock and roll was a corrupting influence on teenagers, and that disc jockeys who used code words for sexual activity were winking at promiscuity. Sadly, there was also a racial angle. Since many of the top artists and songwriters were black, white parents feared that their daughters would be driven by primitive rhythms into the beds of "savage Negroes," to be ruined forever by the experience.

Most of rock's opponents were from a generation tempered by war and economic depression, who just wanted a better life for their sons and daughters and feared losing them to this phantom evil. Some were just frightened of the unknown. The appeal of the music didn't make sense to them. Lyrics were hard to fathom even when they could be heard over the din of the instruments. As Bob Dylan sang (quite clearly over only an acoustic guitar): "Don't criticize what you can't understand. Your sons and your daughters are beyond your command. Your old road is rapidly agin'."

There was also an economic reason for scuttling rock and roll. ASCAP, the longtime licensor of broadcast music on the radio, had failed to anticipate the popularity of rock. As a result, most of the new music was licensed to rival BMI. Since ASCAP considered rock a fad, anything that would hasten its demise would strengthen their hold on the music industry. Their powerful Washington lobby pressured a congressional subcommittee to probe "commercial bribery" in radio to derail BMI and restore ASCAP to its rightful place. Politicians capitalized by jumping on the bandwagon, because America was fascinated watching popular disc jockeys suffer on live television. The new medium gave the pols access to free publicity, and its power with voters was just beginning to be felt—witness the Nixon-Kennedy debates. Constituents could see their congressmen in action, fighting the evils that threatened the next generation.

So when Congress opened up payola investigations in 1959, it wasn't necessarily just to clean up a corrupt system, but to squelch a budding economic and social movement. If rock could be discredited, its perceived negative influence on the morals of modern youth could also be contravened. If its idols could be shown to have feet of clay, then the whole rotten culture could be flushed away.

Alan Freed was the face they chose to represent all that was evil with the scene. Years of drinking had taken its toll on his appearance, making him seem shifty and haggard. A car accident in 1954 had resulted in his face bearing the scars of over two hundred stitches. And he *had* profited from payola by his own admission, although he swore that he never accepted money to play a record he wouldn't have played anyway. Others who were brought before Congress were perhaps equally guilty, but presented a more wholesome image. Dick Clark was accused of having a financial interest in some of the artists he was promoting on his shows. The clean-cut, all-American Clark said he was merely following the standards and practices of the day and would be happy to comply with any new regulations on disclosure. He'd already preemptively divested himself of the conflicting interests. Although Congress was skeptical about certain aspects of his testimony, he was sent away with their kudos as a fine example for the nation's youth. Freed came across more like an organized crime figure in the Kefauver hearings. He testified honestly, but refused to grasp that he'd done anything wrong. He was also on the downside of his career and therefore a worthy sacrifice for an industry willing to name a scapegoat and move on.

So Freed became the target, and the arrows stuck. Although his penalty was a minimal fine, his life's work was in disrepute. He ratcheted downward into more substance dependency and depression until it completely shattered his health. He died at the age of forty-three, broke and largely unappreciated by the millions to whom he had brought the joy of rock and roll. At the time of his death, he was facing federal tax charges and years of time in court and possibly prison. Only in more recent days have film-makers and rock historians given him credit for championing a culture that may have remained hidden from white America for years without his advocacy.

For disc jockeys, the effect of the payola scandal was devastating. Their profession, once the hippest on the planet, was now ranked slightly below used-car salesman. The power to select music was centralized into the hands of program directors, who carefully picked each song and the order in which it was to be played. They justified their picks with a crude form of research, which was more flawed and potentially corruptible than the largely honest ranks of disc jockeys.

Broadcast corporations still wanted to see the justification for playing records in black and white, so that there could be no ambiguity or further scandal. The research techniques, however, weren't sophisticated. They mainly consisted of calling record stores and asking what was selling. National charts kept by publications like *Billboard, Cash Box,* and *Record World* were factored into the mix. The whole process was very unscientific. For example, when you called a record store, to whom did you speak? A low-paid part-time clerk? An owner who had better things to do than spend ten minutes on the phone with a radio station? And how reliable was the information? Could a store owner in 1961 consult his computer and give you precise sales figures on a given record? Or might he just recall four or five copies of something being sold over the time he was at the register? Or was it six or seven copies?

And what demographic information was available? Who bought the records? Teenagers? Grandmothers? Grandmothers for teenagers? Who kept track of such things? And were these record stores located in an area where your target audience likes to buy their music? The final tallies might look good on paper, but the results were practically worthless in determining what music should be played on the radio.

And, just as payola resulted in increased airplay that increased sales, any tactic that could cause a radio station to believe a record was a hot seller would now result in greater airplay. Thus, a number of avenues opened up to the enterprising record promoter. There are legal ways to influence research: store signage, incentive programs, in-store appearances by the artists, dinners with the musician or tickets to a concert, invitations to private promotional parties or conventions. Anything that brings attention to a given record to place it "top of mind" at the point of contact could be very effective in making a record appear to be selling more than it actually is.

But there are also unethical ways. If a minimum-wage sales clerk is reporting to the radio station, how hard is it to offer financial or other inducements that play into human frailties in return for a positive spin? Is a store owner or manager less corruptible? How about some cleans, which could be peddled for pure profit if the record takes off, or returned for credit if it doesn't? This gives store owners an added stake in a particular record's success. The amount escalates with the influence, and exotic vacations and/or hookers were not unheard-of bribes to those who owned chains of stores.

Dave Cousins of the British progressive-rock band the Strawbs tells of how he secured airplay for his fledgling group in England. He gave everyone he knew money to buy his first single at certain stores that reported to the BBC. It worked. Airplay increased, and the song actually did sell, making Cousins's initial investment repay many times over.

But rarely do the principals get involved so directly. Label executives practiced the art of denial long before Watergate. When they needed extra help, it was a simple matter to hire an independent promotion man to work a given record, and wash one's hands of the whole affair. Therefore when the heat came, the little independent guy took the fall, leaving the big man to express his shock, disappointment, and denial to partners and shareholders. The foot soldiers, not the generals, always take the first bullet.

Ironically the job of unethical record promoters was now simplified. Instead of trying to influence six disc jockeys per station, one program director in the pocket was cheaper and more effective.

Some stations still conducted "music meetings," where a board of DJs had a voice in what was played, weighted along with the program director's veto power. Before payola, WABC's music meetings really were about music. Disc jockeys voted on the "pick hit of the week," a device designed to give new artists a chance for some significant airplay to see if the public could accept their music. Jocks were encouraged to bring in records and play them for the program department and the rest of the staff to decide what songs the station would actually air. Music was judged on its merit, not its chart number.

But after 1960, the meetings became such a sham that the staff had to be ordered to join them. No record was even considered unless it had broken *Billboard*'s Top Twenty. Pick hits generally came from established artists whose singles had already climbed the charts before receiving the nod from ABC. The disc jockeys' opinions were ignored, and the meetings were mainly used to explain new promotions or adjust mechanics. Occasionally a jock would defy convention and promote a song, but it was nearly impossible to defy the consensus, either for illicit reasons or just because one believed in a particular record.

Of the staff, perhaps the two who cared about the music most were Scott Muni and Bob Lewis, the overnight DJ. Muni prided himself on his musical knowledge and had become friendly with many artists, especially those who lived locally. Whereas Sklar eschewed promotion men, Muni welcomed them. His interest wasn't financial, but he figured that with the radio market being as competitive as it was, his access to the artists might someday pay off in an exclusive release of a new song or a big interview. He routinely played cards with the promoters, and drank with them on a regular basis. He established many lasting relationships, and his loyalty was rewarded many times over.

Lewis, or "Bobaloo" as he was known, was a big bear of a man. He had a perfect radio voice, silky smooth, deep, and mellow, which resulted in a burgeoning voice-over career. He was an aesthetic soul, sensitive and idealistic, especially about radio. He had curly sandy hair that became Gene Wilder–unruly at times. The overnights gave him a perfect forum to play a wider variety of tunes than the tighter playlist of the higher-visibility time slots. He loved music and championed many progressive bands, his favorite being the Moody Blues. He owned a boat and, in his idyllic later life, would sail to Florida and spend weeks living a seafarer's existence. By the seventies, he was so in demand as a commercial voice that he set up a small recording studio on board and would be messengered advertising copy by major agencies. His versatile style allowed him to record many different approaches on successive takes, which he then sent back to Manhattan.

Aside from involved participants like Lewis, Muni, and Bruce Morrow, taking away control of the music simply meant fewer things to be concerned about. But the effect the congressional hearings had on Rick Sklar, who apparently never participated in payola and professed to know little about it, was to cause him to completely withdraw from record promoters. A shy, intensely private man to begin with, he was probably devastated to see the ruination of his friend Freed, and kept the hordes away from his door. One of the few he did speak with occasionally was Matty

Matthews of Columbia Records. Matthews tells of Sklar picking up the check whenever they dined together, so as to avoid even the appearance of impropriety. Sklar also believed in his research for selecting music and reasoned that all the hypesters could do was cloud the issue.

Shortly after Sklar took over the program director's spot in 1963, a record was auditioned at one of the weekly music meetings. Although the band who made the record would change the course of music and ultimately radio history, the DJs were almost unanimous in their disdain on first listen. "There's no way this will ever make it," said one.

It was soon obvious to the world that the single most of WABC's jocks had dismissed, "I Want to Hold Your Hand," by the Beatles, was destined for greatness. "She Loves You" followed quickly thereafter, along with *Ed Sullivan Show* bookings and a concert at Carnegie Hall. Sklar, never one to hesitate when a promotional opportunity beckoned, quickly renamed the station W-A-Beatle-C. WMCA and WINS rushed in as well, and the Beatles' management meticulously played each station against the other to maximum advantage.

Beatles manager Brian Epstein had been preparing for the assault on the United States for months and had been asking every American band that had played the British Isles who the "movers and shakers" in the States were. He was told to gain favor at WABC, WMCA, and to befriend Murray the K at WINS. The strategy worked—soon Murray had dubbed himself the "Fifth Beatle," and traveled with them to their first U.S. concert, in Washington, D.C. He taped interviews in their hotel room and in the back of limos. Murray, born Murray Kaufman, had been a music promoter for the songwriter Bob Merrill and understood how to sell and market an act. The act he usually pitched was Murray the K, as he presented live concerts in Brooklyn with bands he played on the air. He had invented his own lingo for his show, and thousands of New York teens frustrated their teachers by imitating him.

But Murray and the other stations couldn't match Sklar's unrelenting promotional blitz. He commissioned PAMS, the Texas-based company that recorded all their jingles, to rush produce a new package centered around the band. There were dozens of Beatles contests, Beatles giveaways, anything that would associate WABC with the Beatles. Sklar scheduled Beatles records as often as every fourth tune. He'd play "twin spins" of the band, surrounded by PAMS's slick promotional jingles.

When the group landed in America for the first time, he dispatched

Muni to Idlewild (now JFK) Airport to capture the excitement. Muni was physically frightened for the first time in his life when the crush of thousands of teenage girls plastered him against the chain-link fence separating the tarmac from the arrival buildings. He was wearing a new vicuna wool coat, which was ripped into expensive threads as he tried to extricate himself in time to stick a microphone into Paul McCartney's face as he passed through the gates. Sklar was able to commandeer remote equipment from ABC News, so that Muni could deliver live reports, as opposed to feeding tape into a telephone as the others were forced to. Later, at the band's hotel, where ten thousand teens gathered outside, Muni and Morrow were able to use remote mics to capture the kids singing along with WABC jingles while Dan Ingram held forth on the air. They were able to get live hotel-room interviews first, sometimes resorting to bribing maintenance workers to gain access. They even found a duplicitous way to break new Beatles singles on the air before the competition could—by making a contact in the London recording studio.

The trickery didn't stop there. When Ringo Starr's Saint Christopher medal was snatched away by a female fan, WABC mounted a campaign to recover it. The girl's mother returned the medal to Muni within hours as Scottso promised the girl that she would get to actually meet and hug Ringo and receive tickets to the concert. But Sklar withheld news of the medal's return from the public for an entire day until they'd milked every last drop of publicity from it. It was then presented to Ringo on the air. Bruce Morrow was an emcee at the August 1964 concert at Shea Stadium and presented the boys with a trumped-up medal, "The Order of the All-Americans." Although all three rock stations benefited from the British invasion, WABC was the clear winner in attaching their name to that of the Beatles.

In 1965, WINS decided that the Top Forty competition was too fierce and dropped out to become one of the first all-news outlets in the country. WMCA lasted a few more years before going all talk in 1969. Rick Sklar and WABC ruled the roost as their AM competitors fell by the wayside. Ratings shares were high and revenue rolled in at unprecedented levels. But Sklar's shabby treatment of one of his own stars helped spawn a movement that was to cost WABC dearly—the rise of FM.

Crown of Creation

FOR MOST OF the sixties, it was much easier to get a job at an FM station than at a successful AM one. FM was still viewed as AAA ball, not the big leagues, even in larger markets. Most operators of duopolies were looking to keep costs low, so hiring an inexperienced disc jockey who was thrilled just to have a job was preferable to paying a high ticket for an AM has-been. It's how I got my first professional job.

A few months into my apprenticeship at WALI, I still wanted to be an actor. Through the Adelphi University theater group, I'd become friends with a tall, slender man named Robert Wynn Jackson. A native of Virginia's Tidewater region, he came north on a music scholarship and directed many of the light operas and musical comedies we staged. Bob was an unconventional combination of black, Jewish, and gay. His extensive knowledge of classical music won him the Sunday afternoon slot on WALI. He crafted a highly produced show opening that painted an aural picture of Robert Wynn Jackson as conductor, complete with white tie and tails, the audience bursting into applause as he mounted the podium. He tapped his baton and began to conduct works by the great masters. Of course, he was merely playing records, but his creation was so vivid that one could imagine him extravagantly decked out—a rapier-slim black Bernstein, passionately leading a magnificent symphony orchestra.

Ted Webb served as general manager of WALI to supplement his income while working professionally as chief announcer at WLIR, which, like Adelphi University, was also based in Garden City, New York. A part-timer had left WLIR in a pay dispute so Webb left a note for Jackson that the station had an opening for an announcer trained in the great works. Robert was intrigued by the possibility of taking his program to the next level and asked me if I'd like to tag along with him. I suspect his real reason for asking was that I had access to a car and he didn't, but I was happy to go along. Although he assumed the audition was strictly pro forma and that he'd already gotten the job, I think he wanted company for reassurance, too. Part of him had to be nervous, considering the grandiose future a *real* FM station might promise. We were also curious to see what a professional station looked like, certain that any commercial facility would make our campus station seem dreary by comparison.

Broadcasting from the opulent Garden City Hotel, the high tone of WLIR's programming conjured images of stately men in dinner jackets dining and dancing with elegantly gowned women. In reality, although the aging dowager of a hotel glittered with a prestigious address, the station itself was in the subbasement, along with the linen service, freight elevators, and boiler rooms. As Jackson and I cautiously stepped down the rickety, rusting stairs, we felt like we were descending into Hades. Is this what big-time radio was all about? After searching the winding maze of dank hallways that smelled of bleach and stale urine, we happened upon a solid steel door, trussed with triple locks like a typical New York apartment. Here, in the bowels of the building, was the big time—WLIR.

The open door revealed a mousy secretary who looked like she had just been released from a convent, dark blond hair pulled back in a bun and thick oversize glasses.

"I'm Robert Wynn Jackson, here to take the classical announcer's position. Pleased to make your acquaintance. And you are?" he asked, extending his long bony fingers in her direction. She recoiled as if he'd pulled a knife on her. She stammered out her greetings and gestured us in. "We're looking for Mr. Webb," my friend continued. "Perhaps he's in another part of the complex."

"You're looking at the complex. He's in the next room . . . on the air. I'll get him." She quickly ran off, relieved to be away from what seemed to be her worst nightmare. Jackson was elegantly formal in his approach to strangers, and ultimately very graceful, but upon meeting him, few were prepared for a six-foot-six black man who weighed a scant hundred and forty pounds and spoke with an effeminate drawl. We sat ourselves down on a tattered loveseat and waited for Webb.

In 1959, John Reiger was able to purchase an FM license for WLIR at a cost of fifteen thousand dollars. At the time, there were fewer than a thousand FM stations in the nation, although receivers were selling at the rate of four hundred thousand per year. It was a brave move, since the odds of making a profit on an FM-only operation were roughly one in a hundred. Still, Reiger had foresight. He envisioned WLIR as a high-class item, a luxury appealing to affluent Long Islanders who could appreciate the finer things. His programming consisted of a sophisticated mix of standards in the morning with commuter news and information, followed by a complete original-cast Broadway show album at 10 A.M. Lunchtime fare featured the suave, masculine personality of Bunny Roberts, who mainly appealed to lonely, stay-at-home wives. Afterward, Reiger's wife, Dore, interviewed local celebrities. At 5 P.M., there was cocktail music, mostly treacly piano instrumentals served up for returning suburban breadwinners. Dinner music held forth from six until nine, featuring Percy Faith, Mantovani, and the lush orchestral sounds that tony suburbanites might enjoy with their evening repast. Classical music closed the day from nine until sign-off. By keeping his rates low (often less than ten dollars per sixty-second commercial) and trading local merchants airtime for their wares (mainly cars, meals, and clothing), Reiger was able to eke out a living. Obviously, he paid his disc jockeys very little, often asking them to double as salesmen after their air shift. His methods were typical of many FM owners at the time.

I suppose my initial experience at WALI should have prepared me for what I was to see while waiting near the reception desk. The room was long and narrow with three sets of protruding perpendicular industrial steel shelves. These were stuffed with decrepit record albums, their covers held together by colored masking tape. The prerequisite metal filing cabinets lined the wall behind the tiny reception desk. Another black metal desk with aluminum legs sat parallel to the wall, cluttered with tapes and newer LPs awaiting categorization. The whole area was covered with a ratty red carpet that was as worn and threadbare as Bob Cratchit's topcoat. There was one high window in the entire subterranean room, and any daylight that might have filtered into the window well was blocked by a puny air conditioner. There were three doors off the main room: one to the air studio, another to the announcer's booth, and the third to a private office occupied by Reiger. At least the owner's office seemed better appointed than the rest of the shabby accommodations. The overall impression made WALI look like a penthouse suite on Park Avenue. I could only imagine that the penurious furnishings of the office were sacrifices made to grace the broadcast facility with the latest technology. That illusion would be shattered later.

As Ted Webb emerged from the studio to greet us, I could tell that he had no clue as to whom he'd invited to audition. Since his hours consulting WALI were limited, I doubted that he had ever heard Jackson's weekend show. He only knew that it was the sole classical program on the station and that WLIR needed an announcer well versed in the great masters. Since he was on the air at the time, Webb hurriedly ushered us into the announcer's booth, a small dark room off the main studio. He handed Jackson a sheaf of papers consisting of a job application and some pages of music introduction for his audition.

Robert began to practice reading the copy aloud. To say his approach was disastrous would be an understatement. Although he knew all the proper pronunciations, he embellished the dry script with his over-the-top improvisational flourishes, ones that worked to great effect (and our amusement) at WALI. He had style, but not the kind they were looking for. He turned to me for advice.

"Well, Bob," I said, "if you really want my opinion, I'd tone it down a little. This is FM, so they're looking for a deep voice. Measured tones. Slow and formal. Like this." I proceeded to read a paragraph.

"But my man, that's not me. They brought me in for my uniqueness. My flair." He patted my shoulder and I knew what he meant. When he referred to men as "having the flair," it signified that they were gay, whether they realized it or not.

"Suit yourself, Bob. But I'm not sure that's what they have in mind." I didn't want to hurt his feelings by insinuating that Webb hadn't heard his show, but had merely invited the classical host in for an audition. So Robert proceeded to read it his way. Predictably, as Ted listened from the main studio, he was absolutely horrified by what he saw and heard. Intent upon his script, Robert never picked up on this.

As gracefully as possible, Webb escorted us from the announcer's booth toward the exit, thanking Jackson for reading and asking if he could speak to me privately. Uh-oh, I thought. Was I about to be chided for bringing in a man who had wasted their time? As I followed him into the studio I was already preparing the answer, that I was merely along for the ride. I'd met Ted on numerous occasions at WALI and respected him a great deal. He was the ultimate pro on the air: a great voice with a completely straight-ahead delivery. There was no quirkiness or sense of humor in his presentation and certainly no *flair.* I selfishly hoped this little embarrassment wouldn't hurt me at WALI.

"Neer, I heard you reading with your friend in there. You sounded very good. Do you want to tape an audition?"

"Well, thanks, Ted. But I don't really know much about classical music. I couldn't pronounce all those names."

"First of all, the shift we're talking about isn't all classical. It's Broadway show tunes, Sinatra, even some chicken rock. There's only an hour of classical and I'll help you with the names." He then pronounced "Rachmaninoff" and "Prokofiev" for me. I recognized Tchaikovsky, but Eugene Joachim (OY-gum YO-kim) was beyond me. The copy wasn't difficult otherwise, and I sailed through it.

Webb was beaming. "That was terrific. I've got to run this by the owner, but frankly, I don't think he'll have a problem. Are you free Saturday morning?"

That was like asking me if I wanted to make love to Julie Christie. I couldn't believe that my little good deed of giving a friend a ride would pan out as a job offer at a real radio station. But my adrenaline rush was tempered by the realization that I'd have to tell Robert that I'd gotten the job and he hadn't.

As I thanked Ted, I saw Jackson in the reception area perched on the seedy loveseat, looking nonplussed. Was this worth endangering our friendship? Would he think I deliberately engineered this to steal his job?

To his everlasting credit, he was gracious and kind. He congratulated me from the heart. It was apparent that he felt real joy at my good fortune more than disappointment at his own rejection. The short car ride back to the dorm was filled with his suggestions for the show, all of which were well meaning but 180 degrees away from what WLIR wanted.

As we got out of the car, he sniffed haughtily, "I'm not sure the world is ready for me and my flair yet. But they will be, Dick Neer. They will be."

God, I hated being called that name and Jackson knew it, deliberately tweaking me to affirm our friendship. I had no doubts that someday, in some way, Robert's talents would be appreciated, although at the time my mind was swimming with the whirl of events that had overcome me in the last few hours. I was going to be on a *real* radio station, even if it was only FM.

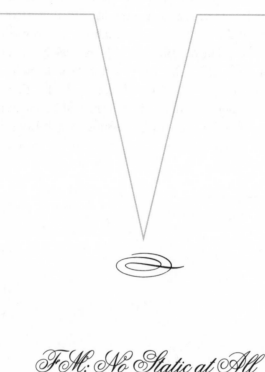

FM: No Static at All

AM RADIO RULED the airwaves for the first six decades of the twentieth century, based on the timeworn business principle of arriving *first,* not necessarily with the *best.* Commercial AM broadcasts began in earnest in the twenties and became solidly entrenched in the public consciousness as the Great Depression neared. Edwin Howard Armstrong was an inventor who pioneered the use of radio transmissions in the First World War and held many of the early patents for AM (amplitude modulation).

But Armstrong was not content with the static and spotty reception that plagued radio in those days. He set about at his own expense to find a better way to transmit words and music in higher fidelity. By 1933, after laboring long hours in a basement laboratory, he came up with frequency modulation, or FM. Upon demonstrating the clear superiority of FM, he expected David Sarnoff's RCA to exercise the right of first refusal on his work he'd given them and begin laying the groundwork for the conversion from AM to FM.

Sarnoff was a longtime friend; in fact, the "General," as he was called, introduced Armstrong to the woman who would later become his wife. But Sarnoff was under the misconception that the inventor had been working on a way to improve AM reception. The General had no intention of junking the massive investment that RCA had in AM transmitters and receivers. He also wanted his company to concentrate its technical resources on television, which he correctly saw as the more powerful of the new media.

What followed was thirty years of legal wrangling, which perplexed and frustrated Armstrong and everyone else who had witnessed demonstrations of FM's clarity and frequency response. At first, the battle was joined over spectrum allocation, or where FM should be located on the dial. Originally, it was granted space at 42–50 MHz and roughly a half-million receivers designed to capture those signals were sold to audio enthusiasts. But RCA fought FM every step of the way, even when the FCC declared that television sound would be FM and dedicated channel 1 to the band. After the Second World War, and after extensive lobbying by RCA using misleading technical data, Washington abruptly switched the frequencies to 88–108 MHz, the area it occupies today. Massive damage was done to FM's cause. Overnight, transmitters and receivers were obsolete, and consumers were reluctant to plunge ahead, fearing that more changes would stick them with more worthless equipment. Also, advances in AM technology had improved its sound to acceptable levels, especially to nonaudiophiles who were content with the status quo.

By 1954, Armstrong was a bitter and beaten man. He'd suffered a stroke and when his wife refused to give up their retirement money to continue the legal battle with RCA, an ugly domestic incident ensued. He realized that his obsession with FM had now cost him the thing most dear to him, and after writing a poignant letter of apology to his wife, he finally gave up the fight, leaping to his death from a thirteenth-story window. His estate settled with RCA for a million dollars, essentially what they'd offered over a decade earlier. FM was left without a champion, although Armstrong's widow continued lawsuits against lesser opponents and eventually won them all.

The next major obstacle facing FM was the dawn of the television era. Consumers were faced with the option of buying improved radio technology at a time when the medium's future was in doubt, or investing in television, obviously the next big thing. To further simplify the decision, manufacturers threw their efforts into television, leaving FM an orphan, abandoned in favor of the newer toy.

By the mid-fifties, vast improvements were developing in phonograph technology. Thirty-three-and-a-third rpm albums, better phonographic cartridges, and improved speakers were reaching the mass market. When ears were awakened to the sparkling potential of near-perfect sound reproduction, AM radios didn't sound so good anymore. Stereo albums were widely released for the first time, and high-end users began purchasing component systems with separate turntables, amplifiers, and speakers. And when consumers heard FM for the first time, they were blown away by its advantages over the muddy AM sound. FM receiver sales grew exponentially and FM converters for the car allowed one to take home-listening preferences on the road until AM/FM car radios became available in 1963. A system for FM stereo was approved in 1961, and the race was officially met.

Still, broadcast fare consisted mostly of the exact same thing you could hear on AM, albeit with increased clarity. With many big-city, network-affiliated stations, FM was "bonused" to advertisers, as an extra incentive to reach a slightly wider audience. Companies saw no advantage in spending money on additional facilities and staff for FM when there was no money to be made. Those who did offer separate programming operated on a shoestring budget, hoping only to break even.

The picture changed in 1964 when the FCC declared that in markets of more than 250,000 listeners, owners of AM-FM duopolies had to provide original programming on FM for at least half the broadcast day. The commission did so under pressure. The AM spectrum was cluttered with over four thousand stations, and there was simply no more bandwidth to accommodate the increasing number of license applications. Since the airwaves were ostensibly owned by the public, if operators were to serve the public interest, more diversity of programming was needed. If FM could be made commercially viable, then formats appealing to more heterogeneous tastes might be carved out.

Amazingly (by today's sensibilities), broadcasters fought the decision tooth and nail. Witness the rights fees paid for cellular telephone bandwidth recently, and compare it to 1964, when untapped gold mines were available with the FM frequencies that companies already owned. Gordon

McLendon and Todd Storz, the radio innovators who were given credit for inventing Top Forty, resisted the order mightily and suffered the consequences. The new technology was repulsed rather than embraced.

Some of this distaste was based on principle: Broadcasters resented the FCC's incursion into programming. They had always been wary of Washington proscribing how they should serve their audiences, anticipating that so-called public service segments would be unprofitable requirements that detracted from their main goals. But perhaps the real reason lay in the simple law of supply and demand. The cash cow AM stations might be devalued by an influx of FM outlets, especially if it meant new competitors who would eat into AM profit shares. Many companies petitioned the commission for waivers, but the only thing that accomplished was to postpone the start date of the new dictum from July 1, 1965, to January 1, 1967.

Again, imagine the businessman of today, faced with a deadline for introducing a new product, realizing that his competitors were under the same time constraints. One would think that enterprising broadcasters would race to get there first, establishing their product in the audience's consciousness before their rivals. But most companies lingered until the very last minute and even *then* their attitude was similar to the mom-and-pop operators: Put out a cut-rate product showcasing their AM talent in prime listening hours, while consigning the rest of the day to cheaply produced filler. After all, weren't all the good format ideas already taken?

The answer might lay in the antiformat: free-form radio. A revolutionary idea, but by 1966 America was ready for a revolution.

Meet the New Boss

AN UNWITTING CONTRIBUTOR to this cataclysmic shift away from AM was WABC radio king Rick Sklar, whose tight format and unrelenting promotions were starting to be out of step with the changing times. With the Beatles leading the British Invasion, America was liberated from the pop confections of the early sixties. The movement spawned an awareness of challenging musical innovations that couldn't be heard on conventional radio. Scott Muni saw this happening and was increasingly at odds with Sklar on how to better serve the still substantial WABC following.

Scottso had always been a big fan of music. At age fifteen, he had wangled his way into a Fats Domino recording session. He watched in awe as the producer explained to Domino how the song went, since no one there read music. He hummed the melody and patiently mapped out the phrasing.

"You made . . . me cry . . . when you said . . . good-bye . . ."

He then talked to the sax player about how to play the instrumental bridge. Take after take, they rehearsed until they were able to perform the song flawlessly. There were no multitrack recorders in studios then; the musicians all sang and played into one central microphone. The slightest mistake by any of the players meant the whole song had to be rerecorded, unless it happened at a spot where an undetectable tape splice could be made. There was a bottle on the floor that the musicians passed around occasionally, a fringe benefit to the twenty-dollar session fee they each received. "Ain't That a Shame" became a huge hit, and Muni felt that he'd witnessed history.

In any case, he was hooked on rock and roll music, quite unlike the sentiment he attributed to his boss. Muni thought that if polka music suddenly became fashionable, Sklar would be equally comfortable programming it.

Tensions escalated between the two men, and things came to a head when Sklar accused Muni, in front of his peers, of receiving payola. On that Tuesday in the spring of 1964, Muni came to the now pro forma music meeting excited by a new record. It was the latest single from his friend Frankie Valli, whose group was one of the few American bands to stay on top through the British onslaught. The Four Seasons, led by Valli's soaring falsetto leads, retained the flavor of the old doo-wops, while incorporating more inventive production techniques. But this one was a little different: plodding, almost dirgelike, and very slow getting to the hook. It was called "Rag Doll."

Only Muni realized that the song was special and submitted it for approval at the music meeting. But now his boss was implying that the only people who would appreciate "Rag Doll" were those who had a financial stake in it. His fellow jocks stood by silently, leaving Muni to twist in the wind.

His integrity sullied, Muni marched into Sklar's office and was summarily fired for his defiant attitude. The move was not without risk to WABC. Rick Sklar had been at the helm for less than a year, and WMCA and WINS were still tough competitors. If Muni defected to one of them, it could hurt WABC in the long run. But Sklar had such an aversion to the mere hint of payola, plus a distrust of Muni's easy relationship with record promoters, that he reasoned he could use those arguments to justify the move to his superiors. Certainly, it made sense to move the popular and more teen-oriented Morrow into Muni's early-evening slot. He believed that his staff was still the strongest and could weather any desertion. It also told the other jocks who was boss, much like a football coach might send a message to his team by punishing a star player. So he went about the business of restructuring the all-American team, sans Muni.

The Federal Communications Commission was coincidentally passing the duopoly rule, by a 5–2 margin, that would radically change the face of broadcasting. Although rejected by many as a bureaucratic proposal that would never take root, a few forward-thinking proprietors of commercial FMs weighed their options. Chief among them was RKO, a conglomerate encompassing the famed motion picture company, General Tire and Rubber, and a string of radio and television stations, among them WOR and WOR-FM in New York, where free-form radio was born on commercial airwaves.

WOR-FM began the day on July 30, 1966, with the Troggs' raucous anthem "Wild Thing," not with the dulcet tones of longtime WOR morning host John Gambling. The station was automated temporarily until new jocks could be signed under a revised AFTRA (American Federation of Radio and Television Artists) contract. "Temporarily" turned out to be almost three months.

Finding disc jockey talent wasn't a problem. Scott Muni, after trying his hand for a year at running a hip music nightclub, was a star player and a radio free agent. Murray the K had been dislodged from his *Swinging Soirée* as WINS decided to go all news. And there was an interesting chap named Bill Mercer, aka Rosko, who'd knocked around several stations on both coasts. By October of 1966, the labor issues were settled and Scott Muni was doing afternoons with Murray the K ruling the early evening hours on WOR-FM.

Some dispute that WOR-FM was free form at all, citing restrictions that the jocks were under and the preponderance of Top Forty music played. But in 1966, musicians had yet to break free of the yoke of three-minute singles. Albums were just becoming the dominant form of record sales, but they were still mainly a collection of potential singles with B-sides that were not considered "commercial" enough to hit the AM airwaves. At the very beginning, no one could just play whatever they wanted, whenever they wanted. The payola scandals were not so distant a memory as to allow that kind of freedom for DJs. But there were listening sessions where a programmer would sit in with the jocks and approve a stack of records that had been brought in. As the days went by, management began to trust the jocks, convinced that their reasons for airing the songs were altruistic, not because they were being paid to do so. Within weeks, the station *was* totally free form.

When WOR-FM started playing "Society's Child" by Janis Ian, many musicians and record executives took notice. AM radio wouldn't touch the record for a number of reasons, chief among them that the subject matter was about a teenage interracial love affair. At over five minutes, it was longer than conventional singles, and who was Janis Ian anyway? She didn't even record for a major label. The song garnered so much reaction that Ian was invited to the studio for a lengthy interview, another no-no on AM radio.

More and more, WOR-FM looked to differentiate itself from Top Forty. They still had jingles, although their production was much more subtle and understated than the exciting PAMS packages that WABC was still using. They merely acted as a buffer between songs that didn't sound compatible, or as a gentle reminder of the call letters. Since commercial announcements were few and far between, jocks weren't compelled to speak between every record: They could program lengthy sets of music. This led to another dilemma. If each song wasn't a separate entity but more a component of a greater whole, there needed to be some tangible reason for linking them together. Thus came about the art of the segue.

The simplest reason to group songs came from Scottso. He called them "miniconcerts" or "Muni-concerts." He would select three or more recordings from the same artist, often from the same album, and bunch them together. Muni could go fifteen to twenty minutes before announcing what he'd played. This created an added, perhaps unintentional benefit. Since listeners at the time were used to having songs identified immediately before or after they were played, they were now forced to listen longer to discover what they'd just heard. Since ratings are based on not only the number of individuals tuned in at a given time but how long they listen, WOR-FM might garner higher ratings as a result.

Obviously, the miniconcert had its limitations. If one disliked the Rolling Stones and knew that Muni would be playing not just one song but five, the temptation to turn the dial would be great. You also needed bands that had a wide selection of good songs. If you anticipated that every time

Scottso played a set of Beatles, the same five songs would be aired, audiences would soon tire of the repetition. Other reasons to segue were needed.

Thematic sets provided one answer. These were songs that dealt with the same subject and/or shared common words in the title—the overused "rain" sets born of that era, simply stringing together a brace of tunes about the weather. One could play the same songs by different artists, like Peter, Paul and Mary's "Blowin' in the Wind," segued with Bob Dylan's original. Another set might consist of Dylan material performed by others. Later in the decade, musical family trees could be examined, like the Byrds, Buffalo Springfield, the Hollies, and Crosby, Stills, Nash and Young.

Broadcasters with good ears found musical cues: songs in the same key, or with similar chord structures. There are also songs that mesh well together—the closing drumbeats of one song flow seamlessly into the opening percussion of another. These became the most prevalent segues because the opportunities were so extensive.

In the summer of 1967, the Beatles released *Sgt. Pepper's Lonely Hearts Club Band,* giving birth to the concept album. On many a night, the Fifth Beatle, Murray the K, would play an entire side of the masterwork. Uninterrupted album sides became popular programming, especially as more artists began to link their songs together in the manner of FM DJs.

It became incumbent upon the jock to have vast knowledge of music, something that Top Forty DJs didn't need or didn't have. It was like homework for the schoolchild—every day, a jock would take new releases home to sample and select songs for upcoming shows. In 1966, this was a large but not Herculean task, since the number of albums by rock artists was still at a manageable level. The success of FM changed that, as more record companies sought performers who could turn out quality album tracks that might not qualify as singles.

Unlike AM radio, where morning drive was where the money was, evenings were the place to be on FM. Baby boomers were now reaching college age, and dorm rooms in early 1967 acted as huge amplifiers echoing Murray's show. His taste was almost unerring on undiscovered performers, and students looked forward to the introduction of fresh new talent. Rating services gave Murray the K audience shares ranging between 3 and 4 percent during his stint at WOR, which was unheard of for FM, and competitive with most AM stations.

But all was not quiet on the management front. RKO was still uneasy with disc jockeys holding so much power. They also pointed to uneven ratings and felt that although the programming could be uplifting at times, it bogged down at others. As the station began to gain revenue, the star jocks wanted their piece of the action: The low pay scale AFTRA had negotiated was already beginning to chafe. Even though FM was making money for the first time, it still was dwarfed by what its AM sisters were pulling in. And RKO General was having even more success with its West Coast FM outlets doing BOSS (a hip expression of the time, the equivalent of "fab" or "gear," meaning the greatest or coolest) radio, and eventually decided to allow the man responsible for that format to control the programming at WOR.

His name was Bill Drake. Drake was born Philip T. Yarborough and like most programmers began as a disc jockey. He worked at several stations around the country before becoming program director of KYA in San Francisco. He dreamed of running a chain of radio stations, and to this end partnered with Gene Chenault. They acquired several California stations as clients, but it was the success of KGB in San Diego that captured RKO's attention.

Drake-Chenault were able to convince RKO to put them in charge of KHJ (which originally stood for kindness, happiness, and joy) in Los Angeles. Today, the idea that a station in such a major market could be experimental is absurd, but Drake perfected his BOSS radio formula there, working with Ron Jacobs, the hands-on program director. With legendary jocks Robert W. Morgan and the "Real" Don Steele leading the way, KHJ was an instant success.

Drake's talent was not so much in inventing a format, but in taking the best of what others had done before and distilling it into his own formula, insisting on precise execution. Drake saw himself as a master architect who hired other top craftsmen to execute his plans. Chenault also helped him foster an image that was to serve him well, that of a powerful, reclusive figure shrouded in mystery. Many of the programmers who worked with him never met him in person, and carried on few telephone conversations with him. He insisted on absolute control of any property he consulted, although he used his dictatorial powers sparingly.

He lived in posh Bel Air in a luxurious Spanish-style mansion reputed to have twenty-four telephone lines. He rarely granted interviews or appeared in public. Much like Howard Hughes, he traded on the image of the all powerful Oz, one who could make or break careers on his slightest whim. He arranged to be able to monitor any of his stations from his villa, and had a direct line to the control room of each. Disc jockeys lived in fear of a "hotline" call from the mysterious Drake. One could picture him—tall and lanky, relaxing by his pool, surrounded by tanned California beauties, arbitrarily dialing up a station in Boston or New York and exorcising something or someone he didn't like. This was largely an image he took advantage of, not the reality. By all accounts, Drake is a soft-spoken, modest Southerner by nature.

Chenault, however, fueled his legend. Many employees left the company frustrated at how Drake had received credit for their hard work and innovation. Indeed, within Drake's framework, individual program directors had wide authority over music and promotions, as long as they stuck to the basic formula. It wasn't hard to identify a Drake-formatted station. The sound was uniform and clean, with smooth DJs who could have been from Anywhere, U.S.A. The jingle packages were spare, merely the frequency, call letters, and occasionally the jock's name. When Drake approached a major jingle company about fashioning such simple fare, they refused, telling him it would never be effective. So Drake contacted the Johnny Mann Singers, brought them into a studio, and produced jingles for KHJ himself.

Fresh from his L.A. triumph, the mystery man was brought in to consult at all the RKO stations, including WOR-FM. Its days as a free-form station were numbered. Drake probably thought he could work with such a distinguished air staff, but the freedom Muni, Rosko, and Murray had tasted was a powerful elixir, and one by one they resigned or were forced out under Drake's constraints. The free-form experiment was completely over at WOR-FM by October of 1967. WBAI, the Pacifica public station in New York, gave the displaced jocks an hour forum to vent their complaints about how the consultant had ruined their station. Critics in the print media, both public and trade journals, joined in. Most gave RKO no chance after dismantling such a work of art. They predicted disaster for Drake and his "West Coast" sound.

Within months, Drake-Chenault had the next laugh. In the Pulse surveys, WOR-FM's share of the New York audience quadrupled to a 16, second only to WABC, which had vaulted to 26 shares under Sklar. It may not have been innovative or exciting radio, but it was consistent and, as *Newsweek* put it, "a smoothly modulated mixture of pop favorites."

The great progressive experiment seemed dead in New York, and critics ate their words, noting the enormous ratings success of BOSS radio. Drake's consultancy grew far beyond the RKO stations, and he picked his spots well, rarely venturing into a situation where the odds were against him. His few failures occurred when hubris caused him to disregard his own formula, or when citizen groups protested his intent to rob them of a beloved format, as they did in Washington, D.C., when he announced the takeover of a popular classical station. Drake-Chenault enjoyed a decade-long reign as kings of the FM radio world.

But despite the devastating dispossession in New York, the hardy seeds of free form had been sown. They already were growing on the West Coast, and the survivors of WOR-FM were merely wounded, and their spirit remained strong.

Growin' Up

IN LATE 1967, I was oblivious to what was happening at the big stations in Manhattan mere miles across the East River from Garden City. I was busy trying to save my fledgling career. I had only a few days to prepare for my professional debut, and since I'd never listened to WLIR, I figured I'd better get acquainted with it in a hurry. It was rough sledding for an eighteen-year-old. I tuned in the night I was hired and heard a man with an incredibly deep voice, extolling the virtues of a quaint expensive restaurant called the Wee Tappee Inn in Old Westbury, Long Island, old-money territory. The announcer sounded so worldly, so knowledgeable—as if he dined there several nights a week. It was intimidating as hell. This guy was probably in his late forties and would regard me as some snot-nosed kid who didn't belong on his sophisticated radio station. The music he played was the very stuff I'd had so many arguments with my parents about—

vanilla, syrupy, soporific instrumentals. For all my suffering, I was paid the rich sum of a dollar ten an hour. I'd made more the previous summer washing dishes at a New Jersey diner and tending the greens at the Saddle River Country Club.

I was scheduled to go on the air Saturday morning from eight until one. Ted Webb had asked me to come in Friday afternoon so he could show me the ropes. I personally doubted that a couple of hours' training would be sufficient but he had confidence that I could handle it and I didn't want to create uncertainty in his mind by sharing my own reservations. After classes Friday, I journeyed through the catacombs of the Garden City Hotel until I reached the station. For the first few weeks, I don't think I took the same route twice; that's how confusing the underground maze was.

Ted knew that I had learned to engineer my own program at WALI, a practice called "combo-ing." Most major stations employ engineers to run the board, or audio console, for the jocks, but small-time radio is able to reduce expenses by having one man perform the tasks of announcing and engineering. It's akin to carrying on an in-depth conversation while driving a stick-shift car in heavy traffic. After a while it becomes second nature but if you're new at it, both skills suffer. Learning to run the board was the least of my worries, I thought. Pronouncing those big foreign names of the composers—now *that* made me nervous.

Little did I know that the symbiosis between announcing and engineering would almost end my employment at WLIR as soon as it began. My first mistake was an understandable one. I had assumed that since WALI was a minor college AM station, its equipment would be as outdated and ineffective as any imaginable. Adelphi wasn't exactly known for its broadcasting curriculum, like Syracuse or Northwestern. Therefore, the equipment had to be whatever they could muster from some commercial station's discards, held together only by the ingenuity of John Schmidt. WLIR's facility had to be light-years ahead. *Wrong!*

As Webb explained how things worked, I was lost in a daze of horror— I couldn't concentrate on what he was saying. The audio console must have predated WALI's by at least ten years. It looked like something Edwin Armstrong had jury-rigged before the war. The Civil War. There were seven huge unlabeled black knobs across the front, topped by little dark switches that resembled telegraph keys. Two VU meters were clipping away above the keys. Everything was channeled through the two large knobs in the center. It actually looked much simpler than WALI's multi-channeled console.

"Where are the cart decks, Ted?" I asked innocently. "Cart," or cartridge, decks, are units that resemble old eight-track tape players. All radio stations play their commercials on these. Generally, there are four or more, rack mounted and run by remote control. The operator simply slides the tape into a slot, punches a button, and boom! instant commercial. The cartridges could also play songs or short programs. Cart decks were commonly used on Top Forty stations for music, since vinyl 45s or albums tended to scratch and deteriorate upon repeated spins, whereas tape could be replayed hundreds of times with no noticeable degradation. Most studios also have them linked together, so that if several spots in a row are scheduled, you merely had to start the first one and upon completion it would trigger the second and so on until the set of commercials was over.

"We don't have any," he replied tersely.

"How do you play commercials, then?" I wondered aloud.

"With this . . . the spot tape machine." He pointed at a ramshackle gray box labeled "Spotmaster," with one pointer and a hundred or so markings: A1, 2, 3, 4; B1, 2, 3, 4, etc. He slid the top lid open to reveal a large flap of celluloid with narrow grooves. It was held on a metal spool by cellophane tape. I was tempted for a moment to think it was some new technology that I was unaware of, but from its appearance, it had to be older than the audio console. Webb explained, "You just dial up the commercial, let's say J3, hit this button, and—"

I heard a muffled voice, followed by rumbles and then a flapping sound.

"Damn, it's come loose again," he swore. The celluloid had separated from the spool and was flapping around the innards of the machine until Webb turned it off. "It's very important to turn the unit off immediately if you hear the flapping sound. Otherwise the tape will shred and we'll lose all our commercials."

I tried to hide my dismay. The cellophane tape obviously had dried up under the heat of the machine's internal works. It wasn't hard to imagine this happening on a regular basis. Plus, there were other problems I could anticipate right away. First, there was no remote control and the unit was three feet behind the broadcast position. Meaning that when you went to commercial, you had to close your microphone, slide back on your roller chair, and locate the start button. That had to take at least a second. Then,

the sliding dial had minuscule markings and didn't click firmly into position. So you might think you were playing J3 when in reality you were
playing J2. You could jiggle the dial over to the proper spot, but if it wasn't
aligned precisely, you got muffled sound at half-volume. But these were
things Webb had to deal with daily so he must have been aware of them.

"Ted, what happens when you have three spots in a row?" I asked.
Most stations had at least that many.

"Well, you can do it a couple of ways. You can wait until the first one is
finished, hit the rewind button, and then slide the dial over to the next
number and hit play again. You've got to wait till the green light comes on
or it won't be fully rewound and the next spot will start in the middle. Or
else you can plan it so that you alternate live reads with taped spots, or use
the spot tape once, then a reel-to-reel spot, then a spot tape again. Got it?"

He pointed toward two ancient Roberts home tape recorders. My dad
had better and newer ones in his basement. Any time there were commercial breaks, you had to find the proper tape from a disorganized pile of five-
inch reels stacked randomly on a desk, thread it onto the machine, cue it to
the beginning, and hit the play button. Again, there was no remote control
on the tape decks and they were a few feet farther back than the spot tape
machine. What a nightmare.

But the biggest problems were yet to come. I noticed there were four
turntables in the studio, a bit unusual because most places had only two.
And they were not the rugged broadcast variety I was used to, but home
units made by a local manufacturer. "Must break a lot of needles cueing
these up," I remarked.

"Uh, Mr. Reiger doesn't believe in cueing up records. Thinks it
wrecks the stylus and scratches the opening of the song."

The Firesign Theatre once released a comedy album entitled *Everything You Know Is Wrong*. That precisely described my feelings at the moment. I had been taught that anathema to all radio was dead air—pauses
when nothing is transmitted. Certainly in Top Forty or BOSS radio, pacing is all important. Everything has to come with machine-gun rapidity,
with no silence—ever! But given the equipment at WLIR, every time you
went from one record to another, there had to be a long moment of noth-
ingness. From live announcements to commercials, a second or two of silence. One commercial to the next—dead air.

Then came the topper. WLIR broadcast in stereo, but each channel
was controlled by a separate knob or fader. All four turntables were on the

same two faders, as were the tape decks and spot tapes. To go from one record to the next, you had to turn both knobs down to zero, hit the switch to go from the left turntable to the right, start the right turntable, and then turn both knobs back up simultaneously as the music started. But this had to be done without cueing the record beforehand—just dropping the needle in the space between tracks and guessing how long it would take before the music started. Good luck!

Oh, by the way, the switches to go from one turntable to the next were old and had long since lost their click stops. So, like with the spot tape, you might think you were on turntable one when you were really on turntable three. And since they were home machines, not professional units, they didn't get up to speed immediately, taking two revolutions to achieve 33⅓ rpm. If you estimated the start time incorrectly, the record would "wow" in. In other words, it would start slowly and gradually accelerate until it reached the proper speed. As Webb explained these eccentricities to me, I broke into a cold sweat.

That night, I lay awake, not able to sleep at all, anticipating the disaster that was to be my professional broadcast premiere.

Fortunate Son

FOR BILL "ROSKO" MERCER, the end of free form on WOR-FM in the early autumn of 1967 was a dream dashed. He found himself out of work again, and was faced with the unpleasant prospect of returning to a format he despised or finding an alternate way to make a living. Muni was given the opportunity to keep his shift, and Drake told him that he could continue to play what he wanted. But Scott's experience taught him that he wouldn't remain an island for long and his oasis of freedom would soon perish in the harsh desert of strict formatics. It was fortunate for both of them that the initial success at WOR-FM had not gone unnoticed.

WNEW-AM had been one of the top stations in New York for de-cades. Boasting such talent as William B. Williams, Gene Klavan and Dee Finch, Jim Lowe, Julius La Rosa, and Ted Brown, it was the city's favorite place to hear all the great standards. They broadcast Giants football on

Sundays and had a full-service news and sports operation. A Metromedia station, they were owned by John Kluge, who has since become one of the richest men in America. Year after year, profits increased and advertising revenue exceeded ratings because Madison Avenue loved the affluent audience WNEW attracted. But WNEW-FM was a different story.

The station was originally headquartered at 565 Fifth Avenue, sandwiched into a small area next to the massive AM complex. Like most owners, Kluge was content to simulcast his AM signal on FM until the FCC's duopoly ruling in 1964. Given no choice by the commission, Jack Sullivan, head of Metromedia's radio division, charged George Duncan with the job of inventing a new format for the FM stations.

George, the general manager of WNEW-FM, was a beefy, florid Irishman who wore his Gaelic heritage and Catholic faith like a banner. He favored crisply pressed dark suits, and kept his bald bespectacled head immaculately barbered. A graduate of Cornell University, the ex-Marine once served as a milkman and a New York State trooper.

Duncan was justly proud of his service record, and Scott Muni had to break up more than a few bar fights late at night when some inebriated patron insulted the Corps or the Catholic church in George's presence. And those who knew of these twin loyalties were not advantaged if they tried to use them dishonestly to advance their cause. On one such occasion, a hotshot young salesman petitioning him for a job had nearly clinched the position when Duncan mentioned in passing that he had been a Marine.

"Oh, yeah. I was, too," mused the job seeker, trying to ingratiate himself further.

"Really?" said Duncan, with a raised eyebrow. He didn't look like an ex-Marine. "What was your serial number?"

"Oh jeez, I don't know. I forgot," came the answer. The man, despite his otherwise impressive credentials, didn't get the job, because no Marine ever forgets his serial number for the rest of his life. The man was a fraud, and if he'd lie about that, could George ever trust him with anything else?

Duncan looked forward to experimenting with something that could generate another profit center for Metromedia when the duopoly ruling came down. His original blueprint was to form a station that played similar music to WNEW, but with this twist: The disc jockeys would all be women.

By today's standards, this doesn't sound so radical, but in 1966, this was a completely alien concept. Women weren't generally accepted in the media at all except as window dressing. There was the token TV weather girl, often the butt of the anchors' sexist humor. But they weren't taken seriously as reporters or disc jockeys. Their voices were thought not to cut through the limited frequency response of AM radio, and on television and in the workplace, they were seen as a distraction.

But Duncan posited that with FM's wider bandwidth, a quality woman's voice could attract male listeners or other women, who might take pride in their sisters' accomplishments. With the civil rights movement and feminism gaining momentum in the sixties, the idea seemed to have merit. Four hundred women auditioned, and among those hired were Alison Steele, Nell Bassett, Sally Jessy Raphael (yes, her), and Rita Sands, who later became a news anchor at WCBS radio.

Duncan's plan never got a real chance. Initially, male reaction wasn't positive and women seemed to resent the idea of their mates being seduced over the radio by female jocks. Madison Avenue firmly believed that women could not sell products to other women. Metromedia Group head Jack Sullivan had told George in a casual meeting that "something is happening in rock music" and suggested that he visit some clubs in Greenwich Village and experience the new phenomenon close up. In addition, Duncan was being handed a gift by RKO's abdication and wasn't about to return it.

The following story ran in *Billboard* on October 28, 1967:

Bill "Rosko" Mercer, the former all night personality with WOR-FM who resigned a couple of weeks ago, has been hired by WNEW-FM for a progressive rock show and will handle a seven days a week stint, 7–midnight. George Duncan, station manager at WNEW-FM, said the decision for the change in the programming and image of WNEW-FM was "made strictly on Rosko's availability." WNEW-FM is "building for the future," he said. The station plays easy listening music. WNEW-FM was the first all-girl station in New York. The girls are being retained for the daytime operations of the station. Duncan said he saw no reason why the combination of the girls daytime and Rosko nighttime shouldn't work. He said Rosko will play "meaningful" music. "Our music has progressed in this direction for some while. Rosko's availability only pushed up our timetable for the change."

It wouldn't be the first or last time that a radio executive misled the press. Duncan had already laid the groundwork for Jonathan Schwartz of

WNAC in Boston to do middays, and Scott Muni was in negotiations to come in to host afternoons. One by one, the women were replaced, with the exception of Steele, who was sent to the Siberia of overnights.

Rosko started on October 30, 1967, followed by Schwartz a month later and Muni in early December. "This Rosko thing has been unbelievable," George Duncan told *Billboard*. "Not only in advertising, and his show was immediately sold out, but in mail pull. In one day, we received letters from a psychologist, an anthropologist, and a physician, all saying they were glad we hired Rosko. The doctor said that he felt that the only station left for him and his wife was WQXR after WOR-FM changed." In that same issue, Duncan admitted that WNEW-FM was going all the way with "meaningful" music.

The very term "meaningful" indicated his naïveté when it came to the monster he was creating. "We spoke Russian," said Jonathan Schwartz, years later at a reunion. "They [management] didn't understand it. It was like we were speaking Russian." Indeed the bosses didn't know what they had; but ironically, neither did the jocks. They were "faking it," according to Rosko, and some did it better than others as they hurried to educate themselves about a brand of music that was foreign to all except Muni. They only knew that there was an audience, a very vocal audience, who appreciated Metromedia's picking up the baton from WOR-FM. They targeted advertising toward the youth market, placing print ads in *The Village Voice* and local college papers.

Mornings continued to be a simulcast of WNEW's Klavan and Finch, until program director Nat Asch hired John Zacherle, who had no radio background but was a familiar figure on local television. Zach was moved to late nights in fairly short order, mainly because his poor eyesight caused him difficulty reading the studio clock. One morning as Duncan commuted from Westchester County, Zach said it was 8:15, causing Duncan to curse himself for being late for an important meeting. After breaking several traffic laws to minimize the damage, he discovered that he was actually early and the Zacherle had overstated the time by an hour—it had been 7:15.

Someone a bit more dependable was needed, so ex–Top Forty jock Johnny Michaels was brought in to hold down the morning gig. Everyone worked six days a week live, but were heard for seven since the weekend shows were taped in advance. Pay was scaled at $175 a week, and in the beginning there was little opportunity to make anything on the side.

It was a disparate group—"the crew of the SS *Motley*," as Muni would often describe them. Jonathan Schwartz, whose father, Arthur, had written "Dancing in the Dark" and a number of pop standards, had grown up in Southern California and New England, enjoying wealth and privilege. A childhood playmate was Carly Simon, of the Simon and Schuster publishing scions and later a talented singer-songwriter. He was able to afford an apartment and maintain an office at Carnegie Hall. A budding writer, he put together a collection of short stories entitled *Almost Home* and penned a semiautobiographical novel called *Distant Stations*. "Jonno," as he was called, liked to dress shabbily in torn jeans and rumpled golf shirts. He was an intellectual and a clever raconteur who took pride in using certain multisyllabic words for the first time on a rock station. His trademark was the stories he would tell on the air, very much like Jean Shepherd did on WOR at the time. Whereas Shepherd rarely played music, Schwartz now was forced to step away from his background as a Sinatraphile and lover of standards—literally moving from Bing Crosby to David Crosby. He loved the sound of his own voice, which retained a slight Boston accent. Often he would play a song simply because he enjoyed saying the name of the band.

Bill "Rosko" Mercer was the star. His show began at six with a set piece, "a mind excursion, a true diversion" and "reality, the hippest of all trips" over the bass line of some cool jazz. He ended every night at ten with the words, "I sure do love you so." He played jazz, blues, R&B, rock; his musical range was the widest on the staff. And he'd read stories by Shel Silverstein or poetry from *The Prophet,* all in a voice that was the most exquisite ever heard on the FM airwaves. He had a mild, barely perceptible Southern lilt, but his sound was pure honey poured from a jar—gentle yet masculine, smooth yet crackling with emotion when the moment called for it. Originally perceived as a black militant, he was certainly the most political disc jockey in the station's history. He didn't hesitate to make his opposition to the Vietnam War known, expressing his criticism of the government in unambiguous language. He and Schwartz mixed like Israel and Iraq. At staff meetings, which Rosko always dominated with his highly opinionated convictions, they were often at each other's throats and more than once had to be separated by Muni.

Zacherle first gained prominence as the host of late-night horror movies on the local ABC-TV affiliate. Made up like Lon Chaney in *Phantom of the Opera,* he'd approach these cheesy offerings with a warped sense of humor, often injecting his image into the film to make cryptic comments. He even had a number six hit record, "Dinner with Drac (Part One)," in 1958. The affection he engendered among the younger generation then translated to an emcee job with an afternoon dance party on a local UHF station. It was a parody on *American Bandstand* gone bizarro, with Zach dressed up as the ghoul, muttering under his breath as precocious high school girls gyrated wildly to the new music.

But the dance party introduced him to the new rock and he formed a lasting bond with the music. So when a friend told him that WNEW-FM needed DJs in their new format, he contacted Duncan and Nat Asch. They originally hired him to do weekends, but the response from the now college-age audience that remembered him from his ghoul days was so great that he quickly moved into full-time. Asch felt they needed someone a bit different to do mornings and after consulting his teenage son who said Zach was cool, he got the job. His broadcasting skills were minimal: He broke every rule in the book and radio mavens were indeed horrified upon hearing him for the first time. When the engineer opened his microphone, he sounded as if he had been aroused from a deep sleep. First, you would hear papers rustling as he scrambled to gather his notes. His sentences featured long pauses interrupted by staccato bursts of rapid-fire mumbling, punctuated with his infectious chortling. Boris Karloff on acid might be an apt description. He very often forgot to keep track of what he played and would spend minutes either trying to remember or finding the scrap of paper he'd scribbled it on.

As a boss, Duncan could be an intimidating figure to some of the jocks who only saw the straightlaced ex-Marine aspect of him and missed his iconoclastic and playful side. But he led the WNEW-FM jocks with a sense of family, even after he ascended to head of Metromedia's radio division. One DJ tells a story of how he was filling in for the morning show host when an FCC inspector showed up at 6 A.M., unannounced. This particular bureaucrat was notorious for his intimidating style and rigid enforcement of even the most arcane rules. He had bullied countless jocks into committing nervous mistakes on the air. The inspector was taking notes and asking detailed questions, making the young man even more edgy than he already was. A radio custom is to sign off the program logs in advance near the end of a shift so that you won't forget. At 9:45, the skittish DJ logged off, stating the time as 10 A.M. The inspector jumped down his throat.

"How dare you sign this log as ten A.M., fifteen minutes early," he scolded. He then extracted an official-looking form and wrote up the transgression. The shaken jock left the studio several minutes later, convinced that he'd not only lost his job but had endangered the station's FCC license. The first person he ran into in the hall was George Duncan, ramrod straight in a blue serge suit, who asked him how he was doing.

This is it, I'm about to be fired, the kid thought. Instead, Duncan placed his arm around him.

"You know that guy from the FCC?" Duncan whispered ominously. "Fuck him."

According to Scott Muni, Duncan later scoured the accusatory report and found several procedural violations in the inspector's tactics. He complained vociferously to his supervisor in Washington, which led to the man's dismissal.

Under Duncan's leadership, WNEW-FM began its wobbly journey from a miscast group with diverse backgrounds to a team of eclectic personalities that made radio history. Their mission was to explore the new world of rock, which was experimenting in art rock, blues, country and folk rock, psychedelia, and other progressive forms. But other radio conventions were left unchallenged.

An odd quirk in those early days was that while WNEW-FM simulcast hourly news from their AM sister station, there was guitar music playing gently underneath it. Most listeners thought that this was some sort of hippie affectation to soften the authoritative tone of the WNEW-AM newsmen, but in reality, it was a technical matter. An FM transmitter triggers a red beacon on most receivers indicating that the signal broadcast is stereo. This was considered a competitive edge in 1968 when some stations were still monaural. But FCC policy stated that the beacon could only remain on for four minutes when the actual broadcast material was not in stereo. Since the mono newscasts were five minutes in length, to avoid shutting down the beacon, they had to find an unobtrusive way to keep it fired up. After scouring the music library, Asch and Duncan found a guitar work by German composer Georg Philipp Telemann that would fit behind every conceivable news story—from the most dire tragedy to the lightest kicker.

General manager George Duncan had a healthy respect for the power of the FCC and an appreciation for the value of John Kluge's broadcasting licenses. Kluge himself saw his stewardship of radio and television stations as a responsibility not to be taken lightly. Whereas others would later challenge the FCC's authority when it came to censoring obscene content, Kluge and Duncan initially believed they had a moral responsibility to provide programming that reinforced positive societal values. They resisted hiring "shock" jocks, and heeded listener complaints when members of their own flock went too far. They were not about to risk their licenses in cavalier fashion, and quickly laid down clear guidelines. "Eskimo Blue Day" by Jefferson Airplane was outlawed for obscenity, as was "Volunteers" for seditious content. "Working Class Hero" came a bit later, and you know that story.

WNEW-FM underwent an early management shake-up, as John Kluge realized what a gem he had in George Duncan, who he now elevated to lead the company's entire radio division. A no-nonsense businessman named Varner Paulsen was named to succeed him as general manager, and Paulsen soon came to the conclusion that Nat Asch was out of his element as program director. He approached Scott Muni for the position, the only staffer who could unite the disparate jocks by virtue of the respect he was accorded for his legendary market status.

Muni had never managed before and was reluctant, but Paulsen convinced him that he would handle the administrative work and leave Scott to his strength—music. And since the music was programmed by the jocks, Scott's main task would be to ride herd gently, to prevent egregious abuses.

Muni did not take to certain aspects of the job readily. His first big test came early, when Varner Paulsen told him that his music director had physically assaulted a saleswoman. Scott told Paulsen that he had been fired many times, but had never fired anyone and dreaded the assignment. He asked his boss to give him some time to think about how he was going to execute the unpleasant task. Varner told him to call the recalcitrant music director to a 9 A.M. meeting in Paulsen's office and that he would ease Muni through the process.

Although not overly lavish, the general manager's office did have a window facing the Pan Am Building and a heavy oak door that shielded any commotion from the outside rooms. When Muni haltingly began the meeting saying that the man's actions had left him no choice but termination, the man leaped from his chair and made a threatening move toward Muni, screaming, "You're not going to fire me, goddamn it. Nobody's going to fire me."

Paulsen quickly moved from behind his desk to back up Muni, but the ex-Marine needed no such assistance. He shoved the man back into his chair and got in his face.

"Listen, you skinny son of a bitch," he yelled. "You'd better get used to getting fired because as long as you can't keep away from those drugs you're using, you're going to get fired over and over. You're gonna be fired so many times the word will be emblazoned on your forehead. And you're lucky I wasn't around when you hit that woman. Because if I was there, I would have coldcocked you into the middle of next week. Now get your ass out of here before I throw you through that wooden door or out that window and they have to scrape you off Forty-fifth Street. I'm firing you and what are you gonna do about it?"

The young music director slinked out of the room, and Paulsen beamed toward Muni. "Now that wasn't so hard, was it?"

Muni's words proved prophetic as years later, the former music director was working for a small station in Westchester and was fired for punching a politician he shared the dais with during a fund-raising rally.

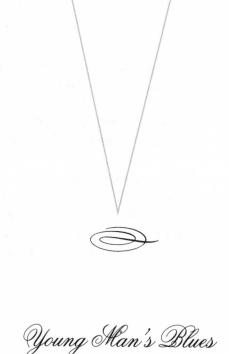

Young Man's Blues

I WAS LUCKY. In 1967, at eighteen years old, I was in the best aerobic shape of my life, having played freshman soccer for Adelphi the previous fall. I'm sure that was the only thing that prevented a fatal heart attack.

Here I was, alone in a dimly lit studio on a cold Saturday morning in late autumn. The hotline telephone was blinking, its red beacon signaling that owner John Reiger was about to fire me. I ignored it and tried to figure out why there had been no audio on WLIR for the last thirty seconds. My hands were shaking as I flipped switches and twisted buttons to no avail. Finally, I goosed one of the turntable knobs and felt a mushy click, and heard the surging strings of Mantovani. Success!

I gingerly picked up the phone, steeling myself for the barrage I knew was coming. It was Reiger, all right.

"What the hell is going on there? Why is there so much dead air? What's wrong with you? Haven't you ever been on the radio before? You're finished. I'm calling your replacement right now. Dore, I can't believe thi—" He slammed down the receiver before hearing my stammering apologies.

As I watched the Mantovani record spin on the aging Empire turntable, I prayed that it would go on forever so that I didn't have to change records again. I jiggled the switch on the opposite side, hoping that it caught in the right position. To hell with Reiger. I cued up the next album in the traditional manner, finding the beginning of the next track and backing it up a couple of turns. As Mantovani faded, I went through the multi-step procedure necessary to change songs and miraculously, there was Percy Faith. I'd underestimated the time it would take to get up to speed however, and the record wowed in . . . unsonorously.

The hotline barked again. He'd already fired me once, so what else could he do? Besides, now I'd locked in the two turntables. I wasn't going to get tricky and switch albums until each side ran out, and even then I contemplated just retreating back to the first cut on each and replaying them.

"Hey, how are you?" A deep voice, not Reiger's, was on the other end. "It's Mike Harrison. Reiger just called and said you're having some trouble there."

Harrison was the man I'd heard a few evenings before while checking out the station for the first time. He had to be a seasoned pro, probably having a good laugh at my amateur bumbling.

"Yeah, he just fired me, I think. Are you coming in now?"

"Forget about it. He must have fired me five times already. He thought your tape was the best he's heard in a long time. Calm down. I'll be there in a little while and help you out."

"Thanks, Mr. Harrison. How far away are you? How long will it take you to get in?"

"Should be about fifteen or twenty minutes. How do you like your coffee?"

I told him, not realizing that caffeine was the last thing my jangled nerves needed now. But Harrison's words were reassuring—maybe he could teach me how to overcome the quirks of WLIR's ancient technical setup. Maybe I wasn't really fired after all. Despite the low pay, the seven dollars I'd take home every week from a regular shift would put gas in the car and maybe allow me to hit the diner one night a week with my friends from the dorm.

My father had made it clear when he sent me away to school that his bank loan would cover tuition, the dorm room, and a meal ticket at Post Hall. Any discretionary spending money was up to me. And the car was due back so that my mother could use it. Living at home the previous summer, I'd managed to salt away almost my entire paycheck from the money I made as an assistant greenskeeper at a local country club. With a couple of Christmas checks from relatives, I should be able to make it through until summer. And if I could expand my role at WLIR . . . I was getting ahead of myself. I needed to keep what I had first.

The next hour went better as I began to get more comfortable with the equipment. There were still gaps of silence between elements, but since they were consistent, the effect was not jarring to the ear. When I signed on, I was so nervous that my voice was a couple octaves higher than its normal range and I must have sounded like the frightened kid I was. Normally, my radio voice was pitched much lower in an attempt to sound older. Gradually, the vocal cords loosened and I found my comfort zone.

Harrison arrived about an hour after he'd called. When he came through the studio door, I was unprepared for what I saw. I had pictured him in a corduroy jacket with patches, suede shoes, and an ascot, with silver hair and an elegant Don Ameche mustache.

But Mike Harrison was a *kid,* a few months older than me, and he was dressed in faded blue jeans and a flannel shirt. Slightly under six feet tall and lean, his black curly hair was long and shaggy. Twinkling brown eyes danced over a hawklike nose. He reminded me of John Kay, the lead singer of Steppenwolf. Did anybody on the radio look the way they sounded?

"Brought you coffee. You sound much better now. Haven't heard from Reiger again, have you?"

As Bogey said to Claude Rains, this was the beginning of a beautiful friendship. Harrison and I worked together at WLIR for the next four years. We romanced women together, ate together, even roomed together for a time. We were best men at each other's weddings. We formed a bond that has lasted to this day. But in 1967, we were the punk kids on the WLIR staff of veterans. Some were destined to stay working on Long Island throughout their careers. Some were clearly on the downside of their radio lives, and had to find other ways to survive. But Harrison and I shared a dream: Someday we would work in New York together. And if we could, we wanted it to be at WNEW-FM.

At the time, it seemed a hopeless fantasy, or at least one that would be decades in the making. Radio had created a hierarchy over the years, much like baseball only less formally structured. You start at the bottom, college or noncommercial radio. Then, a small paid gig in a tiny market. Travel throughout the country, increasing market size with each stop until, if you were lucky and/or had enough talent, you'd arrive in New York—the big time. Only the best radio people were in New York. Not Chicago, L.A., or Boston. New York was A #1, king of the hill . . . top of the heap (sound familiar?).

We found out later that this was utter hogwash. Many smaller markets have people as good as New York has, but for whatever reason, they've opted to stay put rather than challenge the Big Apple. Some folks don't care for the frenetic pace of Manhattan. Many realize that top dollar in a smaller market can afford a better way of living than similar money in New York. And there is the local nature of radio to contend with. A show that wows them in Cleveland might bomb on the East Coast, and vice versa. Humor that works in a big city might sound too elitist for the corn belt, and a midwestern monologue might fall flat in a city of skyscrapers.

At any rate, laboring at WLIR while honing our craft, Harrison and I were like the conspirators in *Papillon*—plotting our eventual escape. We hoped that somehow we could advance ourselves. We hadn't yet figured out how to make the jump from middle-of-the-road music to rock, but that would come later. Although we were less than thirty miles from the city, it might as well have been across the universe.

The air staff held WLIR in such low esteem that more than once it was deliberately knocked off the air. One such occurrence happened with a weekend morning host who was paid an unexpected visit from a friend and coworker at the station. The two were hungry and wanted to have breakfast together, but the 8 A.M. sign-on was approaching. So the jock, knowing that it would take at least twenty minutes for the plate current on the transmitter to recycle, flipped a switch and turned off the transmitter. He then threw it back to the warm-up stage, and left the building for breakfast with his friend at a nearby diner, noting on the station's logs that the transmitter had overloaded and shut down.

One by one, regular hosts migrated from WLIR to greener pastures, and Harrison and I advanced until we were working full-time. We were both drama majors with education minors, and still entertained the notion that we might be great actors someday. I saw Harrison in a production of *Dracula* and he stole the show, playing the evil count for laughs years before George Hamilton did. He did several shows at Nassau Community College with another young Long Islander who wanted to be a comedian and actor. He stuck with it longer than Michael and me, and now we're forced to admit that he also had more talent. It's still hard to believe that Harrison's little friend turned out to be Billy Crystal.

College memories are supposed to be of idyllic times with frat parties, panty raids, football games, and similar shenanigans. But for Harrison and me, it was almost all work. We'd attend class in the morning, work at WLIR in the afternoon and early evening, and rehearse our plays at night. We didn't mind because other than the lectures, we enjoyed what we were doing. I continued to play progressive rock at WALI until my junior year when my schedule didn't allow it. WLIR became a small source of income and a training ground to hone our style. There was also the game of trying to outwit Reiger and get away with liberties, like playing too many vocal tracks in the afternoon instead of boring, sappy instrumentals. We'd try to sneak in someone like Ed Ames or Johnny Mathis covering a rock song. These were the minor victories that kept us sane.

Once, the boss called us in and criticized us for using our names too often. We always figured that if we'd identify ourselves every break, some big-time radio exec who lived on the Island might happen by our spot on the dial and be impressed. But Reiger thought this cult of personality was too much, so to spite him, we remained not only anonymous, but blatantly so. We'd sign off with, "We hope you enjoyed 'Cocktails for Two.' Stay tuned for 'Dinner for Two,' with your next WLIR announcer. I'm your current WLIR announcer . . . wishing you a pleasant evening."

After a few days of this, Reiger caught on and rescinded the earlier edict. All the while, we listened to Rosko and Alison Steele at WNEW-FM and just knew that they didn't have to put up with miserly owners telling them not to say their names. But WLIR wasn't alone in indulging its owner's quirkiness. One owner of a small suburban station called the hotline while Cher's "You Better Sit Down Kids" was playing and harangued the disc jockey. "I'm a believer in family values," he huffed, "and this song glorifies divorce."

The jock explained to him that the song was on the playlist and that although it dealt with a divorced mother's message to her children, it did not promote family breakups. The owner was having none of it, though, and demanded to be put on the air as the song ended. He proceeded to apologize to the audience for playing such a subversive tune and swore that it would never be aired again.

As WLIR grew more successful, benefiting from the FCC's rulings on FM in general, our salaries slowly rose until they were brushing up against eighty dollars a week. And as plans were laid to demolish the old Garden City Hotel and replace it with a new building, WLIR was forced to relocate. Reiger chose a penthouse suite in the new Imperial Square Building, in the heart of Hempstead. New equipment was purchased, and finally we were working in a comfortable, modern environment. There were generously sized offices, storage libraries for the albums, a separate news booth and production space, and a spacious studio that could accommodate large roundtable discussions or even a small band. It was still the same old little station at 92.7, but it felt classier, leaving a subterranean dungeon for a deluxe apartment in the sky.

But the high-rent district had its price. Overhead soared and sales failed to keep pace and rumors flew that WLIR was either on the block or about to declare bankruptcy. Reiger was desperate to realize his vision as the center of Long Island culture for sophisticated adults, but WHLI AM-FM in Hempstead had an insurmountable edge. Just slightly hipper than WLIR, it was everything Reiger's little shop aspired to be. Its ratings were always solid and they paid well by comparison.

There was no way that Harrison and I imagined that we could jump from the low minor leagues of WLIR directly to a dream job in New York. Progress had to be incremental, in baby steps. We were still in school, and dropping out to make a parallel move to a small-market progressive station in another part of the country was risky. The Vietnam War was still raging and we valued our student deferments. Boxed in by our own priorities and fears, we applied for jobs at WHLI. It wasn't our ultimate goal: The music they favored was middle-of-the-road pap, but we saw it as a small step up.

It proved to be a humiliating experience. The haughty program director looked down his nose at our résumés, equating WLIR to some farm-belt AM daytimer. He gave us the bum's rush and we vowed to get even someday.

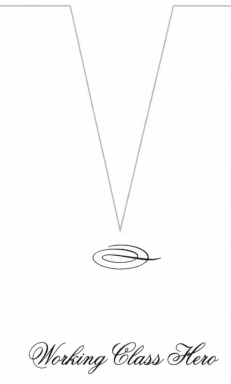

Working Class Hero

As WNEW-FM was opening up the limits of what could be done on commercial radio, a small college FM station in New Jersey was shattering all the rules with impunity. Upsala College had been granted a license for a low-power FM educational station in 1958. WFMU was not concerned so much with educating students who wished to be broadcasters, but with educating the general public, who stayed away in droves. They replayed a lot of boring government-sponsored public service programming, and produced very little original work. Essentially, it was a waste of a frequency— but in those days, no one really seemed to care. But as WOR-FM and later WNEW-FM began to become favorites on campus, some students wanted to try their hand at free form, without the limits that commercial frequencies imposed.

Vin Scelsa was a student at Upsala and, like many, didn't know what he wanted to do with his life. He edited the campus literary review and knew that his future lay somewhere in the creative arts, but wasn't sure exactly where. Scelsa is a short, heavyset man with a pleasant, open face. His hair is usually clipped short, and a bald spot on the top gives him a monklike appearance. He'll alternately be clean-shaven or sporting a dense beard, depending on his mood or the season. Vin favors small, wire-rimmed glasses and speaks in a soft rasp. Scelsa was a big fan of Bob Fass on WBAI, the Pacifica noncommercial station in New York. Fass would record demonstrations, and weave music and commentary amid the sounds of protest. But Scelsa wasn't just a political animal; he loved music of all kinds and eventually convinced the student general manager of WFMU to let him try a free-form program late Saturday after the station's usual sign-off.

He debuted in November of 1967 with a nod to radio tradition. From the thirties until the early fifties, *Fibber McGee and Molly* had been a popular radio sitcom. Often, the final punch line consisted of Fibber opening his overstuffed closet. Regular listeners knew that merely cracking the door would create a landslide of junk that McGee had compiled. Rather than throw anything out, it was tossed willy-nilly into the closet. So at the end of the program when he finally opened the door after many false starts, the sound effects of junk tumbling from its shelves would be heard for several seconds over uproarious laughter. Scelsa began his show by opening such a door, and when the noise of falling debris finally abated, he would calmly sort through the garbage. He'd find a new album by the Kinks— he'd have to play that later. An interview with a noted poet—he'd use that as well. A live guest, et cetera. So by using a variation of Fibber McGee, Scelsa launched *The Closet*. A modern programmer might point out how cleverly he began with a list promoting the show's highlights designed to keep people listening. But he was able to accomplish this without employing a hyped manner that would turn off an audience sensitive to radio tricks. By the end of that school year, he'd assembled a group of like-minded students who wanted to host their own progressive programs.

Unfortunately, like many campus stations, WFMU signed off for the summer after final examinations in May. But Scelsa was undeterred, petitioning the general manager for the right to continue broadcasting throughout the summer. A bargain was struck: If he could raise the money to cover expenses, including a forty-five-dollar-a-week stipend for himself as program director, Scelsa could keep the station running on a limited basis. So he conducted a pledge drive that netted them three thousand dollars, enough to cover the bills until the fall semester began.

A wide assortment of programming was to follow, with outsiders joining students in a united effort to bring creative radio to the metropolitan area. Some shows were politically based, universally opposing the Vietnam War and championing assorted radical causes. Some were just devoted to music, others to books and theater. It was a wildly unpredictable place, but it garnered national attention when *Rolling Stone* magazine featured it. Scelsa and his cohorts never thought about ratings or revenue as his commercial brethren were forced to: They were students having the time of their lives. Some of them actually lived at the station, and sex and drugs on the property were routinely accepted. Although it had its share of internecine struggles for power and influence, it became a truly communal experience with no ambitions to be more than it was. It continued that way for another year and a half, becoming the darling of hip New Yorkers whose activist political outlooks were unsatisfied by the commercial outlets.

The one event that began the glory years for FM rock on commercial radio was seen as the *end* of an era for WFMU. The Woodstock Music and Arts Festival, which legitimized so many artists in the minds of mainstream youth, was seen by the radicals at Upsala as the ultimate sellout or commercialization of a hitherto pure form of music. The subsequent movie and soundtrack album brought the Woodstock experience to the nation, but Scelsa and company weren't around to celebrate it. The administration at Upsala was becoming increasingly concerned with the direction WFMU was taking, receiving numerous complaints from alumni who were shocked at the political viewpoints their formerly harmless little station was espousing. Some of the jocks had no regard for radio standards involving obscene language, and frequently uttered words that even today are unacceptable on public airwaves. More safeguards and controls were put on the students, limiting their freedom until all the fun was sucked out of it. Many were dropouts who needed to find some kind of gainful employment. A few were near graduation and needed to do something else with their lives, including teaching to avoid the draft.

When Woodstock took place, they realized that their exclusive world was now invaded by corporate moneychangers looking for profit and not giving a tinker's cuss about the music as anything but product. The dream was over for WFMU. The counterculture was fast becoming absorbed into the mainstream, and soon wouldn't be worth their passion. Labor Day weekend of 1969 marked the end of the line, and Scelsa resigned along with most of the staff.

Vin wasn't sure what he wanted to do after WFMU, and he temporaily took refuge in his new wife's family jewelry business. Radio was part of his past, he was sure, knowing that he could never re-create the joyous times he'd had in college. Never again would he experience that exhilarating freedom, and he didn't ever want to work for some suit who would dictate what he had to play and say. So he drifted along, hoping that someday he'd find a muse—doing something he could be passionately committed to that would also allow him to make a living.

In the nearby New York City market, WNEW-FM had hired its first young jock, Pete Fornatale, who had made a name for himself doing college radio at Fordam's WFUV. He was installed as morning host, which at that time was a less important day part than any other with the possible exception of overnights. AM still ruled the airwaves in the early hours, so management felt safer hiding their latest experiment there than in a more highly visible time slot.

WABC-FM had become a recent convert to the new music after unsuccessfully filling their days with wall-to-wall original cast recordings of Broadway musicals. They attempted hipness by presenting music hosted by a syndicated personality called Brother John. It came off as insincere and phony—an obvious corporate attempt to cash in on the success that progressive music was enjoying.

But this failure led to an opportunity for Scelsa that came to him in a quite unexpected way. While at WFMU, he'd been contacted by a man named Larry Yurdin, who worked for the ABC-FM stations under Alan Shaw. Yurdin had sold Shaw on the concept that since most markets now had some kind of FM underground presence, be it commercial or college, ABC should find the best DJ in each town and hire them. Dave Herman, host of *The Marconi Experiment,* a popular Philadelphia underground show, was hired immediately, and Yurdin called Scelsa with an offer he couldn't refuse.

Vin couldn't believe his ears: WABC-FM would pay him the princely sum of three hundred dollars a week. Scelsa could play whatever he wanted and there would be absolutely no corporate interference. It sounded too good to be true, and although he had no illusions that it would last, he excitedly spoke to his wife, Freddie, about it. He knew that it was a chancy career choice, and there would doubtless be periods of unemployment and heartbreak, but she agreed to subsidize the family through the hard times so that Vin could pursue his dream. Eyes wide open, he signed on with Yurdin and WPLJ was born.

WPLJ was a suggestion of Dave Herman's taken from a song by Frank Zappa and the Mothers of Invention called "WPLJ (white port & lemon juice)." Many believe that the letters were a cryptic description of male ejaculate, in which case it would be a cruel joke on the staid ABC corporate culture. But WPLJ was undoubtedly the most radical commercial radio New York had ever heard. Other than Herman, the PLJ jocks did not have the deep professional radio voices one expected from syndication. Most sounded like the just barely above adolescents they were, and their musical taste was all over the map. Midday host Michael Cuscuna loved jazz and that was what he played on his show. Scelsa was more eclectic: You could hear anything from folk to standards to show tunes to progressive psychedelia. Herman was more conventional not only in his manner but in his selections. He held down the important 6 to 10 P.M. slot, opposite Rosko. Herman's one eccentricity was his advocacy of underground comedy: He often played lengthy bits from the Firesign Theatre and later was an early devotee of Monty Python's Flying Circus.

"Cousin Brucie" Morrow at WABC couldn't stand what was happening at his sister station. As its competitors fell by the wayside, fully a quarter of New York's radios at any given time were tuned to 770. In terms of the music, the station was tighter than ever, playing fewer than fifteen songs in regular rotation. As a nod to the changing times, Sklar *had* relaxed his policy of banning oldies and records over three minutes. Breakthroughs like Richard Harris's "MacArthur Park" and Bob Dylan's "Like a Rolling Stone" convinced him that certain records were worth stretching out for. But he still maintained his research and refused to play anything that lacked a solid sales history. But Morrow believed that even more than the music, it was WABC's sense of community that garnered its monster ratings. The jocks were out in the city's neighborhoods, promoting the station at any event that drew a crowd. WABC was a palpable presence wherever you went in New York.

But although many AM personalities couldn't see it, FM was fostering a different kind of community. Politics was at the heart of most of this. Conservatives were thought to like AM radio because it was the establishment. Solid, predictable—it stood for the status quo. FM appealed to the left, those who sought to uproot institutions. It wasn't only opposition to the war, which was the litmus test, but an opposition to mindless capitalism. The values it espoused were more spiritual, not in the sense of traditional religion, but the ideals of peace and love. Before these virtues became marginalized by jokes about hopelessly naïve hippies, there were substantial intellects who felt that the country had veered from its founding principles and was embarking on a dangerously imperialistic course, sacrificing young lives for business interests. It wasn't all about free love and experimentation with drugs. Corporations like Metromedia and ABC were walking a bit of a tightrope—on the one hand, they were in it to make money; on the other, their stations were decrying avarice and greed and advocating a more spiritual existence.

Many middle-class kids watched from the sidelines. Although demonstrations rocked campuses across the nation including Adelphi's, most of my peers never participated. They were momentarily excluded from military service with student deferments, and were more concerned with how they were going to make a living when they got out of school. Many minored in education (as I did), knowing that teachers were also deferred. The majority were against the war, and not just on principle. The most active opponents were upperclassmen who were about to be exposed to the draft and would have to make the hard decision of laying their lives on the line for a war that no one was enthused about fighting, or retreating to Canada and giving up any chance of seeing friends or family again. For those graduating in the late sixties, the war loomed as a palpable presence, like a paid assassin relentlessly stalking your consciousness, awaiting an unguarded moment to devour its prey.

The war was partly based on the "domino theory," which held that if the United States allowed Vietnam to fall, the rest of Southeast Asia would topple like a row of dominoes, followed by the rest of the world in due course. The problem was that it was only a theory, not a hard fact. The younger generation couldn't justify sacrificing their lives for a theory that might later prove incorrect. Some historians have also suggested that Communist insurgents were at work on American campuses, stirring up unrest and dissatisfaction with foreign policy. Whatever the cause, many sociological factors came together to espouse "Make Love, Not War" as a marching order throughout the country's student population.

Science was also responsible for changing mores. With the invention of the birth control pill, sex became less feared as having the life-changing consequences of an unwanted pregnancy. The proliferation of television brought beautiful sexy people into the living room, and programs like *Peyton Place* purported to unveil the sexual shenanigans of even conservative New England life. Books that had been banned decades earlier were becoming required reading in modern courses. Magazines like *Playboy* that had once been considered pornographic were now seen as harmless fun and were available on regular newsstands. Sex to many became recreational. The only thing that stood in the way was religion, and millions of adolescents parted ways with their parents on the true meaning of morality. They maintained that the violence of war was the worst sin man could commit, and that sex was a manifestation of love, life's most valued virtue. Perhaps led by the Beatles' example, they sampled alternative religions where the prohibition of sex was not a central tenet. The institution of marriage was under siege: As more parents divorced, it signaled to their children that perhaps monogamy wasn't the natural way people were intended to live. In a sense, this led to a very real crumbling of the dominoes: As one steadfast rule of behavior was rejected, others were called into question and eventually discarded.

My classmates were by and large straight kids—they dressed neatly, drank beer, had sex with their girlfriends on Saturday night with the dorm room door open a crack, but were part of the establishment. They didn't like certain aspects of it, but thought that the best road to change was to attain power themselves, and then shape society toward gentler values from within. They secretly cheered on the campus protesters, hoping that their long hair and unconventional dress would not detract from their message. I don't know who was more naïve, the protesters or those who remained silent.

Bruce Springsteen tells a story about growing up in that era. Through the sixties, he was constantly at war with his father, who disapproved of his long hair and guitar playing. High school grades were not Bruce's forte, and after turning in a bad report card or getting into trouble with the authorities, his dad would often tell him, "I can't wait 'til the army gets ahold of you. They'll make a man out of you." The drone was repeated time and time again as the youthful Springsteen got into one scrape after another. He saw many of his friends and peers sent to Southeast Asia, and some didn't return. As Vietnam escalated and Walter Cronkite recited casualty lists, Springsteen's father remained silent but stoic in his support of the armed forces. Finally the dreaded day arrived when Bruce received his draft notice and was told to report for a physical. Not wanting to allow his father that moment of triumph, he left the house a few days prior. He returned only after taking the physical to find his father waiting for him in the kitchen, smoking a cigarette in the darkness. "Where have you been?" he asked his prodigal son.

"Took my physical. Failed it." Springsteen awaited the displeasure he knew was coming from his stern parent.

All he could see was his father's silhouette, nodding in the cigarette's glow.

"That's good," he muttered. "That's good."

Many of our generation had similar conflicts with parents. Raised during the Second World War, it took most of them a long time to realize that the government didn't always act in their direct best interests or in those of their progeny. But rather than encourage active protest, many tried to avoid confrontation, hoping that Robert Kennedy, Eugene McCarthy, or even Richard Nixon would extract us from the quagmire, hailing "Peace with Honor." Collegians wanted to believe as well, but distrust of anything the government told us was well founded during that era of lies and deception. The dichotomy between the protesters and the straights on campus was how they framed their dissension.

But even though styles of dress and recreation might have differed, there was one thing that united those on campus: listening to WNEW-FM, especially Rosko. The straights and hippies alike felt we had an ally in our concerns and that, just by listening, we were registering our support for what he believed in. His music was a beautiful rainbow of influences, from Sam Cooke and early R&B to the latest fusion of jazz and rock to Eric Clapton's mournful blues. It was totally color-blind and a little daring, but not so risky that it didn't reward those who trusted Rosko's instincts. His poetry reading and storytelling could evoke tears, but he never wallowed in cloying sentiment or obtuse philosophy. His sensitive interpretation of Silverstein's "The Giving Tree" actually made it onto vinyl and sold well locally. But despite the near unanimity of opposition to the war among the New York FM radio community, the charge was led even more voraciously on the West Coast by a former Top Forty jock with bloodlines similar to those of Scott Muni.

His name was Tom Donahue.

We Built This City

THE FATHER OF progressive radio.

That's how Tom Donahue is described in numerous publications and websites. Godfather would be a more appropriate term.

The story of his journey is a commonly told one in radio circles—Donahue was an ex–Top Forty jock who was a star at some major stations, chief among them WIBG in Philadelphia, where he spent ten years as "Big Daddy." Not only was the moniker synergistic with the station's call letters, but it was an apt description of the blond, bearded giant, who weighed over four hundred pounds. In 1961, he took off to San Francisco for another four-year term of hit radio at KYA.

By 1965, Top Forty radio had lost its attraction for him, so he turned to the record business. He founded Autumn Records and signed several local bands, including Grace Slick's Great Society. Donahue began promoting concerts, including the Beatles' final U.S. public appearance, at Candlestick Park in 1965. During those years, he would hold court at Enrico's, a classy bistro in the heart of North Beach that was also the favorite dining establishment of Joseph Paul DiMaggio.

Legend has it that he was sitting in his pad with his second wife, Raechel, listening to the Doors' first album in 1967 when an epiphany came: Why isn't anyone playing this music on the radio? The story is partially true, but a man named Larry Miller was already on KMPX at night playing music in a free-form style months before Donahue came in. The station was foundering, a brokered time-share outlet that played to the city's Portuguese population by day. Donahue and his crew came aboard in April of 1967, and soon generated the same kind of buzz in the market that WOR-FM had done in New York.

There is a contention between East and West Coast factions as to who was more responsible for free-form radio. Obviously, WOR-FM had already been on the air with live jocks since the previous October, so Donahue wasn't the first to explore the new territory of FM. Since he was based in San Francisco, the hub of hippie culture, he generally is given credit by Left Coasters for pioneering the new format, even though Scott Muni and Murray the K were doing it at least six months earlier. To illustrate the schism, Muni offers this tale:

At a Metromedia managers' conference in the Bay Area, Donahue offered to show Scottso the sights, along with L. David Moorhead, the general manager of KMET in Los Angeles. As they prepared to get into Donahue's custom Mercedes, Moorhead drew Muni aside.

"Scott, no offense, but Donahue is my hero. He started this whole thing, and if it's okay with you, I'd like to sit in the front seat with him. I'd like to talk to him, eye to eye. Is that a problem?"

Muni shrugged; obviously, he couldn't care léss. He and the fawning Moorhead piled into the car, and the smaller man pulled his seat forward so that Scott could ride comfortably in back. Donahue moved his own immense body to the driver's-side door.

Both passengers were astonished when the legendary behemoth pushed the specially manufactured seat back on its tracks to accommodate his bulk. By the time it completed its journey, the driver's seat was in the rear of the car. Donahue slid his massive girth behind the steering wheel, which had also been altered to fit his four hundred pounds. Donahue was now "eye to eye" with Muni—in the *back* seat.

In laying out his West Coast antiformat, Donahue did have some rules that were strictly adhered to. No jingles, even on commercials. No talking over the introductions to records. No screaming disc jockeys. Songs were laid out in sets, with no interruptions between records. Commercial time was limited to eight or nine minutes per hour.

Obviously, this is the antithesis of what Top Forty was all about. The music had become an afterthought to most AM jocks, mainly because they had so little choice in what they played. Everything was set at an artificially high energy level that left no space for earnest monologues about anything. Most stations had rules about how long the microphone could be left open without music playing underneath, and some went so far as to automate their systems to turn off a jock midstream if he didn't comply. Rick Sklar's original concepts were taken to a ridiculous extreme, making the WABC program director's iron-fisted reign seem downright benevolent. So even if the DJs did have something to say, their mic time was reduced to spouting one-liners or reading station promotions over the beginnings of records. PDs were frazzled when the Beach Boys' "California Girls" featured a twenty-seven-second lead-in prior to the vocal. Most could fit an entire newscast into that time.

But Donahue's staff became musicologists, taking the time not only to identify each song in their sets, but often commenting on specific musical or lyrical aspects. The "rap," as it was known, came to be the standard against which a jock could be judged. And as the music became more political, reflecting the turbulent times, so did the raps. There was no time limit, and coupled with the conversational approach employed, serious issues could be raised without sounding out of place.

Drugs started to play a large part in the evolution of societal norms. America's youth experimented with substances hitherto forbidden and suffered no immediate consequences. Sex, drugs, and rock and roll got linked together in a rebellious spirit that resulted in the Summer of Love— 1967. With Donahue's KMPX as the soundtrack and Haight-Ashbury at its epicenter, hippiedom reached full flower. Timothy Leary championed LSD, and new designer drugs were sprouting up like weeds: Tune in, turn on, drop out.

Bands were popping up all along the West Coast, led by the Doors in Los Angeles, and the Grateful Dead, Jefferson Airplane, the Jimi Hendrix Experience, Big Brother and the Holding Company, Santana, Buffalo Springfield, and Quicksilver Messenger Service up north. The Monterey

Pop Festival that year exposed many of these artists to a much larger national audience. As *Sgt. Pepper* broke the bonds of what an album should sound like, more and more groups were stretching out their licks and listening to other forms of music as influences—jazz, blues, and Latino rhythms. The Beatles experimented with India's sitar ragas, notably on "Within You, Without You." They all found a welcome home at KMPX. And as free-form radio progressed, not only were the bastardized rock uses of these forms explored, but their original sources: Mingus, Muddy Waters, Tito Puente, and Ravi Shankar. Since there were no three-minute time limits on records or restrictions on the manner required to properly present them, the DJs could actually explain what they were asking the audience to groove on. Listening became educational as well as entertaining.

It didn't stop at merely talking music. Since the subject matter of the material was deeper than "silly love songs," jocks felt empowered to involve themselves in the politics of the moment. Most of what came out in their diatribes were knocks at the establishment, a catchall phrase for anything they disagreed with, the attitude being that anything established should be questioned and torn asunder. Hypocrisy became *the* mortal sin, with materialism close behind. Jocks spoke openly of revolution, of destroying an old order based on hate and replacing it with one founded on love. Hippie communes were proliferating. Dabbling with communism on this small scale strengthened opposition to the war: Maybe Soviet and Chinese communism wasn't the evil the adults preached. A sense of community was developing—the audience felt that the jocks were addressing their concerns in an intelligent fashion, instead of whistling past the graveyard in hard times. The DJs had the power to be catalysts because their words were viewed as having real value or "heaviness," not just as filler between songs. A counterculture was forming that rejected anything remotely tied to the old ways. AM radio was the cultural icon representing the old school.

KMPX further codified some of the rules that defined free-form radio in its early days. Commercials that promoted the armed forces were rejected. Frequent time and temperature readings were excluded to the point where Donahue removed the clock from the studio. The approach was low-key and respectful toward the music. Donahue did have an idiosyncrasy: He hired only female engineers. Whether he was a pioneer in the feminist movement or just liked to be surrounded by women is something we'll never be sure of.

In early 1968, Richard Quinn filled in for Donahue while he was away in Los Angeles trying to expand his broadcast empire to KPPC. Quinn, using the radio handle Tony Bigg, had also worked at KYA and had led a typical radio gypsy's life to that point, working mostly in Top Forty. Upon finishing his work at KYA on Saturdays, he would often hang out with one of the big man's engineers while she operated the audio console and thus he became a familiar face at KMPX. When Donahue went to Pasadena to negotiate for KPPC, he invited Quinn to substitute for him. Strangely, the man known as the father of progressive radio liked to hire former Top Forty jocks, because he felt they better understood how a station is supposed to be put together, with texture—the musical ebb and flow.

But while Donahue was away in Southern California, KMPX owner-ship was laying plans for his demise in San Francisco. Even though the station was the talk of the city and fast becoming an important cultural entity, revenues were not growing to management's satisfaction and the flower children of Donahue's team were having trouble paying the rent, given their meager wages. Upon his return, the air staff met to decide how they were going to handle management's latest salvo. Even though they were hippies who sat on the floor and smelled of patchouli, they felt that they should organize into a union (whimsically calling it the Amalgamated Fed-eration of International FM Workers of the World). One of the ringleaders stood up and insisted that they have unanimity. There could be no strike-breakers, including this new guy, Tony Pig, uhh, Bigg. The rest laughed nervously, as the man had not only flubbed the name but this Quinn/Bigg dude was sitting right next to him. They voted to strike and handed out picketing assignments. Upon leaving the room, Donahue suggested to Quinn that the accidental mispronunciation actually sounded more appro-priate than his current name. So Tony Bigg became Tony Pigg.

During the strike, several bands, including Traffic and Creedence Clearwater Revival (while they were still known as the Golliwogs), came by the flatbed truck that was the center of the picketing activity to entertain and raise money for the striking workers. There was a large benefit concert held, with all the top bands from the Bay Area lending their support. But management held firm, with scabs filling their airwaves in a lame attempt to replace the staff.

George Duncan, who by now had been elevated to the head of Metro-media Radio, was trying to decide what to do with KSAN, the weak sister of the chain. He sought a meeting with Donahue and they agreed to transfer the staff of KMPX to KSAN, almost intact. Listeners abandoned KMPX as word got around about the new station, and in May of 1968, Donahue had a new base of operations.

Like WNEW-FM, KSAN had a prominently placed female (Raechel Donahue) and a politically hip black man (Roland Young, who was also a Black Panther). Young once got into trouble on the air when he echoed the statements of writer David Hilliard, who insinuated that he would murder anyone who stood in the way of his freedom. Young suggested that his listeners sign a petition vowing to kill anyone, including the president of the United States, who might abridge their rights. Three days later, as Tony Pigg auditioned records in his new job as music director, he was horrified to see three gray-suited Secret Service agents accost Young while on the air, and inform him that should any harm come to Nixon, he could be named as an accessory to murder. The Black Panther toned down his rhetoric.

Pigg was then making around three hundred dollars a week to do an air shift and serve as MD, but the money, although it was less than he earned at KYA, didn't matter to him. He reveled in the sense of community that had sprung up around KSAN. The Berkeleyites, who controlled the area's leftist political thought, found a friend in the station, but mostly it was sex and drugs and rock and roll that made it go. Free love wasn't just an expression, and disc jockeys had as many groupies as the musicians did. Drugs were an integral part of the experience, ranging from marijuana to LSD, and in some cases heroin and cocaine. The effect of drugs on the air staff was palpable. Although the morning jock and several others never touched anything harder than alcohol, most did indulge and weren't afraid to fire up on the air. Pigg admits that he loved the effect marijuana had on him while listening to music, and he felt that it sharpened his music sense to the point where he would be unerring in his selections. Of course, in retrospect, it's debatable as to whether grass actually did have such an effect, or if it merely felt that way.

But the station was a labor of love for everyone involved, and Pigg recalls that he listened to it all day, not to scrutinize the music, but because he delighted in the way it sounded. In fact, his duties as music director were essentially clerical. He would listen to new releases and place them in a bin in the studio, to be available for the staff. He never marked suggested tracks to play, and if he didn't add a record to the bin, a jock was perfectly free to bring it in from a personal collection. Music lists were not inspected after the fact either; they were merely kept so that DJs could tell the audience what they'd just played in their lengthy sets.

The music selections, like at WPLJ in New York, completely reflected the jocks' personal tastes. They played everything from dissonant avant-garde jazz, to Indian ragas, to R&B, to the Archies, a bubblegum group that had a number of three-minute hits. Donahue would rarely criticize a jock's choices and his music director never did. The shows were done not to cater to the audience, but to please themselves. They played what they liked, and thought, perhaps arrogantly, that the public would go along. Pigg recalls that he initially hated Led Zeppelin, thinking them a "bullshit English band," and even disliked Santana, wishing that the local group would "just go away and leave us alone."

Segues were also overemphasized to the detriment of the station's overall sound. In the jocks' mind, the segue took precedence to the point that they would play several mediocre songs in a set, only because they meshed well together. But even then, Pigg used the tactic of dropping in his voice briefly to identify the station between songs that didn't flow into each other, trying to play quality music instead of attempting to impress his peers with his musical acumen.

Listeners had the feeling that KSAN belonged to them. Many of them, high on acid, were regular callers. In their drug-induced reveries, they'd say things like, "Wow man, I've been programming your station for the past half hour." Donahue might try to bring them down to earth by retorting, "Oh yeah? Well, what am I going to play next?" Or when they'd call and request a Donovan track, the jock might refuse to play it.

"I thought this was the People's radio station, man," the listener would moan.

"I'm one of the people, and I don't like Donovan," came the reply.

Break on Through
(to the Other Side)

IN LATE 1969, as KSAN became established in San Francisco, Michael Harrison and I were in our senior year of college on Long Island. Our radio careers had stalled with the snobby, offhanded rejection we received at WHLI. WNEW-FM still seemed like a distant dream, and our best hope was to try to make a go of it at WLIR, working on the theory that if we could make this small nonentity a success, New York would have to sit up and take notice.

Harrison put together a package called "Dimensional News." Rather than the rip-and-read style that characterized a nonexistent news budget, we agreed to produce a full fifteen-minute news segment daily, with reporters and live audio from events. We wanted to capture the sound and gravity of a big-city operation. I handled sports, recording interviews with the coaches and managers of the Yankees, Mets, Knicks, Nets, Rangers,

Jets, and Giants. I found that if I caught them in their offices in the late afternoon, they'd agree to talk to me on the phone for five minutes. Harrison did the same with politicians and cultural figures, and soon "Dimensional News" took on the patina of a quality product. We'd get friends or other jocks to call in with reports, essentially expanding on the UPI copy with our own colorful details. Thus, a staff of two used the theater of the imagination to sound like a crew of twenty.

I must admit that we employed our imagination a bit too vividly at times. We couldn't actually go out and cover many events live, so we used the station's phone system and sound-effects library to re-create them. Once, when the offices of Long Island's major daily paper, *Newsday,* caught fire, Harrison stood in the other studio shouting into the phone about the terrible flames and destruction while we played filtered sounds of fire engines and gushing water in the background. When the Knicks won the NBA championship, I was at home in a rented shack in Long Beach (where I had moved after fleeing Adelphi's dormitories), listening on the radio. As the final buzzer sounded, I tuned my radio to a blank frequency and turned the static up loud, pretending it was crowd noise. I screamed a report over the din, as if I were on the court for the celebration. My roommate, playing the role of Willis Reed, shouted in the background, "Right on. Knicks are number one." Part-timer Pete Larkin did reports purportedly from the state capitol in Albany while in his mother's kitchen in Queens. I doubt any one of the dozen or so listening had any inkling it wasn't real.

My association with "Dimensional News" might have actually kept me out of jail on one occasion. On the way home one evening, I stopped at the now defunct TSS store in Oceanside. After rent and food, my roommates and I never had any money, and I'm ashamed to say that we occasionally would shoplift a can of stew so that we could have dinner. It was winter, and I had a down parka that could hide a whole bagful of groceries. When I thought no one was looking, I slipped a container of soup and a loaf of bread into my jacket and stole out into the parking lot. Out of the corner of my eye, I thought I spotted a man following me, but dismissed it as guilty paranoia.

Sure enough, as I opened the car door, that same man came up behind me and said, "Store detective. Would you open your coat please, sir."

Caught. I opened the zipper, revealing the pilfered merchandise.

"Come with me, sir."

I followed him through the back of the store to the executive offices, where I waited as he filled out a report and paged his boss. "What have you got to say in your defense? We're about to call the police."

I thought fast. Summoning everything I'd learned as a drama major, I smiled broadly. "Great job, sir. I commend you. I'm Dick Neer, a reporter for Long Island's 'Dimensional News.' Maybe you've caught our show? Well, I'm doing an undercover report on shoplifting and I wanted to find out firsthand how you deal with it."

I could tell he wasn't buying it. I was still only twenty and wasn't dressed as you'd expect a reporter to be attired, even on radio.

"Young man, I've heard some good ones in my time. That's about the best I've heard. But gimme a break. You're no reporter."

"I know what you're thinking, sir. But I couldn't present myself the way I normally do. I wanted this to be real . . . visceral. To put myself in the place of a thief."

He still wasn't going with the story. So I took a calculated risk, knowing that Harrison was on the air and was quick-witted enough to catch on. "If you don't believe me," I said, "call my news director. His name is Michael Harrison. Here's the station's number. I'm entitled to a call, right? You make it for me."

The skeptical store detective shrugged and dialed the number. I'd given him the news-room hotline, knowing that it was always answered in case a newsmaker was trying to contact us. "Dimensional News, Harrison speaking," I could hear faintly through the receiver.

"Yes, sir. We have a young man named Neer here. He claims to be a reporter. Is that true?"

A moment's hesitation before Harrison suspiciously answered, "Yes. Who's calling?"

He explained that he was a store detective and told him of the shoplifting incident. "Is he working on a story right now?"

The moment of truth. Harrison could have been forthright and said that I had never been assigned such a story. I envisioned a tearful night in the local lockup, with my embarrassed parents driving in from New Jersey to bail me out. Could you still work in radio if you had an arrest record? This was before the present day, when such a conviction is considered an asset.

But Michael picked up the cue. "Well, Mr. Neer works freelance. With a reporter of his stature, I never assign him stories. He does them on his own and submits them to me when they're completed." He embellished it for good measure. "I'm surprised you don't know his work. He's up for a Peabody Award, you know."

This finally convinced the sheepish detective. "All right, sir. Just checking. I admit his story sounded fishy, but I thank you for your time."

He apologized to me before sending me on my way. I tried not to run out of the building, but I didn't look behind me until I was in the safety of my car, speeding away from a store I'd never enter again.

Them Changes

NINETEEN SEVENTY SAW Bill "Rosko" Mercer on top of the world—
he was New York's most respected jock, a prime-time player at WNEW-FM.
Life was treating him well as he and a friend from a record label strolled
down West Fifty-fifth Street, looking for a new restaurant they'd heard
about. It was a lovely summer day and the streets of the metropolis were
bustling with their usual nervous energy. As the two men approached the
Warwick Hotel near Sixth Avenue, a commotion burst out on the street before them.

At the curb sat a sleek stretch limousine, shiny black and resplendent
in the midday sun. Around the limo, a gaggle of excited young women
screamed at the top of their lungs as a colorfully garbed black man with a
large Afro emerged from the hotel, surrounded by an entourage of seven
or eight assorted bodyguards and hangers-on. There was a blue sawhorse

police line separating the women from the car, keeping them at a safe distance from this obviously important personage.

Rosko recognized the rainbow colors of the outfit immediately. He hadn't realized his longtime friend was in town so the normally reserved Mercer yelled, "Hey Jimi."

James Marshall Hendrix motioned him toward the open door of the vehicle and gently shoved him inside to escape the clamor. "Hey man, how are you? I was fixing to give you a call."

"Great to see you, Jimi."

"One question though, man. How did you know it was me?"

Rosko looked down at the tie-dyed apparel his friend was wearing and burst into laughter. Rather than answer what seemed to be an honest question, he merely hugged his buddy.

"Call me at home later," he said, extricating himself from the plush enclosure. He wondered how Jimi Hendrix, then at the height of his popularity, didn't realize what a rock icon he'd become. In his own eyes, he was just a working musician who had a unique style of torturing a guitar.

Rosko never forgot the encounter and he wept openly, as millions did, upon hearing of Hendrix's death some months later. Their friendship had started at Jimi's behest. Rosko was a club DJ and radio personality on the West Coast when they'd met. He'd never befriended musicians, and had a disdain for hanging out and getting high. His life experience left him with an appreciation for all kinds of music, and a solid knowledge of jazz and R&B. Hendrix's rock sensibilities combined the best elements of both, not to mention his deftness in the studio at exploring the sonic wonders of stereo. In the early days of progressive rock, Hendrix was a black man in an almost all-white environment, so perhaps he naturally gravitated to a black DJ in a similar position. The two would talk for hours on the phone at whatever station Mercer was working, often continuing their talks at his home after hours. Bill was impressed by the musicality and lyrical quality of Jimi's speech. He unconsciously spoke in poetry, and there were numerous times in their conversations when he'd have a spontaneous burst of creativity that made its way onto vinyl weeks later.

Whereas Hendrix was the first guitar hero, Rosko was the first superstar of FM underground radio. Scott Muni and Murray the K were well-known legends of Top Forty by the time they arrived at WOR, but Mercer burst upon the New York scene as a virtual cipher. He'd come from the West Coast to DJ at a club called the Cheetah, in a program that would be simulcast on WOR-FM. Relations between the club and the station broke down early on, but Murray the K had taken a liking to him, and convinced RKO management to hire the small, shy disc jockey.

Rosko was a compact man of light color, with a high forehead and noble features. He thrived on the freedom that WOR-FM provided and in a matter of months became one of its most popular jocks. But months were all the pioneering station was allocated. Upon arriving for his program one late summer's night in 1967, he was greeted by a memo, brusquely stating that the station would be BOSS radio soon and that Murray the K had been fired. Mercer immediately called his friend at home and Murray detailed how he'd been sacked as he was told about Drake-Chenault's plans to overturn their sandbox.

Rosko immediately went on the air and resigned, telling the whole story of how he felt he'd been betrayed by RKO. He had been hired on the condition that he could play and say what he wanted and that now that promise had been broken. "I'll stay on the air until they send somebody up to get me, but this is my last show." He segued records for forty minutes until Peter Yarrow of Peter, Paul and Mary came through the studio door to offer his sympathy.

"How did you get up here?" Rosko asked incredulously, knowing of the building's tight security.

"I told the guard downstairs that I was your brother," the pale, balding Yarrow replied. "While he was trying to figure that out, I hopped on the elevator and here I am."

They shared a laugh and played a few more songs on the radio until Rosko's replacement arrived. Mercer never spoke another word on WOR-FM. Bob Fass invited Murray and Mercer onto his program on Pacifica's WBAI to tell their story. Fass used the hour to illustrate how the establishment was squelching free speech and suppressing rock and roll, years after the payola scandal.

Bill wasn't out of work for long. A mutual friend arranged a lunch with George Duncan of WNEW-FM, and the ex-Marine and the African-American iconoclast hit it off immediately. Eventually, the subject came around to Rosko's on-air resignation. This is something all broadcast executives dread. Whenever a station changes format or fires a disc jockey, the existing audience feels disenfranchised, quite simply because they wouldn't be listening if they didn't enjoy what they were hearing. Since terminations only happen when leadership perceives the program to be unsuccessful, listener protest is generally manageable and subsides within a few weeks. However, WOR-FM represented a radio revolution and had garnered the highest ratings FM had ever seen to that point. The ensuing protests presented a nightmare for RKO, which was trying to woo much the same youthful audience, only more of them.

(It has since become de rigueur not to allow disc jockeys to continue working after they've been fired, seeking to avoid the kind of angry harangue Rosko vented. This was something Rosko did again later in his career, and it was to cost him dearly. But now, jocks are generally told after they get off the air that they've done their final show.)

At their luncheon, George Duncan did not admonish Mercer when the on-air resignation came up. "I hope that I'll never do anything to you that will cause you to resign on me," he said.

Rosko actually got misty-eyed. Most managers he'd known wanted to lay down rules and regulations immediately. Here was a boss who was telling him that he had faith in him and that he could do whatever he wanted on the radio, and that he only hoped that *he* could live up to Rosko's paradigm.

As noted earlier, he began at WNEW-FM on October 30, 1967, and immediately became the star of the station. His trademark opening about "reality being the hippest of all trips" was in actuality a strong antidrug message. "A mind excursion, a true diversion" encouraged self-exploration. His philosophy mirrored that of the Robin Williams role in *Dead Poet's Society*—question authority and seek the answers not from others, but from within yourself. He read not only poetry and stories, but also columns and essays ranging from Jimmy Breslin to Russian dissidents. One of his literary heroes was the Soviet poet Yevgeny Yevtushenko, who wrote *You Shoot at Yourself, America*. At the urging of Ted Brown of WNEW-AM, he read the piece on the air. Brown, who knew of Duncan's superpatriotism and strong Roman Catholic beliefs, was mischievously setting Mercer up for a confrontation with his general manager.

When the expected complaints from listeners on what they perceived as an anti-American diatribe crossed Duncan's desk, he called Rosko in for a meeting. "Do you really think this is a good idea, Bill?" he asked.

Rather than debating the intricacies of the Russian's work, Mercer simply answered, "Well, you know, Yevtushenko is Jackie Kennedy's favorite poet."

"Oh, then I guess it's okay," Duncan said, immediately dismissing the matter.

For all his seemingly leftist views, he actually was a supporter and fan of Richard Nixon. He judged him to be an excellent president who did many positive things for the country. He felt it a shame that his personal meanness destroyed what could have been a great presidency. And Rosko wasn't reflexively antimilitary either. He was once summoned to the Pentagon by Major General Winston "Wimpy" Wilson, who solicited his views on why the National Guard was having such a difficult time recruiting America's youth. In the company of the general's aide, a major whose name is long forgotten, Rosko listened to the man's problems. He replied that the National Guard had a bad image; that every time students were protesting, the Guard was called in to bash heads. They were perceived as the enemy.

Rosko then said, "But if a television camera was in this room, kids could see how you honestly care about protecting your country and all it stands for, they'd respect you for it. They would see how a mighty general is humbly asking me, a mere civilian—a mere disc jockey, for advice."

The general's aide angrily stood up and said that he was sick of trying to explain to America's young men that they had a duty to their country, and that they should be grateful for all it had given them. Calmly, Mercer said that perhaps the major should be fired because recruiting was his job: explaining history to young people and why they should be proud to serve. That was his mission and if he was sick of performing it, it could only fail. He looked up meekly at the general, who had taken in the entire confrontation and would undoubtedly sympathize with his aide. But Wilson sided with the DJ and told them that perhaps quite a few majors deserved to be fired. Years later Wilson was in command of the National Guard during the time they opened fire and killed four students at Kent State University. He took early retirement shortly thereafter.

One of Rosko's great traits was his knack for blending seemingly dissimilar songs together. He once segued from the Doors to the Singing Nun, then back to the Rolling Stones, and it all somehow made sense. He liked to work without a net. He once told a colleague that he didn't want to know what he was going to play on turntable two until a record was already spinning on turntable one. He did his show completely by feel and although sometimes bizarre, most of his sets were works of art. And although he was considered a musical guru whose taste many of his peers at the station admired and imitated, he deferred to younger people when it came to new music. His formal education in music was in jazz, so he had to learn about rock like everybody else. He and George Duncan frequently visited area colleges for seminars and learned as much as they taught.

Although Mercer was a powerful presence and extremely popular with his listening audience, he didn't enjoy great friendships with his peers at the radio station. He regarded Schwartz as a spoiled rich kid and an intellectual bully who tried to intimidate and impress with his wordsmith's vocabulary. He attributed this to attempting to live up to his celebrated father's expectations instead of carving his own path. Mercer and Schwartz shared a rivalry that sometimes threatened to break into physical violence when their verbal jousting got out of control.

Alison Steele had alienated him early on with what had seemed to be a relatively innocent encounter, at least to her. When the station moved away from sharing offices with WNEW-AM to its own digs at 230 Park Avenue, working the streets there was a hot dog vendor with whom Rosko had become friends. Every so often he would enjoy lunch alfresco, munching a wiener and shooting the breeze with the man. One day, Steele happened by on her way to the studio and saw them together. She barely nodded a hello, and that night, following him on the air, she said sarcastically, "Imagine the *great* Rosko, outside eating a hot dog."

Mercer was offended. The passing remark told him all he needed to know about Steele. He considered her an elitist who lacked the common touch and was only performing an act on the radio as opposed to investing her heart and soul. With her show-business background, he expected little else.

And he allows that he gave as well as he got. His attitude toward coworkers was simple: He extended the hand of friendship but once. They could embrace that hand and accept him for who he was, the sensitive, cerebral Bill Mercer, or they could reject it and view him as Rosko, radio star and competitor. And once you were on his bad side, he admits, he could be the biggest bastard who ever walked the earth.

He had no problems with Zacherle, who was a kindred spirit. Scott Muni and he shared no common interests, but there was no real bad blood between them. He was cordial to some of the newer members of the staff (he liked and respected Fornatale), but forged no real relationships with most of them.

Mercer's real struggle was with fame, in all its double-edged ambivalence. He once said he spent his whole life needily seeking love. He wanted to be heard and loved by millions, but perform "his craft or sullen art" in solitude. It's a common foible of radio people; otherwise, they'd be on television. He tells a story about how his ex-wife would always introduce him as Rosko and brag about his broadcast exploits. He came to realize that she loved his on-air persona and all the fruits that his fame harvested, but had only a nodding acquaintance with the inner man.

They soon divorced, but he met a woman shortly thereafter who was refreshingly different. Their initial encounter took place while they were walking their respective dogs in Central Park. After their first lunch together, he took her to visit Jerry Moss, an old friend of Bill's and the M of A&M Records. Moss's mother was ill at the time, and the two men engaged in a discussion about her health and Mercer pledged sincerely to offer any assistance he could. Upon leaving, they encountered several promotion men in the lobby, who proceeded to work their shuck and jive on the city's most influential disc jockey, and Rosko gave it right back. His then girlfriend called him on it when they were alone. She asked how he could be such a warm and caring friend in one situation and such a transparent phony in another. Bill Mercer had met his new soul mate and they spent the rest of his days as husband and wife.

What it came down to with him was that he wanted to be accepted for who he was, and not what he could do for someone. Surrounded by record promo men and sycophants who constantly told him how great he was, he appreciated a woman who would not hesitate to criticize him when he transgressed their shared principles. She could help steer him to a higher path instead of silently accepting his flaws. As the relationship blossomed, however, his job left him feeling increasingly empty. He grew tired of the glitz and superficiality that came along with his stardom. He still loved the work, being able to impart what he viewed as the best part of himself to his audience, but if they only chose to see him as a cool guy with a great voice and missed the underlying message, well, that was their loss. It took its toll on him, as well.

Over the three and a half years he spent at WNEW-FM, the showbiz side of it all began to overwhelm him until even he wasn't sure who he was. He'd vacationed a couple of times in the south of France, and was impressed by the French people's indifferent attitude toward him. They couldn't care less about some black American disc jockey who only spoke a few words of their language. The French wanted to know Bill Mercer for the *man* he was, not for his celebrity. It was an epiphany—as if he'd found in France millions of people who shared his wife's values.

So in 1971, at the top of his profession, Bill "Rosko" Mercer decided to walk away. George Duncan had ascended to the top of Metromedia's radio division by then, and he and new general manager Varner Paulsen prevailed upon Rosko to stay with all the usual inducements. But it wasn't about money, as it almost always is, or long-term security, perks, or the other little trivialities we occupy our time worrying about. He wanted to rediscover *himself*. How very sixties it now sounds.

He wasn't closing any doors—he might return to America one day and he might even do radio again. But to the delight of his colleagues, the coveted 6 to 10 P.M. slot was about to open up. There was blood in the water.

Move on Up

IT WAS A CHILLY night in late winter 1971. Mike Harrison had just finished his 5 to 9 P.M. shift on WLIR and I was wrapping up some paperwork in the office. We grabbed a quick cup of coffee and went out to the rooftop of the Imperial Square Building with a portable radio that was locked in at 102.7 WNEW-FM.

"Something's up with Rosko," Harrison said. "I just heard him say something about doing his last show."

"Wow. They actually fired Rosko? I can't believe it. I wonder who they're bringing in." We stared westward into the dark night, looking toward the city. Long Island is relatively flat, and from seven stories up, you could see the New York skyline on all but the most hazy nights. The lights of the Throgs Neck Bridge twinkled in the distance, but our focus was on the crest of the Empire State Building. At that time, most FM antennae were located atop its tower. In the evening, we often retreated to the serenity of the rooftop after working, to mellow out and formulate our plans for WLIR. Those plans had taken a different turn of late.

After "Dimensional News" failed to boost us ahead of our competition, Reiger talked openly of selling the station. His ownership had been a stormy and difficult ride. Since we had become full-time employees, our views had shifted from our initial perceptions of him as a tightfisted ogre. We had pictured him a wealthy man; after all, he drove a luxuriously appointed Oldsmobile, courtesy of a sponsor. He resided in what we assumed was an opulent house near the Hamptons on eastern Long Island. He loved sailing and had, we thought, a large yacht at his disposal. He had chits at some of the finer local restaurants, also in trade with sponsors.

But we didn't realize that everything he had was tied up in the radio station, including the mortgage on what was in reality a comfortable but unpretentious split-level home. The yacht was really a meticulously maintained but modest sailboat. His wife clipped coupons, his sons went to public schools—he really was just getting by, sweating out payroll every fortnight. As Harrison and I spent more time at the station during business hours, we began to sympathize with his plight. He was just a small businessman, a mom-and-pop operator competing in a world of corporate giants with much bigger battalions at their command. We started to see him as a doting uncle, who wanted success in the modern world but was too tied to old customs to achieve it. He began to treat us as his sons, proud of our accomplishments and work ethic.

It was in that spirit in the spring of 1970 that Harrison hatched a scheme that he believed would mutually benefit Reiger and ourselves. We were graduating that June, he from Hofstra, I from Adelphi. We slowly accepted that the odds of making it in theater were narrow. We believed that we had talent but there were thousands of talented actors on the unemployment line or waiting tables. Plus, our upbringings influenced us to seek the security of a regular paycheck, even with the risks that a radio career entailed. No big-city program director was beating down our door, and even WHLI wasn't impressed. As for Reiger, a man nearing sixty, he wanted to be able to create a comfortable nest egg to sustain him in his later years. Clearly, his current format wasn't putting him closer to that goal.

So Harrison shared his plan with me. We would create the nation's first suburban progressive rock station. It was his belief that WNEW-FM, WPLJ, and the rest served only Manhattan. They were too cosmopolitan for suburbia, too focused on city life. Nassau Coliseum was in the works. The Westbury Music Fair and Long Island colleges were hosting concerts with major rock bands. A new entrepreneurial culture was emerging—hip boutiques and head shops were opening almost daily. But there was no radio station addressing this burgeoning community. Harrison believed that if we could fill the void in this radio wasteland, there would be a thirsty audience eager to drink from our well.

Of course, Reiger and his wife were skeptical. They hated rock music and the idea of hippies hanging out in their penthouse. But whereas the salary structure at WLIR kept us from hiring quality talent for news, classical, and easy listening, the low pay scale would attract young broadcasters who actually loved and understood the music and lifestyle, because they lived it. Rather than hire recycled Top Forty jocks, we would bring in fresh talent who wouldn't have to fake their passion for Clapton and Hendrix.

Harrison asked me to prepare a report, showing Reiger the availability of the demographics we sought. I researched the population data at Adelphi's library, extrapolated some highly questionable figures, and tried to weave a compelling reason that WLIR would prosper as headquarters for Long Island's rock culture. A more scientific analyst might have scoffed at my conclusions, but they were fueled by a heartfelt belief in our mission.

Michael was in constant meetings with Reiger while I set about to recruit a staff. I spoke to some friends at WALI, but Harrison judged them too radical for what we needed. His idea wasn't to do free-form radio at all, but a formatted version of what the city stations were giving. We believed that this was the first time anyone tried to give shape to progressive radio without destroying the freedom that made it work.

Thus we came to a crossroads that WNEW-FM and its successors would reach years later. Whereas the concept of total freedom is an attractive one, no one is totally free until they're six feet under. In America, we have control over our lives to a large extent, but we are all governed by laws that we defy at our peril. We theoretically have freedom in the workplace, but management always has the final say on how wide-ranging our discretion is to be. We also put restrictions on ourselves, based on our judgments of what is best for our interests. We sacrifice freedom for security every day. As the Eagles put it, "We are all just prisoners here, of our own device." So Harrison and I saw no contradiction in giving people freedom within boundaries.

We sought to hire like-minded jocks. Although we never codified it in the terms that others would later, our goal was to make money. We wanted to get ratings by playing the music our generation wanted to hear. In turn, local advertisers would purchase commercials, get results, and both would thrive. Although this seems like Radio 101, you'd be surprised at how many managers were afraid to explore this in 1970. Since FM disc jockeys had risen to the power their AM siblings possessed in the fifties before payola, they controlled the content of their shows. They selected the music, the spoken material; they were individual fiefdoms within a greater empire. Alison Steele liked spacey music; Rosko, jazz; Muni, British rock. Their choice of music defined a large part of their personalities on the radio.

Michael and I thought that although they went overboard at times, WNEW was not the prime offender—WPLJ was our target of scorn. Their morning guy did a talk show, their midday guy did a jazz show, the afternoon guy liked country and folk, et cetera. There was less continuity than there was at the old WLIR. You could never be sure of what you were going to hear. It sounded like six separate radio stations, depending on who was on the air at the time. If one jock was on vacation and another filled in, regular listeners to that day part would be jolted by unfamiliar music they couldn't relate to.

Our idea at WLIR was to homogenize the sound so that the station was more consistent. This might strike you as what Bill Drake and Rick Sklar were doing, and you'd be partially correct. But the difference was vast— like that of a democracy versus a dictatorship. To us, WPLJ represented total anarchy. WNEW-FM was a young republic with essentially responsible leaders. WOR-FM was BOSS radio, a smothering monarchy. We sought a middle ground, where each jock had the freedom to highlight music that he liked within a large core of songs that we knew were popular. This was actually the toughest road, and reflecting back, I think that only two kids in their early twenties could have done it. It required total devotion to the mission and seventy hours a week.

We gave each jock a one-page guideline of what was expected of them. We insisted upon a certain percentage of oldies, current popular album cuts, then secondary cuts from those same LPs. There were slots for new unknown artists and a wild-card selection, where the jock could play whatever he wanted. But rather than follow a playlist with songs delineated by category, we left much of this to the jock's discretion. It was freedom with an honor code.

That meant that the scrutiny had to come after the fact and that Michael and I had to trust our hosts' music acumen and integrity. Jocks had to list what they played, and we would go over their selections the next day. We'd have frequent individual meetings with jocks, making general comments that redirected the music when it strayed from our guidelines. Only records that were in our library were eligible for airplay, but we were very open to a jock's suggestions on albums we hadn't added yet. In the early going, we couldn't get review copies from most record companies, so we had to either buy albums or bring them from home. For the first month, the financial restrictions were greater than any philosophical ones we could impose.

But the acid test was what came out of the speakers. Between the two of us, Michael and I listened all day until sign-off at 1 A.M. We didn't believe in terrorizing the staff on the hotline, but we would sometimes make surprise calls or visits to the station during off hours just to let them know we were listening. And since I did the 1 to 5 P.M. shift and Harrison did 5 to 9 P.M., we knew the crux of the day was covered. Don K. Reed (later of WCBS-FM) did mornings and his pop leanings fit perfectly into what we envisioned that segment to be. Chuck Macken started out doing middays, and his tastes were a bit more progressive than Reed's, again fitting nicely into our concept.

Reed was the subject of one of the station's most embarrassing anecdotes. In the years Don K. did the morning show, it was truly a one-man operation. He selected the music, prepared and read the news, and engineered. The office staff didn't arrive until nine, so he did most of his program in complete solitude. The men's room was near the front entrance, quite a distance from the studio. So when Reed had to answer nature's call, he had the option of running all the way down a long corridor or using the women's loo, which was mere steps away. Most often he opted for the latter, since there were no females present until later. For some reason, the handle on the ladies' room door was not installed properly, with a lock button on the outside and keyed on the inside. It was probably the work of an inexperienced carpenter, and Reiger hadn't gotten around to calling building maintenance to rectify the error. So women who desired privacy needed to bring the key with them to lock the door from the inside. Without the key, the only other way the door could be locked was if the button was turned on the outside.

While on the air one morning at around 8:15, Don K. Reed retreated to the ladies' room for a quick respite, but failed to notice that someone had left the outside latch in the locked position. He screamed and pounded on the walls to no avail, as his record ran out and clicked into the inner grooves. It wasn't until a half hour later, when the office staff arrived, that someone released a red-faced Reed from the ladies' room, whereupon he dashed into the studio and introduced the next record as though nothing had happened. Building carpenters corrected the lock problem that very afternoon.

As solid as our full-time staff was, we did have a problem finding part-timers who would go along with the program. We mistakenly thought that we could tame some radicals who wanted WLIR to be to the left of WPLJ. Life with them was a constant battle. They would conveniently forget to note certain selections on their music sheets. A few would even lie outright, denying that they played what we'd actually heard. One guy took pride in finding the most obscure tracks on popular albums. He'd play something by Chicago that even Peter Cetera didn't know. If you just looked at the column listing the bands, his music seemed in perfect balance. But if you listened, you might only recognize one track in ten.

We signed on as the "new" WLIR in June of 1970, and following WNEW's pattern, we kept our full-timers on seven days a week, with weekends featuring the same hosts on tape. Michael Harrison loved Rosko's sound and shortened his radio moniker to just "Harrison" in tribute to his hero. He spoke in Mercer's laid-back tones, until he found his own persona within a few months. With Bill Mercer's success in New York, most rock stations wanted a cool-sounding black man on at night and we were no exception. But we never found our own Rosko. Following Harrison, we wanted a black jock in the worst way. Today, it would be called tokenism—then it was opportunity. Too bad Robert Wynn Jackson only knew classical music.

Our eyes lit up when soon after we signed on, a black man walked into our offices unsolicited and announced that he wanted a job. He even looked like Rosko. He had a very deep voice, and professed to be a big fan of rock music. He'd been working at a small AM daytime country station on the Island, but just had to see us when he heard what we were doing. He brought an audition tape, but it consisted mainly of reading simple copy so we couldn't tell if he had a rap or not. We took him to lunch, and he impressed us with his life experiences in the service and radio. We asked him on the spot to audition for us the following Saturday night, and we thought we'd found a combination of Rosko and Jimi Hendrix, who'd also been a serviceman, in one undiscovered surprise package.

The surprise was on us. After a couple days of orientation running the console for other shows, we judged him ready to handle the technical part. My own experiences had compelled me to worry about that with each new hire. Mike and I went to dinner in Hempstead that Saturday night and sat in a car together at 9 P.M., eagerly anticipating his first words.

"This is WLIR, coming to you from the Imperial Square Garage. I hopes you enjoy the music I'm about to give you."

It was 1970 and "hopes" didn't trouble us too much. But where had the "Imperial Square Garage" come from? We later found out that's what the sign said on the multilevel garage where we parked, so he assumed that was the name of the building. *O-kay.*

He then played a set of obscure songs by famous artists. We'd have to correct that. He came on after the set with, "That was Steven Styles. Next some Led Zeppleman, and some Spooks' Tooth. I hopes you enjoyed the music I gave you. I know I did. Steven Styles is one of my most favorite." Commercials followed.

Stephen Stills and Led Zeppelin were staples on any rock station. Spooky Tooth never achieved great success, but we liked them because they did a killer version of "I Am the Walrus," and their lead singer was named Mike Harrison (no relation).

After that break, Harrison and I looked at each other in shocked disbelief. "Richard," he said, "this guy knows nothing about music."

I agreed. "I bet he played those tracks only because he doesn't know the right ones to play. My God, what are we going to do?"

We were two minutes from the studios. We were with our girlfriends, and had promised to take them to a movie later. The women were very understanding when we said we had to go to the station for a few minutes, and they agreed to wait in the car at the Imperial Square Garage. As we took the elevator to the top floor, we both tried to remain calm, hoping we could salvage something from the night. We decided that I'd be the bad guy if needed, and he'd be more conciliatory.

Our man was in the studio, cueing up his next record. "Hey man, how're you doing?" Harrison greeted him.

"Great. How do I sound?"

I swallowed hard. "Pretty good. But this is the Imperial Square Building, not the garage. And it's Stephen Stills and Led Zeppelin."

"Okay. Well, you understand I never heard of those guys. Ain't like they're the Beatles or nothing. Probably the listeners don't know either." He then busied himself with a stack of LPs, shaking his head in nonrecognition at most of them until he found *Otis Redding at Monterey Pop*.

I was tempted to pull the plug right there but Michael spoke first. "Keep rockin' man. Come in Monday morning and we'll talk about the show. Have a good one." He shoved me out the studio door, a little too hard.

When we reached the corridor out of earshot, he grabbed my shoulder. "Look, the women are waiting in the car. If we yank him now, either you or I do the show. You know how that'll go over with the women. The damage is done, my friend."

"I know. But he's got such a great voice. Don't you think we can teach him how to do this?"

"He's got no clue about the music. He lied to us. We've got to let him go. It can wait 'til Monday, though. Let's just go to the movies and not listen anymore. It's only going to get us upset. Let's forget about it until after the weekend."

We got in the car and drove up Hempstead Turnpike to a cinema in Uniondale. We couldn't resist tuning in on the way, hoping against hope that he'd improve and that we could find something salvageable. But things went from bad to worse, as he immediately repeated the Imperial Square Garage tag, and misidentified another record. We switched to Alison Steele and made our way to the theater, trying to put our dashed hopes out of mind.

Another problem was caused by our own insecurity in the first few months. A loudmouthed engineer from WPLJ arrived on our doorstep one day and bragged about how he could put us on the map immediately. He told us that he had contacts at record labels and could have our library stocked within days. If we would just give him a weekend air shift, he'd use his influence to bag us interviews with Jim Morrison and Janis Joplin, both of whom he claimed were his personal friends. He'd worked with Tom Donahue in L.A., he said, and knew everything there was to know about underground radio.

I was impressed, although I sensed Michael seemed threatened by this guy who seemed to outclass us. Nevertheless, we gave him a Sunday show on a temporary basis. Although he sounded good and was very clever on the air, he proceeded to break every rule we had set down.

We called him into the office the next day and he broke into tears, apologizing for upsetting us and swearing it would never happen again. When he left, Harrison theorized that he was a spy from WPLJ, looking to subvert our operation and steal our secrets. I dismissed the idea as ludicrous, but was troubled by his insubordination.

The next day, he came up to the station with a woman that he introduced as his wife. He was there to practice formatics so that he could improve his work to our standards. He took his wife into the production studio with him and began toiling on a tape. The woman was proving to be quite a distraction around the station. She paraded around in cutoff jeans, just barely covering her bottom and ripped in strategic places, topped by a tight T-shirt with no bra. Her bosom seemed to have a life of its own as it surged beneath a thin layer of cotton. She was an obviously bleached blonde. If our Sunday host had told us he found her soliciting in Times Square, we would have believed him.

He motioned me into the production room and played a tape that he had made—a montage of songs put together to illustrate a political point ridiculing Nixon. Although the station had antiwar overtones in attitude and music, we tried not to be overtly political when it came to specifics. I told him that, although creative, it really wasn't for us but that I was sure that WPLJ would appreciate it. But he'd quit WPLJ, he protested, in anticipation of more work at WLIR. I quickly disabused him of that notion, saying that he was only here on a tryout basis, and in any case, there were no full-time positions available.

He shocked me with his next comment. He said that he noticed me stealing a glance at his wife's boobs. Would I like to see them? If so, he had an apartment in Queens, and Harrison and I could join them later that evening. Just bring some hash, and we could take turns partying with his wife. I was embarrassed for her, but she said that it was cool. I begged off as gracefully as possible, using the excuse that Michael and I were both engaged, but that didn't seem to bother either of them. Bring your women along, too.

As I beat a path out of there, I tried to come up with a justification to get this man out of my life. He seemed more than a little unbalanced but we were still naïvely impressed with the contacts he'd talked about. We were hoping that we could rein in his wild streak and maximize his obvious talent. He had done an interesting show the previous Sunday.

No further incidents occurred involving his wife and he had the good sense to pretend it never happened. He still seemed defiant on the air, breaking our guidelines during every show but always apologizing profusely thereafter. To his credit, he never repeated the errors, but constantly found new ways to tweak our noses. But we were getting our music library filled, whether he had caused it to happen or not. He continued to be an erratic presence, alternately delighting with his creativity and dismaying with his blatant disregard for our rules. But he never did anything serious enough to warrant his dismissal, until he crossed Harrison.

One morning while going over music sheets, Michael told me he'd heard some scuttlebutt about this man's intention to overthrow us and take over as program director. Although we trusted that Reiger would give us the time we needed to accomplish our mission, any dissension within the ranks could only hinder the process. So he asked me to speak to the man confidentially, indicate that I had doubts about Harrison's leadership, and see what developed. He was asking me to be Luca Brazzi to his Don Corleone, and ferret out a traitor. Intrigued, I complied with his request and sure enough, the guy broke free, expanding on how Harrison had no clue as to what he was doing and that I should be running the place. He would be my right-hand man of course, until I got up to speed. He already enlisted other staffers to back him up and I had only to give him the word. I felt like I was in a Robert Ludlum thriller. Any benefits the guy might have offered were thrown aside when I told Harrison my story. The knave never did another show at WLIR.

We also had a problem keeping the place from turning into a flop house. We maintained a strict "no visitors after hours" policy. Don K. Reed, one of the straightest guys in the universe, complained that the studio reeked of marijuana many mornings and that he'd found seeds behind one of the tape decks. We traced the material to a weekend jock and brought him in for a warning: no more visitors or pot smoking on the premises. We also had a minor uproar when Reiger's wife found a used prophylactic in the cushions of the aptly named loveseat in her office. We issued a memo in strong terms, but privately suggested that any amorous encounters after hours be conducted on the roof. The view was better there anyway.

But our weekend guy just couldn't accept our restrictions and one Saturday evening, we were dining out in Hempstead and realized we had forgotten some albums at the station. Harrison and I found not only our jock floating away on a marijuana trail, but several of his friends toking away in the main offices. This time, we did fire him on the spot and Michael finished the show.

We were luckier with most of our other hires. Ken Kohl went on to a successful talk career and is now a highly placed executive for a Sacramento-based ownership group. Pete Larkin became a program director in Maryland and later worked at WNEW-FM. George Taylor Morris, also an alum, went on to run an NBC radio division and hosted mornings at WZLX in Boston. So we did help to start some careers in the right direction.

But most surprising to us was the speed at which WLIR rose to the top of the ratings on Long Island. Within six months, we were number one in total listenership. We knew early on that it was working, but it quickly surpassed even our expectations. Record companies, who initially didn't want to send us their releases, were falling over themselves to visit in person. We got on mailing lists for home service and artists made the station a regular stop when on press junkets. We were asked to broadcast from trade shows, and we actually drew crowds. We crafted commercials for local boutiques and their business improved overnight. People recognized us and asked for autographs.

The zenith came when we cohosted a concert in Eisenhower Park in East Meadow with a jock from WNEW-FM who lived on the Island. He was introduced first, to scattered applause. When our names were announced on the P.A., the crowd went crazy. Had we actually toppled the great WNEW-FM in a few months? That night gave us hope. But we still revered Muni and Steele and of course Rosko, and intuitively knew that they were light-years beyond us.

Although our confidence was growing, we wondered if we ever would get beyond small-market radio and move up to the station of our dreams. We spontaneously called Alison Steele at WNEW on the air one night for guidance. She knew all about us and was gracious enough to come out to Long Island for an interview. She later invited us to rendezvous in the city at a sleek East Side restaurant. When she excused herself during the meal to use the phone, Harrison and I burst out laughing as she walked away. Here we were, two twenty-one-year-olds, just out of college, having lunch with this accomplished, sexy woman in tight leather pants at a trendy Manhattan bistro. Alison was every college boy's wet dream and she was *our* friend. We'd made it to the big time, and if it had all ended there it would have been worth it.

The commercial log at WLIR was sold out for the first time, and rates were raised regularly to reflect its increasing pull with advertisers. Harrison and I had made a deal with Reiger to start at $110 a week apiece in our new jobs as program and operations director, respectively. As ratings and revenue grew, he promised that we could expect hefty raises. It still seemed like short money, even in 1970, but we trusted Reiger so we agreed. We'd even started making some money on the outside for in-store appearances and concert hosting. Our expenses were under control, since Harrison and I had rented an apartment together over a bakery in Oceanside for $175 a month. We weren't exactly driving Cadillacs and living on Park Avenue, but our prospects had improved markedly in a very short time.

While at the apartment one evening, the phone rang and a stilted voice, affecting a mid-Atlantic accent said, "Is this Dick Neer?"

It was the program director of WHLI in Hempstead. I was a bit off balance because WLIR had catapulted over WHLI and with my newly bolstered ego, I considered them a step down. They still played stodgy easy-listening music and, frankly, I hoped we'd left that world in the dust. But I played along, curious to see what he wanted. It seemed their evening host was taking a couple of weeks off next month and they were wondering if I'd be interested in filling in.

I told him that I wasn't interested in filling in, but asked if he was offering a job. He hedged, continuing to act as if joining his station would be my crowning acheivement in radio. After a short time, his arrogance got to me and I reminded him that WLIR had soundly beaten him in the last ratings book. To which he replied that I had a lot of nerve asking for a job that I didn't intend to accept, conveniently leaving out the fact that I'd applied over a year earlier.

I hung up, more satisfied than angry. Revenge was sweet. But that winter, Michael and I were in for a chastening experience when we approached Reiger for raises. Christmas had been a bonanza for WLIR. They'd increased the rates and the spot load several times and still couldn't handle the demand. They were raking it in, and now it was time for us to collect our rewards.

Reiger knew that this day was coming and dreaded it. Despite the revenues surging into the station, he'd incurred such debt running the old format for so many years that he was unable to extricate himself. He candidly showed us the books and indicated that even at this pace, it would take him another year to reach solvency. He could offer us a fifty-dollar raise over the next twelve months but even that was overextending. He was looking for a partner, an investor to inject some capital into his growing business. If he could pull that off, maybe someday he could pay us what he knew we were worth.

Michael and I dejectedly left his office and went down to the building's coffee shop. He stared at me with his intense brown eyes, and stated the obvious. It was so damn depressing. We had set our sights on a lofty goal, and now that we seemed so close to attaining it, we found that it was fool's gold. There was no recourse but to leave. For $250 a week, we could have lived like kings. And we ruled WLIR. We set the format, called the shots. Reiger had no desire to interfere with programming, knowing nothing about it. We had thought that someday we might even own part of WLIR, and have the cars, the house, and the boat that Reiger had. But we hadn't known it all was mortgaged to the hilt to support his business.

Harrison had already moved on. "All right, this afternoon I'll call Les Turpin at CBS-FM. You try to get ahold of George Duncan at Metro-media. Let's find out if there's a station we could program on the West Coast."

I'd grown to love working on the Island, living near the Atlantic Ocean. Pulling up stakes to go west didn't sound all that appealing. My family was nearby in New Jersey. But Michael was right, we had to make a move now while our stock was high.

So we pounded the pavement. We arranged job interviews at CBS. Everyone there was receptive and knew of our accomplishments in Garden City. But we were still kids. George Duncan agreed to see us at Metro-media headquarters. As head of the whole radio division now, he could send us wherever he wanted. But we failed the test he gave us, when we endorsed the uncensored version of "Working Class Hero."

So as we stood on the roof that wintry Friday night in 1971, coats pulled tight around us against the wind, we had no prospects other than to languish at WLIR and hope for a savior to bail out Reiger. The hours we spent working decreased as we became more dispirited and more in search of an escape. As our little transistor radio played gently in the background, it was obvious that something indeed was up with Rosko. His normally silky voice was breaking like an adolescent's and he seemed to be near tears. He reiterated that this was his last program at WNEW-FM, although he'd be on tape the following night. He played "Don't Let the Green Grass Fool You" and sang along, although we couldn't know at the time how closely that song paralleled what was happening in his life. He thanked all his coworkers—George Duncan, program director Scott Muni. He was leaving of his own accord and he'd been treated like a prince by everyone at Metromedia. There was no rancor in his voice, only a strange kind of joy, as if he were leaving one happy phase of his life behind for an exciting new adventure. The last record he played was Lee Michaels's "Heighty Hi," and he sang along with it on an open microphone. He wished us all peace and closed with his patented, "I sure do love you so."

Then he was gone with the wind.

Harrison and I were thinking precisely the same thing at that moment. While sad to be losing Rosko, there was no announced successor and no logical candidate to take the great man's place. We rushed back into the building and began editing our audition tapes. The assault on Manhattan was about to begin.

The Lamb Lies Down
on Broadway

ONCE HARRISON AND I were officially hired at WNEW-FM, after the bizarre interviews with Muni and company, things seemed to move in slow motion. Our first duty was the bittersweet task of informing Reiger that we'd both be leaving. He seemed stunned by the news. He said that he had always allowed for the possibility that one of us would leave, but felt confident that the other would carry on. With both of us gone, he feared that his newfound prosperity would be short-lived.

The fact that he didn't try to retain us with offers of more money confirmed our beliefs that it just wasn't there to give. But we assured him that we'd stay as long as necessary to make a smooth transition, and that we would work with Chuck Macken, our recommendation to program the station. I felt that Macken was a solid man and that it wouldn't take long for him to get up to speed. Michael had already drilled Chuck on the importance of closing ranks and keeping outside forces from corrupting what we'd built.

Meanwhile, our lease over the bakery was expiring and with our generous new salaries, we knew that our days of rooming together were over. I also felt the need to be in the city, although the idea of high rents and parking fees in Manhattan still put me off. A reasonable compromise seemed to be Queens, an easy commute by subway. I settled on a studio apartment in Lefrak City, eight miles from the station. Michael wound up in Lynbrook—it was a longer commute, but had more space.

Our first shot on the New York airwaves came quickly. Zacherle needed two days off in early April. Michael filled in first, and I did my initial show the evening of April 13, 1971. But we were cautioned not to say anything on or off the air about our upcoming roles at the station, since everyone who would be affected by the moves had not been informed of them yet.

Two weeks later, we got a succinctly worded letter in the mail:

I am truly sorry to inform you both that there are no openings in programming any of the Metromedia stations at this time, nor do we anticipate any in the foreseeable future.

However, I have gotten wind of the fact that there may be some changes coming at WNEW-FM in New York and that it might afford an opportunity for you both. I suggest you contact Varner Paulsen, the general manager, at your earliest convenience.

> *Good Luck and Congrats,*
> *George Duncan*
> *Vice President*
> *Metromedia Radio*

We were so afraid of Duncan that his impish sense of humor had escaped us until that letter arrived. But the plan at WNEW-FM finally solidified: Michael would do mornings, bumping the current occupant, Pete Fornatale, to middays. Muni would continue in the afternoons, followed by Schwartz, Zacherle, and then Steele overnight. After having a taste of the daylight hours, Alison couldn't have been too pleased. An aggressive careerist, much of her outside activity took place during regular business hours, and working all night was not conducive to her syndication deals and commercial work. It also didn't leave time for much of a social life. But everyone else loved the new schedule, especially Fornatale. It would allow him an easy rail commute from his Port Washington home, avoiding rush-hour traffic both ways.

Mornings were still the least important shift. Most car radios still didn't have FM tuners, and much of morning listening is spent in the car, trying to glean information and entertainment while fuming through traffic jams. Longtime morning hosts on AM like Klavan and Finch, John Gambling, Don Imus, and Harry Harrison, as well as the all news outlets, were too powerful to be challenged by anything FM could offer. Varner Paulsen expected audience shares in the morning to lag well behind the rest of the day parts, in stark contrast to the philosophy general managers have today. The money time on FM was 6 to 10 P.M., and that was in the hands of Jonathan Schwartz.

My first brush with Jonathan was an uneasy one. I had gone into the studio on my first day as music director to replace a worn LP when he cornered me, almost literally, exhaling garlicky breath in my face.

"Young man, what's your name again?"

I told him, using the radio name I'd been stuck with.

"Ah, Dick Neer. Doesn't exactly roll off the tongue, does it? What qualifies you to be on this radio station?"

Jonathan wasn't trying to be obnoxious, although I didn't know it at the time. This was his unsubtle way of asking me about my background, getting to know me. I had heard his raging ego had only gotten worse since ascending to prime time and replacing his arch rival, Rosko. I was warned by Steele and others to steer clear of him. "He'll eat you for breakfast," she told me.

"I don't want to distract you before you go on the air," I said to Schwartz. "We'll talk another time when it's more convenient for you." I was determined to do everything in my power to ensure that that time would not come soon. With his unconventional radio voice, there was speculation among those who didn't know him that Jonathan was gay. Reading between the lines of the staff's warnings, I feared that his interest in me might not be wholly professional. I would later learn that my fears were completely unfounded, and that Jonno went through women like Muni went through scotch.

"Don't leave, don't leave, young man. Have you ever heard of me?"

This was ridiculous—any answer I might give would obviously be designed to feed his ego or reveal my own ignorance.

"Of course I've heard of you, Jonathan." I made sure to use his first name. Referring to him as "Mr. Schwartz" would have only weakened my already prostrate position.

"Do you know that I do other things, that I'm not just a 'jocque du disques'?" Of course, the appellation "disc jockey" would be beneath him. "Do you know, for example, that I'm a writer?"

"Sure I do. You wrote *Almost Home.*" In every station tear sheet, the minibiography of Jonno contained the obligatory "celebrated author of *Almost Home,* a collection of short stories." I had no idea about the rest of his background, other than that he was from Boston and his family was rich. Little did I realize that his father had penned "Cocktails for Two," the song I was compelled to play for years while introducing WLIR's evening program of the same name.

Schwartz wasn't satisfied to leave it at that. "I don't suppose you've read it. No, I don't suppose you read much at all."

Welcome to WNEW-FM and the big time! I was being insulted by its most powerful host, a man whom I'd just met. At the time, I wasn't a voracious reader, but did I look like that much of a hayseed to this snob? After all, I had just graduated from college. So I lied.

"As a matter of fact, I have read it. Look, the news is ending and your show is starting. I'd better leave." I bolted out the heavy studio door as he shouted something after me. I grabbed my jacket and ran for the safety of the elevator, lest he pursue and interrogate me more about his book.

As I walked across town toward the bus terminal, I seethed. I knew from Alison that WNEW-FM wasn't one big happy family but this was ridiculous. I posed no threat to Schwartz. I respected his air work and wanted him to like me.

But now I was faced with a real test: I hadn't read *Almost Home.* There was no way that I could avoid him following up on it the next day unless I left early, and that wouldn't sit well with my new bosses, whom I was trying to impress with my work habits. To admit that I had lied to him might gain his respect, or it might signal that his intimidation tactics had worked, leading to more of the same. So, as I passed a Doubleday bookstore on the way home, I bought a copy of his tome and began reading it on the bus. I didn't enjoy it much under the circumstances, but I stayed up until two in the morning until I'd finished every last page. I felt like I was back in college, cramming for an exam.

Sure enough, Schwartz ambled into the music library at a quarter to six the next evening. I was prepared for him, not only by my study of his book, but by a pep talk from Alison, who told me not to take any more of his crap. She advised that if I did, he'd only try to humiliate me again, but that if I stood up to him, like all bullies, he'd retreat. She conveyed that even though Rosko gave away four inches and thirty pounds to Jonno, Schwartz had backed down from physical confrontations. I filed that away—not given to violence myself, and knowing that winning a fistfight with a star jock would result in losing my job. Not worth it.

I looked up at him from the pile of records on my desk. "Hey, Jonno, how are you?"

He reacted as if slapped, but quickly recovered. "Young Neer," he said sneeringly. At least he used my name; that was a start. "I noted that you re-treated rather quickly upon mention of my book. It led me to the in-escapable conclusion that you indeed, in fact, hadn't read it at all, as you stated." This was typical Schwartz verbosity: perhaps a test to see if you'd rise to his level of literacy.

"I did read it." I tried to sound unimpressed. And though his prose was not exactly to my liking, he was obviously talented. Plus, as his tear sheet stated, director Peter Yates (*Bullitt*) had optioned it for the cinema.

He looked askance. "Oh, really," he said skeptically. "What was your favorite part?"

I then launched into a lengthy description of my favorite story, and then mentioned some other segments that I had enjoyed. He listened to my entire analysis with his mouth open, as if a child of four was explaining quantum physics.

"I could have sworn you hadn't read it," he muttered, almost to him-self, as he fled to the studio. My feeling was that I had won something im-portant in my little duel with Jonathan. For once in his life, he was almost speechless. Our relationship, though never a close one, was conducted professionally and with respect thereafter, but for reasons unrelated to my perceived little victory. I grew to like Jonno, accepting his strangeness as a sort of quirky charm.

I had misread his intentions as poorly as he had misunderstood mine. Schwartz has always considered format to be the "dust in the air" at any radio station, ready to settle down at a moment's notice. He lived in con-stant fear of anyone in a position of authority telling him what to play. In his obfuscating fashion, he was letting me know that he was not about to take orders from me when it came to music. Even though my impression of his personal wealth was vastly overstated, he wanted everyone to believe that he enjoyed economic independence from the job. His trumpeting of *Almost Home* was his way of saying that he didn't need WNEW-FM, but that *it* needed *him*. His writing had garnered the station oceans of free ink, in the *New York Times, Newsweek,* and other important publications. Along with praise for his work, every article contained the call letters and that impressed the powers at the station. He was also tight with George Duncan, who had told him that he'd be around as long as there was a Metromedia, which was indeed prophetic. Schwartz was defending his territory, fierce in his desire to maintain autonomy and defend free-form tenets.

My agenda was to be accepted as a peer. The only system that WNEW-FM had to regulate music was the "rack." This was a rolling wooden bin, about thirty inches tall, with a partition in the middle. It contained about 250 albums. Similar to what Tony Pigg did at KSAN, my job was to give the rack a semblance of organization. Albums were designated NA (new album) and PA (progressive album), which merely meant that it was a current release. In the back were FA (folk album), JA (jazz), and INST (instrumental). In those days, the station simulcast hourly news with WNEW-AM so instrumentals were helpful in filling time to the top of the hour. At any given moment there might be sixty NAs, one hundred PAs, thirty FAs, twenty-five JAs, and a handful of INSTs. I would listen to the new releases and mark tracks that I liked, although the jocks were under no requirement to heed my suggestions. I might include a bit of biographical material or a brief description of the sound of the record. Weekly memos came from my desk, detailing the new albums added.

The rack was changed every six weeks and this was enough to keep me awake the night before. It entailed winnowing out the NAs, moving the successful ones to PA or FA, and eliminating the ones nobody played. The NAs might then shrink temporarily to ten, before gradually building to sixty again and necessitating another rack change.

To keep the PAs at a manageable level, the less-played ones would be put in the "wall," a massive shelving system along the rear of the studio. All records that achieved PA status went into the wall, regardless of merit or airplay, and stayed there after they lost their designation as a "current." Politics played a big part in deciding the fate of an album. Holy hell would be raised if you removed a record that a friendly promoter was hyping to Muni or Steele. You had to be sure that it was toast before relegating it to the obscurity of the wall, since anything that left the rack saw an enormous drop in airplay. The rack-change memo was my biggest enemy, in that regard. With all the albums available, I figured that I could sneak a few losers out of the system without anyone noticing. But the memo had to state which new records went into the rack, which into the wall, and which just vanished. The jocks then perused the memo and if one of their favorites was eliminated, I heard about it. Muni generally insisted that I return it to the rack or, on a few occasions, suggested that jocks play their own copies.

I also had to check over the taped shows to make sure that the proper albums were pulled from the library and inserted into a cardboard box containing cue sheets. Tom "Tammy" Tracy produced the taped shows, meaning that he recorded the vocal tracks and barked out timing so that the jocks knew how many songs they could play within a given hour. He typed a detailed cue sheet for the weekend engineers, who most often were veterans of WNEW-AM and neither knew nor liked rock and roll. Very, very often, even Tracy's clearly labeled instructions were misinterpreted and disaster followed.

Schwartz tells of one particular tape operator we'll call Lewinski who, in Jonno's words, "would never be confused with Saul Bellow." One evening, a friend had arranged a ménage à trois for the always adventuresome Schwartz. Upon reaching his Manhattan apartment, one of the two nymphets suggested that they videotape the encounter for posterity. Unconcerned that the tape could surface later and cause him embarrassment, Jonno carefully positioned his video camera and adjusted its focus toward his king-size bed. He flipped the stereo to 102.7, where his taped show was about to air. He anticipated a night of ecstasy—listening to himself on the radio while enjoying the lascivious attention of two young women. It just couldn't get any better than that.

Just as they were getting down and dirty, his voice came over the speakers, announcing that he was about to play the Beatles. The unmistakable percussive beginning of the Rolling Stones' "Sympathy for the Devil" stopped him mid-stroke. A triple dose of Viagra couldn't ameliorate the physical reaction it had on him, as he screamed, "Goddamn it, Lewinski!"

The women, wondering if he was invoking the name of an ex-lover and thinking they had uncovered another dimension to Jonno's kinkiness, just played along.

The moment still amuses him whenever he replays the videotape.

Helter Skelter

DAVE HERMAN WAS WPLJ's best and most famous disc jockey. Dave's career had gone the route of so many free-form pioneers: He had started out doing mornings for a tiny station in Asbury Park, New Jersey, playing standards by Sinatra, Nat King Cole, and Tony Bennett along with the typical Mantovani and 101 Strings. He had a small family, and was carving out a respectable middle-class living, one that sustained him for ten years. He never dreamed that major-market radio would come calling. But in 1967, he tried LSD and experienced an epiphany that transformed his entire being. He became a hippie, in appearance, lifestyle, and attitude. He decided that he had something to say, and he felt that he could bring something to radio that he wasn't presently hearing, much like Tom Donahue did in San Francisco. He became a fan of WNEW-FM, and fell in love with the music they were playing, music that spoke to him in a way that Percy Faith never had.

So he trundled off to Philadelphia and pitched Gary Stevens at WMMR, another Metromedia station, on the concept of doing a free-form program. The station was basically an automated music service, existing only to placate the FCC by not duplicating its AM sister, WIP. Herman gave management a fanciful presentation that showed how progressive radio was catching on in other markets, most notably in New York at WNEW-FM and KMPX in San Francisco. They remained skeptical, since Philadelphia considered itself the home of Top Forty radio with Dick Clark's *American Bandstand* and WIBG, where Donahue once worked as Big Daddy. But with little to lose, Dave's persistence convinced them to give him a one-year contract to take over the evening hours at WMMR.

Dave had to give himself a crash course in rock and roll when he was hired. His early days in Philadelphia were spent learning, listening to album after album of the rock that he never played in Asbury Park. In 1968, this was not so daunting a task because there wasn't that much underground music. There might have been two hundred albums that were important to be conversant with, and by listening and reading up on the artists in *Rolling Stone* and the nascent music press, he educated himself enough to get by while developing his own tastes. And he'd learned interviewing techniques in New Jersey, talking to local politicos to assemble newscasts for his morning show.

Within months, Herman's show, *The Marconi Experiment,* was the toast of the town. He was supported by clubs, concert promoters, record labels, counterculture newspapers, boutiques—in short, all the emerging businesses that appealed to the youth market. WMMR was pleased with the buzz it created and sought other jocks to fill the rest of the day.

Herman had become a political animal, holding strongly stated positions against the war and government in general. Revolution was a concept that he supported, and he harbored fantasies of an overthrow of the federal government and its replacement with one more responsive to the people's wishes. Dave spoke at an alternative-radio seminar in Vermont sponsored by Larry Yurdin, which seemed to be more about overturning the system than creating great radio. *The Marconi Experiment* interviewed the radical thinkers of the day, underscoring their words with appropriate music. Dave was keenly intelligent if admittedly somewhat misguided, but never came off as a wild-eyed young radical. He was older than most of his fellow travelers and his professional baritone impacted even conservative listeners who didn't share his politics but were soothed by his measured presentation.

His success caught the ear of Alan Shaw, who was assembling a revamped ABC-FM network. Shaw offered Herman the chance to be heard nationally at a greatly increased salary, but since ABC had no affiliate in Philadelphia, Dave would have to move to New York and broadcast from corporate headquarters. It represented a tough decision and he sought counsel in two areas. First he spoke to his father, a rabbi, who asked Dave the fundamental question: Why did he want to be in radio? Was it for the money? Fame? Politics? Dave said that although he would appreciate higher pay, his main reason for doing what he did was that he thought he had something to say that could change the world in a positive way. His dad replied that if that was the case, he should seek the biggest forum he could find, and that fifteen hours a week on the ABC network and twenty hours live in New York topped doing a local show in Philadelphia.

Although his father's advice made sense, Dave still was torn. Barely a year out of Asbury Park, he was an enormous cultural figure in Philly, and was making more money and having more impact than he'd ever dreamed of. He traveled to the Jersey shore and asked a Gypsy fortune-teller what he should do. She supported his father's counsel. Not without misgivings, he accepted Shaw's offer.

As difficult as it was to make sense of what WPLJ was doing musically, its politics were consistent—radical left. Alex Bennett did a morning show that was mostly talk. Alex had established himself as a weekend talk show host at WMCA as it drifted away from Top Forty before becoming all talk. Michael Cuscuna, the jazz maven, did middays, followed by Mike Turner, Herman, and Vin Scelsa. It became a mecca for the likes of Jerry Rubin and his cohorts in the Chicago Seven. John Lennon had even filled in there when Bennett went on vacation. The language they used was unabashedly revolutionary stuff, and was often coarsely stated. Lawyers were constantly buzzing around the studios in the ABC Building on Sixth Avenue, trying to stem potential libel suits and FCC sanctions.

The transformation of WABC-FM to WPLJ extended to the decor, and was analogous to the clash of the two cultures. ABC had a strict policy of bare walls, stating that no art could be hung without management approval. It was the epitome of a sterile corporate environment, with strict rules about the way the office was to be kept not only free of clutter but also about unauthorized personnel, i.e., female visitors and radical hangers-on. But once the offices closed for the day, posters of Che Guevara went up, tapestries were hung, and hash pipes broken out. Lava lamps and other psychedelia decorated the place, with friends loitering around "doing their thing." The air studio took on the appearance of a murky drug den: dimly lit, smoky, and smelling of incense. Spiritually, it resembled WFMU, a little college community of like-minded hippies bent on changing the world.

There was a palpable disregard for authority; indeed, the inmates were running the asylum. Once Michael Turner was asked by general manager Lou Severin to speak to him on a matter of some importance. Turner replied to his boss that he had to take a crap, so why didn't Severin follow him into the stall and discuss his issues with him there? Orders were ignored as memos from the top went up in smoke, literally and figuratively. Any attempt by management to bring some balance to the operation was met with sneering disregard and acts of defiance that became bolder and more outrageous.

Shaw tried to remain a buffer, shielding his charges from higher management on the premise that they needed this work environment to weave their magic on the airwaves. He tried to school his people on how to express their radical sentiments without incurring legal action. But it had gone too far, and any attempt at direction only alienated Shaw from the staff, who lived in constant wariness of selling out to the corporation. The "suits" wanted to see ratings and revenue, but WNEW-FM was winning those wars handily, and it was becoming harder to justify what management viewed as a repugnant culture when the financial rewards failed to be forthcoming.

At WNEW-FM, John Zacherle liked what he was hearing across town in the spring of 1971. Zach would get off the air at 2 A.M. and, still energized from his show, drive around Central Park for hours with the top down on his VW bug convertible, the radio turned up loud. His contract was expiring, and although he was free to play whatever he wanted, the respective atmospheres at the two stations reflected a stark contrast in the open expression of their political leanings. Upon Rosko's leaving, there was precious little political talk on the station, and most of that was nonspecific. For example, Fornatale reacted with horror to the Kent State shootings, and later he played "Ohio," which was rush-released by Crosby, Stills, Nash and Young a month later, four times in a row. Opposition to the war was a given—by attitude and the music played. Most jocks were in sympathy with the protesters and supported them on their own time. Schwartz and Muni were independent thinkers, allying themselves neither with conservatives nor liberals by rote but reacting to every issue on its own merits. No one seriously thought that overthrowing the government was the answer, basically jibing with John Lennon's line in the Beatles' "Revolution": "We're doing what we can."

Drug use was also something that separated the two stations. Muni was a fan of scotch, as was Schwartz. If either used marijuana, it was strictly to be convivial when someone passed a joint around. In the twenty-five years I'd known her, I never saw Alison Steele intoxicated by anything more than a New York Rangers victory, and Harrison and Fornatale mostly abstained. Zach always seemed to be on something, but I think it was more a case of his flighty personality than any substance abuse.

Zacherle also was at odds with his colleagues' more extravagant life-styles. He was never a conspicuous consumer; he owned a VW Beetle and lived in a rent-controlled apartment with his elderly mother, whom he supported. He was surrounded by Schwartz, who had a perpetual tan from his Palm Springs retreat and "beautiful people" friends among the literati of New York and Hollywood, and Steele, who spent thousands on exotic clothing and her luxurious Manhattan rental. Even Muni, who didn't flaunt his wealth, owned a boat and a beautiful lagoon house in an affluent community on the Jersey shore.

Zach's coworkers at WNEW-FM were more polished in their manner on the air as well. He was more simpatico with the unvarnished presentation at WPLJ, the lack of showmanship and structure. Indeed, he'd agreed with Rosko on the use of the rack. It was Rosko's viewpoint that the music director not even touch the rack, but that records would find their own way into airplay or oblivion. It was a nice but hopelessly naïve thought, just in terms of maintaining order. When a song is reaching its conclusion and one is casting about for a perfect segue, you're never afforded the time to rummage around through unsorted piles of albums to locate the one you need. But Zach didn't worry about that, he just knew that he had found kindred spirits at WPLJ and that when his contract expired, he'd try to join them.

Muni was aware of Zach's dilemma, but was also pragmatic enough to know that ABC, for whom he'd worked years earlier, would not tolerate what was going on at WPLJ much longer. His entreaties fell on deaf ears. Zach had told him that he'd never held any job much more than a year, so it was time for him to move on. Unlike many jocks, John Zacherle wasn't making the standard power play to better himself. He was a true believer who loved his audience and wanted to remain true both to it and himself by working in an environment more suited to his nature. There were jealousies and rivalries galore at WNEW-FM that he sensed weren't present in the more communal atmosphere at WPLJ.

A little insight into the man: When he did the morning show, he sometimes felt isolated from his audience. So one day he told the listeners to gather outside his window at 230 Park Avenue and that there would be a nice surprise awaiting them. As a small crowd bunched up minutes later, eyes to the sky and his thirteenth-floor window, they gasped in amazement as dollar bills began floating down toward them, from Zach's own wallet. Upon being introduced at rock shows, as he took the stage, he pulled off his wristwatch and flung it into the crowd for some lucky concertgoer to keep. He later admitted that it was becoming too costly a habit, and that he switched to an inexpensive Timex when a public appearance loomed. One of his quirks while on the air was to activate the turntables with his toes instead of fingers. The studio ceiling was pocked with tiny black holes where he'd engaged Schwartz in a competition to hurl sharpened pencils upward like darts, trying to stick their points into the soft acoustic tile.

Zach dressed in jeans and work shirts but wasn't a "limousine liberal," as were many of his peers. In fact, one jock who professed to be a man of the people took limos to concerts whenever possible, but asked to be dropped a block away so that he wouldn't be seen by his fans. Not Zacherle—what you saw was what you got. He either walked, took the subway, or came puttering up in his Volkswagen.

So in June of 1971, he bade WNEW-FM good-bye and went to work for the competition. WPLJ was thrilled to have him, and gloated not unlike Americans welcoming a prominent communist from behind the Iron Curtain. Perhaps the tide was changing—the more commercially successful WNEW-FM was losing defectors to the revolutionary cause.

For Alison Steele, Zacherle's move meant a sea change in the course of her career. Although she'd gained a small cachet from her overnight exploits, other than night workers and cramming college students, few had actually heard her, save for the occasions when she filled in during the day, when her Nightbird routine seemed out of place. But now that the coveted

10 P.M. to 2 A.M. shift was hers, she could play to a far wider audience while still working after sunset. It was in this time slot that her legend was born.

This also meant a change for me. As music director, I'd asked Paulsen and Muni if I could come in with Harrison at 6 A.M. This would serve several purposes. Since both of us were frugal with our newfound wealth, we could save money commuting. We could also enjoy each other's company and bounce ideas around on the ride in. And I had the advantage of being able to audition records in peace and quiet for three hours before the phones began to ring, thus freeing me to make more decisions independent of the pressures of record promoters. I'd leave by three, sometimes with, sometimes without, Harrison. I could also assist Michael in putting his show together: fetching albums from the library, offering opinions on new material I'd heard, or helping to sort out commercials. Muni had no problem with the hours, as long as the work got done.

But now I faced a fork in the road. I was offered Alison's old overnight shift. I'd make a few more dollars and work five days live and one on tape instead of seven days a week. But I'd be giving up the chance to stay in management and the opportunity to shape the direction the station went musically. Plus, my life would be turned around and I'd lead a vampiric existence—sleeping by day and working all night.

The choice wasn't difficult. I enjoyed performing more than directing and here was a chance to perform twenty hours a week. I could hone my talents in the relative obscurity of the overnights and, when someone else left, spring into a more prominent spot. Besides, it was becoming increasingly obvious to me that WNEW-FM was not about to offer the jocks any structured musical direction, so my job in the library would essentially be that of a lackey whom the staff would distrust if I aspired to more control. So I agreed to do the overnight show. I would be surrounded by the two people I liked most at the station, Alison Steele at night and Harrison in the morning.

A young contemporary of ours named Dennis Elsas was hired to do the weekend shows I'd abandoned. Dennis was a friend of Pete Fornatale's, and like-minded in his taste for accessible music. So when John Zacherle took the shopping bag that he carried in lieu of a briefcase to WPLJ, we lamented the loss of a well-liked and good comrade, but found ourselves a strong new player.

Things were rapidly falling apart at WPLJ. The uneasy alliance between a large corporation and leftist radicals was crumbling and both sides were growing increasingly militant. Compromise seemed out of the question and decisions were coming from ABC that risked throwing the baby out with the bath water. As Muni had forewarned, shortly after Zach signed his deal at WPLJ, the ax fell. He'd done only a few shows when ABC, tired of the lawsuits and political culture that had developed, brought law and order to Sixth Avenue. The entire staff was called into a meeting on August 26, 1971, and sat silently as general manager Lou Severin outlined the new rules. The music would be formatted (it would later be called "rock in stereo"). There would initially be two or three songs an hour that must be played. A card system would be instituted that would restrict choice somewhat but still offer a wide range. All guests had to be cleared with management prior to airing and no politics would be discussed.

The mood was somber. This was the beginning of the end—no one could deal with any of these restrictions and retain their credibility with the political community. The audience at the time may not have been large, but they were fiercely loyal. The jocks felt powerless to object—after all, it was ABC's candy store. WPLJ was destined to become just another radio station, albeit a far more profitable one.

At a lull in the presentation, Zacherle slowly reached down under the table into his shopping bag and pulled out a vintage machine gun. With a crazed look in his eyes, he aimed it in the direction of Severin and Shaw and screamed, "You've betrayed me, you son of a bitches! I'll get you bastards! You'll pay for this!"

The two men cowered in fear. This was an era when the staff had openly urged violence against the establishment. Times were not far removed from the political assassinations of Martin Luther King, Jr., and Robert Kennedy. A bomb factory run by student radicals had recently been discovered in the Village. Severin and Shaw had always felt that Zacherle was a harmless eccentric, and never thought he was given to violence.

Herman and Scelsa watched in horror as Zach's diatribe continued, cursing the two men and the whole establishment for killing his dreams of WPLJ. He then hoisted the weapon into firing position, locked the clip, and pulled the trigger, as members of the staff dove under the table for shelter.

But instead of a hail of murderous bullets emerging from the barrel, out popped a harmless little flag that simply said, "BANG!!"

The room erupted into relieved laughter as the tension was broken.

The meeting ended shortly thereafter, and the staff retreated into little groups to discuss their next move.

For Scelsa, it was simple. He told Severin plainly, "I'm outta here," and never did another show. Herman said that he was leaving also, but Shaw insisted that Dave had a contract and would not be allowed to quit. He said that if Herman refused to work, he'd sue him and keep him from making a living in radio for as long as he could. Since Herman had a family, he couldn't risk the banishment, so he reacted like Harrison and I had when Reiger had censured us for using our names too often. He did his show, but he spoke as seldom as he could. When he did open the microphone, his voice was a slow monotone, merely identifying the call letters and never using his name. After several weeks of this, management agreed to release him from the remainder of his contract. One by one, the rest of the staff quit or were fired, with one prominent exception: John Zacherle.

After a series of programmers tried to restore order, Larry Berger, a Rick Sklar protégé, was brought in to settle the station. Berger had survived the payola era, but only barely. A story circulated that while at another station, he had agreed to play a certain record and had accepted a large sum of money to do so. But when it came time to deliver on his promise, he reneged. Apparently, the promoter he had cheated was connected to the underworld and sent a messenger to Berger's high-rise office. The burly enforcer then dangled the diminutive Berger out the window by his heels until he relented and agreed to play the record. No one knew if the tale was apocryphal, but legend has it that the experience left Berger scarred for life and that, much like Sklar, he refused to entertain promotion men after that and became absolutely incorruptible.

The noose restricting choice got tighter over time until the jocks had no say in what they played. Berger brought in his own staff, who understood from the beginning that he was the boss and that their opinions on music and politics held little sway with him.

Zacherle remained at WPLJ for another twelve years, obediently toeing the line and playing the hits. He had nowhere else to go, having walked out on WNEW.

Prove It All Night

"WAKE UP, THE RECORD'S OVER."

Engineer Pete Johnson was shaking me by the shoulder. Where was I? *Who* was I? I groggily arose from the uncomfortable sofa and stumbled through the darkness toward the light switch.

Oh, God! I'm working. I'm on the air. Before I could organize my thoughts, I rushed to the studio and pushed the remote button for turntable one, and I watched in horror as the other tonearm spun relentlessly into the center groove with a sickening click . . . click . . . click.

It was coming back to me now. This was my first Saturday doing the all-night shift from 2 A.M. until six. After struggling through the first hour, I told Johnson that I needed a quick nap, just twenty minutes or so to refresh me so that I could make it through the rest of the night. Luckily, the cool new group Emerson, Lake and Palmer had just released *Tarkus,* and all of New York was clamoring to hear it. With Keith Emerson of the Nice, Greg Lake of King Crimson, and Carl Palmer from Atomic Rooster, they comprised a typical British supergroup. Like Blind Faith and Crosby, Stills, Nash and Young before them and Asia, Foreigner, et cetera, later, they were presold as an all-star lineup before recording a note. With Emerson's keyboard pyrotechnics, Lake's sensual vocals, and Palmer's frenetic drumming, they'd scored big with their first album, which featured the single "Lucky Man." The hit was a ballad of manageable length with a conventional acoustic guitar. The only progressive element was the ending, with Emerson's synth swirling from channel to channel like a Hendrix guitar solo. The rest of the album had long, largely instrumental set pieces, which showed the performers' virtuosity to great advantage. On *Tarkus,* they'd decided to go all out with a concept album about some mutant tank that resembled an armadillo with gun barrels. The first side ran almost twenty minutes and would afford me the nap I needed.

I told Johnson to wake me up with about two minutes left on the side, but when I looked at the studio clock, I calculated that the side had been over for nearly five minutes. I pressed the intercom button to yell at Johnson across the glass.

"Pete, what the hell happened? I thought I told you to wake me up before the record ended."

"Sorry, man. I fell asleep, too."

I couldn't stay mad at him. He was working a split shift and was doubtless having the same problem adjusting to the hours. For months, I'd been arriving at the station at 6 A.M. with Harrison, so I was used to going to bed early and getting up at 4:30 A.M.. Michael would pick me up at 5:15, or we'd take my car to the Vernon-Jackson subway stop in Long Island City where we could park all day for seventy-five cents. We would then grab a train to Grand Central, and ride the long escalator up to street level. There was an all-night deli where we'd pick up orange juice and a doughnut, and then walk across Forty-fifth Street to the studio. We felt like coal miners as we commuted with the early morning shift.

Luckily, my adjustment to the overnights came quickly and soon I'd worked out a routine. I'd usually hang with Harrison until six-thirty, then go home and try to get to sleep by seven-thirty. If I got up by one or two in the afternoon, I still had a good stretch of daylight in the summertime to enjoy the weather. The problems came later, in the winter, when if you didn't get to sleep right after getting home, you might think you lived in

Norway, seeing little or no sunlight from November until March. You acquired what Frank Zappa referred to as a "studio tan," a ghostly pallor that
made Zacherle look healthy by comparison.

It was during one of these nights that I got my real name back. I'd always hated the nickname "Dick" but since it was the only one I used in
radio, I figured I was stuck with it. Then while doing my overnight show,
I noticed a new album by "Richard" Betts of the Allman Brothers. I said
spontaneously, "Well, if old Dickey Betts of the Allman Brothers can
change his name to Richard, dammit, so can I. From now on, I'm Richard
Neer."

I never used "Dick" Neer on the air again. It took a little longer to convince my colleagues to make the switch, but within a few months the conversion was complete. I can always judge the age and station loyalties of a
listener these days when they approach me by saying, "I knew you when
you were Dick Neer."

But it was while doing overnights that I learned, almost by osmosis,
how the business was structured and how lucky we all were to be in the
right place at the right time. And how the days of free form were numbered.

The economics of AM radio were changing. The mid-twenty shares
that WABC once enjoyed were now sinking rapidly into single digits as
FM began to flex its muscles. WNBC, with the spoken emphasis on the N,
took up the competitive mantle for years, even managing to steal away
Bruce Morrow after Sklar decided to attempt to impose what he saw as the
new realities. Bruce had been used to the big money of the golden years,
averaging close to two hundred thousand a year in salary and perhaps double that in outside activities. As FM stations began making inroads, ratings
were slipping from their peak in the late sixties. To protect themselves
against falling revenues, management proposed a lower base salary for
Morrow, with incentives for ratings increases, coupled with deductions if
the station's popularity fell. Bruce was incensed, feeling betrayed by the
very people he felt he had helped make into legends. Everyone could read
the writing on the wall: No matter what they did, things would never be as
good as they once were.

Always a canny businessman, Bruce knew that rival WNBC had tried
an array of talent to combat WABC's superiority. The one thing they
hadn't tried was pirating their disc jockeys. So while Morrow told Sklar he
agreed in principle with the new concept, he was secretly being wooed by

WNBC's Perry Bascom, who had no qualms about guaranteeing Morrow's contract at a much higher salary. Bruce allowed that he would consider WABC's new arrangement if they would tear up his existing contract immediately.

What happened next is unclear. Executives at ABC said that they realized that releasing Morrow in this fashion would make him a free agent, but that they were unconcerned. By this time, Sklar considered his jocks to be like "spark plugs." They give you service for a while, then wear out and are replaced by new ones. Whatever WABC's attitude was, Morrow didn't wait to find out, inking a new deal with WNBC the next day. Bruce presented Sklar with a gift-wrapped spark plug as a going-away present. But both stations continued to lose numbers as more listeners flocked to FM.

Even though it was winning over hearts and minds, the progressive era was an anomaly for several reasons. Chief among them was the FCC, who took almost worthless FM stations and by decree gave them profit potential. The duopoly and the AM-FM receiver rulings opened up a wealth of possibilities, through no fault of the broadcasters themselves. It would be as if the FTC had declared tax rebates were available to anyone who bought the Edsel. It was a gift from the gods to radio-station owners, whose main purpose was to make money.

And since owners suddenly had all these frequencies to fill and with all the good formats taken, they had to be creative. The music industry realized they could make more money selling long-playing albums than singles. They in turn pressured artists for more than just a few three-minute songs a year—now they needed forty-minute albums. So recording artists began to experiment. Some got the idea that rather than come up with twelve short tunes, they could write five short ones that might work as singles and four long ones that allowed them space to jam. So now you had a new kind of music on record that wasn't being played on the radio, and progressive programmers swooped in to give it exposure.

Also, to staff the new stations, there were a bunch of young broadcasters who hadn't ever held a job and were willing to work for a tenth of what stars like Cousin Brucie were drawing. In addition, there were legions of burnt-out Top Forty jocks who were willing to work for less money to revitalize their sagging careers. So a whole staff of FM disc jockeys might cost less than one Top Forty personality. Plus the AM sales staff could sell FM time on the side, and the AM general manager could mind the cash register. Since production was an artifice scorned by the new medium, money could be saved on jingles, promotions, and contests. A program director merely had to ride herd, since no real direction was given. So no FM station had to pay Rick Sklar–type money for a programming genius. Any profit would be pure gravy.

And new businesses were emerging that could take advantage of FM's low rates to reach their target audiences. Record companies didn't need to dish out payola to individual jocks; they could buy inexpensive commercials on the stations that played their records. Boutiques and head shops couldn't afford WABC and would sound out of place there if they could, so they gravitated to FM. Concert promoters and publications that sought credibility with a young audience could find it with low-key ads read by hip FM jocks.

With the combination of low overhead and a ready-made marketplace, FM owners began to see water transformed into wine. So managers didn't know or care if jocks were playing unfamiliar, noncommercial music. Most of the DJs were making more money than they needed. They got free dope from admiring fans. Sex was there for the asking. They were in hog heaven. Why sell out and play something that some suit ordered you to when you already had everything you needed?

I grew to admire the way Muni ran the station. He was effective in keeping the corporate wolves at bay. I don't know if it was because he is such a keen judge of human nature or that he is just lazy, but his loose-reined approach was right for the times. As he hired new people, I began to realize that his rambling interview technique was actually pretty cagey. The key to finding good jocks was assessing what kind of people they were, which he was able to do in the long sessions, without their knowledge of his agenda.

He once told me how he approached audition tapes. If he heard something memorable in the generally slick productions he received, he asked the applicant to sit down with a tape recorder and, in six to ten minutes, explain why they thought they were good enough to be on WNEW-FM: "If they started out in a staccato, 'Mr. Muni . . . I feel . . . that I should be . . .' I could tell they were just a reader and I threw their tapes out. But if someone could put his feelings on tape in a cogent manner, and showed an all-around knowledge of the music, then we might have a keeper."

Unlike Top Forty, where what you do on the air is an act, manufactured to fit a style of forced excitement, on progressive radio you couldn't fool the audience into thinking you were something that you weren't. One veteran jock told me, "The key to all of this is sincerity. Once you learn to fake that, the rest is easy." It wasn't easy to fake it on FM, however, and those who tried were generally found out in short order.

To succeed on progressive radio you had to a) know the music, b) understand and preferably share the listeners' politics and lifestyles, and c) have a delivery compatible with a and b. Of course, these elements won't guarantee fame and fortune, but without them there is little chance of success.

Knowing the music was first and foremost. In those days, the slightest slip could undermine your credibility with the audience. While Alison Steele was still learning and making the transition from Frank Sinatra to Frank Zappa, she introduced a cut by saying, "Here's some new music from a band called Flowers." She didn't realize that *Flowers* was the title of the new Rolling Stones record, because *Flowers* was in large letters on the front jacket and the band was merely pictured on the sleeve. This story haunted her for ten years among serious music lovers, well after she had learned the ropes.

In the progressive era, a jock was often attracted to music that wasn't popular yet. One could get behind an artist and with enough airplay, the public might follow the lead. This advocacy might not be limited to the life of one album. Take Peter Frampton. While performing in the band Humble Pie with Steve Marriott, he released several acclaimed but modestly selling albums. As a solo act, his first two records were good, but didn't really make a dent in the marketplace. Upon releasing *Frampton Comes Alive!*, basically live performances of his previously issued material, he sold over fifteen million copies and was an instant superstar. WNEW-FM played both Humble Pie and Frampton's early solo stuff, knowing that he had talent but not knowing how popular he'd become. But for every Peter Frampton, there are ten Warren Zevons, who, despite a long career of quality work, has never achieved much commercial success.

So when choosing music, the (traditionalist) progressive jocks balanced the artists they liked with quality material they knew was selling. The decisions were harder with popular bands that weren't considered any good. The consensus on Grand Funk Railroad, among music cognoscenti, was that they had very little original talent. They sold a lot of records, though, and a disc jockey had to carefully weigh the perceived lack of quality versus the commercial value.

To Muni, it was no contest. He played the FM hits his audience wanted and if that included Grand Funk, so be it. His oft-repeated quote were the words he lived by: "There are no experts, Fats." But on the other side of the coin, Jonathan Schwartz didn't seem to know or care about what was selling. The music he played was for his own entertainment, as a musical scholar. His famous quote was: "There are only two types of music—good music and bad music. I prefer good music." If the public didn't like it, so what?

The sixties culture bred a brand of disc jockey who didn't care about ratings—they were an anathema. These jocks were interested in self-expression, which often translated into self-indulgence. It's the elitist attitude that "I know better than the marketplace. I know what's good, the great unwashed public doesn't." Most of the jocks with that posture had other means of income and could afford their arrogance. They attracted cult followings who were extremely loyal. But although they opened creative pathways hitherto unheard on commercial radio, in the long run they threatened ruination for the format.

Let's use the analogy of the "auteur" filmmaker, who wants control of every element of his vision. He demands the final say in every aspect of work, even those where he's not an expert. He makes often interesting but commercially failed pictures. This approach only succeeds financially when you have a rare director like James Cameron, who is able to blend artistic vision with commercial sensibilities.

In film, auteurs are eventually forced to scale back their works for lack of financing. So a Woody Allen can make small gems with a tight budget and remain viable. Highly paid actors are willing to work for scale to participate in one of his films because they believe in the quality of his craftsmanship and want to enhance their own artistic credibility. One understands going in that you'll never make a fortune doing a Woody Allen film.

Progressive FM jocks started out making Woody Allen films—low-budget, highly personal masterpieces that stretched the creative envelope. Ratings were never huge, but neither were expenditures. But as disc jockeys began to have financial responsibilities of their own, like families and mortgages, their repulsion toward commercialism was tempered by an understanding that they couldn't build sandcastles without getting their hands dirty. And fortunately for them, America was undergoing a transformation from greedy capitalism to the belief that there were higher values outside financial goals.

Even management drew the line at advertising products they found socially irresponsible. Ads for the armed forces were not even considered, either as a moral stance or because they realized that doing so would alienate the audience and the rest of their sponsors. They had to walk a fine line between risking their credibility by presenting an element that might undermine the image they'd sold to the savvy student community, and limiting their revenues by being "too hip for the room."

There were borderline decisions to be made. In the early seventies, Bob Guccione was infuriated by Alison Steele's refusal to read commercials for *Penthouse* magazine on the air. The college-age men Guccione was courting were listening to Steele, perhaps with his magazine in one hand, but the feminist contingent in the audience saw the magazine as exploitive. Mindful of Guccione's protests, management arranged a meeting with Steele to allow him to plead his case. Although not a bra burner, Steele was offended by much of the content of *Penthouse* and told the publisher flat out. Tempers escalated as he refused to accept her arguments until she brought the dialogue down to his level.

"Look," she said, "I don't care about naked women. I hate *hair.* The only hair on my entire body is on top of my head. Even my eyebrows are shaved, and I'll leave it to your imagination what else. I can't stand those hairy-looking women, spread-eagled in front of the camera. And until you do something about that, I won't read your spots." Guccione retreated, and the day was hers.

The line had to be walked with music as well. Playing too many hits was perceived as being just as dangerous as not playing enough. In 1971 on progressive stations, commercialism and ratings often took a backseat to credibility.

Ratings have been determined in essentially the same manner for decades. Arbitron selects a representative sample of the population and sends them diaries. On these pages, a listener is to mark down what radio station he listens to, and for how long, for which he is paid a token fee. Phone calls are made to follow up to ensure that the diaries are being attended to. At the end of the week (Arbitron weeks go from Thursday to Wednesday), the diaries are mailed in and the results tabulated, weighted against the market's demographic and ethnic makeup. That's why most big radio promotions are done on Thursdays, the day the diaries are sent back in— because if someone has been negligent in their recording duties, they hastily fill them out on the day they're due in. Every three months in major markets, a book comes out, detailing the hourly listening habits of the region. On a monthly basis, "Arbitrends" are released, which are less dependable, mid-course samplings. A common mistake is to overreact to trends and make changes, only to find that statistical errors render the trend's findings unreliable.

Although ratings are king now, in 1972 credibility was more important to most FM programmers. And the demise of WPLJ, with its highly credible but low-rated jocks, was to soon have a major impact on WNEW-FM, and especially on young Michael Harrison.

Dirty Water

THE EARLY WORLD OF progressive radio was a small and incestuous one. Even though they were then owned by another company, WBCN in Boston was always regarded as a sister station to WNEW-FM.

WBCN was the first station to broadcast in stereo as engineers at nearby MIT discovered how to multiplex with the "aural exciter" (broadcast in stereo). T. Mitchell Hastings owned the station in its early days, along with WHCN in Hartford and WNCN (later WQIV and WAXQ) in New York. The three comprised the "Concert Network," and all were respected classical stations until Hastings became seriously ill with a brain aneurysm in 1968. He underwent a partial lobotomy, which required a lengthy rehabilitation. By the time he returned to work, he owned an underground rock station in Boston, which his employees had surreptitiously implemented on WBCN while he had been recuperating. It seems the old man never recovered enough to fully understand what had happened, and the staff had free run of the place. They would explain things to him as if speaking to a child, since despite his corporeal presence around the offices, much of his intellect had been left in the operating theater.

WBCN's most celebrated jock was a fellow named Charles Laquidara. He's done mornings in Boston on and off for almost three decades, and his story has some eerie parallels to those of many other early progressive jocks. Charles wanted to be an actor and did radio part-time, playing classical music at Pasadena, California's KPPC. Like WLIR, the suburban station was located in a basement, this time the cellar of the Pasadena Presbyterian Church. His approach was revolutionary in that he viewed the classics as "the people's music" and not just serious work for intellectual snobs. He distilled the essence of what he did to this: explaining opera to plumbers. He'd take an aria and break it down—translating the story, noting the technical prowess of the performances, and using his keen sense of humor to make it accessible for the hoi polloi. He continued to pursue an acting career after graduating from the Pasadena Playhouse.

Like Tom Donahue, he hated what Top Forty radio had become. The high-energy disc jockeys who seemed oblivious to the changes the country was going through in the mid-sixties, the inane promotions, the senseless jingles—it all offended him. He and his friends used to smoke grass on the hilltops of Encino and talk about what radio should be: the best of all genres of music, put together intelligently.

His dream came to fruition when Donahue consulted KPPC and transformed it into KMPX South. But like its San Francisco counterpart, KPPC's ownership couldn't make it work financially with Donahue over the long term, and they also were struck by the jocks. Metromedia had a station in Los Angeles, KMET, and before long George Duncan had repeated the magic trick that had worked in New York and San Francisco. KMET became a progressive station and hired Raechel Donahue. In 1968, KPPC started over again with a new staff, which included Laquidara doing overnights.

True to his vision, he mixed Orff's *Carmina Burana* with the Grateful Dead in his sets. Originally, he knew nothing about rock but learned to love it. Within months, aided by his ambition and promotional skills, his legend grew in L.A. Fresh from his West Coast triumph, he returned home to New England for the holidays to visit with family. It was there that he first heard WBCN in Boston, and was so impressed that he called the station and introduced himself, hoping that his reputation had traveled east.

"Oh yeah," they answered. "You're the crazy bastard who mixes classical with rock and roll. Come on in."

As with everything, timing is crucial and Charles happened upon WBCN just as their afternoon jock was preparing to leave for a career with a rock band. Management liked his rap, so in 1969, Charles Laquidara replaced Peter Wolf, who would achieve his own measure of fame and fortune with the J. Geils Band. He was also one of the first rock stars to marry a famous actress when he wed Faye Dunaway.

Besides having a lighthearted approach to radio, Laquidara was extremely active politically, another trait more intrinsic to West Coast commercial radio. He refused to participate in anything remotely related to the war effort. In fact, he and WBCN were once sued for his remarks after reading a camera shop commercial. President Nixon decided to invade Cambodia in an attempt to clear out Vietcong sanctuaries and bring the North Vietnamese to the peace table. But most leftists felt that the incursion only prolonged the war and extended the killing fields to an innocent neutral country, and Laquidara wasn't shy about saying so on the air. A local sponsor called Underground Camera asked that he read a live ad for Honeywell's newest 35mm offering. He refused (Honeywell was a major arms manufacturer), but management prevailed upon him to read the spot anyway. He did so professionally, extolling the virtues of the new Honeywell Pentax camera exactly as the copy stated. But at the end, he added his own fillip: "That's right, run right out and support Honeywell, the company responsible for killing all those Cambodian babies."

Laquidara wasn't aware that the chief executives of Honeywell were in Boston, listening intently to hear the great WBCN host praise their new camera. WBCN was not pleased with the $200,000 legal action that followed, but publicly supported Charles and eventually won the lawsuit. On another occasion, after several major universities had gone on strike protesting the war, he lamented the fact that no school in Boston had followed suit. So he read a fabricated news story stating that the students at every school in the country had decided to boycott classes, with the exception of Boston University. The BU students, who were meeting at the time to decide upon a course of action, were thus moved to strike, lest they be out of sync with their peers.

After three years in various time slots, Laquidara accepted the morning show on a dare. WBCN's female morning host was venting to him in the studio one day, complaining about the treatment that women received in radio, always getting the worst shifts. She ranted on obscenely about her lousy hours until Charles opined that mornings weren't so bad.

"Oh yeah?" she challenged him. "Why don't you try it, then?"

"As a matter of fact, I will," he replied.

In trying to find a memorable handle for the morning show, he envisioned all of New England waking up on a big mattress. So, in 1972, *The Big Mattress* was born. His attitude was typically irreverent: He did a parody of an AM morning show, using all the bells and whistles normally associated with Top Forty, but with a twist. He had a game show called "Mishegas," a Yiddish expression for craziness. Karlos, his version of HAL, the computer in *2001: A Space Odyssey*, occasionally took over his show without warning. He brought in Tank, a sports guy who reminded everyone of a character who hangs out at a local bar and has an opinion about everything. He did spoofs of commercials using the fictitious company Dutchko ("If it's Dutchko, it's so-so"). He invented words like "schloony," which meant foggy or demented. It was almost as if the Firesign Theatre had come to morning radio. For the first time, FM morning ratings achieved double digits, and Laquidara became a wake-up fixture in Boston until 1976, when he decided that the show got in the way of his cocaine use. He "retired" with much fanfare and spent the next two years in self-imposed radio exile.

During this time, he was wooed by WNEW-FM. He interviewed with Scott Muni, who was impressed with the fact that someone had finally broken through the FM morning barrier. But Laquidara valued his freedom and needed to be assured that Metromedia wouldn't attempt to control his content. As a litmus test, he asked Muni if WNEW was playing Lou Reed's "Walk on the Wild Side." Muni, still executing Duncan's conservative edict when it came to possibly obscene lyric content, told him that the line "even when she was given head" disqualified it from consideration. Charles decided then and there that WNEW-FM wouldn't be a cool place to work and removed his hat from the ring. He preferred unemployment.

The End of the Innocence

WITH THE DEMISE OF WPLJ as a free-form station in late 1971, Dave Herman and Vin Scelsa were out of work. With nothing in their pocket but the support of a small but loyal following, they pondered their next move.

Scelsa had his wife's income to fall back on. He also knew that he had writing talent but had never really harnessed it to make money. There was a vague chance that some radio station would come calling, but Vin had been burned twice already, at WFMU and at WPLJ, and wasn't eager to get fooled again. He'd wait it out until the right opportunity beckoned.

Dave was not so fortunate. He'd accumulated enough to live on for a few months, but he had a wife and children who were dependent on him. He weighed going back to Philadelphia, but his prospects were suddenly enlivened by a call from Scott Muni. Would Herman be interested in having lunch with him and Paulsen? Why not? Scottso had approached

Herman once before, years earlier. But at that time Dave was making double what Muni could pay him because his taped show also ran on the ABC-FM network.

At lunch, both sides expressed their reservations. Dave had worked for Metromedia at WMMR, and Muni wanted him back in the fold. His concern was whether Herman could lighten up on the politics. For his part, since Dave had always viewed WNEW as competition, he wondered if he'd be welcomed onto the staff or viewed as an interloper. Knowing the discord already present at the station, Muni had little worry on that account. Some would like him, some wouldn't—just like any new recruit. Schwartz would feel threatened, as he always did. After all, Dave had been on opposite him at night, and when Jonno had tuned in to PLJ one Monday evening while his own show was on tape, he'd heard Herman say, "It's a stormy Monday in New York, and it's good for nothing but the blues." He then launched into the Allman Brothers' lengthy rendition of "Stormy Monday," and Schwartz thought, this guy's good. It was just the way he said blues. He sounded like he believed it.

Leave it to Jonno to pick up on an inconsequential opening that Herman didn't even remember the next day. But there was something to what he observed. Dave sounded in tune with his music and, in his short time at WPLJ, had met and become friendly with a number of musicians. PLJ had started a live concert series at a nearby recording studio and the station's hip reputation attracted a number of top artists. The most famous of these concerts became an album whose title merely noted the date of the performance: *11-17-70*. Muni was particularly incensed that PLJ had scored this broadcast because it involved a musician whom Scott had personally thrown his support behind—Elton John. But Dave's politics remained the main sticking point.

Herman convinced his two suitors that his days of heavy politicking were over. He still would support the antiwar effort, but it would be in subtler fashion than WPLJ, where they would air a Nixon speech and follow it with "Liar, Liar" by the Castaways, or punctuate the address with rude noises like toilets flushing. Economic reality trumped idealism— Herman realized that if he was to remain in New York, WNEW was his only real choice. He might catch on as a staff announcer at some boring easy-listening outlet, but his three years in progressive radio had made that an unsavory alternative.

Schwartz was scheduled to vacation in Palm Springs for his annual two-week stay that fall, so Paulsen dreamed up an ad campaign to introduce Herman as his substitute. Using his trade space to take out a full-page ad in *The Village Voice* and various college newspapers, he composed a terse note, supposedly in Schwartz's hand, asking:

Dave Herman, where are you? I'm going on vacation and I'd like you to fill in.

—Jonathan Schwartz

It took a lot of reassurances from Duncan, Muni, and Paulsen to convince the insecure Jonno that he wasn't being set up to be replaced permanently. Herman passed the test with flying colors, breezing through the two-week stint to glowing reviews. Under the more professional atmosphere at WNEW, his strengths—a mellow delivery and vast musical knowledge—shone through. He filled in for Alison when she vacationed and did some weekend work in the ensuing months.

This presented management with a problem. They wanted Dave on the air full-time in the worst way. But where would they put him? Nights seemed the logical place, but head to head, Schwartz had scored higher ratings than Dave had while at WPLJ. Alison was settling into a nice groove at 10 P.M. and Herman would be wasted in the overnights. Muni wasn't about to budge from afternoons, and Fornatale was now a three-year veteran with credibility of his own in middays. Did mornings make sense?

Although Harrison had been doing the show only a year, his numbers increased in every book. He'd helped Muni set up a series of free concerts in the city's parks the previous summer. Michael had become friendly with important record promoters and gotten to be pals with Lou Reed and David Clayton-Thomas of Blood, Sweat and Tears. He had visited countless area colleges, and had been praised in local newspapers and magazines. He'd done a good job and his reputation was spreading.

His show reflected what we did at WLIR. He had a theme song: "Pick Up in the Morning," by the New York Rock and Roll Ensemble. He essentially did an FM version of what John Gambling was doing on WOR-AM. He played a lot of three-minute FM hits, did frequent time and temperature, and was a friendly, upbeat presence. Sounds like a perfect morning host, no?

But some didn't consider him "heavy" enough for the morning. His breezy attitude was intentional, because he felt that most people didn't need to be pounded over the head with major issues upon waking. They merely wanted to know the time, weather, and key stories of the day, mixed in with their favorite familiar tunes. Michael repeated songs more often than most using this philosophy, and it was getting results with his growing numbers. But free-form purists at the station thought this was too formulaic, and wondered if Harrison had the breadth of music knowledge to range wider.

He was also low man in terms of seniority (other than myself), and was deemed the most expendable after a year's experience. So one Friday morning after his show, he was called into Paulsen's office and informed that he was being replaced by Dave Herman, effective May 22, 1972. Paulsen praised his efforts and emphasized that this was not to be taken as a negative reflection on his work, but that Herman represented an upgrade, having been in prime time in New York for two years. Paulsen offered Michael a strong letter of recommendation for future employment within or outside the company.

Harrison was crushed. He'd just gotten married, and thought that his two-year contract provided him with a measure of security. However, like most radio contracts, his money was not guaranteed, so after a small severance was paid out, his income from the station abruptly halted. He had done everything asked of him and boosted morning ratings higher than they'd ever been, and now he was being replaced by someone who had worked at a failed competitor.

It was a huge blow to a twenty-three-year-old who had achieved his dream, thrived on it, and then had it taken away capriciously. When he told me about it, he tried to put a brave face on things, but I could tell he was deeply hurt by the experience. I also knew that with his intellect and ambition he'd land on his feet and achieve even greater success somewhere. But it all seemed unfair. What did he want me to do? Should I quit in sympathy?

He told me that Muni and Paulsen were afraid of that happening but were prepared to deal with it. He didn't see that my resignation would serve any purpose other than to put both of us out of work. And having a friend on the inside couldn't hurt if things were to change, as they often did. So when I was called in to the inevitable meeting, I bit my lip and told them that I could continue on with a positive attitude and that I understood their position.

Vin Scelsa was hired a few months later to do weekends and fill-ins.

On his Sunday morning show, he created a series of humorous essays entitled "Me and Razoo Kelly," which found their way into book form years later. The premise was that Vin would find these letters awaiting him upon his arrival at the station, so he'd read them on the air. They were also a clever way for the always rebellious Scelsa to cast his cynical eye on the rock scene and say things that he couldn't in his role as disc jockey.

One of the most curious stories about his weekend gig was how he got the world premiere of Springsteen's *Darkness on the Edge of Town* album. A listener had purchased the new Barbra Streisand album and in its sleeve found *Darkness,* the result of an obvious mistake at the pressing plant. He called Scelsa on the air, who offered him an entire box of rock albums if he would meet and slip him the Boss's latest offering. The listener complied, and WNEW-FM had a week's jump on the competition, as Columbia scrambled to rush-release it. Nobody believed Scelsa's story then, thinking that his Jersey connections somehow fed him an early release of the album, but he swears the story is true to this day.

Vin hadn't changed his act much from the WFMU days. He still had eclectic tastes, and would play anything and everything, except music that he considered "corporate" rock. He hated bands like Foreigner, Journey, and Kansas, and shied away from prefab supergroups like Asia.

He formed an alter ego named "Bayonne Butch" and while in character, he refused to acknowledge anyone who called him Vin. In some ways, the Butch character was more reflective of his real thoughts and attitudes, and might have been created to protect the real Scelsa from retribution when the corporate villains disapproved of his rap. He was self-conscious about appearing onstage at times and, to cover up that fear, invented "The Bayonne Bear," a boisterous figure in a bear costume who would dance to rock music at concerts while emceeing shows.

At the time, we were all charmed and amused by Vin's planned schizophrenia, but later it would prove problematic to the station and his own career.

I Am the Walrus

WITH THE CHANGES happening fast and furious at WNEW-FM, Dennis Elsas became music director in early 1972, after less than a year of part-time air work. Dennis was only a couple of years older than I and a devoted Beatles fan. A graduate of Queens College, he'd had a lifelong ambition to be a disc jockey in New York. He especially admired WNEW-FM, which afforded him the chance to work with men like Scott Muni and Bob Lewis, his heroes from an earlier era when they were stars on WABC. Lewis, whose real last name was Schwartzmann, had grown up in Dennis's neighborhood in Queens and his mom still lived in the same house. Lewis used to talk on the air about his Corvette, and so every time Dennis walked down the mother's block, he checked her driveway to see if the car was there, hoping that Bobaloo would be visiting.

One night, when he was sixteen, he and a friend noticed the Corvette parked in front. His buddy insisted they ring the doorbell, and Dennis reluctantly tagged along. When Mrs. Schwartzmann came to the door, they explained that they were huge fans and would love to meet Bob. She invited them in for lemonade on the sweltering July night, and they sat at the kitchen table grilling Lewis about WABC. He patiently answered all their questions, although he was probably peeved at his mother for allowing these two strangers into her home. Years later, when Dennis followed Lewis on the air at WNEW, the older jock winced when told of the incident that had made such a thrilling impression on the younger man. Nobody likes to be told that someone grew up listening to them.

Elsas had almost done his career a worse disservice in his initial job interview with Muni. In an effort to ingratiate himself, he told Scottso that his mother was a big fan, almost more so than he himself was. Muni was prepared to let the innocent flattery pass for just that, but Elsas repeated it several times during the conversation. Finally, Muni had had enough.

"I didn't want to bring this up, Dennis, but how old is your mother?"

Elsas answered and Muni continued, "And how old do you think I am?"

Dennis replied with an age very near that of his mom. "Well," Muni rejoined, "I hate to tell you this, but I knew your mother . . . very well."

Dennis blanched when he considered the possibility that his mother and Muni not only were acquainted, but implied in Muni's tone were issues he wanted no part of. Scott enjoyed the retribution he had exacted, and Elsas never discussed his mother's fandom again.

Elsas revered the Beatles as a result of Muni, Lewis, Morrow, and all the jocks on W-A-Beatle-C and could cite chapter and verse every phase of their career. Interviewing one of the Beatles became Elsas's Holy Grail, and from his position at the radio station, he was uniquely situated to attain his goal. Record labels respected Elsas and the power he had over their fare. Much like food companies vie for shelf position in supermarkets today, promo men would bend his ear to gain a coveted spot in the rack. And if Elsas deigned to scrawl a positive comment or two on the album jacket, like "really rocks" or "sold out MSG in two hours," well then, heavy airplay was almost assured. The rest of the staff generally accepted the sincerity of Dennis's selections, and trusted that he was not susceptible to bribery or hype, heavy promotion on a record that failed where it counted the most, "in the grooves."

That didn't mean the man was immune to persuasion. Promo men dealt with Elsas as they would a prince, and Dennis didn't balk at the royal treatment. In fact, few disc jockeys resisted much. To get them to see an artist perform in a dingy club late at night, hypesters felt it their responsibility to treat the jocks to a sumptuous dinner at the Palm, Chandler's, or the Assembly Steak House. Many lobsters and Angus steers sacrificed their lives for radio exposure.

It was all legal, of course, at least at WNEW. Metromedia spelled out strict guidelines as to what could and could not be accepted. Christmas gifts were limited in value, and an evening's entertainment could not exceed a certain level or it was considered payola. WNEW-FM stayed remarkably clean of that during the seventies. In an industry rife with stories of drugs and hookers, Muni and Elsas were incorruptible when it came to accepting improper favors. But the one favor Elsas wanted more than the lavish dinners or limousine rides to concerts was an interview with a Beatle, and John Lennon lived and worked in New York.

But the record companies weren't able to help him in his quest to interview Lennon, so he worked it on his own. A friend of his was producing a rookie band at the Record Plant, a legendary recording studio where many great sides were cut. Knowing of Elsas's desire to meet Lennon, his friend tipped him off that the great man himself was remixing what later was to become the album *Walls and Bridges* in an adjacent room. He invited the young music director to sit in on a session with his band, knowing that Lennon would often peek in while on a break.

On a Tuesday night in late September, Elsas snuck in and sure enough, big as life, there was John Lennon, working diligently on his latest release. Silently, Elsas watched his hero through the glass like a boy watching model trains in a store window before Christmas. After what seemed like hours, Lennon stopped in for a brief, stumbling introduction before quickly retreating back to his mixing console. After the flurry, Elsas noticed a pretty Asian woman in the hallway, also reverently watching the ex-Beatle at work. She introduced herself as May Pang, whom he knew was Lennon's assistant and rumored mistress. Of course she'd heard of WNEW-FM and knew of his work, but what stunned the normally unflappable Elsas was her offhand assertion that John was aware of him as well. Emboldened by the rush of adrenaline at the idea that his hero actually knew of his existence, Dennis ventured the unthinkable. He asked

May if John wanted to see the station sometime, or maybe wanted to hang out with him on the air. She gave a perfunctory nod, took his name and number, and said she'd run it by John.

Dennis floated out of the Record Plant on that cool but glorious night, dizzy with the dream that John Lennon might even *consider* appearing on his radio show. As he sat in his office the following day, the gleam had still not worn off. He told everyone he talked to about meeting his idol, but held off explaining about the interview invitation. As the hours wore on, he realized that May Pang was probably just being nice and that Lennon, who'd rarely if ever sat down for radio interviews, would undoubtedly not give it a second thought, if indeed May had even brought it up.

Two days later, still buoyed by the experience but realistic about his chances, he was screening albums in the music library when his extension rang.

"Dennis Elsas?" asked a small, accented voice on the other end.

"Yes."

"This is May Pang. I spoke to John and he told me he would love to be with you on the radio. When would be a good time?"

Elsas waited a beat. This couldn't be a practical joke, although this was just the sort of thing Muni or Schwartz would do. But neither Jonathan nor anyone else could have gotten wind of his invitation. He hadn't even told Pete Fornatale, his closest friend on the staff, about the possibility of an interview. It had to be the real May Pang.

"Well, May, I'm on Saturday from two to six and Sunday from noon to four this weekend. Do either of those times work for you?" His voice trembled a bit and was slightly higher than normal.

She said that she'd check with John and call him right back. The room spun on him for several minutes but she was as good as her word, returning the call to specify Saturday at four and could John bring in a few R&B tracks he'd like to play on the air? Elsas stammered that it would be perfectly fine. She asked if there was anything else she could bring. He thought for a second of saying a cheesecake would be nice but wasn't sure she'd appreciate the attempt at humor. He'd settle for the biggest rock artist in the world. She asked the address and how they could get into the building and Dennis gave her instructions before ringing off.

He still couldn't tell anyone. What a laughingstock he'd be if Lennon developed a headache or was in a cross mood or something else struck his fancy that afternoon and he didn't show. So, fairly bursting at the seams

with his secret, Elsas tried to patiently wait two more days, hoping a me-
teor wouldn't strike the Earth before then and spoil his dream. Even coming on the air at two on Saturday, he would only hint that he had a big
surprise awaiting his listeners later in the show as he counted the excruci-
ating 120 minutes until 4 P.M. arrived.

Sure enough, at four o'clock, there was Lennon. He was every bit as
charming and irreverent as he'd been with the Beatles. For some reason, I
had lingered in the music library at the station for a couple of hours after
my show, suspecting something was up. When I came back into the studio
at 4:15, there was John. He was gracious upon being introduced, and left
me with the feeling that he knew who I was. Whether he actually did or
whether he'd perfected the act to ingratiate himself with the media, it did
have the desired effect.

Lennon demonstrated during the interview how he still could relate to
the feelings of everyday people. When Elsas said, "You can't possibly
understand how exciting this is for me," Lennon replied, "Yes, I can. It's
like when I met Chuck Berry on the *Mike Douglas Show.*"

He revealed for the first time that at the end of "I Am the Walrus," ex-
cerpts from a BBC production of *King Lear* were used, simply because it
was playing on a radio in a room next to the studio. He talked about the
original cover of *Yesterday and Today,* which was pasted over because it de-
picted bloody scenes of the group in a butcher shop. They peeled back the
covers on the LP at the station to determine if it had been done to their
copy. Lennon remarked on how they all look put out on the new cover, because they were annoyed at having to reshoot it for American sensibilities.

Since John was present to promote *Walls and Bridges,* Elsas asked the
obligatory questions about the latest solo work, all while itching to ask *the*
question, "Will the Beatles ever reunite?" To this John hedged, not denying the possibility but not encouraging it either. He read live commercials,
did weather reports, and seemed to thoroughly enjoy the two hours.

Just over a year later, Dennis accomplished phase two of his dream
when he was granted a brief audience with Paul McCartney backstage at
Madison Square Garden, prior to a concert on the *Band on the Run* tour in
1976.

By this time, Dennis was getting used to brushes with celebrities. Before he even did his first show at the station, he was introduced to John
Denver. Denver invited him to his show at the Bitter End. He then accompanied other WNEW jocks in a limo to Shea Stadium, where they

hosted a Grand Funk Railroad concert in front of fifty-five thousand fans. Although he didn't go onstage that night, he did make his on-air debut after the concert. For Harrison and me, it was even wilder. Having arrived at WNEW less than two months before, we were shocked when Muni sent us out on our own to introduce Grand Funk.

By the time he met McCartney in 1976, Elsas had already met and talked to Lennon, Pete Townshend, Elton John, and a host of others. He was still a little nervous about finally meeting the "cute" Beatle. What if McCartney was arrogant or curt and brushed off his questions as inconsequential?

His fears were baseless. Paul was a gracious guest, and the only time during the interview he grew impatient was when he cut off Elsas as he asked about a Beatles reunion. He recited a piece of doggerel he'd composed for the hundreds of times he'd been asked the same question. In his best Muhammad Ali impression, he neither refuted the possibility nor encouraged it.

Young Dennis Elsas felt like a made man.

Hotel California

WNEW-FM's CHANGE to Dave Herman in the morning didn't do much for ratings, and whether it affected the station's credibility a great deal is intangible. But interestingly, the castoff Michael Harrison took less than twenty-four hours to land on his feet after his sudden and devastating dismissal.

Within that time he was on the air in New York again, doing Top Forty radio, largely due to a man named Neil MacIntyre. Neil was the program director of WPIX-FM, a low-rated station owned by the New York *Daily News*. They had tried an easy-listening format called the "PIX Penthouse" for years, affecting the same sort of pseudosophisticated approach that WLIR had failed with. Their only claim to any market identity came during the holiday season, when they played nothing but uninterrupted Christmas carols for twenty-four hours, in a simulcast with WPIX-TV, which showed only a blazing Yule log on the screen. Now, Top Forty wasn't going well at PIX either, as WOR-FM and WABC dominated the ratings.

But Neil was a veteran radio man with a solid staff, and he tried anything and everything to get his station on the map. So when he heard of Harrison's fate, he immediately called the twenty-three-year-old and asked him to fill in that night on the overnight shift.

Despite his economic situation, Harrison had to think twice. As a Top Forty fan growing up, he had learned through bitter experience that he wasn't any good at it. Until progressive radio came along, the hyper-energized approach was the only way to play the rock music he loved on the radio. He'd tried to get a job at WGBB in Freeport, Long Island, a tiny hit-oriented AM station, and was rejected. His voice just sounded forced and unnatural when he tried to rev it up, and he expressed his misgivings to MacIntyre.

"Come on, try it. Just give me a little more than you did on NEW in the mornings and that'll be enough."

What the hell? Why not? So Michael trooped into the station a couple of hours before the overnight shift was supposed to begin, and was shown the ropes by Al Gee, a DJ with a speedball approach. Harrison was in awe of Gee, and how the man could be so relentlessly up-tempo on the air for four hours. He was the most nervous he'd ever been in radio as his hour to debut on WPIX drew near. Doing his first show in New York at WNEW, he'd had some initial jitters but ultimately he was confident in what he was doing and settled in quickly. The irony struck him that a couple of years earlier he wasn't good enough to work at a small Long Island Top Forty, and now he was doing it in the biggest market of all.

By his own estimation, he was terrible. He found a better groove as the night went on, but to his ears he sounded like a fish out of water. But others disagreed with his assessment, most notably Neil MacIntyre, who called him as he was getting off the air at six.

"You were great. I knew you could do it. I've got a lot of work for you, doing weekends and fill-ins. I can promise to keep you busy."

Even though the money wasn't much, it paid the rent and would give him free time during the week to explore other endeavors. Plus Neil was a great guy to work for, and all the jocks he'd met at PIX were supportive and friendly, possibly because they didn't consider him a threat. So Harrison went to sleep that morning, still shaken by the events at WNEW, but heart-ened by the fact that he wouldn't exactly be destitute.

He was awakened in the early afternoon by a phone call from the pro-gram director of another struggling New York station, WCBS-FM. "Why are you working at PIX? What about your credibility? Come work for us."

Was he still dreaming? Another job offer? He sleepily agreed to come in for a meeting Monday morning and marveled further at the turn of events. Eighteen months earlier, he and I had pitched CBS for a job and were politely sent away. Now they were calling him on a weekend. WCBS-FM was a Top Forty station with progressive aspirations that favored a more up-tempo approach than WNEW, but required nowhere near the frenetic pace of WPIX. Michael would be a better fit there, not only with his presentation but with their wider range of music.

But he felt guilty about Neil MacIntyre, who had rescued him off the scrap heap in his darkest hour. (In a typical radio horror story, Neil MacIntyre was fired from WPIX a few years later. He was on vacation in the Caribbean and was notified by telegram at the hotel in which he was staying.) When he expressed his reservations about PIX to the managers at CBS, they encouraged him to work at both stations, which he gratefully did. With two stations now in the mix, he was averaging four shows a week and making a decent living, although not up to the salary level he had achieved at WNEW.

But even that station wasn't completely in his rearview mirror. Scott Muni called him a few months later and said, "Hey Fats, you're sharing the talent with all these other stations, why not help us out?"

With that, he added another fill-in job to his burgeoning résumé, which included teaching a class in radio programming at NYU and a record he produced on a small independent label. He sometimes wound up doing a program on all three stations in one day, leaving one gig a few minutes early to shoot across town and slide into another chair just under the bell. But even though he was busy in spurts, he was leading a shadowy existence. Most of his shifts were after hours—weekends or at night. And he never actually felt part of the stations where he worked—he was a hired gun, brought in to clean up when the regulars were away. But by living one year in that disquieting uncertainty, he was able to complement his radio education. Since he'd never actually worked in Top Forty, he was learning its rules for the first time. He discovered when to schedule commercial breaks to maximize ratings, something that progressive stations never thought of. He understood the importance of playing the most popular songs at the most critical times. He got his virtual master's degree in all the time-honored tenets of successful broadcasting that the progressives had cast aside in their quest for total freedom.

As he worked within the tighter formats, he began to formulate a plan. Refining what we had done at WLIR by applying a few Top Forty rules, he came up with a format that would sound free form, but could get the type of ratings that the progressives could only dream of. His idea would also retain credibility with listeners and sponsors, who didn't understand the mechanics of radio anyway. By combining the best of both worlds, he felt he could assemble a station that would not only be successful commercially, but would have respect and authenticity in the community.

So he spread the word throughout his contacts in the music business that he was available with a great new concept that could overturn conventional thinking and bring great rewards to some forward-thinking station. Almost immediately, he was contacted by KPRI in San Diego, which needed a program director and morning man. Harrison fit the bill perfectly.

There were a few problems. Money headed the list. KPRI was willing to pay $200 a week for the dual role. Had he stayed at WLIR, he'd probably be making that or better now. But unlike Long Island, he was able to find a luxurious apartment in San Diego for $135 a month, and the station's owner was willing to offer him ratings bonuses in writing, which the confident Harrison knew he could attain. But Harrison's family was on the East Coast, and moving thirty-five hundred miles away was still a frightening step.

The second problem was a thornier one. Ron Jacobs, the prodigious BOSS radio programmer who had run KHJ in Los Angeles for Bill Drake, was in San Diego at the monster KGB AM-FM combination, and was piling up big numbers. The big, bearded Jacobs had taken a sabbatical in Hawaii to recharge his batteries before returning to Southern California. But more distressing to Harrison was the fact that through a different path, Jacobs had come to the same conclusions he had about progressive radio. He had given KGB Top Forty structure, and it sounded very much like Harrison's concept. He also had a staff of top-notch jocks featuring Brad Messer, Bob Coburn, and Gabriel Wisdom, all men who later went on to even bigger things. And Jacobs had a big ally in the publishing business to expand his legend.

Claude Hall was the radio editor at *Billboard* magazine, the bible of the music industry. Hall wrote a weekly column called *Vox Jox,* and it was required reading for everyone in radio. In it, he detailed the comings and goings, hirings and firings, ratings highs and lows—all the gossip and minutiae that we lived by. He had connections in every major market, and a positive write-up from Hall could mean big-time career advancement. Hall loved Ron Jacobs and, like a latter-day Walter Winchell, built Jacobs into such a legend that Harrison felt he was up against Goliath, without the benefit of David's slingshot. Hall's relentless advocacy of his favorites created a larger-than-life aura about them, which in turn could intimidate potential rivals. But despite the odds, Harrison and his wife, Sharon, packed up all their belongings, hopped into their car, and headed west.

Wars are won in the trenches, not in the press, and Harrison soon found vulnerabilities at KGB. Despite what some of the purists at WNEW-FM felt, Michael was very knowledgeable when it came to rock music, and was better than Jacobs at instinctively knowing what his audience wanted. He crafted a mammoth record library, and used a Top Forty–inspired color chart to direct the jocks. He kept their presentation low-key and loose, and gave them great latitude on music selections, stressing segues and meaningful sets, but not at the expense of quality. He always believed that if the jocks were fully engaged in programming their shows, they would sound in sync with what they played, as opposed to being handed a list of songs to play sequentially. The jocks needed to be an impassioned force in programming their own shows. Michael believed in this and called it the X factor: that if a jock is totally into what he was playing, the commitment will come across and sell to the audience as well. It was akin to Dave Herman's natural gift of sounding at one with the music. It might sound like some worn-out hippie concept now, but the proof is in the pudding: Listener loyalty is much weaker with the disengaged jocks of today.

So even though there were restrictions, the DJs had enough choice to give their shows individuality, but there was enough in common to make the station sound like a unified force. This concept of unity has come to be known as "stationality." It's something that the great progressive stations came by naturally. Since the jocks at a Donahue or Muni station were so involved in what they did, they listened frequently to their colleagues and unconsciously picked up cues and catchphrases from them. They actually mimicked one another in subtle ways that caused the listeners to recognize what station they were tuned to without prompting.

But as progressive radio grew and the jocks became more involved in divergent outside interests, they drifted apart and many stations wound up with no stationality, sounding only like whomever was on the air at the time. So Harrison reinforced his message with certain phrases that the jocks were to work into their raps whenever they felt it appropriate. These in reality were rudimentary slogans, which aided recall when ratings were taken. They were never formalized into liner cards, which are standardized lines to be read at prescribed intervals.

Slogans have been a part of radio almost since its inception. WNEW-FM started as "the New Groove," and when that became embarrassingly outdated, it was ditched for "Where Rock Lives." ABC-FM had their "love" format replaced by "Rock in Stereo." CBS-FM had the "Young Sound." The key is to carve out an identity that doesn't sound corny or forced. Very often these phrases will bubble up naturally from the staff, and those are really the best kind.

Problems arise when these catchphrases are too omnipresent. If you mandate a DJ to parrot a phrase frequently, in evenly timed intervals, it becomes stale and predictable. That's the Top Forty approach and most educated radio consumers resent this manipulation. Harrison and I, dating back to WLIR, had guidelines instead of rigid formatics and hired intelligent people to seamlessly integrate the structure and style into something of substance. Too often the substance gets lost in trying to create a style, or the structure shows through and sounds artificial.

Harrison knew that the substance would always be the music and constantly turned it over to keep it fresh. But he didn't see his formula as the show itself, but only a means to eliminate negatives and harness the human element. He used sales research to buttress his own instincts, but basically flew by what he believed. The music spectrum was broad: rock, R&B, jazz-rock fusion, country rock, and folk rock.

He also learned at WNEW-FM that free concerts were a great way to promote the station while reinforcing a sense of community. Like Cousin Brucie at WABC a decade earlier, he got the jocks out among the people. Store openings, trade shows, concert emceeing, sporting events, television appearances ... anything to promote KPRI. With San Diego boasting probably the best weather in the country, he could do free outdoor shows for the audience on a year-round basis. The acts were bands like the Outlaws, Jimmy Buffett, Jim Croce, the Average White Band, Dr. Hook, Al Kooper, Bloodrock, Mandrill—all willing to perform without pay to build their careers. Some never achieved mainstream success, but who in the audience could complain? It was all for free.

Harrison was pecking away at the competition with hundreds of little promotions, but he wanted to go for a big score. KGB had a very successful promotional tool in the KGB Chicken, which later became simply the San Diego Chicken. This was tough to combat, so Harrison hatched a bold plan: He'd reunite the Beatles.

First, he needed a local venue and the only one big enough for such an endeavor was Jack Murphy Stadium, where the Padres and Chargers played. But the conservative city council didn't want their ballpark torn up by a bunch of raucous hippies, so they banned rock concerts from the stadium. The only performances that could take place there had to be in conjunction with a sporting event—halftime at a football game, between games of a doubleheader, or after a day game. Harrison approached the Padres, whom he knew from personal experience were having attendance problems. He'd attended many games when only three hundred people surrounded him as the Padres played his hometown New York Mets.

So the Padres were especially receptive when Harrison proposed that he put together a Beatles reunion after a Sunday game. True to the model at WNEW, he designated a portion of the receipts for charity. For their three-dollar ticket, fans would get a ballgame and a concert, and KPRI would promote the event heavily—without mentioning the Beatles—in the weeks leading up to it. As with many concerts, there was an implied rumor that more could happen at the show than could be legally stated.

Harrison contacted May Pang in New York and told her that Yoko Ono's Plastic Ono Band was huge in San Diego and that he could almost guarantee a packed house of fifty thousand if she'd come out for this giant festival. Michael also knew that George and Ringo were working on a record in Los Angeles. He called his friends from Jefferson Starship and asked if they'd perform, hoping to make the show so cool that the other Beatles would have to migrate down the coast to catch the action. At which time, Michael would use his considerable powers of persuasion to convince them to join John and Yoko onstage.

Unfortunately, there were flaws in his scheme. Firstly, John and Yoko had split, unbeknownst to Michael. They were in the trial-separation stage and John was spending his nights in Los Angeles in a continuous drunken orgy with Harry Nilsson. The woman in his life at the moment was May Pang. Lennon's attitude was that if Yoko wanted to embarrass herself in front of a huge audience, let her. George and Ringo weren't about to see Yoko perform solo, and she was still being vilified as the woman who had broken up the Beatles. The Starship were too busy as well, so they sent their septuagenarian protégé, Papa John Creach, to perform his violin blues.

So instead of his fantasized Beatles reunion, Michael got an earnest but challenging set from Ono, a competent performance from Papa John and the incredible Jimmy Smith, funking out on the Hammond organ. Ten thousand people showed, which was huge for a Padres game but far from the sellout Harrison had hoped for. But it got the station a ton of publicity—some negative, but publicity nonetheless.

Harrison was also dabbling in other fields. While attending a party at a record promoter's home in Los Angeles, he ran into a man named Bob Wilson. Wilson had been programming KDAY—a dying progressive AM station, but was getting out to start his own business. He wanted to challenge Claude Hall's supremacy by forming a trade newspaper that would cater exclusively to radio, and not primarily service the record business as the big three (*Billboard, Cash Box,* and *Record World*) did. He'd heard of Harrison and had read a few guest columns he'd written for different industry publications and proposed that Michael be the editor of the rock section for his new venture, to be called *Radio and Records,* or *R&R.* Harrison, never one to turn down an opportunity, agreed to give it a try.

He recruited his wife, Sharon, to make calls to radio stations for reports and they ran the operation out of their living room. It was then that he formalized the guidelines of what he was doing at KPRI into a cogent philosophy with an appropriate handle: AOR, or album-oriented rock.

He eschewed the terms "progressive" and "free form" because they were exclusionary. He believed that the terms had come to symbolize only things you *can't* do: You can't have slogans or jingles, you can't do promotions, you can't direct the jocks. As early as the WLIR days, he was uncomfortable with what progressive radio was becoming.

In the next two years, he wrote a series of articles explaining his philosophies and attracted owners and programmers across the country who wanted to have freedom *and* make money. They believed, as Harrison did, that the two need not be mutually exclusive. Of course, one couldn't produce masterpieces using the paint-by-numbers approach. Programmers had to adapt Harrison's ideas to their own situation and some did it better than others. But in the end, Michael became the unofficial consultant to a host of radio stations, now grouped under his appellation of AOR.

All the term AOR really meant was that the station emphasized albums over singles. Traditional Top Forty would take an LP and only play singles as they were released. AOR would take a new LP, designate four or five cuts to be played (depending on the artist's reputation and the album's overall strength), and work them into various categories with different emphasis.

Finally, after two years of often cutthroat competition, Ron Jacobs made one of his infrequent calls to his crosstown rival. Could Harrison meet him for lunch? Michael was curious and agreed to see the man he had fought in a neck-and-neck battle over the years. Jacobs bought him a meal at Burger King.

Ron Jacobs had had it. He was getting out of KGB. It had become too much of a grind. He offered Michael his job, at a large increase over what he was making at KPRI.

But Harrison had his own surprise for Jacobs. He was leaving KPRI. His column for *Radio and Records* had become so huge that he could no longer manage it from home with only his wife and a couple of interns for help. He was exiting radio completely, moving to L.A. for a big office in the big city to be managing editor at *R&R* for big money. San Diego, which had been the battleground, was being deserted by the two generals in exchange for fresh challenges up the coast.

So Michael Harrison was out of radio again. His latest exile, although this time self-imposed, again lasted for one day.

Band of Gypsies

MICHAEL HARRISON WASN'T the only jock whose entire life was uprooted on a regular basis. Most disc jockeys lead a nomadic existence and typical are the stories of Pete Larkin and Charlie Kendall. Their histories briefly intertwine, and their sagas are familiar to anyone who has made a living in radio. Both men had theatrical training and considered acting as a trade at one point. Kendall gained his most success as a manager, Larkin as a jock, although he did program two stations on his way up the ladder. Both had successful voice-over careers and are on the outskirts of broadcasting today, with Kendall very active in new media.

Pete Larkin first worked at WVOX in Westchester County, New York, before joining the staff of WLIR as a part-timer in 1969. He taught school for a while to make ends meet before plunging ahead with radio. When Harrison and I converted WLIR to rock in the summer of 1970, Larkin was not in the original lineup. Being left over from the old format, his style seemed too slick for the more natural approach we encouraged. But he loved radio and saw potential lurking at WLIR, so he agreed to come in after sign-off and work with me on modifying his style.

After several weeks of late-night sessions, Larkin had broken his glib habits and become a valued member of the staff at WLIR. But as bad as our full-time pay was, the part-time stipend was worse. Part-timers essentially worked for free, if one were to deduct food and commuting costs from take-home pay. But Pete had an asset that none of the rest of us did: a first class radio telephone operator's license, or as it is more commonly known, a first phone. By virtue of a rigorous course of study and a tough examination, a first phone allowed you to be a sole operator of a powerful AM station due to supreme command of the technical aspects of broadcasting. To be an FM jock merely running your own console, all you needed was a third phone, roughly the equivalent of passing a driver's license test. (Rules have since been relaxed.)

WAYE in Baltimore was an AM day-timer (a station that broadcasts only while the sun is up). Pete's background and first phone qualified him for a job as program director and morning man. A strictly low-budget operation, he worked the winter months from 7 A.M. until noon, with but one other jock, who worked noon until sign-off. In the summer months, another staffer was hired to fill the midday gap necessitated by the longer hours of daylight. WAYE was a completely free-form station, so as program director, all Larkin had to do was mind his own show and make sure he and the one or two other jocks were roughly on the same page. There was no competition, and despite the limited operating hours and the AM signal, WAYE was able to score ratings in the four range, very respectable for a progressive format. And like other stations of its ilk, the music wasn't confined to pure rock. When Igor Stravinsky died, the station did a lengthy musical tribute to the maestro, and when Tammy Wynette issued "Stand by Your Man," Larkin liked it so WAYE played it. They once did a phone-in contest, asking listeners who they liked more: Sinatra or Presley. They played neither, but were flooded with callers voicing their preferences.

After eighteen months, WKTK in Baltimore came calling. They saw the impressive numbers Larkin had achieved under severely handicapped conditions and offered him more money. But the real lure was their powerful FM signal. Despite the fact that they were a part-time religious station airing God Squad programming in the morning, Larkin's afternoon show and the effective nighttime staff piled up good ratings. Again, this demonstrated the relative unimportance of mornings in FM's early days. The freedom wasn't quite as complete as it had been at WAYE, but restrictions were few. Jocks would reach a consensus on recommended cuts from new records, and Larkin once had to scale back a nighttime personality who took on a Satanic persona for his show. Larkin didn't feel comfortable with the slogan "God in the Morning, Satan All Night," which might have described what was beginning to develop, so he nipped it in the bud. Other than that and short of murder, it was almost impossible to abuse the freedom. Almost anything was acceptable, including long raps, which were encouraged as expressions of personality rather than diminished as they are at music stations today. For most of the day, there was no competition— WAYE handed WKTK many of its listeners after sign-off. And many of these would stay once they sampled FM's aural superiority.

After eighteen months, Larkin was on the move again, this time to afternoons at WMAL-FM in Washington, D.C. The market was bigger and the money better, even though he wasn't brought in as program director. Interestingly, the network of record promotion men was instrumental in acquiring the job. Baltimore and Washington are considered one territory, so when an opening occurred or was rumored in either market, the hypesters were aware of it and didn't hesitate to recommend their favorites. Since promotion men help jocks advance their fortunes, these same people could be expected to return the favor when a record came out that needed help. Quid pro quo.

Owned by the *Washington Star* newspaper, WMAL-FM was already formatted in 1973, but very loosely. Its main restrictions were a result of dealing with labor unions. For the first and only time in Larkin's career, he had an engineer with total control over the technical elements. So rather than program spontaneously, as most progressives did, Pete had to plan his show in advance and type up a play sheet for the engineers to follow. There are obvious disadvantages to this approach. From the management side, it added an extra salary, along with the attendant benefits package, so it made it harder to show a profit. From a programming aspect, in addition to the loss of spontaneity, the "feel" for the music was missing from the engineers' often heavy-handed segues. Some of the younger techies might understand how one song should flow into the next, but some of the veterans transferred from WMAL-AM had a strong distaste for the music, which could manifest itself in many negative ways. The split-second timing—when a song like "Suite: Judy Blue Eyes," with its abrupt ending, was played, another song had to begin precisely at the right moment—just wasn't there. Another downside was the lack of Michael Harrison's X factor. Since a jock could preprogram twenty-minute sets, he was free to roam the station while the engineers ran the show, which came at the expense of the symbiotic relationship with the music. A jock would sound like he wasn't listening carefully, because in many cases, he wasn't listening at all. The sizzle was missing from the delivery, and ratings could suffer as a result.

Contemporaneously, WNEW-FM had the best of both worlds. Engineers were eliminated in 1972, but prior to that point, the turntables were in the air studio and under the jocks' control anyway. Therefore, the commercials and other necessary annoyances were handled by the engineers, leaving the staff free to concentrate on the music. After the engineers' original union contract expired, WNEW-FM went into a full combo operation, which actually was less desirable. It became a more lonely existence during off-hours, and the presence of another mind for stimulation was missed, especially if it was one simpatico with the culture. The jocks then had to perform the mundane tasks of keeping the program log and refiling commercials, which also took away the total concentration on the music. But the segues would always be the way the jock wanted them, and some preferred the privacy to the company of another collaborator.

WMAL-FM was Larkin's longest-running radio job, lasting almost five years. The program director was a man named Terry Hourigan, who had come over from WMAL-AM and had all the sensibilities of an easy-listening jock—every bad habit that Larkin had rid himself of in becoming a credible progressive jock. He was a nice man but clueless in the intricacies of rock programming. The station was called the "Soft Explosion," an oxymoronic slogan with the accent on moronic. Hourigan had the problem many superficial jocks do—handling every record with an equally sunny approach. This entailed treating an apocalyptic song like "Eve of Destruction" with the same upbeat outro as "Afternoon Delight." Listeners saw through this very quickly.

Janis Joplin's final album, *Pearl*, contains a great driving lead track entitled "Move Over." In my mind, it is still far stronger in its condemnation of an insensitive lover than anything Alanis Morissette has expressed. Joplin scats over the closing fade, "and you expect me to fuck you like a goddamn mule." The music director at WMAL-FM brought this line to

Larkin's attention, but told him not to tell Hourigan, because if he knew, he'd pull a very strong record.

So it was Larkin's little secret. Congressman Harley Staggers was spearheading a campaign against obscene song lyrics, and since the station was based in Washington, there was always the danger that the congressman would catch wind of "Move Over" playing on D.C. airwaves. But like most iconoclasts, Larkin took pleasure in tweaking pompous politicians with a holier-than-thou attitude. He almost drove off the road one day, however, when Hourigan, who preceded him on the air, played the song and came out of it with a sunshiny, "Hey, there. Nice, nice thing from Janis Joplin," having no clue of what she'd just sung. Pete wasn't about to take musical direction from this man, and thankfully, little was offered.

ABC bought the station and soon converted it to their Rock in Stereo format, bringing in their own jocks and, in time, firing Larkin. It was as if Wal-Mart had come in and bought their little general store. The call letters were changed to WRQX and they battled powerhouse station DC-101 for market supremacy. Pete knocked around D.C. doing commercials and fill-ins at other stations for a while, until an opportunity arose in New York.

Charlie Kendall's travels were even more circuitous than Larkin's. Charlie was working in radio in Mississippi at the age of fourteen, then worked at several different jobs at West Coast stations before alighting at WMMS in Cleveland in the early seventies. Charlie was a morning host and a music director in Ohio, but his real success came in management. He was programming WBCN in Boston by 1977, crossing paths with Charles Laquidara. It was Kendall who first introduced a structured format to that legendary station, but Kendall, having risen through the talent ranks, appreciated the difference between a station that emphasized systems over people.

Charlie could be his own worst enemy. He was an original whiskey and cocaine guy, which endeared him to some members of the staff, but his tendency to behave erratically and miss too many workdays hurt him with upper management. He had a low threshold for boredom, which meant he rarely was content to leave well enough alone. It seemed that he was only happy in battle, and once a fight was won he wanted to move on to new challenges. He'd pick turf wars with his bosses, struggles that he would have easily won with his intelligence and radio acumen had his destructive habits not impaired his perceptions. Once, sitting in the back of a limo, he became so angry at a subordinate that he bit him viciously on the shoulder, drawing blood.

His talent allowed him to get away with such behavior temporarily and his superiors would tolerate it as long as the numbers were strong. But within a couple of years, WBCN was sold to the fledgling Infinity Group, which refused to keep bonus incentives in Kendall's contract. Since Charlie will almost never compromise on principle, he was gone in a flash.

Kendall quickly got a job as station manager of an Indianapolis station, but soon realized that managing a sales staff and a group of accountants wasn't for him. After two months, when the program director's job at WMMR in Philadelphia became open, he leapt at the opportunity. Like Pete Larkin, that made five stations in less than a decade, the Gypsy lifestyle of a radio person.

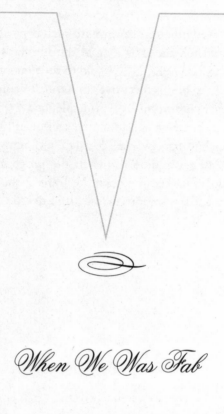

When We Was Fab

AS CELEBRATED AS John Lennon and Paul McCartney were, the "quiet" Beatle, George Harrison, had surprised many with his popular success. George had released a triple-record set called *All Things Must Pass*, produced by Phil Spector, that had sold far better than any solo Beatle effort to date. It featured several hit singles, including "My Sweet Lord" (for which Harrison was later sued because it sounded like the Chiffons' "He's So Fine"). But as George continued his solo career, including his *Concert for Bangladesh* in 1971, the critics began to sour on him. Although Harrison's solo material was solid, he was dismissed as a lightweight, and Lennon remained the media's darling.

Dave Herman had always enjoyed George's work, and eagerly accepted an invitation from a friend named Rich Totoian to catch Harrison's show at Madison Square Garden in 1975. The concert was transcendent, one of the finest the now established morning man Herman had ever seen. He was outraged at the savage treatment the press had accorded George and told his friend that he'd like to meet Harrison and tell him personally that many in the media sincerely enjoyed his work. In fact, Dave wanted to interview the former Beatle for his wake-up show.

Dave's friend Totoian was a national promoter for A&M Records, which distributed Harrison's Dark Horse label, and he got word to George that Dave was interested in an interview. Dave wrote an impassioned letter, expressing his feelings on how shabbily George's work had been treated. Shortly thereafter, he received word that the media-shy artist consented. He was to fly out to L.A. the following weekend and interview Harrison at his home. Herman immediately booked his trip, which included a red-eye flight Sunday night so that he could return for his Monday morning show.

Upon arriving at Harrison's Los Angeles digs, he was escorted back to the pool area to meet the Beatle. After their introduction, he began to set up his tape deck and microphones, but Harrison looked disappointed.

"I thought we'd talk and get to know each other a bit before we started work. Is that all right?"

Dave agreed, and George's soon-to-be wife, Olivia, brought out a bottle of wine, and they chatted like old friends, striking up an instant rapport. After a few minutes, though, Dave said, "George, maybe we should do our taping now before we get too deeply into this wine. You're telling me some great stories and I want to share them with our audience."

They rolled tape, and for the next two hours Dave was enchanted by this man's views on life and stories of the years when he was fab. He had more than enough material to fill two shows. As he thanked his host, George again looked troubled, as if his play date was over and he had to return to school.

"Aren't you going to stay for a while? I've got more of this excellent wine, and we have a guest room if you'd like to stay over."

On the red-eye back to New York, Herman was angry at himself for being so rigid. He'd really blown it. Upon being offered a chance to spend the night in the company of a man he'd admired for years, the call of duty was too strong for him to ignore. He cursed his decision and felt that he'd wasted an opportunity to bond with an artist.

Contrary to public perceptions, most disc jockeys don't hang out with rock-star friends. Like many of my colleagues, I've been fortunate enough to meet just about every rock star who ever lived. But I can count the number of friendships I've made in single digits. Rarely are home phone numbers exchanged, and even if you feel like you enjoy a relationship with an artist, you generally have to go through the same entourage of managers and agents to make contact. When they have records or tours to promote, you can be sure of getting a call, unless they feel their fame has surpassed yours and they need a larger forum to publicize their endeavor. The sad truth is that you never know if your entreaties are being spurned by the artist or are being short-circuited by intermediaries trying to protect their pampered star from grubby disc jockeys.

In his four decades of broadcasting, Dave Herman would count only three musicians as true friends. Therefore when he had a chance to form a bond with Harrison and walked away, he immediately regretted the decision. *What a schmuck I was,* he thought. Through Totoian, he got word that Harrison thought the interview had gone well and wanted the chance to hear it. Dave sent him a copy of the completed program, along with a brief note containing his home phone number if he had any questions.

A few weeks later, Dave, who had just separated from his wife and moved out of his house, got a phone call from his ten-year-old daughter. "Dad, some guy with a British accent just called. He said his name was George."

"Jenny, do you know who that was? That was George Harrison."

Now Dave's daughter felt foolish. "Oh my God, Daddy! He left a number."

Dave calmed her down and returned the call. Indeed, George Harrison himself answered the phone. "Dave, I just want to tell you. I feel all these years that I've been misunderstood by the press. That program you sent me captured my feelings perfectly. I really appreciate it. It's the best interview I've ever heard. Where can I reach you when I'm in New York next?"

A stunned Dave gave Harrison his new number and after a few more pleasantries, rang off. He held out little hope that Harrison would ever call, but felt good about the compliment. And after broadcasting the interview on his morning show, the good vibes continued as he received a call from a syndicator.

The *King Biscuit Flower Hour* was a syndicated concert series produced by Bob Meyrowitz and Peter Kauff with their company DIR (Dig It Radio). The program ran weekly, generally on Sunday evenings, four times a month. The four months of the year that contained a fifth Sunday presented a problem, but upon hearing Dave interview Harrison, Meyrowitz had a solution. Why not have Herman host an interview program highlighting a major rock star on those odd Sundays? Surely, between Meyrowitz's leverage as a syndicator and Herman's influence at WNEW-FM, they could put together four programs a year with artists that all the syndicated stations would clear. Thus, *Dave Herman's Conversations* was born.

Several months later, Dave's soon-to-be new wife, Drea, received a frantic call from Olivia Harrison. "I need your help urgently," she said. "George has been suddenly called into New York to testify in this trial over 'My Sweet Lord.' I've been calling for two whole days and we can't find an empty hotel room in the entire city."

"I'm not surprised," Drea replied. "The Democratic National Convention is in town and there hasn't been an opening here for months."

"We have three options," Olivia continued. "One, blow off the court date. Two, stay at John and Yoko's, or three, ask if you have a spare room." George, for whatever reason, clearly favored the third.

Dave explained that their guest room was in the basement of a brownstone and had no windows, but the Harrisons gratefully accepted the accommodation and stayed with the Hermans for four days. Dave was even called upon to be a character witness at the trial, which ended with a settlement being paid for Harrison's "unconscious" plagiarism. While in New York, George played tracks from his forthcoming album for Dave and Drea, and even treated them to a session with his acupuncturist.

Dave mentioned that they were planning a trip to Europe to visit Drea's sister in Paris and Harrison insisted that they stay at his country house while they were in the area. So arrangements were made to see Paris for a couple of days, and spend the remainder of the week with their newfound friends in England.

But when George's brother Harry picked them up at the airport, he made effusive apologies that George and Olivia were due back in L.A. almost at once. Dave felt naïve to have tailored his vacation around a man he barely knew, and he was now being blown off and left to his own devices in a foreign country. When they reached the elegant estate, the Harrisons were just awakening. They came down for coffee and explained that the new album *33⅓* was past due, and that George had to complete the mix in L.A. and turn it over to the record company. They were able to chat for only a few minutes, and as George and Olivia went upstairs to pack, Dave and Drea sat alone in the kitchen weighing their options. Go back to Paris? Try to find a hotel in London? Go home prematurely?

When George reemerged, Dave was about to ask about getting a ride back to Heathrow when Harrison handed him a set of keys. "This one is for the green BMW. This one is for the side door of the house. Help yourself to anything you like. Stay as long as you want. My brother's in the guest house. Call him if you need anything at all. We'll call you from Los Angeles. We're really sorry about this but we'll make it up to you. 'Bye."

With that, they were off and Dave and his wife had the mansion to themselves for five days. This was awkward for them, because they felt they really didn't know their hosts well enough to feel at ease in this opulent house with its priceless appointments. They marveled at the authentic Tiffany glass, the Persian carpets, and George's Grammy award, carelessly displayed on the mantel. But a discovery Dave made while rummaging in a drawer for a kitchen knife impressed them more than anything.

"Drea! Come here!" he shouted.

Buried in the drawer was a set of snapshots of the Beatles, in their very early days, cavorting around in goofy poses.

"Do you realize, if we were the dishonest type, what we could get for these?" Dave asked. "Thousands! These belong in a vault."

"Dave," she said solemnly, "we're in the vault."

Dave and George have gotten together on many occasions since then, remaining friends to this day. Several years back, while Dave and George were dining in Los Angeles as the Traveling Wilburys tour was in progress, Dave recounted the story of "the vault" to Harrison. "George, I've always wondered, whatever possessed you to leave us, relative strangers, alone in your home?"

Harrison smiled. "If you had done anything you shouldn't have, we wouldn't be sharing this marvelous dinner tonight, would we?"

"But that's not the point."

"What *is* the point? That you'd take some pictures from me and sell them? Do you think you'd be the first person to rip me off and screw me while I wasn't looking?"

With that, they both shrugged and went back to their wine.

Magic Man

IN THE SPRING OF 1975, a scatologically worded memo was issued from the offices of George Duncan. It stated, in Duncan's typically irreverent fashion, that Varner Paulsen had decided to step down as general manager at WNEW-FM, and that his replacement would be a salesman from AM named Mel Karmazin. Little did any of us know that twenty-five years later, this same man would be the most powerful individual in broadcasting.

Karmazin wasn't impressive upon first sight. He had none of Paulsen's intimidating Nordic presence; he seemed to be an average-looking salesman who would be equally at home hawking refrigerators at Sears or used cars in his native Queens. With his black curly hair clipped short, active intense brown eyes, medium height and build, he seemed like just a regular guy. But after one spends a few minutes in his company, it becomes obvious that Mel is no ordinary salesman. In fact, Karmazin might just be the best salesman who ever lived. His total focus is on making money. He never takes his eye off the ball in that regard; his concentration and dedication to that end are formidable.

Dave Herman recalls first meeting Karmazin the day he was appointed general manager. Mel walked gingerly into the studio where Dave was doing his morning show, bearing a gift: a six-pack of Dole grapefruit juice. When Dave looked at his new boss quizzically upon presentation of the juice, Mel replied that while listening the preceding week, he'd heard Herman comment that whenever his voice felt furry or when he lacked energy, he chugged a six-pack of this particular juice and it revitalized him. He said that he'd like to take Dave out to breakfast soon—would today be too early?

Herman was immediately taken with the new young general manager. He never had the feeling that Paulsen enjoyed listening to the station, or had any connection with the staff on any level beyond business. But Karmazin's gift indicated several things to him. First, that he paid attention to detail. After all, he hadn't brought just any kind of juice, but the type that Herman specifically had mentioned. Second, even though the gift was an inexpensive token, it was a gesture that indicated he cared about the health and happiness of a key employee. And finally, he had chosen to have his first meeting with Herman. It was a sign to Dave that his opinions would be increasingly influential as mornings grew in importance on FM.

That morning's breakfast brought further revelations into the man's character. Across the table, Mel admitted something to Herman that had been an unstated belief among the jocks but had never been verbalized by management.

"Dave, let me be honest with you. This station seems to have a special place in radio history. Listeners talk about it with a reverence and respect. The numbers are just not there. Frankly, I don't get it. The revenue far exceeds what it should be, based on your ratings. I'm at a loss. Explain it to me."

That clinched the deal. The fact that a new general manager, trying to earn the respect of his crew, could have enough confidence in his own abilities to admit that he didn't understand how the place functioned was a breath of fresh air. Subsequent bosses would come in and pretend they knew everything about WNEW-FM, when all they actually had seen was a compilation of its ratings over time. They then decided on their own what was wrong and set about to change it before understanding why things were the way they were. Herman had also seen it happen at other stations, but was floored by Karmazin's honest admission that he had a lot to learn. (A postscript to this story occurred over two decades later, when Dave was doing a show for his twenty-fifth anniversary at WNEW-FM. On his way to negotiations for his ascension to CEO of CBS, Mel stopped by the studio and dropped off a six-pack of Dole grapefruit juice. Dave had to be reminded of its significance.)

Mel might have known little about WNEW-FM when he got the job, but he learned fast. Upon joining Metromedia, Mel went straight to the top and took lessons from owner John Kluge. He continued some of Kluge's company traditions, like supplying turkeys to the staff of all his stations at Thanksgiving. Again, it was a small token, but it sent a much larger message. Like Kluge, Karmazin never seeks personal publicity, although he is intensely aware of everything written about him. You never see items in the gossip columns about his relationships, his living quarters, lavish parties, or what kind of car he drives. His personal life is intentionally cloaked in mystery. Any time his name does appear in the papers, it is in correlation with a company objective. In many ways, he is the antithesis of Donald Trump. Mel's business relationship with Kluge ended in 1981, when Karmazin wasn't given the job of general manager at Metromedia's WNEW-TV. He then became a partner in Infinity Radio, the machinations of which will be covered later. But Kluge still believes in his protégé, to the extent that he purchased a large block of CBS stock when Karmazin took over as CEO.

A CEO can't know everything in his domain, but Mel tries to learn and manage every detail. From that initial breakfast with Herman to his last days at WNEW-FM as general manager, he never stopped asking questions. He admittedly didn't know the music when he first came aboard, but he listened constantly and soon was conversant enough to know what was appropriate and what wasn't. Many years later, when he ruled not only CBS radio but television as well, he was listening to a New York Giants pregame show I was hosting on WFAN. The second to last segment was a scoreboard of NFL games in progress, several of which were in their waning moments. As we signed off, he noticed that we hadn't updated the final scores of those close games. The next morning he was at the station and pointed out the flaw to the program director. By the following weekend, the scoreboard segment had been moved to the end of the program.

From the very beginning, he would not brook no for an answer. Early in his tenure as general manager, the Rolling Stones sent notice that they were going to announce their upcoming tour from a flatbed truck on Fifth Avenue in front of the restaurant Feathers. "How are we going to cover this?" he wanted to know.

When told that we'd probably just send a reporter from WNEW-AM down to the event who would send in a phone report, Mel said that wasn't good enough. He insisted we install feed lines to the location and broadcast the event live. The engineers objected, giving him a hundred technical reasons why it wouldn't be possible. "I don't want to hear excuses," he replied, "just do it." Needless to say, it got done and resulted in an exclusive event for the station.

Karmazin was very good at winnowing out the right brains to pick, people whose perception of reality was not skewed by their hubris or ignorance. Polite but cool to those he considered fools, he efficiently managed his time in the counsel of those who could broaden his knowledge. He was also a fair man who would vigorously defend his position, but when proven wrong, he would quickly admit his error and move forward. An example of this is the first time (of many) he almost fired me.

The station had gotten involved with doing live concert broadcasts from remote locations like the Bottom Line in Greenwich Village, the Capitol Theater in New Jersey, or the Academy of Music on Fourteenth Street in lower Manhattan. These were indoor locations with fixed sound systems that were easily adapted for radio. But many larger acts were playing outdoors under more challenging conditions. Pat Dawson was a weekend personality at the station then (he's since become a major reporter at NBC television). He and I decided to form a company to produce these larger concerts for radio. We'd arrange for a sound mixer and set up a system so that these notoriously unreliable rock shows would start on time and run smoothly. Our price varied, depending on the complexity of the task, but most often we would pocket a hundred and fifty dollars each, after expenses. Generally the record company covered the production costs. It reached the point where Pat and I would approach the station with the complete package, just needing Mel's approval.

Muni, through his friends at Atlantic Records, had set up a live broadcast of Yes from the now defunct Roosevelt Stadium in Jersey City. This was a major coup and the record company took the position that the station should pay for the technical arrangements. They reasoned that a band of Yes's stature assenting to a live broadcast constituted doing the station a favor. We spoke to Mel about producing the show and he immediately balked. Since we already worked for WNEW-FM, why should we be paid extra to produce a station event?

The answer was that it required days of preparation time and that this task had nothing to do with our jobs as disc jockeys. We'd have to lease a truck, set up lines to the stage, pay our technical whiz David Vanderheyden to mix the show, et cetera. It was a big undertaking, and we weren't getting rich by doing it.

Mel didn't see the need to have a separate mix for radio. Why didn't we just take a feed off the mixing board? That was possible, we said, but highly unreliable since what may be acceptable audio for a thirty-thousand-seat stadium wouldn't necessarily work on a stereo broadcast. Plus we'd be at the mercy of the mixing engineer's skill level.

Mel wasn't buying it. He decided that we'd just take a feed off the board. What about the production? we asked. Coordinating stage cues for radio? Not necessary, he ruled. You guys will be there as hosts anyway. I'm sure you can handle it on the fly. We offered a third way. We said that for $125, we'd oversee the whole operation so that the show would run crisply, but not take responsibility for the mix, which was out of our control. He said no, and that ended our discussion. We decided to merely act as announcers for the event—and let the chips fall where they may on the production end.

The night of the concert was a disaster. The station's chief engineer brought a couple of microphones out for radio introductions and set them up in the huge infield area behind the stage. We had no means to communicate with the stage manager, so we had no idea when the band would be ready to begin. We made several false starts. The lights went down and we came on, described the scene, and told our listeners the concert would start momentarily. After a few minutes killing time with banter about the group, the lights went up again and we threw it back to the station. Muni was angry.

"Why is this so poorly organized? What's going on with you two?"

"Scott," I said, "we're not in charge here. Mel decided not to hire us to produce, so we're just here to help you host."

"Why didn't he hire you to produce?"

I then uttered what could have been fatal words. "Because he's a cheap bastard who doesn't care what this sounds like. He's just trying to save a couple of bucks, and we're the ones who look bad."

Pat added, "Yeah, we tried to talk some sense into him but the hard-headed bastard wouldn't listen."

Unbeknownst to us, Karmazin was back at the station, supervising the broadcast from that end. While we were talking to Muni, holding the microphones at our side, the overmatched engineer had kept them active. A live feed of everything we said was beaming back directly to the station, where Mel listened on the cue channel.

We finally got the show on, and the mix, although not up to our standards, wasn't bad. During intermission, we got word that Mel had heard our conversation and wanted to see us the next morning, ostensibly to fire us.

Scott said that he'd handle it and indeed he did. He later told us that Karmazin was furious and wanted our heads, but had to admit that we were right and that he should have used us to produce the concert. And from that point onward, any live broadcasts we did were under control and came off flawlessly.

Mel wasn't completely against his people making a little money on the side, especially when it didn't come directly out of the station's pocket. When Dave Herman did his first George Harrison interview, he'd flown across the country at the station's expense. When DIR asked him to do a syndicated program, Herman knew that his contract clearly stated that it would belong to Metromedia. He asked Mel for permission to farm it out.

"You know we own the rights. But are there a few extra bucks in it for you?" Mel asked, and Dave nodded. "Go ahead, take it."

The straightforward approach works best with him because it's impossible to bullshit Karmazin. If you marshal the facts on your side, he'll listen to any argument with an open mind and rule accordingly, but if you try to finesse him to your own advantage he'll ferret you out in a minute.

Although no one would confuse Mel for a Knute Rockne type, he did know how to motivate in more ways than just by intimidation. One day after another ratings loss to WPLJ, Dave Herman emerged from his morning show downcast. As he passed Karmazin's spacious corner office, he merely waved instead of exchanging pleasantries as he traditionally did. Mel rose and followed his morning man down the hall.

"Hey Dave, stop in for a minute." Herman hung a U-turn and joined Mel in the office.

"What's wrong? You look down," Karmazin began.

"I just don't understand what it takes to win anymore. We've done a great show, with great music and information. We've done great contests and promotions. I've listened to tapes of the competition. I know we're better than they are. I just don't know what it takes to beat them and I'm bummed out about it."

Karmazin picked up the phone and called the business office. "Herb," he said, "I'm coming down in a minute. Have the books for the last three months ready." He hung up and turned to Dave. "Walk down the hall with me."

Dave followed his boss to where the accountants kept records. There were no computers then, so everything was organized in large ledgers, in which clerks painstakingly recorded profit and loss. Mel opened one of the heavy books and flipped pages until he found the one he was seeking.

"Now Dave, the numbers you're aware of are ratings. PLJ has a 3.5 and you have a 2.8. But the real numbers that count are these." His finger scrolled down the column to the monthly bottom line, a steadily rising figure. "And here is last year at this time." He pointed to another number, substantially lower than the previous entry.

"These are the only numbers that count. The hell with Arbitron ratings. Don't you worry about that. You just do the best show you know how. But if *these* numbers ever change, then believe me, you'll hear from me right away. Then you can worry."

Dave walked away, his spirits lifted. The next time the ratings came out, they showed improvement, and Karmazin heartily congratulated Herman. He'd found a clever way to raise Dave's confidence and yet let him know the criteria against which he'd be judged.

Herman's relationship with Mel underscored another tenet that has made Karmazin the giant he is today. He is able to identify the stars—the chief moneymakers—and he treats them like kings. They are accorded generous contracts, complete with perks that most companies would never extend to talent. If a Don Imus or Howard Stern gets in trouble, he'll back them to the hilt. But he also is hard-nosed when it comes to union contracts or pay scales to those he deems replaceable. There is never fat in a Karmazin-run enterprise, dating back to his time at WNEW. When I was his operations manager, there originally was no music director. That fell under my domain until much later when I proved to him I needed assistance in that area. There was no promotions director, and only a part-time production manager. Now, radio stations have whole departments employing several people in each of those areas. But Mel wouldn't expand the staff unless you could absolutely convince him that it would improve the station's revenue picture. Likewise, he pares away jobs he sees as superfluous. One of his least popular but effective moves was to eliminate salaries for salesmen, making the position a "commission only" situation. By doing this, he drove away the timid and kept only those willing to hustle. Perhaps this dates back to his early days in radio sales at WCBS when he turned a $17,500 salary into $70,000 in yearly commissions.

As I said, I was almost fired by Mel a number of times: One of my most vivid recollections concerned a conversation in which he accused me of not working hard enough. He didn't have the feeling that I was willing to go that extra mile for the company. I equated my attitude to that of a baseball player, who played hard but wouldn't risk injury diving for the ball. I felt that my talent would make up for that.

He replied, "A lot of people have talent. I guess I need somebody that'll dive for the ball."

At that point, WNEW-FM had never cracked a three share in the ratings. We were then at a 2.7 and seemed to be bumping against a glass ceiling. But after that talk, I worked harder than I ever had, giving up evenings and weekends in a single-minded pursuit of that three share. When the numbers came out, we'd bounced up to a 3.1, and Mel took us all to our favorite watering hole to celebrate. Before we left the station, he put his hand on my shoulder and said, "I want you to know that more than anyone else, I hold you responsible for our breaking a three share. I've never seen anybody work as hard at this station. See what happens when you dive for the ball?" That was probably the best compliment I've gotten in four decades of radio.

I had very few problems with Mel after that. He's extremely loyal to his people once they prove themselves, and he expects that loyalty to be returned.

A story told by Charles Laquidara illustrates that point. When Mel's Infinity Radio bought WBCN, Charles was in contract talks and things weren't going well. Karmazin flew to Boston and drove to Laquidara's home to handle negotiations personally. The longtime morning man was surprised at how easily Mel agreed to his terms, and the two went out to dinner afterward, becoming fast friends. Karmazin even included stock options in the deal, something he said he'd never done before.

Subsequent contracts went smoothly as Charles dominated Boston's ratings in AM drive time. But he noticed over time that his dinners with Mel were becoming more infrequent, and that whenever Karmazin came up to the station, Charles barely merited a quick hello.

Laquidara championed BCN's workers when they had disputes with management and lent his voice to political groups that supported gun control, environmental issues, and generally liberal causes. His need for approval included Mel and he felt that their personal friendship extended beyond a typical employee-employer relationship. So when his boss next visited WBCN and ensconced himself in the general manager's office, Charles wrote him a note.

"Dear Mel," it read, "I know that since I met you the first time, you've succeeded in business far beyond anyone's imagination. You are a very busy man. I realize that your time is valuable. I estimate it to be worth a thousand dollars a minute. So enclosed please find a personal check for three thousand dollars. I humbly request three minutes of your time before you leave today." He asked an intern to deliver it.

The kid returned a moment later. "He said, 'Fine.' Should you meet in the office he's in now, or in yours?"

Laquidara, always one to tweak authority said, "Tell him that since I'm paying, he should come here."

Moments later Karmazin appeared, closed the office door, clicked the stem of his watch and said, "Clock's ticking."

Charles proceeded to outline his case: He'd been hurt by Mel's indifference and he wanted to know what he'd done to deserve such disregard.

"Charles, when I bought this station, I didn't treat you like an employee. I treated you like a partner and a friend. I gave you stock options. I pay you ten times over scale. I never tell you how to run your show. And yet, anytime there's a labor issue here, you're always against me. The people here have unions, they have a mechanism to fight their battles for them. They don't need you. You should be on the company's side. You're invested in the company, part of management. And yet every time something comes up, you're on the other side. Also, it's eleven-thirty now and you're packing up to leave. Do you know that Howard Stern almost never leaves the station until three? He's always listening to tapes and trying to improve his show. Do you think you're better than him? Time's up." With that, he left. Charles had to admit that the words had resonance, yet he felt a moral responsibility to the support staff to use his leverage to better their lot. His contact with Mel has been limited since.

Two months after the three-minute encounter, Laquidara's accountant called. It seemed Charles was missing a check that hadn't yet been cashed. After retracing his transactions, he realized that the missing check was the one that he'd written Karmazin.

"Oh, forget about it," he told his man. "He'll never cash it."

Shortly afterward, Laquidara received a letter embossed in gold ink from the White House. It was an invitation to meet President Bush, who wanted to personally thank him for the generous contribution to his re-election campaign. Also included in that day's mail was a form letter from Wayne LaPierre, then president of the National Rifle Association, thanking him for the largest donation they'd received from a private citizen that week.

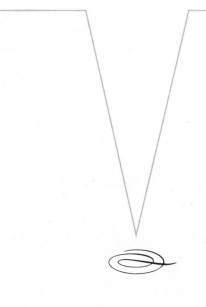

Good-bye Yellow Brick Road

JONATHAN SCHWARTZ WAS TIRED.

The grind of working seven days a week had become too much for him. He was entangled in a romantic situation that was strangling him, and he always had taken such attachments very seriously. One of them had landed him in a mental ward two weeks before he was supposed to start at WNEW-FM in 1967. This time, it was a young coworker, and Schwartz was feeling trapped.

His quest for love in many of the wrong places could be traced back to his childhood in Beverly Hills. His famous father wasn't around much and his mother was often bedridden, so he spent his early years largely unattended by family. It was here where he developed his radio skills, closing himself inside a closet and practicing play-by-play for his beloved baseball. As he grew older, he began to break into houses in his neighborhood, where many people left their doors unlocked. He would rifle through his neighbors' personal items, perhaps in search of some kind of human connection. (He once rummaged through a house he later discovered was Gene Kelly's.) He always left everything as it was, but he admits to stealing a few 78s.

He was also tired of rock and roll. Like anything new and uncharted, the gradual revelation of its mysteries had been fascinating at first. Schwartz probed and experimented, exploring its limitations and taboos further and further. He defined rock as "jazz, under pressure." But he was rooted in Sinatra and the standards of his father's era and eventually found playing the Doors wanting. The music rarely spoke to him anymore—it was time to move on.

He'd come to the realization in the spring of 1975 that his radio work was interfering with his writing. It was all too easy to put in a full evening behind a hot microphone, have a late supper and stay up until nearly dawn, sleep away the day, and then get up and do it again, without ever putting pen to paper. He was earning a nice living between the two stations, AM and FM, and was revered by the fans of each.

But the old gang wasn't around much anymore: Paulsen was gone, Duncan was on the road a lot; he even missed fighting with his old nemesis, Rosko. His new boss, Mel Karmazin, wasn't enthralled by his habit of dialing up the radio station that carried the Boston Red Sox games and listening in while doing his show. But it was that and the alcohol that kept him going. His relationship with Alison Steele had never been good—he'd never had much use for her other than as a target for derisive flirtation. His appreciation for Scott Muni was only as a comrade in arms, a fellow drinker; but he was disdainful of what he saw as Muni's substandard intellect.

Muni regarded him as a spoiled eccentric with peculiar tastes in everything but scotch. One of the characteristics Scottso found most disquieting was Jonathan's habit of eating food from garbage cans. Other jocks would be appalled when Schwartz would steal into the newsroom, spy a pizza box crammed into a waste bin, and help himself to a half-eaten slice. One of Muni's apocryphal tales, retold so many times that it is accepted as true, regards one such incident. Schwartz vehemently denies the veracity of the following:

Early in Jonno's tenure at WNEW-FM, the station employed a young

woman at minimum wage to answer phones at night and keep track of requests. One evening while leaving work, Muni found the woman sobbing
softly. As father-confessor to everyone at the station, he tried to comfort
her and see if there was anything he could do to alleviate her distress.

"Mr. Muni," she wept. "You know I don't make a lot of money here.
I'm going to school during the day and I can't afford to order out for food.
So I make a sandwich every day and put it in the refrigerator here at the station. I bring in a can of soda, too. Well, today, when I went to get my sandwich and soda, they were gone. I'm hungry. I haven't eaten all day. I'm
short of money and don't have enough to order out."

Muni empathized and gave the woman some money. He then headed
back to the studio, where he saw an empty soda can and crumpled paper
bag in the area where Schwartz had been sitting before going on the air that
evening.

Muni decided to get some vigilante justice. The next morning, he prepared a treat for Jonathan—a peanut butter and jelly sandwich with a special added ingredient: a crushed slab of chocolate-flavored Ex-Lax, a
powerful laxative. He wrapped it in wax paper and stuffed it into a brown
bag, much like one the receptionist had used. He surreptitiously placed it
in the small refrigerator the station provided for its employees' convenience and waited for Schwartz's arrival.

It was a Friday evening and when Muni finished his show and got
ready to depart for the weekend, he checked the refrigerator and the bag
was missing. Schwartz, who claims in thirty-five years of radio never to
have missed a show due to illness or to have even been late, dragged himself into the studio the following Monday.

"Bad weekend, Fats?" Muni asked him. "You look a little green around
the gills."

"Horrible case of diarrhea," Schwartz said. "Must have been something I ate."

Muni never let on the source of his malady. He was gleeful in his revenge, but the incident didn't curb Jonno from devouring anything that
wasn't nailed down.

Despite his boyish mischief, Schwartz was feeling out of sorts playing rock music for kids. He told Karmazin that he didn't want to leave the
station in the lurch, so he was handing him a year's notice. May 1, 1976,
would be the date of his final show on WNEW-FM. Mel tried several times

to dissuade him, but his mind was made up and he never looked back. He was financially secure and free to write what and when he wanted. He kept his part-time gig at WNEW-AM, where he could play only what he wanted. He could flit in and out of exotic women's lives without having to face them at work. But he would miss the free food.

Thunder Road

JUST AFTER THE FOURTH OF JULY in 1974, an obscure musician from New Jersey played the Bottom Line, an intimate but prestigious music club on West Fourth Street in Greenwich Village. On his second album, he'd written a song about the holiday and his manager thought it would be a good idea to book him to play New York near the Fourth. Unfortunately, although it sounded good on paper, it turned out to be a bad idea, since many city dwellers flee for the shore or mountains to escape the heat at every opportunity. The house was half full, but despite the lackluster gate, the club's owners, Allan Pepper and Stanley Snadowsky, saw something during those shows that made them believe that someday Bruce Springsteen would revolutionize rock and roll.

I developed a friendship with Bruce through an odd series of coincidences. I was a big Rangers hockey fan and I attended most of their home games on Wednesday nights with the rep for Columbia Records, Matty Matthews. It seemed that after every game, there would be an artist Matty had to pay his respects to, and since I wasn't on the air until 2 A.M., I generally accompanied him.

I must have seen Springsteen play Max's Kansas City a dozen times. I really wasn't too impressed with those early shows. Bruce had presence and the band had a lot of raw energy, but it was too much for such a small club. Whenever we went back to his dressing room to say hello, he treated each introduction as if I was meeting him for the first time. A bad memory or drugs, I thought, not knowing at the time that he didn't indulge. Maybe he had met so many DJs in the course of his touring that he didn't remember me. Or maybe he was just shy or simply didn't care.

Our real relationship blossomed not in person, but on the phone. During that era, all the jocks felt that it was important to answer the request line to stay in touch with the audience and get a sense of what they wanted to hear. And frankly, we often got lonely, sitting by ourselves in a small room filled with records. Nights could be especially long—meeting Matty for dinner at six, seeing a hockey game, catching a live performance, and then doing a program until six the next morning. The juxtaposition of all the social activity followed by the imposed solitude made for a difficult transition, and the phone was the only way I got any feedback. Talking into an open microphone in the middle of the night is like trying to have a conversation with a golden retriever. Occasionally we'd flirt with female listeners; some even became friends or lovers. Dave Herman met his second wife via the request line: She'd called to ask a question, they began talking, hit it off, and agreed to meet for lunch at a promotional party. A couple of years later, they were getting married at his country home in Connecticut. There are other less wholesome stories I could tell about the listener line, but I made some lasting friendships with some of the regular callers, and one of these was Bruce Springsteen.

I must have given him the hotline number a dozen times, but he'd jot it down on some scrap of paper and lose it, so he always called on the request line. We'd talk about sports, women, music; whatever was on our minds. He's an amazingly self-educated man. When you hear him interviewed today, he is so articulate and chooses his words so precisely, it would seem that he's the product of a Princeton education. In reality, the closest he got to Princeton was Ocean County Community College in Toms River, New Jersey, which he attended for one semester before dropping out. But back then he had trouble putting words to his feelings, although he did it better on the phone than in the flesh. I was always astonished that this man, who struggled so mightily to express himself in normal conversation, could author the lyrics that he did. I think sometimes that he crammed his verses with so many syllables in an attempt to overcompensate for his lack of formal education. As his confidence grew, his later work got simpler and more elegant. The more he traveled and read, the more he refined his art, until he now can say a lot by saying very little.

He was a big radio fan, and once confided that his friends would tease him by calling him Cousin Brucie. He often listened at night, and not only knew the major rock groups, but was aware of R&B and new stuff as well. Our talks were often rambling two-hour discussions, with long gaps while I had to change records or set up commercials. He'd wait patiently and we'd pick up where we'd left off. Often, I could tell he wasn't alone, as he whispered his words into the handset so as not to disturb the sleeping body next to him. Sometimes, if six A.M. came around and we were still on a roll, I'd continue the conversation in another room as Dave Herman did his morning show.

Springsteen's first album, *Greetings from Asbury Park, N.J.*, had received tepid airplay, and many of my colleagues thought he was a low-rent Bob Dylan. The hype coming from Columbia didn't help, since they were comparing him to the poet from Hibbing and projecting him as "the next big thing." Bruce himself resented the comparisons and told me so, and I defended his talents whenever the staff would get into a music discussion, blaming the record company, not the artist, for the overaggressive promotion.

He didn't even feel that the record captured what he was doing. "I was always with a band," he told me. "When I auditioned for Columbia they were into this singer-songwriter thing. But at the time, I was so desperate to get a contract that I'd have done anything. But I was into playing guitar, loud."

Greetings sold modestly, mostly in the Northeast, and won some loyal followers like myself and Ed Schaiky of WMMR. Certain influential people became believers, but none were more devoted to Bruce than Schaiky. He'd actually schedule his vacations around tour dates and follow Bruce from city to city. If Murray the K was the Fifth Beatle, Ed could lay claim to being the ninth E-Streeter (or tenth, or eighth). The mere mention of Bruce would incite a lecture on his latest song or performance and minutiae about how Bruce changed the set from night to night. Ed almost got to be annoying in his devotion to the Boss. Another early disciple was Kid Leo (Lawrence Travagliante) at WMMS in Cleveland.

But most radio people didn't see what the fuss was about. "Frankly, I didn't see what the big deal was," Dave Herman said in *Newsweek*. "The record was okay, but to compare this scruffy New Jersey kid to Dylan was ridiculous. I saw him as a pale imitation and I resented the comparison."

When the second album, *The Wild, the Innocent and the E Street Shuffle,* came out the following year, the resentment only increased. Vin Scelsa and I were its champions at the station, and I thought it was getting decent support, but apparently Springsteen's manager, Mike Appel, didn't agree. He sent everyone on the staff a postcard asking, "What does it take to get airplay on this station?"—the clear implication being that the only way to get his artist exposed was through payola. One by one, the jocks tacked their postcards up on the station's bulletin board under the legend: "Did you get one of these, too?" It was hard for me to do damage control, especially since I remember getting Xeroxes of hundred-dollar bills after the postcard came in the mail, and I was *supporting* the record. We complained to Columbia, and they publicly disavowed the postcards while privately telling us that Springsteen's manager was an idiot who thought he could use intimidation to get his acts on the air. I told Bruce about the mail campaign, but he knew nothing about it.

That incident set Bruce back in a market that should have spearheaded his drive to the top. I loved the record, even though it showcased more of Bruce's jazz and classical side than his straight-ahead rock and roll roots. I savored the opportunity to play the entire second side, consisting of "Incident on 57th Street," "Rosalita," and "New York City Serenade" on the overnights. I thought it captured the city at night so perfectly, with lines like, "It's midnight in Manhattan/This is no time to get cute/It's a mad dog's promenade." "Fourth of July, Asbury Park (Sandy)" was another song of quiet desperation that I relished playing year-round. Overall, if Bruce had stayed mining that vein, I'd have been a fan for life. But I knew that he'd never achieve mass popularity going that route.

In late 1974, my brother Dan was attending Syracuse University and working part-time for Columbia Records, promoting their artists upstate. He'd obtained a bootleg copy of the title song from Springsteen's forthcoming album, *Born to Run,* which was scheduled to be released in August

1975. When I played it for the first time on the overnight show, I knew that my midnight telephone conversations with Bruce would soon be over because he'd belong to the world and would outgrow the need to call radio stations in the middle of the night.

The song was a breakthrough, an homage to the production techniques of Phil Spector, with densely layered instruments echoing over a relentless driving beat. The theme was classic Bruce—the lonely rider, desperate to break loose from his meaningless blue-collar existence to find his place in the sun, all the while doubting his ability to break the ties that bind. After a few weeks of exclusive play on my show, other jocks were getting requests for it and asking me for a copy. His doubters on the staff were slowly being converted into believers.

Kid Leo in Cleveland had gotten hold of the record around Thanksgiving of 1974 and immediately gave it heavy airplay on his afternoon show on WMMS. He loved the song so much that he played it as he was signing off every Friday afternoon, and it became his anthem leading into the weekend. Bruce played Cleveland again in February of 1975, and was trying out a few of the songs from the forthcoming album. He played "Thunder Road" (then called "Wings for Wheels") and "Jungleland," both of which were received with enthusiasm. But when the band went into "Born to Run," the entire crowd rose to its feet and sang it along with him. When the show ended, Bruce asked the promoter how this audience knew every word to a song that wasn't scheduled for release for at least six months. He was told about Leo's unbridled support, to which he said, "Bring him to me!"

Leo was led backstage and was a little unsure if he would be excoriated and possibly sued for pirating the record, which technically wasn't supposed to be aired. But Springsteen was overwhelmed by the response of the crowd and thanked the young DJ profusely. They spoke for about ten minutes, and Leo became Bruce's friend and biggest champion in Cleveland.

But 1975 was make-or-break time at Columbia. Bruce's contract was coming to an end and if his third album continued the disappointing sales of the first two offerings, the label would drop him. I had begun to cultivate a friendship with Mike Appel's personal assistant, a stunning blond woman. Upon hearing *Born to Run,* I was convinced that it would be a smash and I wanted WNEW to be there at the beginning, and not let the payola postcards destroy the relationship. There was a buzz starting about the album, and Appel's assistant played me some other tracks that convinced me that Bruce was about to explode. Through her and Michael Pillotte, the national promotion director at Columbia, I found out that the band had been booked for the Bottom Line in mid-August, right after the album was to be released.

I found other allies in strange places. Michael Leon of A&M Records, who had no tie to the group other than as a fan, had obtained an advance copy of the record and was promoting it to his legions of friends in the business. Pepper and Snadowsky saw national prominence for their club if the dates turned out to be as monumental as we hoped they'd be.

So I sent a memo to Mel Karmazin stating that I'd put my reputation on the line that this Bottom Line concert was going to be historic and that we should arrange now to do a live broadcast before someone else beat us to it. Pat Dawson and I would do all the legwork—coordinating with the record company, the club, and the band—if he would just give us the airwaves for two hours. Mel sensed my passion and gave the nod.

The alliance was an uneasy one from the start. Whereas Columbia was willing to underwrite some of the costs of the broadcast, their funds weren't limitless. They saw this as a favor to the station. Mel was going on my word that the prestige of this event would make up for the lost revenue we'd suffer by presenting the show commercial-free. Even if we had found a sponsor, we'd have probably made more money with regular programming. I couldn't push him for a contribution above that. The club generally was paid a usage fee whenever they hosted a broadcast and I had to convince them to waive that, explaining that the attendant publicity would more than make up for the few dollars they lost. Pepper and Snadowsky were smart businessmen and agreed quickly. But with all these ducks in line, we still had objections from Appel, fearing that bootlegs of the concert would harm record sales. Pillotte smoothed him over, or so we thought.

I tried to talk directly to Bruce about this, but his management drew a tight wall around him. I was hoping he'd call, and I eagerly answered every ring on the request line hoping that it would be him. But he never called and although he'd once given me his home number, I'd been as careless with that as he had been with our hotline number.

As the show dates grew nearer, tensions mounted as I sensed we still had a few loose ends. He was booked into the club for ten performances—five nights, Wednesday through Sunday, with shows at 8:30 and 11:30 P.M.

We were scheduled to broadcast the early show on Friday. That way, any technical glitches or early jitters could be worked out, and the print journalists who reviewed Wednesday and Thursday's shows would be able to increase the anticipation with what we knew would be glowing accounts.

I attended a couple of the early performances and they were fabulous. Bruce had really found himself onstage, borrowing from Elvis, James Brown, Little Richard, and others, but still adding his own special panache. They were the best rock shows I've ever seen, before or since. He sprinkled in a collection of oldies like the Searchers' "When You Walk in the Room," Manfred Mann's "Pretty Flamingo," Ike and Tina Turner's "I Think It's Gonna Work Out Fine," and the Beach Boys' version of "Then I Kissed Her." He played with the full band, he played with solo guitar or piano, and in guitarist Steven Van Zandt's words, "We kicked ass."

In addition to the music, Bruce told stories. I don't know to this day where that came from, but he presented his songs like an FM jock, explaining and embellishing their meanings. The sets lasted just over two hours. I found it impossible to leave after the early show and begged Allan Pepper for standing room for the eleven-thirty performances. I was psyched that this would be like Muni and the Beatles at Idlewild—that's how exciting the shows were.

That's why I was destroyed when Mel Karmazin awakened me that Friday morning with the terse message that the show was off. I groggily tried to make sense of it. It seems that Appel was reneging on his agreement to let David Vanderheyden, the Bottom Line's regular broadcast engineer, mix the concert for radio. He was demanding a professional mobile recording studio (a truck costing thousands of dollars) with himself at the controls. Of course, no one was willing to pick up that expense and, therefore, the broadcast was canceled.

I was livid as I hastily drove into the city. I tried to figure out if there was a hidden agenda behind Appel's demand. Did he think that Bruce wouldn't deliver the goods? That was hard to believe after having seen the show. Was there a possibility that Bruce had gotten cold feet? I recalled my conversations with him and how he'd always felt ambivalent about being a rock star. On one hand, he wanted to be recognized as a great artist and have all the attendant fame and riches, and on the other, he saw himself as just an average kid from Jersey and didn't want to be changed by the experience. He didn't want to be isolated from his fans, playing only cavernous halls where he couldn't see their faces. He wanted to be able to go out in public and do the things he normally did—hang out at the beach or go to a ball game, without an entourage. He hated the mansions and trappings of fame that would cloister him away from the average people that he cared and wrote about. He didn't want to spend the rest of his life writing songs about how tough life was on the road. He wanted success, but he also feared it. He felt the star-making machinery itself was corrupting; he'd had a taste of it in the hype surrounding his first record and he didn't like it. I hoped that if he were revisiting these doubts I could give him a pep talk that would assuage his uncertainties.

The first person I encountered upon entering the club was Appel and after talking to him for only a minute, I knew that Bruce wasn't the problem. Dawson and I corralled him in a quiet corner of the room and played good cop/bad cop. He told us his fears were grounded in the fact that the Bottom Line's mixing console was in a very noisy location near the stage. You couldn't get an accurate mix from there.

"Right," said Dawson. "All the more reason to let David do it. He's mixed dozens of shows from there."

"Why should I trust my artist's future to some kid from NYU I just met?" Appel asked.

"Mike, we gave you tapes. Did you listen?" I wanted to know. "David even did some tapes of Bruce last Fourth of July."

We could tell that he hadn't heard the tapes as he responded by changing the subject. "Have you seen that rinky-dink board he uses?"

Vanderheyden's console was far from state of the art but he was very proud of how he'd cobbled together a system that turned out sound rivaling that of the quarter-million-dollar trucks. His system had quirks, but he had them under control and his tapes were grand.

"Mike, you almost blew it for Bruce last year. I don't have to remind you about the postcards. You want to hazard a guess at what your airplay at Metromedia stations will be in the future if you blow us off now?" Pat said ominously.

"Is that a threat?"

I tried to be conciliatory while Pat played the tough guy, a role he relished and came by naturally. "Mike, look. We're all fans of Bruce. We want the best for him. We don't want a crappy-sounding broadcast on our airwaves. You've got to trust David."

"For you, it's one bad show. For me, it's a man's career. How do I explain it to him if the shows sound bad and I tell him that some college kid mixed it? I need to be in control."

He had a point. "Let's try this. Let's go up to David's booth. Listen to the tapes he made from the first two nights."

We climbed the rickety ladder behind the stage and David slapped on his tapes. They sounded as good as I'd remembered. But Appel was too stubborn to back down now. "All right, the equipment works. But this show is going live to New York and Philly." Sure enough, WMMR had hastily petitioned Columbia for a simulcast, and Ed Schaiky had driven up to represent them. Could Kid Leo be far behind? "This is a tough mix. I've got to be at the board. That's it. Take it or leave it."

He was holding the cards. We were bluffing with our threat at pulling the record. We'd only be hurting ourselves and we weren't in a position to speak for Metromedia. "Give us a minute," Pat said.

He went down the ladder into the club and we explained the situation to David. "He's been in my booth the last two nights," he told us. "He doesn't have a clue. If he mixes this, it will sound like crap. I don't want him touching my equipment."

Now we were surrounded. I didn't fancy explaining to Karmazin that my grandiose idea was now dead, especially since he'd since found a sponsor. We brought David down to see Appel. I ventured a middle ground. "How about this? David will be hands-on. You direct him. He'll do anything you want."

"I'm hands-on. He can help."

No point arguing further. We had the show back, and even though we knew that it wouldn't sound as good as it could have, the raw power of the E Street Band should shine through any technical limitations. We shook hands and called the station to tell everybody that the show was on.

It was one of the least enjoyable Springsteen shows I've ever attended. Not because of Bruce, he was superb. It started with the onstage introduction by Dave Herman, who had been to one of the earlier performances and had been converted into a rabid Springsteen fan. "And now everybody, please welcome Bruce Springstreet and the E Steen Band."

Yeeesh. Dave still laughs about that intro. Pat and I retreated to Pat's car to hear what the broadcast sounded like. It began very badly. There was some clicking noise underneath the whole thing that was noticeable during soft passages. Clarence Clemons's sax was not miked, and the whole thing did not sound properly balanced. But after a few songs things fell into place and it was vintage Bruce. We could finally sit back and enjoy the rest of the show.

As it ended, I made my way backstage and interviewed a heavily perspiring Springsteen. He sounded like a boxer as he described how he "felt real good out there." He was doing his best Muhammad Ali, and I couldn't help laughing as the tensions of the night came spilling out. I wished him luck and he retreated to his dressing room.

A sweaty Mike Appel came down from the booth and mopped his brow. Pat and I gave him a wry thumbs up, and then climbed the ladder to see David. "It sounded pretty bad at first but it got better," I said. "How was it for you?"

He then told us what had happened. Appel had originally taken the mixing console, but after struggling through the first notes, frantically motioned for David to take over. Vanderheyden mixed the lion's share of the show, with Appel prodding him occasionally to boost the audience mics. Much ado about nothing.

Almost twenty years later, when Mel Karmazin was well on his way to controlling a broadcasting empire, he must have been cleaning out his files when he came upon a copy of the memo I'd written to him, pleading to do the Springsteen broadcast. He sent me a copy, with a note stating, "That's why I never liked working with you. You had no foresight."

Bruce was to me what the Beatles were to Dennis Elsas. A proper interview became my Holy Grail, but his management team, now headed by Jon Landau, comes from a print background and shields him from radio people. Initially, I could understand Landau's need to protect Bruce, since he was not a great wordsmith while not onstage. But whether it was on Bruce's own instruction or overly conservative management, our contact has been limited. Management continues to hold him at arm's length from radio, and as a result, many stations don't play his new records. Today, he is such an articulate voice on so many diverse issues, one would think that an extensive radio interview would benefit all concerned, even if it had to be conducted on a talk station. It's a shame that so many artists who have nothing valuable to say are frequently accorded open forums on radio, and one whose words would be esteemed is strangely silent.

Mike Pillotte at Columbia helped put Springsteen and me together a few times. Mike and I rode up to West Point to catch one of the best shows I've ever seen Bruce do. After the concert, a man came out to the front of the stage and paged me. When I identified myself, he said, "Follow me," and led me through the backstage catacombs to a small room where Bruce stood alone, toweling off after a typical three-and-a-half-hour show. We had a ten-minute chat before we both had to catch our rides back to the city.

In the summer of 1976, Springsteen and I went to a baseball game with a group of mutual friends. Amazingly, here was a man who months before had been on the cover of both *Time* and *Newsweek,* but as we walked through hundreds of young people on the way to our seats at Yankee Stadium, not a soul recognized him. Of course, Bruce was always changing his appearance then: His hair was long, short; he had a beard, a mustache, he was clean-shaven; he was skinny, he was muscular—he always looked a little different.

In November of that year, he played the Academy of Music and he and Pillotte popped into my Saturday afternoon show unannounced. He hung out for two hours, selecting his favorite records and playing disc jockey. I had no chance to prepare for the impromptu interview. My natural affinity and knowledge of his career enabled me to ask good questions, but as I listen to the tape now, there are so many more I would have liked to have addressed. But other than a telephone interview a decade later and a brief dressing room conversation before a Meadowlands show I did along with my brother in the early nineties, I have yet to do the definitive Bruce interview.

Kid Leo's friendship with the Boss deepened throughout the seventies as well. In fact, E Street guitarist Steven Van Zandt's protégé, Southside Johnny Lyons, had been so grateful to Leo for his support that he played the Kid's wedding. On the Darkness tour, Leo was asked to emcee Springsteen's performance at the Agora, which was coupled with a live radio broadcast. He contemplated his introduction for days, memorizing a dozen ideas that were eventually discarded. Leo was a big sports fan and he knew that Bruce had used boxing metaphors coming offstage in the past, so he crafted a Michael Buffer–type opening.

"Ladies and gentlemen," he intoned. "Round for round, pound for pound, there ain't no fighter this world around, who can stand toe-to-toe with Bruce Springsteen and the E Street Band!" The crowd went wild and the broadcast soared from that point onward. After intermission, as the band came out, Max Weinberg hit the cymbals and Bruce yelled, "Round TWO!"

That show was part of a trilogy of dates in smaller venues that were regional live broadcasts. The other two originated from the Capitol Theater
in Passaic, New Jersey, and the Roxy in Los Angeles, and were designed to
build excitement for the first arena tour, which was beginning in Cleveland
three weeks later. Now in a twenty-thousand-seat hall, Leo was again
called upon to bring out the band. He began his boxing litany, and this time
he was carried away by the power of his amplified voice filling the cavernous space. The crowd was screaming as the band entered, but Bruce
held up his hand for silence, turned to Leo, and asked, "What's the matter
Leo, can't you think of nothing new?"

I do recall a more peculiar encounter. New Year's Eve live broadcasts
of concerts from the Capitol with Southside Johnny and the Asbury Jukes
had become a tradition in the late seventies, and whenever Johnny played,
there was always the hope that Springsteen might join him onstage. We
ushered in 1980 with "Havin' a Party," a Southside staple, and signed off
forty minutes later. But the Jukes' manager was acting skittish all night, and
when Johnny Lyons finished his last encore, came back to our broadcast
location and asked pointedly if we had signed off. We assured him that we
had, but by then it was obvious that something else was up. We called the
station and told them to keep the line open, since we'd seen members of
the E Street Band around, and we figured they might be gearing up to play.
Bruce had gone over three years before releasing another album after his
breakthrough *Born to Run* as he disengaged from Mike Appel's management and signed on with Landau. Legal problems caused him to keep a low
touring profile as well, so any chance we might get to air even a few songs
was a huge scoop.

As we suspected, about twenty minutes after the Jukes finished, John
Scher took the stage and announced a special surprise—a live set from the
E Street Band. Over half the audience had left the theater, but those still in
the street outside rushed back in to catch their hero. We hastily reactivated
the lines and broadcast the first couple of songs, causing ticket holders who
were already in their cars to turn around and come back.

Johnny Lyons was livid. He called me every name in the book, and his
manager accused me of lying when I told him we were off the air. I replied
that we indeed had been off when he asked, but that such a major event
was big news and nobody officially told us we couldn't air it. Lyons lunged
as if to hit me, but was held back. He swore that he'd kill me if we didn't

end the broadcast immediately. Somehow, I found the fortitude to tell him that unless I heard it directly from Bruce, we'd continue.

As the next song ended, the irate manager snuck onto the stage and whispered into Springsteen's ear. The Boss shook his head violently, and I could tell that he was denying us permission to broadcast further. We had to respect his wishes, and told our radio audience that we regretfully had to sign off due to contractual reasons.

Johnny calmed down after that—we talked and shook hands and both of us said there were no hard feelings. I was morose though, because we had potentially damaged our relationship with two artists we had supported and believed in from the beginning. I had hosted the first nationwide Asbury Jukes concert from the Stone Pony in Asbury Park several years before, and saw Lyons not just as a satellite of Springsteen, but a man with considerable talent of his own.

As a New Year's party started onstage after the brief E Street Band set ended, I said good-bye to my friends at the Capitol and prepared to go home. As I started out, Bruce grabbed me from behind and spun me around, giving me a big hug. "I'm sorry, my friend," he slurred, drunkenly. After all, it was New Year's and we'd all imbibed a bit.

"Will you forgive me?" he asked plaintively.

"Forgive you for what?"

"I don't want you to be mad at me. Please don't be mad."

"Bruce, I've got no reason to be mad at you. I just hope you're not mad at me. You understand we wanted to broadcast your set for our listeners, that's all."

"Don't be mad," he repeated. This was making no sense. Was he apologizing for cutting us off when he had every right to do so?

"Johnny's a good guy. Don't be mad at him, either." He gave me a warm embrace.

I felt that he was appealing not to the representative of a radio station important to his career but to a friend, and I was touched that he seemed genuinely concerned that I thought well of him personally. He is extremely sensitive and expresses himself from the heart, and I think that's one of the reasons he's such a great artist. As I drove home, I felt pangs of guilt, hoping that I hadn't betrayed him and that when we both drew more sober breaths, our strange sporadic friendship would survive.

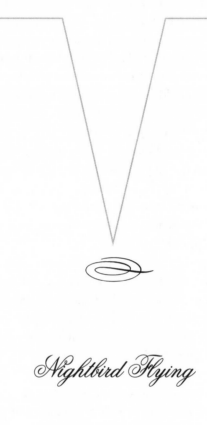

Nightbird Flying

ALISON STEELE IS PROBABLY the most revered woman in radio. She's been an inspiration and role model for hundreds of other women in the business. And like Frank Sinatra sang, she did it her way.

There was always an aura about her. Men that she reportedly dated included the aforementioned Francis Albert, Sean Connery, and William Holden, all many years her senior. She reputedly caused an Emerson, Lake and Palmer concert to be canceled because Greg Lake couldn't tear himself away from her charms. In the twenty-five years I knew her, though, her steady companion was a muscular assistant district attorney named Roy Kulcsar, who would pick her up in his Mercedes convertible many nights after her show. He accompanied her to hockey games, often with her friend Dani Greco, whom she introduced to everyone as her sister. There was a period in New York when she was considered the most desirable woman in a city filled with them. But the talent responsible for her seductiveness didn't come from any of the typical areas, although she was no slouch in those either. Quite simply, it was her voice. Deep, sexy, provocative.

Her mother was an opera singer, and young Alison (née Celia Loman) grew up around music, both classical and big band. She never talked about her father. Alison married and divorced bandleader Ted Steele at a very early age and it was that relationship that gave her a new name and began her career in television and radio. Her alliance with WNEW-FM came about in 1966, when she was selected from among four hundred audition-ees to become a disc jockey on the short-lived all-female format, originally doing afternoon drive. When the switch was made to progressive rock in 1967, she was fired three times by Nat Asch, but refused to leave. In fact, it was possible that the only reasons she was able to retain her job when the others were let go were her willingness to work overnights and her deter-mination to learn a style of music that had been completely foreign to her until then.

She began doing overnights on the progressive station in January of 1968, and quickly attracted a following of college-age men, who were suckers for her sexy presentation. Although in person she displayed a tough, slightly New York accent, on the air there was a distinct mid-Atlantic feel, most apparent in her pronunciation of "buhhd" as in "Night-bird." The voice of actress Kathleen Turner comes to mind.

She came up with the Nightbird in December of 1967, when she was on a two-week hiatus, having moved out of afternoons to make way for Scott Muni. It showed a side of Alison that would alternately haunt her and benefit her throughout her life. Whereas Schwartz and Muni had no shtick, Alison came up with an alter ego. In person, she was as hard-edged and pragmatic as anyone I've ever known. She smoked thin Nat Sherman cheroots—smelly, dark brown cigarettes that aspired to be cigars. She liked leather, and her outfits weren't bashful about showing off her lean build. You'd never see Alison less than completely made up, even at two in the morning. Her red hair was perfectly coiffed, a perpetual tan gracing her well-toned physique, even in the dead of winter. She could curse like a sailor. In the company of her fellow jocks, she was like one of the guys—laughing at their crude jokes, telling some herself, and showing no signs of vulnerability. I don't think I ever saw her in tears.

But on the air, she was spiritual, sensual, and gentle. As she began her show with some new-age poetry, read over Peruvian pipes, one was instantly transported to another sphere. Perhaps it was her classical background that caused her to favor bands like the Moody Blues, Yes, Renaissance, and Vangelis.

They say that the character "Mother" in the 1978 film *FM* was based on Alison. There was a certain nurturing quality about Alison when it came to young talent. She certainly was kind and helpful to Michael Harrison and me in our early days at the station, and she later took a mentoring role with Jo Maeder, who was known as the Rock and Roll Madame on various New York stations. But she also could be competitive and even fight dirty if her role as queen was threatened.

An example of this happened in 1973, when Carol Miller from WMMR joined the station. Carol came from Long Island, and was a pretty, dark-haired college girl working on a law degree. Unlike Alison, she was without pretense on the air, at least in her early days. She grew up with the music and was good at the technical aspects of presenting a program, something Alison could be lax with on occasion. Carol began working weekends, soon impressed Muni with her talent, and seemed to be a rising star.

Not long after Carol had been hired, WNEW-FM hosted a benefit concert for WNYU, the radio station at New York University, where she was attending graduate classes. Held at Town Hall, it featured David Bromberg and a host of artists from the Village folk-rock scene. As was his custom during the intermission, Muni came out onstage to introduce the troops. Alison was brought out last, since she always got the biggest ovation. Some of us took this as an indication of our relative popularity, but comparisons to Alison were discounted because of her spectacular appearance, especially from a slight distance. Alison played this to the hilt. There was once a summer concert in Central Park when she wore a thin leather halter top, a leather bikini bottom, with high boots and a bare midriff. Boys were literally falling out of trees to get a closer look. No telling how many dramas inside their pajamas it later inspired.

But that night at Town Hall, Carol, dressed simply in a granny skirt, got a huge ovation when brought onto the stage early on. When Alison came out, there was a noticeable chorus of boos amid the normal raucous applause. She stormed off with fire in her eyes; it was the first time she'd ever been upstaged by another woman and certainly the first time she'd been booed.

While doing her show a couple of nights later, Alison took requests.

She always liked to answer the phones and develop personal ties with her audience. That night, some callers claiming to be from NYU told her that Carol had deliberately incited some of her classmates to boo Alison. Since Steele had some acolytes at WNYU, she investigated further and others confirmed this. Alison immediately complained to general manager Varner Paulsen, and issued an ultimatum—either Carol goes or I go.

To be fair, no one really knows if Carol had anything to do with the response to Steele. At the time, it seemed pretty obvious why Alison was upstaged—Miller was twenty years younger, very attractive, and more accessible sounding on the air at a time when some college students were appreciative of that approach. But Alison was able to prove her case to Paulsen's satisfaction, and Carol was dismissed.

It was difficult for me to fully understand what Alison had to deal with because I had always respected her and saw her as a larger-than-life figure. But for her, life was a constant battle for acceptance in a male-dominated world. She always kept her age a closely guarded secret. Whereas Muni was seen as an éminence grise and the rest of us were fairly young (except Zacherle), Alison was fearful of being portrayed as a middle-aged woman playing kid's music. She also had credibility problems with her musical knowledge in the beginning, and even when she had caught up, she went out of her way to impress with her acumen in a manner that indicated insecurity. She was nearly fired several times in her first year, and I think that spurred her to work even harder to not just be an equal to the guys, but to be better.

Of course, male chauvinism did rear its head. There were those who just refused to accept that a woman could know and love rock, and present it properly. These people, many of them coworkers, were constantly seeking out chinks in her armor to prove that she was a fraud, whereas if a man showed similar weaknesses, it would be dismissed as minor. Her sex life was gossiped about in salacious tones, whereas a man sporting the same adventures would be admired.

Her liaisons with rock stars were legendary. One night, soon after young Marty Martinez had been hired by the WNEW newsroom, Alison asked him to do a favor for her. It seems that the building guard had called up to the station, saying that a dangerous-looking man was demanding to be let up to see her. He was driving an expensive car, and swore that he was friends with Steele but refused to reveal his identity. Would Marty go down and find out who the man was?

"Dangerous-looking" was right. The man wore an expensive custom-tailored suit, Italian loafers, silk shirt, and with his slicked-back black hair appeared to be the very image of a stereotypical mobster. The black Mercedes he drove completed the image.

"Can I help you, sir?" Martinez asked meekly.

"I want to see Alison. I'm a good friend."

"Can I ask who is calling?"

"Here." The man pulled out an elegant pen and scratched out a note, which he folded and gave to Martinez. "Take this to her."

As Marty turned to go, the man said, "Wait a minute, kid. Take this." He extracted some bills from a wallet and pressed them into his hand. Martinez was insulted at being treated like a bellhop, but since he wasn't sure who he was dealing with, he merely thanked the dark stranger and tucked the cash into his pants pocket. He brought the note to Steele, and as she read it, she burst out laughing.

"Oh, damn. Bring him up, Marty. It's my friend Gene."

Martinez looked at her quizzically, and then she whispered, "He doesn't like people to know who he is without his makeup. It's Gene Simmons from Kiss."

Not being a fan of the band he was unimpressed, and further bothered that a rock and roller would treat him like a servant. It wasn't until later, when he reached into his pocket to get some cash to pay for a sandwich, that he unfurled the wad Simmons had given him—three hundred-dollar bills. Martinez was less offended.

Steele had a way of breaking the ice with her rock-star interviews by posing questions that no man would ever ask. In 1978, Columbia Records finally convinced Bob Dylan, during a very cold phase of his career, to extend himself to radio in hopes that his latest venture might get some airplay. He reluctantly agreed to grant an audience surrounding his shows at Nassau Coliseum. Several WNEW jocks were driven out to the arena and ushered backstage, where they were seated in a semicircle around the diminutive legend. Dylan was clearly uncomfortable with the attention, and some of the jocks felt sorry for him, that this icon had to be subjected to relentless fawning from his admirers. This clearly wasn't the time to ask who "Sad-Eyed Lady of the Lowlands" was about. But Alison complimented him on his boots, and got him into a discussion about the best shops in the Village to get exotic footwear. Although some of her colleagues rolled their eyes, the exchange loosened Dylan up. He became much more comfortable in the setting, and actually seemed to enjoy himself as the dialogue continued.

Later, other women came into the market to challenge her title. Unlike Carol Miller, Meg Griffin was able to work at the station contemporaneously with Steele and to my knowledge there were never any problems between them. Maxanne Sartori, Carol, and Pam Merly all followed Alison, and Mary Turner made noise on a national level, but they all represented the next generation of women, who didn't have to overcome quite the same obstacles, largely because of the pioneering work done by Steele. She made it de rigueur to have at least one prominent time period reserved for a woman. That may sound like tokenism today, but in her time it was an accomplishment. And whereas she did fend off challenges from other women early on, she fought hard for her sister broadcasters later in her career, offering advice and encouragement to all who asked. None of her successors at the station achieved the legendary status that Alison did.

All in all, she deserves a huge amount of credit for paving the way for women to be taken seriously in broadcasting. Sadly, some of the beneficiaries of her struggle now only see the superficial trappings—the leather outfits and such—and are unable to understand the context of the times. There may have been other paths, but Alison Steele got there first.

L. A. Woman

IN 1975, METROMEDIA'S KMET in Los Angeles was ready to make a move. The station was completely free form, with jocks like B. Mitchell Reed, Raechel Donahue, and Tom O'Hare leading the way. The celebrated Shadoe Stevens had once been its program director but now ratings languished in the 1.2 range, although they were still marginally profitable. ABC's Rock in Stereo entry, KLOS, was dominating the market by a 4–1 margin. The time had come for a change, meaning its free-form days were over, at least temporarily.

L. David Moorhead was the general manager of KMET, and his appearance was similar to that of comedian Mike Myers's character Austin Powers. A man of sizable intellect, he wore thick glasses and his brown hair fashionably long. Unlike Powers, he favored modest business suits rather than psychedelia, but he shared Powers's propensity for being a bit on the chubby side. His personal life was also the subject of delicious rumor—divorces, drugs, scandal—but no one knew for sure. In some purely business ways, he was similar to his counterpart at WNEW, Mel Karmazin, in that he was a brilliant, ambitious man with an underperforming station.

When Michael Harrison left San Diego and landed in Los Angeles to work with Bob Wilson on the trade journal *Radio and Records,* the very real possibility loomed that his direct involvement with radio was over. But the first call that greeted his arrival was from L. David Moorhead.

"So you're out of radio, Michael?" he teased. "Do you miss it?"

Harrison was intrigued by Moorhead's question enough to join him for lunch the following day. Although he'd enjoyed success at KPRI and his WNEW morning ratings had not been forgotten by Metromedia, Michael had found his niche in publishing. Bob Wilson had become an intimate friend, and the two men and their wives spent the majority of their waking hours together. *Radio and Records* was providing a service specialized for radio's specific needs, not as a music business publication that treated radio as a sidelight. Although Harrison wasn't involved directly with any one station now, he was working with a host of stations on a number of levels. Managers, upon reading his work in the magazine, constantly called him for counsel, and many extended this to a formal arrangement where Harrison would consult their stations. He provided research, designed formats, tweaked marketing plans, and gave pep talks to their sales staffs.

But ever since he'd left WNEW, his sights were set on one job—programming KMET. His time in San Diego had convinced him that he could guide the sleeping giant to new heights if given the opportunity. Indeed, years before, Varner Paulsen had recommended him for the position, but at that time Moorhead had eschewed structuring the station, preferring to stay free form. At their lunch, he offered Harrison the job.

It was tempting, but his relationship with, and commitment to, Wilson prevented him from accepting. He felt he was building a lifelong business with *Radio and Records,* and program directors tended to last only a few years. But Harrison desperately wanted to involve himself with the struggling station, and he appreciated Moorhead as a visionary who saw radio in much the same terms he did. So he formulated a unique proposal—he would consult KMET in a confidential manner, in an arrangement that would only be known to Moorhead, sales manager Howard Bloom, and Moorhead's assistant, Samantha Bellamy.

Bellamy was involved in running the programming already, along with

Raechel Donahue and, until recently, Tom O'Hare. They made an odd troika. Raechel was estranged from her legendary husband, who was to pass on at the age of forty-six in April of that year. She was still a vital woman, but radio didn't seem to consume her life anymore. She enjoyed the freedom a show on KMET afforded her, but wasn't really interested in becoming a radio executive. O'Hare was a large, intimidating-looking man, with a droopy mustache and long, dark hair tied back in a ponytail, usually underneath a ten-gallon cowboy hat. He looked almost like a Cossack, with a brooding persona that belied the gentle man inside. He was a child of free form and had left in 1974 to program WQIV in New York. But much like Scott Muni at WNEW, programming a progressive station was a largely ceremonial position that involved hiring the right staff, gaining favor with the record labels, and developing ties with the local purveyors of culture. Very little attention was given to actually directing the jocks or the music.

But Sam Bellamy had ambition. She was a businesswoman who had little radio background, but was a quick study and was willing to do what it took to achieve success. She was selected to be Harrison's alter ego at KMET—she would act as program director and execute his plan.

And what was that plan? Much as he had done in San Diego, he first conducted some market research. To Harrison, research is best done informally, seeking the big picture rather than easily quantifiable details that don't help to achieve the objective. A common tool of scientific researchers is the focus group. Quite simply, a focus group is a select body of eight to twelve average people. They are gathered into a room, placed in front of a two-way mirror, and asked questions about the product being investigated. Politicians use them to gauge public opinion and corporations use them to market their products. Safeguards are taken to ensure that the answers given are honest and not influenced by outside forces. Most groups are not told of the sponsoring organization, although smart members can guess within minutes if the leader of the discussion doesn't carefully mask his intentions. They are paid a small fee, and walk away feeling that their opinions count.

The problem with focus groups is that they put their subjects in an artificial environment that is influenced by a group dynamic no matter how carefully they try to avoid it. An outspoken member can lead the others in directions they might not go on their own. People also tend to respond the way they are expected to, as opposed to revealing what they really think. Focus groups can be costly, so few stations can afford to do enough of them to reveal much of what they don't already know. But they look good on paper—an official-looking document that draws conclusions on people's opinions of a given product, in this case, a radio station.

One of Harrison's gifts is his universal taste, and by this I don't mean anything cosmic. It's his ability to think like Everyman when it comes to popular culture. He genuinely likes what's popular without passing judgment on it. His taste generally mirrors that of his audience because he *is* the audience. He could essentially program to please himself and be right a large percentage of the time. Michael could listen to an album and select the proper tracks for airplay instantly. He knew what people liked because he knew what *he* liked. But rather than rest on those laurels, especially in markets that were unknown to him, he'd perform his own brand of research. He'd walk through malls, hang out in clubs and bars, and talk to people in record stores. He wouldn't announce that he was Michael Harrison of KMET, but just engage everyday people in conversation to see what they liked and didn't like. It could be as simple a foray as, "Hey, I'm new in town. What's a cool rock station to listen to? Oh yeah? Why is that?"

More scientific types would dismiss this as anecdotal, but radio stations win or lose on intangibles that can't be easily quantified by formal research. After a few days of this informal polling and compiling the results in his head, he could get a handle on what people wanted. Combined with creativity, Harrison could then forge a radio station that would appeal to the masses, without condescending, because he liked what he was hearing as well.

To further gauge what was happening in Los Angeles, he asked Moorhead to give him a show on the station—a talk show. But L. David Moorhead did his own listener feedback show at KMET, "Mangle the Manager," which aired 10 P.M. to midnight Sundays following the popular Dr. Demento. He offered Harrison the Saturday morning, six to noon shift—6 to 9 A.M. being a talk show, and nine to noon, a music show. He was also free to do fill-ins whenever called upon. The talk show soon became known by the catchy moniker *Harrison's Mike.*

With Sam Bellamy programming under Harrison's governance, the station grew and within two years eclipsed KLOS in the ratings. Michael met with Moorhead on a regular basis, and would sneak into the station at night and mark tracks to play, organize the library, and refine the formatics.

The staff suspected that Harrison's involvement was more than that of a part-time jock but he had no other official title. He was content to let Bellamy take credit for the station's rise, happy to accept the remuneration and inner satisfaction of knowing that he retained control. There was a system to direct the music, but the jocks were encouraged to develop their own wacky personalities. Promotions and tie-ins with local concerts and sporting events abounded. In many ways, Harrison was refining Rick Sklar's formula for success at WABC a decade earlier for a new generation of FM listeners.

Harrison had some bizarre experiences while living in Los Angeles. Through *Radio and Records,* he began a series of artist interview programs that would be syndicated to stations across the country. The first was done in 1976 with a reunited Jefferson Starship, looking to make a comeback with their *Red Octopus* album. He traveled to KSAN territory, to the famous Starship house in Haight-Ashbury, to interview each member separately. An old Victorian manse with dozens of rooms, it accommodated the band's business offices and studios, additionally serving as a crash pad for the group and their entourage. Grace Slick insisted on being interviewed while in bed, with Harrison sitting alongside. Therefore he can always brag about how he went to bed with Grace Slick.

But he took a few useful lessons away from the encounter. First, it taught him how splintered a successful rock band can become—how petty jealousies and slights are magnified until they collapse the band's structure from within. Democracy rarely works in rock; too many talented leaders generally pull in different directions until the whole is shattered. The group dynamic is like a corporation—everyone tries to take credit for success and likewise distance themselves from failure.

The second thing he learned was how easily two hundred stations could be signed on to take the program nationally. Unlike the situation today with consolidation, stations who didn't take a special program back then risked losing it to their competition. An ambitious entrepreneur could hustle for exclusive interviews and be heard across the country. Now, since large groups control multiple stations in each market, there is no incentive to take premium programming from outside sources. Competition is squelched and quality can suffer as a result.

By far, the strangest journey he took involved the mysterious Cat Stevens. He was commissioned to put together a special program, high-

lighting the final album the reclusive singer was to make before becoming
an Islamic minister. He was warned that Steve (his real name being Steven
Georgiou) could be difficult, and that Michael might not get much out of
him during the interview. But Harrison was a huge fan of the man's music,
and was prepared to write off any eccentricities as the vagaries of artistic
temperament. He'd seen such behavior a hundred times before, with
friends like Lou Reed and David Clayton-Thomas of Blood, Sweat and
Tears.

He was flown to Minneapolis, where Stevens was mixing the final
tracks in a stately old mansion on the outskirts of town. His flight arrived at
midnight, and he was met at the airport by a chauffeur in an antique Rolls-
Royce. As he traveled forty minutes through the snow-covered Minnesota
hills, he felt like a modern Renfield on his way to visit Count Dracula. The
whole nighttime journey took on a foreboding nature as the Rolls pulled
up to the majestic gated residence. He was led down to a cavernous studio
where Stevens sat behind a prodigious mixing console, tinkering with the
single "Remember the Days (of the Old Schoolyard)." The handsome
artist greeted Harrison warmly, and bade him to sit while he put the finishing touches on the track.

Michael watched in awe and wonderment as the black-bearded Rasputin
attended the details of the final mix. Stevens paused several times to ask for
Michael's opinion, but the young broadcaster would only issue encouragement, feeling it was inappropriate to criticize a sensitive performer who
made such meticulously crafted records.

Finally, at around 3 A.M., the song was finished and the two men retreated to another room to set up for the interview, with comfortable
leather chairs and a bottle of whiskey, two glasses and two expensive cigars
carefully set out on an oak table. As they fired up the cigars and sipped their
drinks, Michael asked questions. Stevens responded freely and openly, discussing his childhood, romances, and music. As they spoke, Harrison was
puzzled how anyone could consider his subject to be difficult, since it was
the most candid dialogue that he'd ever had in a professional situation. The
conversation rambled on for nearly two hours, and when it concluded,
both men seemed enraptured with the outcome.

Harrison was chauffeured back to a hotel, and plans were made for
him and Stevens to be picked up later that morning for flights to their separate destinations. Stevens's flight departed first, and Harrison helped him

carry his guitar cases and kept him company until takeoff. As they said their farewells, Michael sensed that he'd formed a lifelong bond with an artist he held in high esteem.

Back in Los Angeles several days later, he received the raw tape for editing and was impressed again with the quality of the interview and the kindness of his new friend. He also knew that he had a winner of a radio program, and hoped that his efforts would help boost the career of the artist he genuinely admired.

The next day, he was very surprised to receive a stern call from Stevens's management. The interview was never to see the light of day, he was told. He would be sued if any part of it aired anywhere in the country. He was denied permission to mention anything he'd been told, and was asked to immediately return or destroy the tape. When he protested that the interview would only do favorable things for the artist, astonishing news was delivered. Stevens was maintaining that Harrison had hypnotized him without his consent during the interview, and that he'd forced him to say things that were either untrue or too personal to be revealed.

Although Michael had hoped that the talk would be spellbinding, this wasn't what he had in mind. He sadly filed the tape in his archives where it has gathered dust for the last quarter century. Although he has recently agreed to do interviews, the most notice Stevens (now Yusuf Islam) has received was when he explained why Islamic law declared that Salman Rushdie must die. His statements were misunderstood by the media to mean that Stevens supported slaying the novelist, when in fact he advocated no such thing. As punishment, many radio stations publicly burned his albums and banned them from the scant airplay they were receiving.

Not all his experiences with major rock stars ended so badly. Dark Horse Records had asked him to produce a special for George Harrison's *33⅓* (a double entendre based on the speed at which an album revolves and Harrison's age while recording it). Much like Dave Herman during the same period, he was invited to meet Harrison at his home in the Hollywood Hills. George was then spending a lot of time with Monty Python's Eric Idle, both in friendship and as executive producer of the Python films. The plan was for Michael to spend a few days in get-acquainted sessions with the ex-Beatle at his abode, and then conduct the interview in a relaxed, trusting atmosphere. The twenty-seven-year-old broadcaster drove alone into the hills, knocked on the massive door, and was amazed when George himself answered, barefoot and clad in blue jeans and a T-shirt. He gave Michael a tour of the property and made small talk about their shared surname. As their initial conversation wound down, he suddenly exclaimed, "I've something to show you, if you have the time."

Unlike Herman, Michael had no flight to catch and readily agreed to stay as long as his company was welcome. George led him to a guest bedroom, dominated by a large-screen television. He popped a cassette into the VCR and explained, "This is something new. Have you heard my song 'Crackerbox Palace'?" Michael had done his homework and was familiar with the entire album, so he nodded.

"Good," Harrison continued. "My friend Eric Idle and I put this together. It's the first of its kind . . . a little movie about a song. We're calling it a 'rock video' and it'll run on *Saturday Night Live* next week. Tell me what you think."

Michael was blown away, sitting on the edge of a bed with George watching the tape. He was agog with the idea that just years before, he was a teenager idolizing the Beatles. Now, here he was hanging out with George Harrison and chatting like old friends. His head swirled as he mused that he was seeing a firsthand preview of something that could revolutionize the music world. Later, he realized that the Beatles movies could actually be viewed as full-length rock videos on film, adding to the band's rich legacy. George fully understood that this new genre would be a major force in exposing music, as it was to become some five years later when MTV debuted.

As with Cat Stevens, he could only offer praise for the extraordinary footage he had just witnessed. The actual interview for the project was done at the MCA studios in front of a small audience. Most thought the show was tremendous, although critics suggested that he was too soft on George. Remember, this was a time when the quiet Beatle was being dismissed by the media as a lightweight, but Michael had far too much respect for this gentle, cerebral man to ambush him with confrontational questions.

Harrison was doing well with his syndication but the cozy consulting arrangement between him and Sam Bellamy at KMET began to chafe. Bellamy resented Harrison's authority over her, and petitioned Moorhead for more autonomy. He gradually weaned her off Michael's tutelage. She had proven a good student, and with her quick mind and full-time concentration, she took the station to heights beyond what it had reached when Michael called the shots. For his part, he was happy to relinquish control since he was involved in so many other activities. He would meet with Moorhead and Bloom a couple of times a month for general strategy sessions, but as time rolled on, it was clearly Sam Bellamy's station. Ratings reached the six-share level and KMET was making John Kluge a lot of money.

Meanwhile, Harrison and Bob Wilson were having their problems. They were constantly arguing over philosophy and direction for *Radio and Records* until their once tight relationship was breached beyond repair. Harrison splintered off to form his own company, Goodphone Communications, which published a tip sheet aimed at AOR stations. He worked with Norm Pattiz and Westwood One Radio Network to develop more syndicated programs, while continuing his Saturday morning involvement with KMET, which was now garnering monster ratings. It proved so popular that the mayor of Los Angeles was moved to proclaim a Michael Harrison Day in his honor.

But as the sun began to set on the seventies, hubris caused KMET to lose its way again. Intoxicated by their success, the jocks were demanding more musical freedom and Bellamy was giving it to them. KLOS remained a steady AOR presence, and KROQ had signed on to champion the new-wave and punk-rock movement. KMET was now outflanked—one station was steering down the middle of the road, picking up casual listeners who were turned off by KMET's eclecticism, and the younger listeners seeking new music were flocking to KROQ.

By 1979, KMET had become totally free form again, with all the wonderful creativity that offered. But the station was also subject to the maddening musical inconsistency that undisciplined progressive jocks fall prey to. In a highly competitive market, ratings were sagging with the onslaught of the two other stations, not to mention the emerging popularity of Rick Dees and his revitalized Top Forty concept on KIIS. Los Angeles was the market where Bill Drake's BOSS radio was fostered, proving that a well-executed Top Forty station could always be a potent force in the market. KMET needed help, and Moorhead was lost in a morass of personal problems. He'd been unable to bring Bellamy back to the formula that had given the station its initial success. He was fired, and longtime sales manager Howard Bloom was elevated to the general manager's post to stanch the bleeding. It seemed that free-form radio in Los Angeles was doomed once again.

I Didn't Expect the Spanish Inquisition

IN THE LATE SEVENTIES, overnights weren't subject to Arbitron, not that ratings seemed to matter much anyway. Between 2 and 6 A.M., I was able to play and say whatever I wanted. Management rarely was up that late, and I felt I could push the envelope with impunity. One night I met a woman who happened to be a jazz fan. She didn't like WNEW-FM—she felt it was too sterile because we didn't play enough jazz. In reality, I played almost none, only the Mahavishnu Orchestra and an occasional Chick Corea or Herbie Hancock fusion piece. But that night, I told her to listen and she might be surprised.

I dug out every jazz album in the library and devoted two thirds of my show to it. It worked and she was demonstratively impressed, but I later felt that I had cheated my audience to satisfy my libido. I never sank to that level again, but it was an early lesson in the power we all had to affect people simply by playing a song or mentioning their name on the radio.

But there was a price to pay for working in the relative obscurity of the overnights. It was safe in terms of job security but you would never be a star or even a major player. If you did well for an extended period, you could attract a loyal following. Most listeners to the station would know your name but would rarely actually listen. You could draw fans at colleges, where students stayed up late studying or partying, and fellow late-shift workers, but the average nine-to-fiver would never know what you did. Management tended to forget you. This could be good and bad. They never would hassle you for doing something that might get you into trouble in another day part. But when it came time to advance, you were rarely considered.

So I endeavored to expand my role past overnights almost as soon as I started doing them. Within the first two years, I had managed to land the Saturday 10 A.M. to 2 P.M. slot, and a Sunday evening program to go along with three all-night shows. For some unexplained reason, the Saturday midday shift was the highest rated on the station. I kept the music very up-tempo and familiar, limited my raps, and boosted my own energy level from the laid-back style I employed overnight. Sunday nights became my time for interviews and I closed the show with a classical piece, usually something accessible like the *1812 Overture* or "Jupiter" from *The Planets*.

It was on this show that I did the first American interview with Monty Python. I discovered them strictly by chance. While sorting through albums one day in my Lefrak City apartment, I came upon this strange-looking record that I couldn't make heads or tails of. But since WNEW-FM believed that it was our continuing responsibility to break new artists, I dropped a needle on it. At first, I couldn't understand what I was hearing. Something about the Spanish Inquisition. The liner notes were some prattle about the Swedish prime minister, so I found nothing there to enlighten me about this group, if in fact they were a group. Maybe it was just one man named Monty Python. By the time the first side was over, I was pounding the floor in laughter. I couldn't wait to play some of their bits on the air to expose this bizarre brand of humor to our audience. Since WNEW and its listeners were predisposed to like anything British, I figured this would be a home run.

I played cuts from the album on the overnights and got little reaction from anyone. But when I played some of their stuff during the Sunday show, the phones went crazy. The following week, I was contacted by their record company. Did I think that this could make it here in the States? They had planned to release the record with very little publicity and see if it found an audience before they would commit to any major promotional campaign. I gave it an enthusiastic thumbs-up, and before long, other jocks turned on to their antics. The record began to sell, and they were brought over to America to do press. I wasn't sure if they were nervous, jet-lagged, or what, but the interview was peculiarly serious and not very funny. It was a disappointment but subsequent visits went much better and their success was almost unparalleled in the annals of British comedy.

But that's just one example of the influence we all had to make something happen. Since most of the major record labels were based in New York, the support of WNEW could mean more to an artist than that of a station with higher ratings in another market. Most of the big record executives listened to WNEW all day, to check their own airplay and to monitor what competitive labels were promoting. But it took more than the advocacy of one jock to make a record successful. If the support ended with one individual, nothing much would develop. But everyone on the air listened to everyone else's show (stationality), and therefore Dave Herman, who always appreciated and played good comedy, adopted Python, as did Alison and Muni somewhat later. With that kind of support, a record company is encouraged to throw its weight behind a project and you might have a smash.

It's no wonder, then, that the record promoters took us all seriously, even the lowly overnight man. It was important to get DJs to listen to new product by any means possible. There were a few standard ways to do this, the most basic being a listening party.

For a small investment, the record company would rent a restaurant on a night when they might normally be closed, provide a sumptuous meal, and invite key DJs from all the important stations. Sometimes, they'd do this in every major market, and sometimes they'd hold one in New York and one in Los Angeles and fly in programmers from other cities. Rarely will any member of the media decline free food and entertainment. The artists themselves were generally present, to perform live or just circulate while their record played in the background.

A variation on listening parties were receptions held after performances. Dinner at six, show at eight, party at eleven. Generally, a team of promotion men would divide up responsibilities. Sometimes, when there were heated rivalries with competing stations, one man would squire the WNEW jocks while another would handle WPLJ. At other less warlike times, a group of people from several stations would be taken to dinner collectively, whisked to a concert, and then brought to a postperformance bash.

Monty Python had one of these in the Time-Life Building on Sixth Avenue after a performance at City Center. In addition to DJs, key celebs were also invited so that newspapers would pick up on gossip and further publicize the group. At the Python party, Dennis Elsas and I were talking shop in a corner of the spacious room when a flamboyant-looking man with a shock of distinguished gray hair approached us.

"And who might you be, you handsome young fellow?" the man asked Dennis, swirling his long black cape. He'd obviously had a bit too much to drink, but there was something familiar about him.

"I'm Dennis Elsas, sir. It's an honor to meet you." Dennis is a polite fellow, but I never saw him be this deferential to a stranger. The short man in the cape and tuxedo beamed at him, and proceeded to flirt mischievously.

Elsas looked a bit uncomfortable, but said, "My mother is such a big fan of yours. Wait until I tell her we've met."

The man mumbled something as he realized that Dennis was not interested in anything more than conversation. He gracefully whirled away from us and glided across the room to chat up another group.

"My God, Dennis. Was that Leonard Bernstein?"

"It was. I never knew he was so short."

At these parties, you could meet anyone—from the mayor to famous athletes to performers in all fields of entertainment. Schwartz and Fornatale weren't into that scene. Dave Herman lived in Connecticut at that time and had to be in early, so you rarely saw him. You might encounter jocks from PLJ, but as their power to program their own music diminished, their invitations dwindled proportionately. It was all legal, as long as you kept the entertainment below the financial limit imposed by Metromedia as protection against payola. And we all had to sign a disclosure form on a yearly basis that affirmed we hadn't received special favors for airplay.

Lunches with artists were another means of promotion. Usually, the performer was scheduled for an interview with Muni in the afternoon. The entourage would arrive at noon, and Scottso and the music director or any other jock who happened to be around would be taken to lunch at the

Palm or "21" or any prestigious restaurant within walking distance. The artist and Muni would get to know each other over the meal if they hadn't been previously associated.

I'll never forget my first experience with this. José Feliciano had made a record that his label believed could be played on rock stations and they were bringing him around to promote it. He was a major star on the easy-listening stations and the subject of some controversy for his rendition of the national anthem at the World Series in 1968. We sat in a fancy restaurant with his German shepherd guide dog lying at his feet. Many of the other patrons, not recognizing Feliciano, complained to management about the well-behaved dog's presence until it was explained to them. They nodded and proceeded to gawk at José for the remainder of the meal.

It always amazed me how shy most artists are when not performing. At a similar lunch with Roy Orbison, he was monosyllabic. It wasn't that he was standoffish or unfriendly, but he was uncomfortable putting words to his feelings with strangers unless it was in song. So many other musicians were the same way. The exceptions were folks like Elton John and Pete Townshend, who were hams at heart and loved pressing the flesh with the media, although often fortified with alcohol while doing so. Elsas once interviewed Townshend about a solo release, but soon found him talking about the Who with such reverence and respect that it became obvious that Pete was the biggest fan the band could have. Townshend knew and appreciated what his group meant to the public, and always made himself available to radio people. He once excoriated WNEW producer Marty Martinez for wearing headphones. "They'll make you deaf, they will," he expounded. "Wore 'em meself onstage for years, now I'm deaf as a post."

"What?" Martinez replied.

Muni interviewed Jimmy Page of Led Zeppelin one afternoon and was stunned when the colorful guitarist collapsed onto the floor in mid-sentence. Scott quickly put a record on and rushed to the musician's aid. No harm was done—Page had been out partying for days on end and had merely fallen asleep while talking with Scottso. They placed the guest microphone on the floor, and Page did the remainder of the interview from a supine position.

One of the most enjoyable nights I ever had was in the company of Rick Springfield, who had several hits and was a huge soap-opera star but had little credibility with AOR stations, which saw him as just a pop star. Springfield, local A&M promoter Rick Stone, and I went to a small Indian restaurant, where we got rip-roaring drunk and spent most of the night re-creating Monty Python routines. Springfield, for all his fame at the time, was a down-to-earth fellow with a lively wit and a lot of talent who happened to be cursed/blessed with a teen-idol face. Like a buxom blond actress who no one takes seriously, his skills were underestimated by AOR stations swayed by his pretty-boy appearance.

There were many times when you'd be wined and dined by record promoters when no artist was around, or taken to a sporting event when there was nothing specifically to hype. I went to the 1973 World Series games at Shea Stadium with Herb Alpert of A&M, just to create goodwill toward the label. And that was important. During the early seventies, there might be ten albums a week that were ticketed for rock airplay. Even with our liberal policies, scattering airplay among that many records did no one any good.

During that era we might play a song or two an hour by totally new artists. There might be thirty-six slots a day when a nonestablished performer might get airplay. With forty records a month, if everyone got equal spins, each artist might get exposed once a day, not nearly enough to mean anything. Six plays a day at minimum were needed to make any kind of impact. At a progressive station, that meant at least four jocks solidly behind the record—no easy task, given their diverse tastes. So a record company had to hope they'd created enough credibility with the jocks so that a promoter could ask that his offering be considered above the others.

This put us in a tough spot sometimes. When promoters became your "friends" they would ask for favors, like playing a record you didn't like in order to "help them out." You'd hear entreaties like "My job's at stake, man," and you'd want to be sympathetic. But ultimately, playing a bad record helped no one. The listeners would turn you off, or at least question your taste. And if the record was truly bad, no amount of airplay would cause it to sell, so the promoter didn't benefit much. And you hurt other artists who deserved the play more. So most of us took our responsibilities seriously and tried to judge what we played impartially, without succumbing to pressure from the labels. We all had moments of weakness, though, where we tried to help out friends when the decisions weren't so clear-cut.

Imagine auditioning all that new music and trying to decide what was good enough for attention and what wasn't, often based on one listen. And how did the mood you were in affect how you responded? A soft, sensitive ballad could speak volumes to you when you're feeling low, but might get dismissed as sentimental pap if you're in the mood to rock.

You also had to separate your personal feelings toward an artist from your aesthetic judgment. Over the years, you do become friendly with a handful of performers, and sometimes they don't make records that your station can support.

A good example was Styx. James Young of that Detroit band became a buddy of mine for a period in the early eighties. He was interested in drag racing and took me to Englishtown, New Jersey, on several occasions to hang with Shirley Muldowney, a friend of his and a truly extraordinary woman. But Styx never really got the kind of airplay at WNEW that they had in the rest of the country, where they were considered the biggest band of the seventies. Most of our jocks dismissed them as hopelessly corporate.

My advocacy did help the career of a man who made records that no one considered to be rock and roll. A&M records had invited me to check out one of their new artists at a late-night club date. The previous overnight, I'd played Harry Nilsson's rendition of the great standard "As Times Goes By." A favorite of mine since first hearing it in the film *Casablanca,* I was delighted when Nilsson's version gave me an excuse to play it.

The following evening, I went to see A&M's latest find at Reno Sweeney's. The small Greenwich Village club was packed for the late show, and the audience included celebrities like Candice Bergen. In the middle of a rollicking set with his small combo, the artist stopped and said, "You know, I heard this song on the radio last night, and I've been thinking about it ever since. So here goes." I got chills, knowing he must have been talking about my show. He then proceeded to do a killer performance of "When Time Goes By." I went backstage to meet him afterward, and immediately fell in love with his outrageous personality. I spread the word of his talent to all my colleagues and unlike the situation with Styx, they gladly piled onto the bandwagon. My friend reached enormorous heights, from his humble beginnings as an Australian singer-songwriter playing bars in the Far East to his own Broadway show. I saw dozens of his live performances—each one more flamboyant than the next—and I was proud to have a small part in introducing the world to Peter Allen.

Likewise, your disdain for an artist's personality shouldn't be a factor in deciding airplay, but it's hard to ignore. When the Pretenders' first album was released, the station played it heavily. Warner Bros., their record label, pressured us to interview Chrissie Hynde on Scott Muni's program months before she arrived in the States. We felt that she needed a greater body of work before putting her on with Muni in the afternoon. But we liked the record so much that I agreed to interview her on tape and replay it during Scott's show while I filled in for him. The taping was set for 2 P.M. and would be aired the next day if all went well.

At 2 P.M., no Chrissie Hynde. Hours passed with no sign of her. Finally at four-thirty, the harried Warner's rep appeared and apologized profusely. "Chrissie was delayed," he said. "She really is into this but the print people have kept her longer than we thought and she's on her way. Set up your tape and she'll be here in a minute."

Ten minutes later, a bedraggled-looking Hynde walked into the station with another promotion man. She stank of sweat and alcohol and was so rumpled it appeared as if she'd just rolled out of bed. She half sneered upon being introduced, and our offer of coffee was met with a rude "Don't want any of that shit."

I raised my eyebrows at the rep and guided her into the production studio, where I sat her behind the microphone.

"How long will this shit take?" she asked.

"We've been ready to go since two. We can start now," I said, feeling the anger rise.

"Right. Let's get this shit over with, then," she snorted.

After waiting over two hours, I was in no mood for a hostile interview. It wasn't like we were doing this for our benefit. It was a favor to the label since I was content just to play the album. I said that I was under the impression that she welcomed the exposure such a forum would provide.

She rolled her eyes. "Who told you that? The frigging record company? I was out late last night, drinking and screwing around with my mates. I just got up. This is the last place I want to be right now with a bunch of frigging radio people, doing a frigging worthless interview." ("Frigging" was not the exact word she used.) Angrily pulling off her headphones, she bolted the studio, stomping right past the astonished promoter.

"What happened?" he said to me. "What did you say to tick her off?" He was torn between finishing his business with the station and pursuing his fleeing diva.

As much as I wanted to shove the Pretenders' album into a place where only Hynde's proctologist would discover it, it was too good to ignore or penalize. I just shrugged and we continued to support the Pretenders.

Love over Gold

THE MOST FEARED, respected, and hated man in FM radio for almost two decades was Lee Abrams. The very mention of his name incited controversy wherever he went, and to this day his contributions are viewed by some with admiration and by others with contempt.

Lee grew up in the Chicago area listening to AM radio from stations across the country. Since the city is centrally located, he was able to hear not only the great stations of the Midwest like WLS and WCFL, but WABC, WBZ, and some of the powerhouses from the East Coast and Southern regions as well. Abrams was something of a child prodigy, playing and managing in rock bands in high school, and he designed a radio format based on his experiences.

He was an early advocate of research, initially doing a crude form of exit polling as people left concerts or club dates. In the mid-sixties, he picked up on the disenchantment many felt for Top Forty, and foresaw the rise of progressive radio on FM. He envisioned a modified Top Forty station that didn't play bubblegum music, featured a broader playlist, and eschewed screaming, mindless jocks. However, he didn't embrace the free-form stations of the time, considering them too political and too extreme in their bizarre music. He felt that there was a third way—to change the familiarity factor from the songs to the artists. Therefore, although listeners might not recognize a particular tune, they would be comfortable identifying the artist. Spending his summers in Miami, he was able to latch on as a gopher at WQAM and learn how the business worked firsthand. WMYQ gave him his first shot at programming in southern Florida, and the ratings were impressive.

Abrams is a promotional wizard above all. When he sets his sights on something, he blitzes it with every technique known to man. When WRIF, an ABC affiliate in Detroit, was going through the same kind of political mess that was occurring at WPLJ in 1971, Abrams hit them with a direct-mail campaign to sell his services to them as a program director. Armed with the success in Miami and a speaking voice that belied his eighteen years, he convinced the brass to meet him in Florida, whereupon he dazzled them with a one-hour presentation. They asked for another meeting in Chicago, and finally offered him the job. Although they didn't allow him the freedom to wholly implement his plan, he did take the station from a 1.6 share to a 4.1 within a year. By this time, he'd been contacted by a Raleigh, North Carolina, FM station, which he agreed to consult on the sly. When ABC found out about his outside activities, they issued an ultimatum—either us or them. Abrams chose consulting, and quickly picked up another station, WRNO in New Orleans.

By now, his success was being noticed throughout the business, largely through his own promotional efforts. Superstars, as he dubbed his programming system, paralleled what Harrison had refined at KPRI and KMET and was not far philosophically from what we did at WLIR, although it was far more rigidly structured. Abrams was still small-time, though, and had to turn down jobs because he lacked the resources to fly into other cities and consult. He needed an infusion of capital and a partner, and he found one in Kent Burkhardt. Kent had been running an old-school AM consulting firm out of Atlanta, and Abrams met him at an industry convention. He convinced the older man that FM was the coming thing and that in order to have a more complete consultancy, Burkhardt needed to expand his horizons. It took them less than twenty minutes to hammer out a deal.

With the money and power of Burkhardt/Abrams behind him, Lee was able to annex dozens of new stations to his broadcasting empire, including the Taft Group. Each situation was different, but since he still only had a limited staff, much of his research was aimed at a national audience as opposed to many local ones.

His prime area of knowledge came from "call back" cards. He arranged for certain key record stores to include cards with every rock album they sold, which the customer would fill out and send in, and after two weeks, a representative of his company would call back the purchaser with several questions. They were along the lines of "Now that you've had a couple of weeks to live with *Thick as a Brick* by Jethro Tull, what do you think? What cuts do you like? What radio stations do you listen to?"

With these calls, he was able to find out some interesting things. One early example concerned Miles Davis's *Bitches Brew,* which was selling very well and getting airplay on progressive stations. Abrams was able to glean that although its purchasers really enjoyed the album, they were inclined to listen to jazz stations, not rock, and therefore it shouldn't be played. Earth, Wind and Fire posed a similar dilemma for FM programmers, and Abrams was able to provide some clues. The unfortunate side effect of this research was to eliminate a lot of the R&B music that had found its way onto progressive stations as spice. In most circumstances, this wasn't an outcropping of racism, merely the myopia of the research. What dry research fails to grasp is whereas listeners might indicate a partiality to Led Zeppelin, hearing too many of the same songs by that band could turn them off. It is analogous to surveying diners on their favorite food. They might tell you that they prefer steak. But if you serve them steak every night, they will tire of it and beg you for anything else. Their response when questioned would still be that steak is their favorite. But like any positive reinforcement, you get better results when you reward Pavlov's dog intermittently, instead of every time he performs his trick. Zeppelin blended with other popular genres will work better than a monotonous mix of Zeppelin, Whitesnake, and all their other imitators.

Another method Abrams used was to hand out questionnaires at concerts and asking the attendees to fill out specific questions about what songs they liked and what other bands they wanted to hear on the radio. Obviously, much of this was subjective, and had to be interpreted by someone who knew the music and understood the lifestyle issues of the audience. Like Michael Harrison, Lee believed in mixing with average listeners and getting a feel for what they liked. The problem was, as his business grew, he was able to spend less time doing that and more time in airports and hotels, sequestered away with radio insiders who would skew his perceptions.

The obvious problem with this broadband approach is that every market has local eccentricities and that Abrams's research doesn't allow for these. His standard reply was that the 90 percent of the country who liked FM rock favored the same songs by the same bands. The remaining 10 percent reflected local differences and were up to his individual program directors to decide. The 90 percent seemed an arbitrary figure, but the point was taken.

For consultants like Abrams and his stations, the delegation of authority could be a thorny issue. Lee's deal was made with an individual general manager or a group manager of stations. Abrams would have final say, and could hire and fire the program director and jocks. At these stations, he bore total responsibility for what happened, good or bad. But many stations had existing PDs and jocks in place and were doing well, and only wanted suggestions from Burkhardt/Abrams for fine tuning. This could alternately be frustrating and affirmative for both parties. If ratings improved, the consultant would take the credit; if it failed, he could always tell management that his orders were not being followed properly. Either way, with Abrams's ability to spin events in his favor, his firm looked good.

His greatest successes came in markets where he could regiment a self-indulgent free-form station musically, while allowing the jocks to be creative between the records. Sets and segues were not important in Lee's scheme, only the right mix of music that gave the station the consistency, or stationality, he sought. He used a card system and clock, so that the individual jocks were limited to playing what was selected by the program director. Jocks hated to hear that Lee was coming in to consult because they knew that it meant the end of their freedom musically.

One could make a case that if the freedom had been used responsibly in the first place, there would be no need for people like Abrams. Radio is not rocket science, and anyone who was even modestly perceptive could figure out how to be successful in the seventies. But there was an attitude shared by many jocks that their show was an extension of their personalities, and that they had to select their own music to perform at their highest potential. Once that freedom was taken away, they merely became voices relating to nothing.

I've seen this from both sides. When I was just a disc jockey, after a few self-indulgent months of total liberty doing overnights, I came to realize that if I did a show to please only myself, I was pleasing an audience of one. Like Harrison, I believe that most of my choices are universally applicable to a mass audience. The difficulty comes with a record that you know people want, but you don't particularly like. The reverse is when you like something that isn't going to appeal to the masses. A responsible free-form jock will exert the self-discipline to limit or eliminate personal favorites that lack commercial potential, and concentrate on songs that are popular. If you can't appreciate most of those, then it's time to seek another form of employment.

But when the freedom is taken away completely and one is left with a computer printout, it completely kills the jock's involvement in programming music. As much as consultants can tell you that DJs should focus on their talk segments, so much of what was talked about in progressive radio sprang directly from the music. Without its inspiration, many jocks descend into vapid talk about the weather. At WNEW, where we were billed as "musicologists," the idea of having no choice diminished the personalities into wanna-be comedians, and many weren't skilled in that area.

Program directors are in a similar box: If they don't control the music, they risk the mistakes that an inexperienced jock or an arrogant veteran might make. If they totally strip their staff of its musical discretion, they can wind up with a bland jukebox. They also ignore consultants at their own peril, knowing that they'll be criticized to upper management if their digressions from the formula aren't fruitful. The other option is to blindly follow the consultant's lead, and hazard the reprobation that they aren't perceptive enough to call their own shots when the advice is leading them in the wrong direction. They also have to fight off the perception among the jocks that they are merely puppets, following some out-of-town bully's directives.

Stations choose to handle this in different ways. If the program director and general manager have a strong, trusting relationship, the consultant's input is merely weighed in with several other factors and can be contravened. But other PDs are told that since "we're spending all this money on a consultant, we should heed his counsel." These programmers usually don't last long and are replaced by someone in the consultant's stable of disciples who is willing to move up the food chain with him.

For all of the flaws that a consultant might bring to the table, Abrams at least understood the good things about free form and tried to incorporate them into his plan. "Perfect album sides" were an endorsement of when jocks were legitimately excited about a record and wanted to play a side in its entirety. Abrams merely identified the albums worthy of this and scheduled them at strategic times. He liked "Twofer Tuesdays," where a station would play two songs in a row from each featured artist—a scaled-down version of Muni's miniconcerts. He subscribed to occasional thematic sets, but selected the songs on their individual merit and not just because they fit the theme. These elements sprang from early progressive radio; the difference was that under Abrams, they were planned and selected by the programmers as opposed to the jocks. At a skillfully executed Superstars station, it was hard for the average listener to tell it wasn't free form. If the jocks played their roles properly, they could manufacture enthusiasm and make it sound like these preconceived elements were actually spontaneous. And if the jocks did discover a band or song independently, they could run it up the chain of command and their input might be heeded and even valued.

Some of Abrams's Superstars elements were original, but many of them were the creation of individual jocks and programmers at the stations he consulted. One of the benefits of working with a consultant is that each week you receive a newsletter that alerts you to programming and promotional ideas that have worked in other markets. The challenge is then to adapt the ones you fancy to your individual situation. That's why you hear many of the same features on different stations across the country, with only minor variations in their execution.

Some program directors found a way of dealing with Abrams that kept his reach away from their territory. In the seventies, Lee suffered from common human weaknesses involving sex, drugs, and rock and roll. If a programmer could keep him supplied with enough of each, Abrams wouldn't have enough time in his short visits to critique the programming, and the PD could enjoy more autonomy.

Lee's bitter rival was Jeff Pollack, who began his consultancy after achieving success at WMMR in Philadelphia in the early eighties. According to Abrams, the difference in their approach was that Lee wanted talented jocks who could do much more than just read liner cards promoting the station's activities. He encouraged personality, always believed that if two stations played the same music, the vital, jock-driven one would outdistance the sterile "shut up and play the music" outlet. He wanted "cinematic" radio with scope and dimension, whereas Pollack required tightly controlled automatons who reverberated the call letters with maddening frequency. Although Lee was rigid in his insistence that the jock be kept away from the music selection, Pollack took it a step further with presentation. In some ways, this reflected the differences between Rick Sklar's strategies at WABC versus Bill Drake's BOSS radio concept. Sklar, before he came to see jocks as "spark plugs," valued their individual personalities, whereas Drake saw them as replaceable parts from the beginning.

But to disc jockeys who didn't appreciate these minor differences and were vexed at their musical freedom being quashed, Pollack and Abrams were equally detested. In fact, at some stations, the DJs weren't even told about the participation of a consultant, who would be squirreled away for clandestine meetings in hotel rooms, the hidden hand that moved the chess pieces. Most jocks had enough contacts within the industry to know that their station was being consulted even if upper management chose to keep it secret, and often would plead their cases directly to Abrams, going over their immediate bosses' heads.

Both Pollack and Abrams licked their chops at getting hold of WNEW, WBCN, KSAN, and KMET. They believed that their formulas could take these underperforming progressive stations and bring them into new levels of glory. The difference was that Pollack wanted to clean house and replace all the jocks with his loyalists, and Abrams was willing to work with the existing talent. The jocks at the Metromedia stations saw both of them as barbarians at the gate, and lived in fear of the day when the assault would bring an abrupt end to their freedom.

Eve of Destruction

RATINGS AT KSAN in San Francisco had achieved high levels in the early seventies. But since the salesmen's hands were tied in terms of the station's refusal to accept jingle commercials, the only advertisers were local head shops, boutiques, and leather crafters. National sponsors like Coca-Cola weren't about to give up their expensive, highly produced spots to please the hippies at KSAN. Cash flow became a problem, as small businesses were notoriously lax at paying bills, especially for something as ephemeral as radio advertising.

Under Tom Donahue and his protégée, Bonnie Simmons, an eclectic band of hippie broadcasters turned the station into a virtual commune. When an interim manager issued a memo instructing the jocks not to bring their dogs to work because the carpets were being ruined by excrement, he also sent out a reminder that marijuana was still illegal and would not be tolerated on the premises. On his desk the next morning was a pile of dog feces with a roach stuck artfully in the middle. At WNEW, Mel Karmazin would have had the offenders hunted down and strung up in Times Square.

The station actually went so far as to broadcast drug reports on a daily basis. They forged a cooperative deal with a laboratory that analyzed the safety and purity of whatever substance was sent them. The subjects would deliver a small sample of their stash to the lab and be assigned a random six-digit number. A few days later, KSAN would announce the number and the results of the test. There was no fear of FCC reprisal. They had their own news department and the reporting was far from the objective presentation that WNEW displayed in its simulcasts with its respected AM news department. KSAN did a death count every day during the war, and their vehement opposition to the conflict was not hidden.

KSAN was so politically charged that when the Symbionese Liberation Army kidnapped Patty Hearst, their manifesto was delivered for broadcast on KSAN's airwaves. The jocks were totally free to invite whomever they wanted onto their shows—musicians, filmmakers, activists, or just people off the street with a crazy story to tell. For the most part, they were able to craft the interviews to be entertaining and informative. Music was completely of their own selection, and individual taste prevailed over sales figures. The only attempt at formatting came when the station designated certain albums with a red dot and suggested that these be played more frequently. But the dots weren't based on research or sales reports; they were just the records the station felt should be supported. But even this was ignored, and no one took them to task. Donahue might mention to the afternoon jock that he was playing too much of the Marshall Tucker Band, but that was the extent of the musical direction. They tried to have music meetings, but they were sparsely attended and deteriorated into complete wastes of time. Selections that became popular at KSAN would not be dictated by Donahue, but arose naturally from the staff's collective preferences. Stationality was achieved naïvely since everyone listened to each other's programs and they frequently socialized. If one jock heard another playing a great track, the rest would soon follow suit.

Money wasn't a big factor either. The music librarian in 1970 was paid ninety dollars a week, but practically lived at the station out of devotion to the cause. The jocks were all paid roughly the same amount, about three hundred dollars, and there was little jealousy and backbiting as a result.

Since many of them were working their first radio job at KSAN, the egos were kept in check in the early days.

George Duncan held the reins very loosely at KSAN. It is doubtful that he would have been able to countenance this kind of activity if the station could be heard regularly by John Kluge. The old man paid attention to his complaint mail, and his conservative values were reflected in the content at the stations within his hearing. But from a distance, Duncan understood the necessity to provide a comfortable working environment for these hippies, and gave them great latitude. It wasn't until Tom Donahue passed on in April of 1975 that Metromedia took a more direct interest in running the station. The old axiom "If it ain't broke, don't fix it" applied until then and since KSAN was making them money on a shoestring budget, they acted autonomously.

The big man's death shook the station like an earthquake, and staff members to this day are emotional when his name is brought up. His four-hundred-pound bulk was a constant health risk and, combined with the drugs in fashion at that time, it is regrettably understandable why his heart stopped beating at the age of forty-six. It is likely that Donahue's days at KSAN were numbered in any case, as he was in negotiations with film-maker Francis Ford Coppola to buy and manage his own station to compete in the San Francisco market. Always the astute businessman, why should he make money for John Kluge when he could be maximizing profits for himself and his allies? Simmons was appointed program director after his death.

Given the lack of album-rock competition and the politics of the times, KSAN remained the hub of the city's popular culture for some time. Bill Graham, the Bay Area's preeminent concert promoter, gave them tie-ins to all the major shows. Van Morrison, the Grateful Dead, Santana, Jefferson Airplane, Quicksilver Messenger Service, and the other top bands that lived in the area would drop by for impromptu interviews. But even when the visits were scheduled in advance, the jocks often forgot to promote them and frequently neglected to record them for posterity. Each jock was issued one reel of production tape, and since it cost fifteen dollars, they were careful about how they used it and which interviews they decided to archive.

This careless spontaneity actually had a beneficial effect. The listeners never knew what was going to happen next and were discouraged from changing the dial for fear they'd miss an important event, like a visit from

Mick Jagger or a fistful of Grateful Dead tickets about to be given away. Since the promotional budget was less than twenty thousand dollars yearly, cash giveaways or expensive vacations were not even considered. The prizes awarded included dinners, albums, or concert tickets, given to them by record companies. Any promotions that KSAN did were linked to the lifestyle of the audience and often played on its creativity.

One campaign that worked beyond their expectations was a contest staged to design a billboard for the radio station. Anticipating only a handful of entries, the jocks figured they could determine the winner at a quick informal meeting. But upon receiving over five hundred entries, they actually had to convene a panel of art critics and marketing gurus as judges. One submission that almost took top prize was a poster depicting an explosive battle scene with the caption, "Oh KSAN you see, by the dawn's early light." But a few nights before the winner was to be announced, an explosion took place at Metromedia's Foster and Kleiser billboard offices in Oakland. The proximity of the bombing made the judges uncomfortable, worrying that the destruction might have a connection to the contest. So they awarded the grand prize to a cartoony space moose that had to be seen to be appreciated. The best of the other entries were rounded up and turned into an exhibit that toured the country.

One crazy promotion that backfired was designed by Warner Bros. rep Pete Marino to publicize the release of Randy Newman's "Political Science." Marino was a flamboyantly gay figure who owned a Rolls-Royce that was elaborately emblazoned with colorful vignettes of San Francisco. He reputedly was a close and personal friend of Liberace and they exchanged clothes on occasion. He also frequented the North Beach strip clubs and was a friend of the Condor's Carol Doda, a busty exotic dancer. He recruited her for the promotion, centered around the song's repeated chorus, "Let's drop the big one." The idea was to simultaneously release hundreds of doves from atop KSAN's downtown building, literally covering the sky with birds. What this had to do with "dropping the big one" was certainly a stretch, unless the doves relieved themselves en masse. Local TV stations were notified and cameras were all out, awaiting the big moment. KSAN jocks trooped up to the roof with Doda, who wore a Randy Newman T-shirt stretched so tightly over her enormous bosom that Newman's picture was distorted beyond recognition. On the way up the stairs, the jocks fired up joints and exhaled the smoke into the birdcages. Cameramen craned their necks to catch a glimpse of the spectacle, although

I'm not sure which they thought was the more spectacular, Doda or the doves (maybe she embodied the "big one[s]"). But at the crucial juncture, the birds had inhaled so much smoke and were so stoned that they refused to move from their perches. So Marino and the staff reached into the cages and began tossing them off the roof, with grotesque consequences. The birds were too looped to fly and fell to the pavement like mini–lead zeppelins, where they were run over by trucks and buses. The ASPCA got involved and the station had a full-fledged embarrassment on their hands. The incident was fictionalized years later on the TV show *WKRP in Cincinnati,* with turkeys dropped from a helicopter replacing the doves.

But the station wasn't always cruel to flying creatures. KSAN had a great ability to galvanize its audience during times of crisis. When an oil spill devastated Stinson Beach, the station put out the call for its listeners to help to save the shore wildlife. The next morning, five thousand of them showed up to rescue injured birds. They did a "Turkey Exchange" every Thanksgiving morning, where listeners would post messages like "I'm new in town and have no place to go for dinner. Call this number if you're willing to open your home to me" or "My husband and I have room for four more at our house. Call 555-1333 if you're hungry." Thousands shared dinners over the years and the station never was informed of one ugly incident.

Lee Abrams tried to crack the market in 1975 with KYA-FM, but it was a dismal flop, mainly since the music was not reflective of the market's vagaries. Things changed shortly after that with the advent of KMEL in July of 1977. Armed with an enormous promotional budget, they made ratings inroads very quickly. Riding a wave of boastful publicity claiming that they would immediately annihilate KSAN, it took them longer than they figured to finally surpass them. KMEL took the best elements of what their competitor was doing and gave them form and structure. Popular favorite songs, which might turn up once a day at KSAN, appeared with regularity at KMEL. Like most free-form stations, the programming at KSAN could be erratic, rising to the level of art but too often wallowing in self-indulgence. The jocks were losing sight of their audience and were paying too much attention to their peers in the industry, who had a tendency to be too far ahead of the curve, always seeking the new and adventurous, even at a time when the audience was searching for the safe and familiar. The spoils of success infected some of the jocks with inflated egos and they were not working as hard as they once did to keep up with the music. Stationality was broken as musical tastes diverged; the new-wave movement caused a rift between AOR aficionados and punk rockers. Drugs were also a major distraction, as their grip on some staff members distorted priorities.

At the root of KSAN's success was their strong tie to the cultural and political identity of the city. But the Vietnam War had ended, and there was a sympathetic Democratic president in office, so radical politics became less a factor in choosing radio stations. And the best values of the hippie counterculture had become absorbed into the mainstream. Bonnie Simmons reflects, "I don't think that radio makes the culture, but mimics the culture. Your success can be judged on how well you mirror what's going on outside. And for ten years, I think we made a pretty good stab at it. Maybe ten years is the life cycle of a radio station, and nothing can stop the inevitable evolution. The audience changes and seeks other things from their radio."

Metromedia saw these signs and was alarmed by the erosion that KMEL was causing on the ratings. Management was pressed to make massive changes. Simmons saw the handwriting on the wall and knew that the free-form days were coming to a close. She had come up through the ranks under Donahue and had too much respect for his memory to be the one to format the station and shut down its freedom. She resigned at the end of 1978. Still in her twenties, she accepted a national promotions job in Los Angeles with Warner Bros. Records and started a new phase in her career. It was time.

Total free-form radio was in trouble in Boston as well. The newly formatted WCOZ was quickly threatening WBCN in the ratings and scooped them on some major shows, establishing instant credibility. The most notable example was a Who concert at the Boston Garden on a snowy November day. There had been an afternoon basketball game at the venerable old arena and afterward, bleacher-style concert seats were hastily rolled out over the ancient parquet floor. The debris from the game was merely swept aside under the risers since there wasn't time between events for a thorough cleaning. After the opening act completed their set, smoke began to rise from beneath the bleachers. The doors to the adjoining alley were opened and the wind and snow came pouring into the building, actually fanning the flames. Some of the concertgoers panicked at the terrifying sight of flames crawling up the wooden bleachers, but the Boston fire department quickly snuffed out the blaze and restored order. The fire delayed the Who's entrance by at least an hour as the arena was partially evacuated. The fans were in a foul mood from the acrid smoke and lengthy wait and were pounding their seats for the show to begin. But as the band finally hit the stage, something was clearly wrong. They stopped midway through their first song as Pete Townshend apologized and started over. As soon as they began again, Keith Moon collapsed and fell from his drum kit, completely incapacitated. The band beat a hasty retreat with Townshend promising, "We'll be back."

It seems that the delay caused by the fire had upset the delicate mix of drugs and alcohol that Moon needed to fortify himself for each performance and he was now hopelessly stoned.

The band trooped back onstage and Roger Daltrey made an announcement. "Keith has been taken ill. We'll have to come back another time. We promise to return in April." The crowd booed mercilessly and hurled garbage and ugly obscenities toward the stage as Daltrey threw the microphone down in disgust and stomped off.

Mark Parenteau, a flashy jock who had just arrived at WCOZ but had known the band from his Detroit days, was backstage during all the drama. He asked Daltrey if he'd like to join him on the air at WCOZ later to explain what had happened. The lead singer paused for a moment in thought and then replied, "I just might do that, mate."

Parenteau had to practically bribe the building's security guards to call him if any scruffy-looking rock and rollers showed up, since they were on strict instructions to protect the station from any such intrusions. But Daltrey did materialize that evening, and talked candidly for hours about the problem, taking phone calls from listeners and promising a makeup date later on in the tour. When WBCN got wind of the exclusive, PD Norm Winer was furious. Parenteau took special satisfaction in his cold revenge; he had originally auditioned for Winer upon coming to Boston and had been rejected.

In 1977, after two years of damage wrought by WCOZ, under the theory that "if you can't beat 'em, join 'em," WBCN hired Parenteau. Laquidara was still into his early retirement and Winer had left to pilot WXRT in Chicago. Charlie Kendall was now the program director and his task was to give the station structure and instill some needed discipline.

Kendall's theatrical training gave him impetus to institute some simple formatics: His concept was called "Center Stage." Distilled to its essence, Center Stage represented core FM artists, which at the time were Bob

Seger, the Kinks, the Rolling Stones, et cetera. These artists made up the crux of the broadcast hour. Rules were set up so that the further you deviated from the center, the sooner you had to return. Sheets were attached to album covers, and the jocks had to initial and date them every time they used a record to avoid too much repetition.

Already possessed of a talented staff, Charlie needed to focus his crew away from their self-indulgent ways and toward ratings success. There was also a practical reason behind his single-minded striving for numbers—his contract called for him to be paid twenty-eight thousand dollars, plus a 3 percent share of the station's net profits, which were nonexistent at the time of his hiring. If WBCN could net a million dollars, Charlie could double his salary.

In 1978, Charles Laquidara rejoined WBCN. His cocaine problem was under control, but he initially resisted their entreaties to return because he didn't like it when people announced their retirement to great ballyhoo, only to return later. So he came back as Duane Ingalls Glasscock, a seventeen-year-old alter ego, and did a Saturday morning program. He was convinced that the listeners didn't know who it really was, because Glasscock affected gay mannerisms and talked more than Charles ever had. Soon, his program was pulling thirty shares in its time slot and he even ran a mock campaign for president. Laquidara was convinced to return to the mornings (as himself), but he still kept Glasscock on Saturday.

Parenteau maintains that he and Laquidara had a fierce rivalry, born from their divergent views on where they saw the station going. Parenteau was a fast-talking Detroit rocker, who talked up records almost in Top Forty fashion. He could be outrageous on the air, irreverent toward the music, and lacked any political motivation. Although Charles could be downright loopy at times, he favored the more laid-back approach that WBCN was known for after the Peter Wolf gang left. Charles let his characters do the outrageous things and took his political stands seriously. In some ways, he used Glasscock to fight Parenteau on his own turf. Parenteau was also a Kendall supporter, whereas Charles had his differences with the new PD.

Laquidara hated the idea that ratings ruled his life. He refused to celebrate when they rose, because he believed that it would give them credibility and thus power over him when they went down. This caused him problems at WBCN, as some of his superiors took it as a sign that he didn't care.

Charlie Kendall made an enemy of Charles Laquidara early on

through no fault of his own. Laquidara was like a method actor too deeply absorbed into a role—while on the air on weekends, he *became* Duane Glasscock. Playing his alter ego, he demanded to be addressed as Glasscock by everyone, including Kendall. One Saturday morning, just after ratings came out, Duane Ingalls Glasscock hit the airwaves in full fury.

"The Arbitron ratings have just come out," he started, "and they say that WBCN has no listeners. Well, I say Arbitron is for shit." To this day, that is one of the forbidden words on radio. And although Glasscock might have been the first "shock jock" on FM, this was clearly crossing the line. "Here's what I want you to do. I want you to send a bag of shit to Arbitron."

He proceeded to detail mailing instructions, with Arbitron's address and how to package the bundle. Kendall did not happen to be listening at that moment, but quickly heard about it from upper management. This was still Harley Staggers's time, when the FCC was not the toothless old tiger it is today. Owners lived in fear of losing their licenses for even minor violations. This obscene rant in prime time triggered listener complaints, not to mention the obvious damage it could do with Arbitron. Their contracts with radio stations clearly forbade any mention of the name Arbitron, for fear of skewing the ratings.

Luckily, Kendall had a friend working for Arbitron who called him when packages of the smelly substance began to arrive at their Maryland headquarters. He was able to convince his friend to quietly dispose of the residue for a price. Fortunately, his friend was not skilled at blackmail and only asked for a few albums, which Charlie was happy to provide.

But Kendall had to discipline Laquidara, which took the form of a suspension. He tried to explain that if the station didn't take strong measures to distance itself from this rant, the FCC could fine it heavily or even pull the license. Laquidara took this as a sign of management's lack of support for him, and rallied the troops behind him and against Kendall. The resulting power struggle hurt both men, and undoubtedly the station in the process.

Like most progressive program directors, listening to the station was the key to its flow. With the wide latitude afforded the jocks (much like in the early WLIR days), it was possible to follow the format to the letter and still do a poor job. During the daytime hours, Charlie would actually come into the studio and tell a jock that his show wasn't entertaining and give suggestions on how to improve it. In off-hours, he'd use the hotline to direct the staff. This caused problems.

Progressive jocks tend to view what they do as an art form. Blending music and talk elements into a powerful whole is indeed like creating a painting—using words and music instead of oils and canvas. No artist would tolerate the interruption of a critic while halfway through a work, denigrating what he'd seen so far. The old saying goes, "Art is like sausage, best not viewed during its making." But radio is a constant stream in which progress is evaluated in quarter-hour segments. Whereas an artist can paint over mistakes on canvas to achieve a successful result, one misstep on radio can cause listeners to flock to the competition, perhaps never to return. Consistency is critical, and Kendall monitored WBCN at all hours to ensure that consistency.

The problems result because the temperaments of jocks and artists are similar. The egos are every bit as delicate, and Kendall was not one for subtlety. He also had no qualms about ruling through intimidation and fear. His hotline calls were as dreaded as those of Bill Drake's. Charlie could be very undiplomatic, and one scathing call could ruin a jock's psyche for days. One would think that, as a former jock himself, Kendall would realize this, but his early experiences were with abusive managers and he learned early on to accept that the critiques weren't personal. But many creative types don't respond to that kind of pressure and Charlie was either loved or hated at WBCN; there was little ambivalence.

This made him a great quick-fix program director, or as another of his employees later characterized him, "a great wartime consigliere." Like a football coach who terrorizes his players, they tend to have success initially because of the instant discipline they instill. But over time, the stress builds on both sides and these leaders become ineffective or lose all their best players. The problem would dog Kendall in years to come.

Like WNEW-FM, WBCN put women in prominent time periods, the most famous being Maxanne Sartori. Maxanne first made her mark in Seattle at KOL-FM, where she was the first female progressive jock in that city. Sartori loved hard rock, and her fast-paced approach was quite different from that of the sensual, laid-back Alison Steele, but it served her well. She became friends with Steven Tyler of Aerosmith, and her advocacy of his band was largely responsible for their success. A frequent clubgoer, she once saw a group she liked called Cap'n Swing. She befriended their leader, who coincidentally had attended Antioch College at the same time she had. As their rapport grew and he became more impressed with her knowledge and contacts in the music business, he asked her to manage the band, but her plate was full and she turned him down. She did suggest that their singer play an instrument, but she was told that he really could only play bass in a rudimentary fashion. Seeing big things in their future, she said that he'd better learn.

They recorded a demo called "Just What I Needed" that she played daily on her program, and that led to a record deal on Elektra. By then they'd changed their name to the Cars.

My Aim Is True

BY THE LATE SEVENTIES, the problems that plagued KMET, WBCN, and KSAN were affecting WNEW. Ratings now became more than just a yearly memo; they became of paramount importance and Mel Karmazin wouldn't tolerate another winning ratings book from WPLJ. The Rock in Stereo format, under the direction of Larry Berger at WPLJ, had tapped into a strong vein.

Berger had assembled a solid staff of veterans, led by Jim Kerr in the mornings. They also had lured Tony Pigg in from the West Coast to give stability to the lineup. Carol Miller, who'd gone back to Philadelphia radio after leaving WNEW (she also worked briefly at WQIV), was rolling up numbers in the evening. Pat St. John gave them a quality afternoon presence. Zacherle had come to terms with his mistake in leaving WNEW and was doing well in the late-night shift. The format made them all sound too mechanical, repeating the call letters every few seconds, but the numbers were sturdy, generally in the high-three range.

WNEW was still strong in the key eighteen- to thirty-four-year-old demographic, and WPLJ's massive 12+ (the twelve and older demographic) share was aided by their dominance in teenage listeners. There was now a new force to be reckoned with. WPIX had given up their Top Forty format and were mimicking KROQ in Los Angeles, playing exclusively punk and new-wave music with an upbeat approach. They had taken Meg Griffin away from us, and had hired my brother Dan for his first major-market gig. Although that station never achieved big numbers, the combination of the two (like KLOS and KROQ in L.A.) imperiled WNEW's share to the point where Karmazin had to contemplate changes.

True to his word, Jonathan Schwartz had departed in 1976 and Dennis Elsas took over the coveted 6 to 10 P.M. slot. Dennis was the polar opposite of Schwartz—he had a pleasant, conventional radio voice and very mainstream tastes in music. His rap was limited to pertinent music information, telling no rambling stories in the style that Jonno favored. While not governed strictly by the clock, Dennis was very conscious of talking too much and not playing enough music. His ratings stayed consistent with the rest of the station, which had to be all Muni and Karmazin could hope for.

Dennis by now was a cottage industry. Always desirous of a voice-over career in addition to his DJ work (like his hero Bob Lewis), he was voicing and producing countless record-company commercials as well as doing his show. His production deal with Atlantic Records led to a meeting with Mick Jagger.

Peter Tosh, a reggae artist, was releasing the first album on Rolling Stones Records, called *Don't Look Back,* and Jagger sang the title song with his latest discovery. Dennis was commissioned to produce the radio spot to promote the album. He knew that he wasn't going to be the voice on the commercial, so he tried to come up with a creative way to frame it. He contacted his friends at Atlantic, the company that distributed the Stones' private label, and suggested that Mick Jagger be the one to voice the commercial.

Expecting his request to be a long shot, he was surprised when they got back to him quickly and said that Jagger would be happy to do the spot. Dennis and an engineer brought a portable Nagra tape deck to the offices of Rolling Stones Records at 75 Rockefeller Plaza and interviewed Mick about Tosh, using bits of the interview interspersed with the music to create an effective ad. After the taping was over, Mick asked if they'd like to hear Keith Richards's new solo single, a version of Chuck Berry's Christmas song, "Run Rudolph Run." Of course they agreed, and Jagger popped it onto his stereo. As the record played, Mick began to dance to it, and Elsas was treated to a private performance by one of rock's biggest stars. As he watched Jagger go through his wild gyrations, it seemed as if he were watching a Rolling Stones parody on *Saturday Night Live* as opposed to the real thing.

Although Dennis's presence didn't hurt us, audiences were shifting, moving away from nights toward AM drive time as the preeminent time slot on the station. Now that FM radios were common in automobiles, the morning commute could be eased by listening to familiar music. Dave Herman was starting to take root as an established morning personality in his own right, and we expanded our news and traffic features to rival those of most AM stations.

Muni had no desire to format in any way and Karmazin realized that Scott's main value was his presence, both on and off the air. However, Mel believed that the station needed an active program director and not just a caretaker who would passively keep the status quo. But to relieve Muni of the title would be a slap to his ego, and Mel was very careful to keep his biggest star happy. So he came up with the idea of hiring an operations director, who would theoretically report to Muni, but in fact would call most of the daily shots. He considered bringing in someone from the outside, which would have resulted in cataclysmic changes. Consultants were beginning to feel their oats by this time, and they all had prescriptions for how to bolster WNEW's numbers, most of which involved taking the freedom to program music away from the jocks and changing half the staff.

Karmazin wasn't ready to commit to that. He wasn't eager to be seen as the ogre who had destroyed one of the last bastions of free-form radio in America. WNEW still had absolutely no structure, and the music lacked focus. Herman's tastes were a little left of center, Fornatale favored country and folk rock, Muni was fairly mainstream, as was Elsas. Alison's show was more progressive but that suited the concept of her late-night slot. But we still made too many mistakes minute by minute against WPLJ's heavily researched playlist.

I wrote Mel a long memo proposing that I take the position. I stressed my experience at WLIR and the fact that my concert production work had given me strong ties within the local music community. I was tight with the owners of the Bottom Line, and friendly with John Scher, who produced concerts at the Capitol Theater in Passaic, New Jersey, and also managed the Grateful Dead. I knew all the key record people. Most important, I was an insider who got along with everyone at the station and knew the ropes and could dance politically around some of the stickier issues. The job was carved out of nothing in the budget, so I wouldn't be permitted a music director or promotions manager. I also wanted a weekly show to keep my disc jockey options open if this didn't work out. Karmazin agreed to give me the job, although it seemed he had some reservations.

Almost as soon as he'd hired me to run the programming, he called me in and grilled me about our music.

"Do you think we have better disc jockeys than WPLJ?" he asked.

"Of course I do. There isn't one of our people I would trade straight up for one of theirs."

"You're obviously aware they always beat us in the ratings. So if we were to play the same music that they play, with our superior disc jockeys, wouldn't we win? Just asking."

By then, I knew that Mel's "just asking" constituted a challenge. He would often extend a proposition innocently, but in reality he was stating his position and wanted an explanation of why it wasn't valid. I thought hard for a moment, knowing that he wouldn't brook me just giving the answer I thought he wanted to hear.

"Part of what makes our jocks better than theirs is the ability to choose our own music. Their people have great voices, like ours. That's a subjective thing anyway. But whereas they just go off a playlist, our people have to plan their shows. So when they talk about the music they choose, it comes from the heart. And the listeners pick up on that and respect them for it. If they just read off liner cards like they do at PLJ, we'd be reduced to what they are and they'd beat us worse. We have to play on our court to have a chance to win. If we play on theirs, it won't be close. Also if we went to a playlist, Scelsa and maybe two others would just quit."

"Okay," he said, still appearing unconvinced. "You're the programming expert. We'll do it your way. I'm just a salesman, I don't know anything about programming. That's your responsibility."

Meeting over. Message sent.

He wouldn't argue with me but I knew deep down that he might be right. If ratings were our only objective, duplicating our competitor's format of rock hits might get us higher numbers in the short term. But we'd be just another radio station and that sizzle that helped us rise above the crowd would be gone. And for all his hard-edged business sense, Mel understood this intangible mix and stayed the course. He avoided bringing in consultants and let us have our head.

One aspect of the job I wasn't prepared for was the reaction of my "friendly" colleagues. The people who loved me as a coworker reacted quite differently to me as their boss. The first problem I had was with Dave Herman.

When I did overnights, Dave and I got along famously. I'd been to his house a few times socially, was friendly with his wife, Drea, and even worked out an accommodation to cover his morning show so he wouldn't be inconvenienced. Since Dave lived in Connecticut and didn't want to drive in and incur the expense and hassle of parking in the big city, he took mass transit. The first commuter train from his area didn't arrive at Grand Central Station until a few minutes after his 6 A.M. start time. So Dave offered to pay me twenty dollars a week to stay until 6:20 and program his first few records. He had a recorded opening on cartridge that said, "Good just barely morning, I'm Dave Herman at WNEW-FM." I played that, segued three or four tunes, and then Dave slid in as if he'd always been there.

But immediately upon taking the new job, my relationship with Dave changed for the worse. He seemed to resent everything I asked him to do. He couldn't understand how the overnight guy was now his boss and could give him instructions on how to do a better morning show. He openly defied any direction I gave him, knowing that he could complain to Mel or Scott if I suggested something he didn't like. Fornatale and Elsas were eager to please, but handling Muni became an art form that all subsequent program directors would have to deal with.

I was always deferential to his wishes, but I knew that he'd have to make some changes if the station was to rise above its share in the low-two range. Every morning, I'd spend at least a half hour in his office, talking sports or what needed to be done at the station. Scott was the station's personal ambassador to Vin Scelsa. Vin was working weekends and had all the potential to become a star on the radio, but had always resisted anything remotely commercial. His music was too eclectic and I felt that it got in the way of his engaging radio personality. Muni and I were constantly of the belief that if Scelsa could be coaxed into playing more accessible music, he could be as big as anybody in the country. As it was, he had a fiercely loyal cult following but was constantly quitting the station over one minor directive or another. Muni was always dispatched to smooth his ruffled feathers and woo him back into the fold. Scott was tiring of the efforts and was beginning to wonder if Vin was more trouble than he was worth.

But Scott himself could be truculent, perhaps a residue from his old Rick Sklar days. He refused to take direction and could be contrary if you rubbed him the wrong way. If you told him he was playing too many Rolling Stones songs, he'd play an hour of them the next day. He would roar and flex his muscles on occasion just to show that he could. I began to realize that the only way to get Muni to do something against his initial instincts was to convince him that it was his idea in the first place. I sometimes lacked the skills to accomplish that.

Scott and I got along well overall even though I never had been much of a drinker and his consumption was prodigious. We went to lunch together almost daily, either with or without record people. With his meal, he'd knock down four or five Johnny Walker Red Label scotches on the rocks, his drink of preference. In the studio, he kept a 1.75-liter bottle of the same distillment, which he tapped into once an hour. Most nights, after he got off the air at six, we'd go to a local watering hole where we'd grab a bite to eat and a few more scotches. He usually didn't eat that much, only picking at his steak or burger. As beneficiary of Uncle Scott's spotty appetite, my dog, Paddington, ate better than most humans.

Amazingly, in all that time, I never saw him drunk. He had the most incredible tolerance for alcohol of anyone I've ever seen. Occasionally, late at night on a Friday, I might hear him slur his words slightly, but generally Scottso was the same guy at nine in the morning or at midnight, regardless of his tippling. He almost never missed a day of work for any reason, and had the constitution and strength of a bull. It wasn't until 1986, when he had a near-death experience because his lungs had filled with fluid as a result of his profligate ways, that he stopped drinking. He overcame his demon and has been stone-cold sober ever since, one day at a time.

But our main concern in the late seventies was Alison. Her activities outside the station were so consuming that by the time she reported for work at ten, she had very little left in the tank. She had television spots, syndicated programs, commercials, and public appearances that were draining her energy and detracting from her work. She'd won *Billboard*'s Radio Personality of the Year in 1978, but her show was sliding downhill at an alarming pace. Her sensualist technique was beginning to sound forced, and it wasn't holding up well against the less contrived approach of Meg Griffin. It also seemed that she'd lost interest in the music. Upon playing a long track, she'd wander into the newsroom and chat with a desk assistant, only to let the record run out and click into the final groove for minutes on end. Sometimes a record would begin skipping and she'd be in the studio on the phone and wouldn't notice until someone brought it to her attention. She refused to wear her glasses at work, and her myopia caused her some embarrassing gaffes on the air. Her production work was becoming sloppy, with the rustle of papers foreshadowing her every appearance on mic.

Mel was on my back constantly about her. He felt she was hurting the station, and I couldn't argue with him. We sent her memos, brought her in for meetings, at which she was always a perfect lady. She denied having any problems on the air, and when they were pointed out to her, she maintained that everyone had the same occasional lapses and it was no big deal. I met with her privately, and together with Muni and/or Mel, but eventually the results were the same—she'd improve for a few days and then slide right back into her bad habits.

The way radio works today, there would be a simple solution—hire a producer at minimum wage and have him run Alison's board and keep her energized and prepared for each break. But in 1979, I couldn't even have an assistant to help screen music so an extra body just to cater to Alison was out of the question. In retrospect, it seems penny-wise, pound-foolish.

I attempted to buy her time, but the excuses were wearing thin. After a final warning, I tried to relate to her how thin the ice she was skating on really was. She took it rather casually, until one morning I was called into Karmazin's office. There was fire in his eyes—always the way I liked to start my days.

"Did you hear Alison last night?" he asked.

I could sense what was coming. "Parts of her show. Why?"

"Do you know that she let a record skip for a full fifteen minutes?"

Ooops. I hadn't heard that and I sheepishly told him so.

"It's time to make a move, one way or the other. What do you think?"

"I think we should wait until Scott gets here and discuss it with him."

"No. I want to know what you would do. You wanted this job, and the responsibility that comes with it. I'll deal with Scott. I want to know what you recommend."

I was clearly being tested and this was the part of the job I hated. Alison was a legend. She had always treated me wonderfully and had been instrumental in my getting the job in the first place. To be the implement of her firing would constitute a betrayal of the highest order in her mind. But I had an obligation to the station, and there was no way I could rationalize her recent performance.

"I guess that we should let her go. Do you want me to tell her?"

"No. Scott and I will handle it. You're sure that she's been warned? You've spoken to her about this? This won't come as a surprise?"

I told him that I'd done all I could. Muni obviously was in agreement as he confirmed to me later that morning. Mel and Scott gave Alison the bad news, and she was gone without saying good-bye. Who said programming a rock station with your childhood heroes would be all fun and games?

Scelsa inherited Alison's spot. He and overnight man "Father" Tom Morrera soon formed a coalition called the *Butch and the Brick Show.* In addition to Scelsa's alter ego as the Bayonne Bear (who danced onstage at concerts), he also took on the persona of a punk known as Bayonne Butch. Like Charles Laquidara's Duane Glasscock at WBCN in Boston, when in character, you had to refer to him as Butch or the Bear or he wouldn't speak to you. He talked about these figments of his imagination as if they were real people, and Muni thought that Vin might have serious problems with schizophrenia. Morrera was generally a mellow sort; his nickname, "The Brick," was given to him by Columbia promotion man Matty Matthews, who called marijuana "The Hashish Brick." Given Morrera's affinity for the substance in those days, the name stuck. Vin and Tom were devoted to new wave and punk, and were almost like a rebel outpost on the station. Since they occupied the hours between 10 P.M. and 6 A.M., we felt that their more experimental approach, replete with lengthy cross-talk segments, would enhance our progressive image while doing us little harm in the ratings, which now were in the high-two to three range for listeners over age twelve.

One time we let the two of them do a twenty-six-hour Butch and the Brick marathon. They pretended to barricade themselves in the studio and they wouldn't come out until their "demands" were met. All of this was preplanned and seemed like innocent fun, recalling Scelsa's earlier radical days at WFMU. But halfway through the marathon, the lack of sleep and incessant interruptions from secretaries and salespeople entering the studio to attend to bookkeeping began to wear on Morrera. The two actually did block passage into the studio by bolting the heavy airtight door.

Sales manager Mike Kakoyiannis needed to add a commercial to the log and was frustrated when he found the door bolted. So he summoned a building custodian who let him in with a master key. Morrera was furious. He reached into his bag and extracted a huge hunting knife that he always carried with him (living in the city, he often walked to work in the late-night hours and felt that he needed the weapon for protection). Morrera warned the sales manager to back off or he'd cut him. Although he was smiling, Morrera had a reputation for being somewhat crazy and you never knew for sure if he was serious.

"I warned you," Morrera screamed. "Now get the hell out of here."

Kakoyiannis thought he was kidding and approached the log to make the necessary changes, when Morrera brandished the knife and chased him down the hall. Cornering him, he pushed the frightened salesman against a wall and lashed out with the knife, severing a button on Kakoyiannis's expensive French-cuffed shirt and nearly drawing blood.

"I'll slice your little Greek souvlaki heart out and throw it on the floor," Morrera threatened. The salesman beat a hasty exit and never attempted to enter the studio again.

At the first Hungerthon, an event cofounded by Harry Chapin and Bill Ayres for World Hunger Year, Scelsa invited Patti Smith to join him as a guest. The idea behind Hungerthon was to raise money to help feed the needy or educate them to feed themselves and still continues today under Ayres's leadership. Scelsa was a huge fan of Smith's and loved the new album she was promoting, *Radio Ethiopia*. Before she hit the airwaves he gave her the prerequisite speech that we give all the invited guests. "Just remember that you're on the radio, Patti, and there are certain words you can't use. You're cool with that, right?"

Smith nodded and as the record ended, he introduced her. "You know, they tried to censor me before I came on the air," she began. "But fuck that. This is Radio Ethiopia, and we don't let anyone fucking censor us, man. Radio Ethiopia lives."

Karmazin was listening across the glass in the engineering room and went ballistic. Scelsa and Harry Chapin were able to calm him down, after he initially demanded she be taken off the air right away. Vin had a heated discussion with Smith, and the rest of the interview passed without incident.

Any attempt to rein in Butch and the Brick usually resulted in Scelsa resigning and Muni driving out to New Jersey to convince him to stay. On one such occasion, Scott had a serious accident while braving icy winter conditions. He smashed into a stalled car in the fast lane at forty-five miles an hour. His head hit the windshield and required almost two hundred facial stitches from shards of shattered glass. His mouth was so shredded that he had to drink his meals through a straw for almost two weeks. It affected his speech temporarily and caused him to miss several weeks of work. He drove a full-size Lincoln, but the force of the impact pushed the engine into the front seat. Fortunately, it only resulted in severe contusions on his knees. The crash served as a wake-up call on two levels: First, it alerted Scott to the fact that there were nights when he was in no condition to be driving and that he'd been lucky so far; and second, that babysitting a temperamental DJ would soon be erased from Scott's job description. Vin's upside often had made us overlook the high-maintenance aspect of his personality. But even Muni's tough love wasn't working and there would soon come a time when we'd need to call Scelsa's bluff.

But for Scelsa, events at WNEW-FM were eerily echoing what had happened to him at WPLJ almost a decade earlier. A corporate decision was handed down from Metromedia that all artwork on the walls had to be selected and approved by upper management. All the gold records and rock posters were removed in favor of tasteful Olympic posters from John Kluge's personal collection. Black-and-white photos of the jocks, deliberately overexposed, were encased in Lucite squares and hung in an alcove greeting visitors to the station, now at 655 Third Avenue.

With the aid of Marty Martinez, producer, desk assistant, and aspiring jock/newsman, Scelsa found an album cover featuring weird, spooky eyes and ordered a hundred copies from the record company. They cut out these eyes and carefully glued them to the back of the clear acrylic panels protecting Kluge's Olympic posters. Each morning became a game of discovering where they had placed the self-proclaimed Spooky Boy pictures before any corporate rep saw them. After a couple of warnings from me failed to quell the tampering, I decided to ignore the insubordination and just chalk it up to "boys being boys." But one morning, the eyes, which had now spread like a virus throughout AM and FM, were pointed out jokingly to Karmazin. Mel hit the roof, and demanded that the offenders be fired for desecrating Kluge's priceless posters. Muni calmed Mel down enough to issue an edict—the posters must be cleaned up within twenty-four hours or anyone having any involvement in the graffiti would be axed. It took a massive effort, but by the next morning Scelsa and company had removed all the eyes from the posters. They pasted them on Mel's door, with tears drawn in under them, bearing the caption, "We're sorry." It wasn't until years later that I found out about the similar occurrences at WPLJ and understood this oblique form of rebellion against authority.

Some on the staff harbored the hope that if I was deposed as the station's enforcer, things would go back to the laissez-faire state they'd enjoyed under Muni. They didn't see the bigger picture at Metromedia and that I was their last chance at self-governance. The next step almost certainly would be a more authoritarian regime run by an outsider. Scelsa told me he'd made a secret pact with Karmazin that he could be the staff bad boy with impunity, as long as his ratings were good.

But the constant battle he had within himself to keep any interloper from affecting his "art" was wearing us down and endangering his job. His constant resignations over trivial matters were becoming tiresome. His ratings weren't any better than Dennis's or Pete's, who required almost no maintenance.

We'd been in competition before with two other stations in the market playing rock. In 1974, the classical station WNCN had been sold and turned into rocker WQIV, under Tom O'Hare, formerly of KMET in Los Angeles. Their hook was that they broadcast in quadraphonic sound, an early form of surround sound. Like later incarnations of that same idea, the problem was that there were two competing systems of quad transmission, and consumers were reluctant to buy either until a standard could be agreed upon. O'Hare was called the "Quadfather" and hired Carol Miller and Al Bernstein (both former part-timers at WNEW-FM). They were making modest inroads until a listener coalition of classical fans successfully sued to rescind the FCC's permission to change formats. The commission ruled that the presence of only one part-time classical station in New York (WQXR) was contrary to the public interest. Imagine that ruling standing up today.

But WPIX was another matter and although they never got big numbers, they squeezed us musically. We could never hope to score heavily with the new-wave crowd with PIX in the mix, and if we moved to the right, toward more conventional rock, we were playing on WPLJ's home turf. We had to balance ourselves delicately, playing the best of the new music that wouldn't alienate our core. Although overall we were successful at doing this, our ratings were compromised and we all breathed a sigh of relief when WPIX's management decided to go in another direction.

The WPIX days were short-lived and although the demise of that format was welcome news, it also created some difficult decisions. Meg Griffin was now available and wanted to return to WNEW-FM, and my brother Dan was out of work as well. After dabbling with WRNW and WLIR, he had become fairly well known in the rock community and brought a fresh, energetic approach. But there were political considerations.

First, there was the nepotism issue. I already had enemies within the organization who would use the hiring of Dan against me, especially if I had to fire someone else to make room. And I also had to consider the makeup of the staff attitudinally. Dan would become the ally of Butch and the Brick from a music standpoint, pushing us farther left, and Meg Griffin would take that a step farther. I hoped that if I hired Dan, I could count on our relationship to keep him from straying too far off the ranch with his choices, but I knew the temptation from his industry contacts and friends would be powerful. I pulled the trigger and prayed for the best.

So Dan Neer, going by the name Dan-o, joined the staff on weekends. Meg Griffin was rehired to do some fill-ins, and also to bring back more female presence, lacking on the station since Alison left. Ironically, the new cool-jazz format that WPIX picked up (changing their call letters to WQCD) hired Steele to do evenings some time later.

But after importing two new-wave advocates in place of two traditionalists, I thought it was important to bring some balance back to the mix by finding a solid AOR jock. Pete Larkin was out at WMAL-FM in Washington, so I asked him if he'd consider coming back to New York for some fill-in work. I'd known Pete since his days at WLIR and had kept in touch as his career leapfrogged from small stations in Baltimore to a successful AOR in D.C. Since there was nothing steady available, he agreed to commute from Washington whenever we needed him. For my part, I tried to bunch his shifts together to minimize his travels, and offered to let him stay in my spare bedroom when he needed to. Pete was an avid runner at the time and he and I would often take treks together and also enter 10K races, which helped me cope with the tensions at work.

We entered the eighties with a volatile coalition of two opposing forces: the "artistic" personalities who resented any encroachments on their freedom, and the pragmatic ones, who believed that our "art" must be balanced with commerce to survive. Within two years, the battle would be joined and one side vanquished. But first, a completely unpredictable tragedy would occur that would define the station's finest moment. And although it marked WNEW's artistic zenith, it presaged the end of its free-form days.

Across the Universe

MARTY MARTINEZ WAS DRESSED in his punk finest, festooned with a bright yellow skinny tie with the XTC logo on it. He was finally feeling that he had been accepted as an equal by his peers, not just the token minority hire. He was going to the Christmas concert.

Marty had been hired two years before as a desk assistant, amid the typical confusion that reigned whenever Scott Muni conducted a job interview. A friend of his had been contacted by WNEW-AM's veteran news director (and sports play-by-play announcer) Jim Gordon, who was looking for some night help on the news desk. Desk assistant is an entry-level position, essentially a learning experience that paid poorly but could lead to better things. The job entails preparing copy for the anchor, collecting various sound cuts sent by the wire services and street reporters, and basically doing whatever it takes to make the anchor's job easier, including writing some items when time constraints require it.

Martinez's friend had gotten another job the day before his scheduled interview with Gordon, but rather than cancel the appointment, he sent Marty in his place. Gordon wasn't sure that his qualifications fit what WNEW-AM was looking for, but FM had broken away from the AM news operation by hiring Ed Brown and Robin Sagon, and they also needed some help. Gordon sent him down the hall to talk to a man he simply referred to as Scott. Although Martinez was a big fan of the station, it didn't occur to him that the "Scott" in question was Scott Muni. Upon entering his office, it wasn't until the older man spoke that Marty realized whose presence he was in.

But in typical Scottso fashion, Muni's rambling stories dominated the discourse until he suddenly held up a hand to silence Martinez as the younger man attempted to get a word in edgewise. Muni slowly reached into a desk drawer and withdrew a pistol. Marty recoiled in fear but quickly regained his balance when he realized that Muni now pointed a water gun toward the open door, arms extended in a classic firing position.

"You bug-eyed motherfuc—" A corpulent older black man sprung from behind the doorway and fired off a couple of rounds, but Muni was prepared and doused the intruder with a steady spray from his larger and more powerful weapon. The man beat a hasty retreat down the hallway, yelling racial epithets behind him with Scott in close pursuit, drenching his foe down to his socks.

When Muni returned several minutes later, he was panting from the exertion but wearing a smile. "Robinson, you tired old sack of shit," he yelled out the doorway. "You're too fat and old to sneak up on anybody. Go back and cry to your mother Tammy." He then proceeded to extract several squirt guns of all shapes and sizes from the drawers of his notoriously cluttered desk.

"You gotta be prepared around here, Fats," he said to a still bewildered Martinez. "You seem okay, kid. Go down and talk to Gordon."

When Jim Gordon asked him how it had gone with Muni, he replied, "Good. I guess I got the job." With that, he filled out some forms and started his long, strange trip working for WNEW, a journey that would last twenty years and see him go from newsman to jock to producer to morning sidekick and back to producer. After his bizarre initiation, he was later to find that Robinson was Chuck Robinson, an elderly black man who had worked in the WNEW mailroom for decades and an ally of Tom Tracy's against Muni in their many water gun battles. Marty could see that this was going to be no ordinary job.

Blessed with a roguish personality that everyone at the station loved, he was quickly made part of the Butch and the Brick Show with Scelsa and Morrera. Marty liked to say that he was "invited to every party to make sure there was a party, if you catch my meaning." I always assumed that his bark was worse than his bite when it came to his stories of late-night drug-induced revelry at the station, but I was later to discover that the wild accounts were understated.

But on this winter's night toward the end of 1980, Marty had broken through from being an outlaw on the outskirts of the station, who technically serviced the newsroom, to a full-fledged staff member. Muni had personally invited him to the party that night. It was WNEW's annual Christmas concert, and the party afterward would be held backstage at the prestigious Avery Fisher Hall in Lincoln Center. When Muni had seen Martinez in the hallway the previous week, he'd casually asked, "Going to the party Monday, Fats?"

Upon being told that he was on duty that night, Muni replied, "I think we can arrange for you to take off a few hours. Party doesn't start 'til eleven or so. Stop by then."

He handed him an invitation, and it was the first time that the young desk assistant felt that he actually belonged. The Christmas shows were part of a rich tradition at the station, starting in 1971, when for sixteen thousand dollars the band Genesis was imported to do their first U.S. concert. There was a grand party at Tavern on the Green afterward, and every year since, WNEW hosted a major concert at venues like Madison Square Garden, the Beacon Theater, the Westchester Premiere Theater, the Academy of Music, or Philharmonic Hall. Over the years, we had artists like Melissa Etheridge, Renaissance, Hall and Oates, the Kinks, Yes, and Meatloaf perform for no charge, save expenses. Net proceeds went to United Cerebral Palsy, and Scott would dress up like Santa Claus and bring out a couple of the UCP kids to sing carols between acts. Before the concert, the staff would gather around a large tree in the lobby and accept gifts for needy children. It was a warm and fulfilling experience, and it gave the staff a chance to get together for a classy affair at an elegant location.

Muni had gotten on board with charity early on as a result of a singular experience that had caused an epiphany in his life. He had been asked to accompany Geraldo Rivera to Willowbrook, the infamous Staten Island mental facility whose exposure catapulted Rivera into national prominence. Muni realized that the cerebral palsy children, who had been carelessly thrown in with the mental patients, responded to his voice and some of the older ones knew him from the WABC days. Rather than regard them as wards of the state who couldn't be helped and merely had to be cared for, he believed that with research these unfortunates could have more meaningful lives. So when WNEW initiated the Christmas concerts, or Bikeathons, or a station calendar, he found a willing partner in United Cerebral Palsy. He discovered that most of the executives were retired or semiretired business or professional people who drew no salary, so the money raised all went to where it could help the most, rather than to administrative fees. Unlike most radio stations that used such events to enrich their coffers, WNEW made sure that the net proceeds from all of its nonradio activities went entirely to charity, including the revenues from the softball games that reached out to communities each summer.

Martinez was working at the station until a concert with the Marshall Tucker Band ended, and then planned to go to the party. He probably could have skipped work entirely, but he didn't want to desert Vin Scelsa, who often needed hand-holding to help him make it through the night. Depending on his mood, Scelsa would come in, sequester himself in the studio, do a four-hour show, and resent any intrusions, or he might arrive full of piss and vinegar and invite Marty into his inner sanctum to rail against the station's oppressive management. Martinez's upbeat personality would often soothe the undirected anger residing in Scelsa and convince him that he still had one of the best jobs in the world. But Vin was becoming increasingly bitter about the music business, which he saw as a bunch of corporate exploiters bent on making a profit over the broken backs of poor artists. He hated most record promoters, rejected their company, and despised the ornate parties that they threw. He easily could have taken the night off and attended the show, but preferred being on the air to celebrating with a bunch of hacks whom he felt were destroying the music that he loved. This attitude made it increasingly hard to work at a station that was feeling the economic pressure from Metromedia. But other than noncommercial radio, there was nowhere else where Scelsa could still play whatever he wanted with only occasional brushes with management.

Marty was sorry that his friend couldn't share his excitement about

going to the party. Warner Bros., which was footing the bill for the festivities, boasted many of his favorite artists, so he didn't feel he was betraying any of Vin's principles by attending. As he spiffed up at his desk, he
heard the distinctive warning bells of the police scanner proclaim a bulletin
coming.

He pulled the story off the wire and shrugged it off, making only a
mental note that the incident reported was near Avery Fisher Hall and that
he might have to tell his cabby to use Broadway instead of Central Park
West. A man had been shot on West Seventy-second Street, near the park.
Shootings were not an uncommon occurrence on the night shift in the
city, so Martinez merely left the page for the AM news anchor. There were
no details, other than that several shots were fired.

Monday Night Football was softly providing the background din, but
since no one on the premises was a sports fan, they paid it little mind.
But as he was on his way to the studio to say good night to Vin, Marty
heard Howard Cosell say something about John Lennon being shot. The
AP and police-scanner alarms went off, almost simultaneously, confirming
that the former Beatle had been the victim. Scelsa came bursting into the
newsroom—a listener had called after hearing Cosell make the announcement at the football game. He had just put Springsteen's "Jungleland" on
the turntable, and he agonized over what to do. "I can't tell people that
John Lennon is dead. I just can't do it." Both men went back to the studio,
unsure of how to treat the situation on the air.

As "Jungleland" reached a quiet passage, Marty finally said, "Either
you tell them or I'll have to tell them, Vin."

Scelsa faded down the record and for the first time in his career was at
a loss for words. As Martinez stood behind him, he reported that Lennon
had been shot and that details were sketchy. Both of them found tears
welling up in their eyes as their throats grew thick with emotion. Martinez
went back to the wire room where the grisly story was being confirmed—
not only had Lennon been shot but he had died on the way to the hospital.
He brought the news to Scelsa, and the disoriented disc jockey called Muni
at Avery Fisher Hall for counsel.

The show had just ended and Scott and I were just walking back into
the room for the postconcert celebration when Vin's call came through.
The news went through the small gathering like a windblown shroud of
fog, spreading from one group to the next. I've never seen a room empty
so quickly. Robin Sagon and Andy Fischer, our FM news people at that

time, were dispatched to gather details and confirm the story through other sources. Everyone quietly filed out, at a loss for what to do, say, or where to go. There would be no party and the tables laden with gourmet delights went untouched. The food would later be distributed to the homeless.

I knew that my place was back at the station, and without prompting, every jock reacted the same way. When I got back to the studio, Scelsa was playing only Lennon's work, pausing to recapitulate the tragedy tersely before breaking down in tears again. Dennis Elsas sought out a copy of his famous interview with the former Beatle. He also recalled the time that he had filled in for Muni on the Friday after Thanksgiving in 1975. Elton John had been a guest on the program, during which he told him of a bet he had made with Lennon. Elton had recorded "Whatever Gets You Through the Night" earlier that year with Lennon on backup vocals. Lennon considered the song a throwaway B-side, but Elton insisted it was a number one record. The ex-Beatle swore that if it ever reached that vaunted chart position, he'd sing it onstage the next time Elton played the city. The previous night at Madison Square Garden, Lennon had kept his promise. That would be the last live performance that John would ever give before an audience in New York.

Muni was completely shaken. Although he'd met all the Beatles when the band first came to America in 1964 while Muni was still at WABC, he felt a special kinship with John. Several months after the Elsas interview, Lennon released *Rock 'n' Roll,* and came to the station to debut the album on Scott's show. But their bond went deeper than that. When Muni was anxiously awaiting the birth of his daughter Tiffany, he found another expectant father in the same hospital. Yoko Ono was about to give birth to Sean and it was not an easy delivery. Lennon and he sat together for hours, drinking coffee and sharing stories of fatherhood. John had become a full-fledged New Yorker by then, often seen strolling through the city's streets during his battle with immigration authorities. He loved Manhattan and wanted to live in the city, fighting the government as it sued for his deportation due to prior marijuana convictions in England. Muni chose to honor his departed friend by starting his show with the Beatles every day thereafter.

The night of December 8, 1980, was the single most important in the history of the station. Still free form, we were able to react instantly to every nuance of the story. We had long talk segments with each jock and their personal reminiscences of Lennon. We took phone calls from grieving listeners, and played nothing but John's music for the next twenty-four hours. WNEW-FM became the heart of the story, a sanctuary for a generation stunned beyond belief that such a beloved musician, that *any* musician, could be assassinated. Raw emotions overflowed as we reflected on the unfairness of it all, how this single violent act could strike down a titan. As the man himself had sung in "God," "The dream is over . . . What can I say?"

It marked the end of so much. Beatle babies who prayed for a reunion realized that it could never happen now. Those of us he had touched were outraged at the waste of it all, that a man with so much yet to give was cut down, just as he was starting to get his life on track again. The bitterness of the split with McCartney was dissipating, and his music was taking on a more optimistic tone. He'd reconciled with Yoko and was revisiting the joys of parenthood with a boy he absolutely adored. Just as his life and art were about to enter a happier phase, his mortal being was cashiered in a pool of blood outside his Dakota apartment.

Newsmen for local television stations came to WNEW to cover the story. Some, like CBS's Tony Guida, came to express their sorrow on our airwaves. He was elegantly turned out in a stylish trench coat and suit, but he sat on the floor of the studio next to Martinez, listening and preparing to read a poem he thought might help to ameliorate the grief. Time seemed to move in slow motion and although we were mouthing the words on the air, we couldn't accept the reality that John Lennon was dead.

The shooting cast a pall on the entire holiday season. There was no joy, no peace on earth. The following Sunday, the station went off the air for a moment of silence, followed by a specially commissioned live performance by a former E Street Band keyboardist, David Sancious, in a beautifully played outpouring of melancholy, a variation on "Across the Universe." As the last note reverberated over the spare stage of the Capitol Theater, we told ourselves it was time to put away our grief and celebrate the man's life and all the happiness he'd brought us, but we were unable to do so for many months thereafter. The senseless killing left a scar on our souls that still invokes pangs of anguish today whenever we relive the events of that cold winter's night.

I Love L.A.

BY 1980, THINGS were changing at upper management at Metromedia. Owner John Kluge was sold on the idea that cellular telecommunications was going to be the cash cow of the future, and to that end took the company private so that he could have the freedom to maneuver his assets in that direction. As one of his right-hand men, George Duncan was shifted from radio to Metromedia Telecommunications, the newly formed division created to acquire cellular properties. Former WNEW news director and KRLD general manager Carl Brazell took over the radio division, along with Vicky Callahan, who'd worked under Duncan at corporate. Brazell soon made the move that Duncan had resisted for so many years— he hired a consultant. Lee Abrams was brought in to advise the entire group.

Sam Bellamy's loose hold on KMET had allowed the station to sink into the nether regions—under a two share. The punk-rocker KROQ, run by Rick Carroll, and Tommy Hadges's AOR outlet, KLOS, were beating it handily. Howard Bloom had ascended to the general manager's chair at KMET replacing L. David Moorhead. He immediately sought to put his own stamp on the station.

Bloom had dark hair and intense green eyes, and was a touchy-feely sort. He wanted to be deeply involved in the psyche of all his players and worked very hard, the first to arrive and the last to leave every day. The short, slightly overweight Bloom believed strongly in group dynamics and spent hours locked in his office conferring with the jocks and salespeople. He'd always gotten along well with Michael Harrison, and quickly came to the conclusion that the station enjoyed its best days when Harrison had an active hand in programming.

Michael's participation at KMET had pretty much dwindled to his hosting *Harrison's Mike* on Saturday mornings. Although he still consulted, his advice was seldom heeded. His own life was going through some changes. His acrimonious breakup with partner Bob Wilson in 1978 had led him to exit *Radio and Records* and form his own tip sheet called *Goodphone Weekly,* as in "you give good phone." *Goodphone* differed from the trade papers of the day in the way it charted album tracks. A traditional chart would list the top albums, but not address the priority each cut was given. Harrison charted the tracks as if they were singles, before they were released as such by the labels. Therefore, you might have three songs from *Exile on Main Street* in the top ten, even though only one was the actual Top-Forty hit single. He also came up with the term "JAZZZ," or triple-Z jazz. This heralded the coming of Kenny G, Grover Washington, Enya, and the next phase of the melodic cool-jazz wave that the new-age crowd savors.

For his part, Wilson invented the term "CHR" to replace Top Forty. Contemporary hit radio more accurately reflected the genre—it had been decades since any station actually played forty current records. A cold war existed between Wilson and Harrison, as the two former friends became the bitterest of rivals. Wilson even fought Harrison over ownership of the term "AOR."

By 1980, Harrison had sold *Goodphone Weekly* to *Billboard,* along with its systems and conventions. He gave that trade magazine a blueprint on restructuring for the eighties and consulted for several radio stations on the side. Harrison also hosted *The Great American Radio Show,* a countdown of AOR hits, one of Westwood One's first syndicated programs. But the workaholic in him was not used to this somewhat lighter load, so when Bloom approached him to take over programming at KMET, he couldn't resist one last shot at restoring the "Mighty MET" to its former glory. He didn't relish working with a consultant—but he had no personal animosity toward Abrams, and their philosophies didn't seem that far apart.

Their plans for KMET were in direct opposition, however. Harrison believed that new wave, heavy metal, and traditional AOR bands could all work on the same station. He was alone in this belief, since the consultants posited that each one of these subgenres had distinctly different fans. They believed that by mixing them together at one station, no one would be served. Harrison won out with Bloom on this point, but his neck was definitely in the guillotine if his instincts proved to be wrong. He needed results and he needed them fast. He assembled a staff, hiring his right-hand woman from *Goodphone,* Christine Brodie, as his assistant. He elevated Cynthia Fox, a beautiful blond protégée, to do mornings with hippie newsman Pat "Paraquat" Kelley. Jeff Gonzer hosted afternoons and Jim Ladd was on at night. They were all encouraged to be wacky and outrageous and play only the songs Harrison placed at their command.

Within one ratings book, KMET catapulted to a four-plus share and surpassed KROQ and KLOS. Harrison had given the audience credit for being broad-minded in their tastes and willing to accept all forms of rock, contrary to what the consultants believed. Harrison played much more heavy metal than anyone thought would work, devoting fully a quarter of the playlist to Led Zeppelin, Ozzy Osbourne, Def Leppard, Mötley Crüe, Ted Nugent, Scorpions, and the like. With this, he blended the Go-Go's, Dave Edmunds, Elvis Costello, the Pretenders, Missing Persons, and the best of the new wavers. He added a healthy dollop of Journey, Kansas, the Rolling Stones, and the Eagles and came up with a musical stew unlike any other in the country. He never fell into the trap of eliminating subgenres as long as he featured the best and most accessible songs from each. He spent a lot of time hanging out in video-game parlors, and his informal research gleaned a firsthand look at what his audience wanted.

In an interesting programming tack, Harrison would commission his production department to design elaborate promos, sometimes lasting as long as three minutes, highlighting the premiere date of a greatly anticipated new album on KMET. Much as one would promote a motion picture with trailers, the highly produced announcements would feature snippets from songs and bill the individual musicians like movie stars.

Abrams and Harrison did share their cinematic vision for what radio should be.

KMET was very publicity oriented and involved itself in television cross-promotions as the music-video era dawned. Their street billboards were innovative, sometimes deliberately placed upside down so that people would talk about them. Michael finally reached an uneasy rapprochement with Bob Wilson, who chronicled his success at KMET in a feature story in *Radio and Records*. The two men had seen too much water flow under the bridge to become friends again, but they were able to resume professional courtesies.

But despite the early and continued success, Carl Brazell at corporate headquarters was not content with just defeating his two rock competitors. He had his eye on Rick Dees and the Top Forty station KIIS. Dees, the creator of "Disco Duck," was a huge phenomenon in Los Angeles in the early eighties and was pulling double-digit morning shares, leading his station to continual market dominance. When Brazell asked Harrison how to achieve Rick Dees's numbers, he replied, "Simple. Hire Rick Dees."

His answer was not meant to be sarcastic. He had realistically appraised the situation and knew that if KMET tinkered with what they were doing just to chase Dees, their current success would be lost and they'd only be another pale imitator.

The intense pressure to increase profits filtered downward—Brazell pushed Bloom, who pressed Harrison. Burkhardt/Abrams had been trying to convince the general manager that too much heavy metal was the main reason the station couldn't achieve KIIS-type ratings. Bloom was very supportive of Harrison and was grateful for the growth the station had shown. He thought it unfair that management was exerting so much stress on KMET to carry the load for the other less successful stations in the chain. But Brazell was paying the consultants for their advice and they had his ear, with more frequency and persuasion than Harrison and Bloom could exert from three thousand miles away. So Abrams scheduled a meeting with Harrison to try to change the dynamic of the station so that it could challenge Dees's Top Forty powerhouse. That meeting would decide the future of the radio station, one way or another.

Badlands

THE NIGHT OF John Lennon's death was symbolic in that it illustrated what WNEW-FM could still do as a progressive radio station, how we could galvanize a community in grief to warm itself around our fire. But it also signified the end of an era, and things were to go downhill from there in a fairly rapid fashion. Now that George Duncan had departed the radio division for Kluge's new cellular company and Carl Brazell and Vicky Callahan were running things, neither seemed to be big fans of Mel Karmazin. By 1980, Mel was general manager of both WNEW-AM and FM, but was ready to take on more responsibility within the company. When the general manager job at Kluge's WNEW-TV opened up, Mel was the logical candidate to ascend to the position. The company didn't see it that way, and for Mel it was a clear signal, knowing that he'd gone as far as he could within the current political structure of Metromedia. He set about seeking other options, and soon found himself with an offer to become the president of Infinity, a small radio company that owned three stations at the time, founded by two ex-Kluge employees. Mel would be paid $125,000 plus stock and given a red Mercedes convertible to drive.

Rather than immediately name a successor in early 1981, Callahan took over the station in an attempt to understand how it worked on a day-to-day basis and why its ratings lagged behind some of the more successful stations in the chain. She also had to quell the chaos created with the departure of Karmazin, who had been a driving force behind the station for five years. The two main candidates for Mel's job were Tom Chuisano, a young sales manager in from Chicago, and Mike Kakoyiannis, who had also served in sales.

After some initial feeling out, it became obvious that I could have the program director's job on more than a de facto basis, and that Callahan was less worried about ruffling feathers than in giving the station a more conventional structure. Scott could be given an honorary title and his influence was always a factor in anything the station did, but he didn't want the hands-on responsibility of doing some of the nasty work that had to be done—instituting some kind of music control.

With Vicky Callahan, I attended my first focus groups and met with Dwight Douglas, who was assigned as a consultant to our station by Burkhardt/Abrams. It was clear that the station wasn't going to remain free form, and I could either take the job and try to formulate a structure that would allow us to stay true to our roots, or they could bring in an outsider who would likely trash the place. I never gave any thought to not taking the position, although I should have. Some members of the staff, who already regarded me as a scoundrel, would only grow to vilify me more as they resisted the changes I knew were inevitable.

Mike Kakoyiannis was given the GM job and I officially became program director in 1981. The first step was to adjust the music, and we came up with an unobtrusive way to do that. Similar to what KSAN had tried with their red-dot system, we designated sixteen songs for hot rotation by placing red stickers on the fronts of the records. They would go into the rack, and twice every hour, each jock would have to play one of these songs. After playing the record, they were to put the album in the back of the bin, and couldn't use it again until it moved to the front. The DJs were not forced to play the first record—they could dig three or four deep if they didn't like the selection. This only ensured that the top songs would be played three times a day, something we probably were doing already. But we also could track if certain jocks were avoiding certain records, and react accordingly.

However mild this system was, it effectively marked the end of commercial free-form radio in New York, and given the fact that KMET, KSAN, WBCN, WMMR, and all the other Metromedia outlets had instituted systems years before, we were considered the last holdout in major-market radio.

At the meeting announcing the system, most of the jocks sat ashen faced, knowing that they were witnessing the end of an era. We expected a negative reaction, but most were strangely passive, as if they had seen it coming and realized that they were powerless to stop it. Some were expecting a more draconian format, but I hoped that wouldn't be necessary.

We knew that Scelsa would be the biggest objector but we were prepared to deal with whatever consequences the change inspired. Vin dismissively regarded Pete Larkin and Jim Monaghan (my music director) as "Neer's pissants," so I knew any attempt made to give the music stationality would not be taken lightly.

As the gathering broke up, Scelsa walked right by me without so much as a glance and asked to speak with Kakoyiannis alone. It was déjà vu for Vin, as the events of ten years earlier repeated themselves. While in the privacy of Mike's corner office, Scelsa quit, using his terse WPLJ abdication speech, "I'm outta here." But time had caught up with the boy who cried wolf and his resignation was accepted. The *Butch and the Brick Show* was over, although Morrera stayed on in the safety of the overnights. Vin reconsidered and attempted to rescind his resignation a week later, but still wasn't willing to abide by the rules. If we were serious about competing, we couldn't allow freedom for one and not the others, so Scelsa was irrevocably out.

We couldn't afford to play games anymore. The company was serious about boosting ratings, as I knew directly from Harrison at KMET and as KSAN found out the hard way. After Bonnie Simmons left the San Francisco station, the promotions director, Abby Melamed, took over the programming and tried to instill some discipline. She didn't last too long in the position. Tom Yates, a friend and disciple of Michael Harrison, tried to clean up the mess, but it was too late. Low ratings caused management to blow it up and change it into a country station. Until the end, they still retained a small cadre of intensely loyal listeners who remembered its grandeur. On the day they switched formats, a group of them erected a tombstone bearing the legend KSAN—RIP. At its base was a pile of cow manure.

The same factors that killed KSAN were at work at WNEW-FM and we were wary of suffering the same fate. Drugs were the most insidious. Jocks were doing coke while on the air on a regular basis, and even some of our major players were guilty of staying out all night on a binge, and taking quaaludes to come down. Muni was just drinking, and it never seemed to affect his air work. Pete and Dennis were straight arrows. But almost everyone else, at one time or another, let the grip of drugs distort their reality.

Why? Never having been part of the drug culture, I've never really understood it. Since drugs were so easily available from record promoters or just industry hangers-on at little or no cost, I guess the temptation was just too much to resist, with everyone in the immediate circle doing it.

Marty Martinez recalls a night at John Scher's rock club, the Ritz, where Iggy Pop was performing. David Bowie entered the club, clad in a dark trench coat, long hair swept back from his pale face, looking like a young S.S. officer. He flitted around the room, kissing several of the male patrons on the lips before visiting Iggy in his backstage dressing room between sets. After spending several minutes alone with Pop, he emerged and pranced off with his entourage.

Iggy had done a dynamite opening set, but when he came out for the late show, he seemed transformed. Half of his face was grotesquely painted green, and he appeared to be on something powerful. He staggered to the mic and struggled through his opening number.

"Thas it," he slurred. "Thas all I'm doing unless you pay me. You want more, you gotta pay me."

The late-night clubgoers threw money at the stage—dollar bills, coins, whatever they had.

"Right," he said, and stumbled through another song. "I need more money." As the well-lubricated crowd reacted poorly to this appeal, his mind leapt to another subject. "How'd you like to see my dick?" he asked the shocked crowd. Raucous applause and catcalls broke out, as Pop lowered his leather pants to fulfill his promise in front of the astonished audience, many of whom were impressed by the size of his equipment. Jim Morrison had to flee the country for doing less.

Although this was a high point of outrageousness, the club scene became a staple with the jocks at WNEW. Their faces were their backstage passes, and they were glad-handed by promoters who were happy to cater to their every pharmaceutical whim. This led to ego problems, which had a hand in the station's undoing.

Surrounded by sycophants, the jocks thought they were radio gods. They saw their every program as inviolable art that was beyond the reproach of these barbarians who only saw radio as a business and wanted to make money. When Dwight Douglas of Burkhardt/Abrams first addressed the group, he was met with resistance at first, and then open defiance.

Douglas began his speech with a premise that he believed rhetorical, and he assumed it would be accepted by acclamation without debate.

"Let's face it, the reason we're all here is to make money. For ourselves, for the company—that's the bottom line. We're in business to make money. And the way to make money is by getting ratings. That's as simple as it gets, right?"

No one argued, but reading the faces of the staff I could tell they disagreed to varying extents. At one extreme there was Pete Larkin, who had given me his radio philosophy for the eighties in parable form shortly after he came aboard. He related a story he had heard about the program director of DC-101, the top AOR station in Washington. The man was being wooed by WHFS, the free-form station in nearby Maryland. Although they couldn't pay him what he was making at DC-101, his suitor had avoided the subject of compensation scrupulously and was extolling the freedom his jocks had. He wasn't impressed by the pitch and asked, "What's the figure?"

The recruiter ignored him and proceeded to talk about how he would be free to play anything, a side of Frank Zappa if he wanted. He continued on about the cultural importance that WHFS held among the rock community until the PD finally burst out impatiently, "Look, what's the figure? Frank Zappa, Frank Sinatra, I don't care. What's the figure?"

Although Larkin, Elsas, Fornatale, and Muni would much rather play Lynyrd Skynyrd than Leonard Bernstein, they knew that their jobs rested on making money for Metromedia. They saw their role as putting together a program that would attract and please listeners, even if they didn't love every record they played. This was reality. The others on the staff wanted to create works of art, even if the numbers weren't sufficient to justify their salaries.

So Dwight Douglas's gambit was rejected out of hand by half his audience and it only got worse. When he stressed the value of preparation—making the point that Johnny Carson would never walk in five minutes before *The Tonight Show* was set to tape and wing it—he asked why radio should be viewed any differently. Every time the mic was opened, the jock should have a clear objective. If it was to tell a story, the story should have an ending. A joke should have a punch line. A music rap should have a point.

Dave Herman challenged him in front of the entire group. Dave's argument was that this form of radio had thrived for fifteen years flying by the seat of its pants, and that Douglas obviously had no understanding of what made it great. Douglas replied that Dave was making several times what he had made fifteen years ago and that now there was a highly paid support staff at the station. There was also smart competition, who used extensive research to program their station to optimal advantage. Things were different now.

Dave said that to preplan everything would ruin the spontaneity that made the station come alive. Others chimed in their support and soon we had a full-fledged Boston Tea Party on our hands.

I stepped in and said, "I think what Dwight is saying is not that you have to script everything, but you should practice in your head where your rap is going before you actually say it. Just decide in advance if what you're about to talk about is worthwhile so you can eliminate the bad stuff."

"What's wrong with scripting if that's what's necessary?" Douglas interjected.

He'd uttered the magic phrase. "To be continued. Just some food for thought," I said, preempting any pelting with rotten vegetables, wrapping up the meeting. The idea of having the consultant address the group personally was a complete failure. Our objective was to show the staff that Burkhardt/Abrams didn't have horns and weren't responsible for personally destroying the medium. The meeting only served to strengthen that perception among the unconverted. Perhaps if we had heeded our own advice and rehearsed with Douglas, we could have headed off the revolution by phrasing things more diplomatically. It was as if the staff was still speaking Russian and the Abrams people had read the English translation and found it wanting.

The jocks who considered their judgments sacrosanct were guilty of the same hubris that KSAN's staff suffered from—hanging out and drugging every night with their clubgoing peers was distorting their view of the general listening audience. Avant-garde hipsters might love Iggy Pop, but the majority of WNEW's audience was not as impressed.

WBCN in Boston had similar fast times, but their ratings during this period thrived despite the pharmaceutical consumption. Mark Parenteau relates a story about John Belushi, who was a huge fan of the station, listening to it as he vacationed on Martha's Vineyard. While in town, he would hang with Peter Wolf and David Kennedy, the late son of Robert. David was utterly charming and sweet but liked to party in the rock world, using his connections to get him backstage at all the major shows. He brought Belushi to Boston to make a presentation for the Kennedy Center's Honor Society, at a time when John's career was ablaze. *Animal House* had just been released and had swept the nation by storm. *Saturday Night Live* was creating brilliant satire with its original cast. Belushi was on top of the world but both he and David were hopelessly attracted to the worst combinations of drugs imaginable. Their tragic overdoses were no surprise to those who knew of their proclivities. Before the Honor Society event, Kennedy and Belushi visited Parenteau's afternoon show on WBCN and snorted everything they could get their hands on, sharing their bounty with their on-air host. Belushi joined Mark for a four-hour radio free-for-all, taking calls, playing some unreleased Keith Richards tracks that John had gotten his hands on, and breaking every FCC rule in the book. Scattered throughout the festivities were many of the seven deadly words you can't say on the radio. But since it involved a Kennedy in Boston, and since it was John Belushi, the biggest comic actor of his generation at the time, it was all right.

WBCN was now dominant in the the market with double-digit shares. Charlie Kendall left in the early eighties when Mel Karmazin's Infinity Group purchased the station and refused to honor the bonus clauses in his contract. After a brief stop in Indiana, he landed a PD job at WMMR in Philly. A former weekend jock named Oedipus succeeded Kendall at BCN and built on Charlie's success, keeping his format largely intact. Like Harrison in Los Angeles, they were able to play the best of new wave and blend it with acts that later were categorized as Top Forty like Duran Duran and Madonna. With their large college population, they could walk the line between the classics and cutting edge and make it work.

In New York, however, the music seemed hopelessly splintered. Disco had taken away some of our blue-collar audience, as "Disco 92" WKTU hit the airwaves and went from a one share to an eleven in the course of one rating period. But new wave was our real problem. It was embraced by the cognoscenti but the mainstream rejected most of it as nihilistic garbage. The punk image of purple mohawks and pierced body parts wasn't playing well in suburbia, and that's where the AOR audience lay in the metropolitan area. We had to fight our natural inclination to gravitate toward the adventurous and balance it with the increasingly conservative atmosphere that Reagan had ushered in. But along with the new prosperity and optimism for the future, average people were now dabbling in recreational drugs.

The drug culture particularly affected our news department. One parttime newsman had developed a heroin addiction, and was stealing albums to support his habit. For months, Muni, savoring his role as amateur sleuth, tried to determine who was robbing the station of records we needed to play on the air. The news guy kept a syringe, telling everyone that he was a diabetic who needed to inject insulin several times a day. His big boo-boo was coming into the studio to chat with Muni one afternoon, while scarfing down several Hershey bars. Scott immediately suspected something was afoul.

But his Marine background and boyish conspiratorial side wanted to catch the fellow red-handed. So he convinced Marty Martinez to walk by our suspect with a box of twenty-five shrink-wrapped Led Zeppelin albums, and ostentatiously place them on the desk in the music library. The man's eyes widened as Martinez strolled by with his treasure trove, and sure enough, minutes later the box was gone. Muni positioned Tammy Tracy on the back staircase and within the hour the guilty newsman stole down the stairs with his stash. Tracy grabbed him from behind, alerted Muni, and the man was fired on the spot. We tried to set him up with counseling, but it would take years before he finally cleaned up his act.

Tom Morrera was fired a year after Scelsa left. The building was having a problem with its heat in the off hours. It was constructed such that when they turned down the temperature in the outer offices to save energy, the studios got cold as well. Morrera complained about this several times, and each time we spoke to building maintenance who assured us they had solved the problem. One night after a particularly bad Rangers loss, Father Tom was in a foul mood. He'd brought a hockey stick with him and proceeded to pound it harder and harder on a newsroom desk, until it shattered. He then went to work, and as the overnight wore on, the studio got colder than the water around the *Titanic*. This was it. He took one of the discrepancy forms kept for reporting technical problems and wrote:

Dear Mike . . . you mother f—ing Greek son of a bitch. I'm freezing my ass off here, you little cocksucker. What the f— are you going to do about it?

Despite Marty's advice not to post it, the angry Brick slid the note under Kakoyiannis's door. The next morning when I arrived, I was greeted with, "Call Pete Larkin. I've just fired Morrera. Look at this note." Indeed the memo was so coarse that, coupled with the knife-wielding incident, there was no convincing Mike that Morrera was just having a bad night.

One of my most naïve mistakes as program director was to believe I could, through a logical presentation of the facts, convert the disbelievers to understand and adhere to the current music philosophy. But the truth was that the only way to get them to act more responsibly about the music was to tighten the system so that they couldn't abuse it. The consultants suggested harsh measures like removing the library from the studio so that they had no access to anything we hadn't approved. Symbolically, I thought that went too far, since I wanted the jocks to have some hand in programming, so that they would be engaged in, and enthused about, the music. But it wasn't like working at WLIR with a bunch of young people united in a common cause. Some members of the staff thought they were holding back the barbarians and that I was allowing them in via a Trojan horse. I saw my efforts as a compromise position—to accept the consultant's advice that made sense for us and reject the ideas that wouldn't work in New York. In reality, I was fighting a war on two fronts, and both sides were girding for battle by entrenching themselves in positions that gave no quarter. "Live Free or Die" was not only New Hampshire's motto.

Since everyone there had done this for so long, they thought they were radio icons. But in reality, they weren't humorists. They weren't great raconteurs. They were generally skilled interviewers, but people were beginning not to care what rock musicians had to say, given that the average listener could not relate to the excessive, overblown spectacles that many rock bands had become. All we brought to the table was a knowledge of music that was now compromised by the different directions rock was taking. My goal, like Harrison's in Los Angeles, was to play the best of each subgenre. But by allowing the jocks freedom, they were distorting that goal to their personal tastes.

Ronald Reagan had made it fashionable to be capitalistic, and the whole country was becoming proud of their materialism. People were beginning to flaunt their wealth, instead of hiding it, as our generation had. The stock market was not just for a few Wall Street types, but the average person was now investing and wanted to see his pet companies pay dividends. In mainstream music, art took a back seat to enterprise, and we were slow in reacting.

My biggest disappointment was Meg Griffin. I thought she had the makings of a star. She was bright, attractive, and had a great straight-ahead delivery. Unthreatening to other women and appreciated by men for her intelligence, we thought she gave us a perfect nighttime presence. In May of 1982, she was awarded the still potent 6 to 10 P.M. shift at the expense of Dennis Elsas. It proved to be one of the biggest mistakes I made as program director.

Dennis wouldn't fight the system, played the music the audience wanted, and his pleasant personality never got in the way. His interviews were well prepared and he enjoyed good relations with some of the staples we were playing. In fact, Pete Townshend was so impressed with the chat they had that he asked a friend to tape Dennis's shows so that he could listen to them while driving his daughter to school in the morning. He executed the format well and didn't babble on endlessly with no plan. His ratings were generally just below a three share, even with or slightly under the rest of the station. Firing him completely would have been patently unfair, so he was demoted to weekends for slightly less money. The timing was especially bad on a personal level, because the longtime bachelor was scheduled to be married the following month and had laid out a big deposit on a house.

But Meg was a hot item, in that she was a champion of new wave, sharing her knowledge and friendships with the musicians in a very unpretentious manner. I had long talks with Meg about the music. I was in sympathy with her tastes, but stressed that she was being handed a great opportunity to maximize her talents. If she played by the rules and didn't let her own preferences for punk and new wave subvert her, the sky was the limit. She nodded in agreement and then proceeded to break every guideline we set out for her. Worse yet, when caught, she lied about it. I tried to convince myself that she didn't fully understand the concept, but she was far too intelligent. She would support the format publicly, and privately do everything she could to undermine our efforts. Within a year, fully a third of the audience Elsas had left her was gone.

A concurrent move had equally bad results. Since Dave Herman's ratings had never reached Laquidara's levels at WBCN, or even Cynthia Fox's at KMET, we thought that it was time for a more exciting morning show. Even if we could afford to go after a big-time program from another market, the audition tapes we heard consisted mainly of puerile T&A jokes, and we were seeking a funny but intelligent presentation that wouldn't insult the audience's sensibilities. Unfortunately, although Dave had a great ear for good comedy, he wasn't a funny guy himself. In retrospect, the smartest thing we could have done would have been to team him with a wacky sidekick earlier on, so that Dave could be the straight man and music maven and the sidekick could play the fool. But Dave had an ego, and didn't want his star diminished by a foil who might attract more attention than he did. So along with Vicky Callahan and Kakoyiannis, I tried to come up with a solution. The only person on the staff who we thought was even moderately funny was my brother. He certainly was more high energy than Dave and by virtue of that alone, we hoped to improve on Dave's increasingly low-key delivery.

What I didn't know was that Dave had joined the party crowd and was coming to work at less than his best. All I knew was that our morning show dragged and had no pace, and we felt that Dave was the wrong guy for that slot and that he'd fit in better from ten to two at night. Dan-o was given mornings at the same time as the Meg Griffin move and to put it quite simply, it didn't work. Within six months, his ratings were half of what Dave's had been. We were trying longer talk segments and importing professional comedians to work with him, but listeners used to Dave's laidback approach weren't ready for a wacky morning show. A panicked Kakoyiannis was constantly pressuring me to try new combinations but nothing seemed to work. The old way didn't cut it and the new one made it worse. Was this a hopeless situation?

Finally, after another devastating ratings book, Mike told me it was time to pull the plug. I was charged with the unenviable task of firing my brother after only six months and putting him back on weekends. He saw it coming and took it well, but was disappointed in the support he'd gotten. The truth is that we spent more on trying to help him in six months than we'd spent on Dave in years. It was just the wrong show at the wrong time.

So it became my job to find a new morning show, while filling in doing the old one. We asked our sister stations to make us tapes of their competition in hopes of killing two birds with one stone—eliminating a competitor in another market and finding ourselves a great show. I traveled up and down the East Coast, checking into motels and listening to morning shows. Unfortunately, there was nothing out there that we thought would be appropriate. We liked John DiBella at WLIR, but in his initial conversation with us, he threw out a number so high it immediately disqualified him. He told us what he was making on Long Island and I couldn't believe it. My skepticism was well founded when WMMR brought him in a few months later for considerably less than we would have paid. His show worked for them and their morning problem was vanquished soon after his arrival. My interim morning job stretched into the new year, and by some quirk of fate, the ratings immediately were restored to the level Dave had left them at. Mike and Vicky were starting to see me as less a program director and more as a morning host.

I'm afraid I clinched that decision with another programming move. A new station, WAPP, had hit the market on May 3, 1982—debuting with 103 days of commercial-free music. Abrams believed that with WPLJ playing a tight AOR list and WAPP doing a variation of the same, we couldn't survive by straddling the fence, playing some new wave and some traditional AOR. He'd just invented a new format called Superstars 2 that was having some success in the Bay Area. It was based on the premise that the traditional AOR stations were burning out all the classics by playing them endlessly, and that the adult rock audience was ready for a blend of new wave and alternative tracks from the big artists. For example, rather than play "Born to Run" by Springsteen endlessly, we should play "Backstreets." It sounded good to me, and most of the jocks embraced the idea, tired of playing the same hit records that everyone else was. Lee and I combed through the library for days and I came up with a list that I thought made sense for us in New York. He agreed with my choices, and we entered 1983 with hopes that our latest innovative approach would save the day.

Highway to Hell

THE ONE CONCRETE benefit we received from WAPP was Mark McEwen. He had been imported along with E. J. Crummy to be part of their morning team, but the combination didn't work and he was axed rather quickly.

He called me the day he was fired and I agreed to meet with him. Although I didn't know it at the time, Mark is black. After all that time at WLIR and five years programming WNEW, I finally had the opportunity to work with another black rock-and-roll jock. Race was about the only thing he had in common with Bill Mercer, though, because his style was completely the opposite of Rosko's seriously cerebral and political bent. Mark was a personable guy who had started out doing radio and some stand-up comedy in Maryland. His humor was gentle and inoffensive. I liked him at once and told him that we'd make some space for him on weekends, and try to find a more permanent place as things shook out.

Superstars 2 was interesting radio, but the only place it worked was in San Francisco at KFOG. We were guinea pigs, constantly refining and re-defining the format. Coupled with the new jock lineup and changes within the market, it clearly was going to take some time to gel. Unfortunately, it wasn't given time. Carl Brazell was pressuring us for instant results, and this new format wasn't going to provide them. It probably was an idea ahead of its time, since nowadays there seems to be a clear place in most markets for an adult rock station. But after two down ratings books in 1983, I was called into a meeting with Kakoyiannis and given a choice.

The station needed a full-time program director. The job was mine if I wanted it. But frankly, Mike and Vicky Callahan thought I was having more success in the morning than I was at programming and recommended I stay with that, for the good of the station. PDs were easily found, but successful morning shows were hard to come by.

The decision wasn't a hard one. Mornings would pay me twice the money for half the work. I could go home at eleven most mornings and have the entire day ahead of me. I'd already had a taste of what mornings could do for me on a social level. All my work behind the scenes might give me a nod of recognition from some listeners, but in the prominent morning slot, everybody knew me and couldn't do enough for me. It felt strange, because I was the same guy doing the same thing on the air I'd always done, but now I received star treatment, whereas before I was barely noticed. All sorts of sponsor freebies came flying in, and I was given discounts and special consideration by scores of merchants. Where were they when I didn't have money and had to steal food? Now that I could afford to pay my own way, everyone wanted to give me things. I was asked for autographs everywhere I went. By contrast, programming required a twelve-hour day and every shift on the station was my responsibility. I was paid much less and everyone on the staff saw me as a real or potential enemy. Any success I might have was only known within the industry. The few reservations I had were quickly dispelled by Kakoyiannis. I didn't like leaving the job in programming undone and I was leaving myself and the station vulnerable to outside intervention, but I was assured that I would be involved in approving my successor and that they wouldn't hire someone I wasn't comfortable with.

I swallowed that one whole. I began to set up interviews with prospective program directors, and soon winnowed the field down to three. First, there was Dave Logan. He'd been a Burkhardt/Abrams programmer in Seattle and was the consultant's choice. I liked Dave, but thought he was too inexperienced for the job, especially dealing with the gigantic egos at the station. I also didn't think he knew enough about New York music. I filed him away for the future, thinking prophetically that someday he'd grow into the job.

Norm Winer was the longtime PD of WXRT in Chicago, a station that paralleled WNEW in many ways. He'd had continuous success there, and had also worked to great acclaim in the seventies at WBCN. Winer was a nice man who ruled with a strong but wise and compassionate hand. He was extremely intelligent, and seemed suited to easily win the respect of the jocks. His vision for the station linked with mine perfectly, and I recommended him to the powers above as my choice.

The third candidate was Charlie Kendall. My personal encounters with Charlie were at company conventions and I got along well with him. He had visited us when he hired John DiBella to do mornings at WMMR, and I was impressed with his thoroughness and subsequent success at making DiBella's *Morning Zoo* a hit in Philly. He worked at Metromedia, and that was a plus in advancing someone from within. Any telephone contact I'd had with him on cooperative matters within the chain was constructive.

But Charlie was someone I couldn't recommend. His reputation was not good—people said he played dirty, fast, and loose with the truth, and was seriously unbalanced because of his drinking and use of cocaine. Record promoters and former jocks who knew him told me horror stories about his reign of terror at WMMR, where they had nicknamed him the "Prince of Darkness." Many who had worked with him at WBCN had nothing good to say about him.

Imagine my surprise when Mike Kakoyiannis told me without prior discussion that he had hired Kendall. I felt betrayed and told him so. I was supposed to be consulted every step of the way and have veto powers over any candidate. Too late, Mike said, it's done. I slammed the door to his office, shouting at him to find another morning man because I wouldn't work for that "drug addict."

After I had cooled down, Muni and Kakoyiannis sat me down and said that I was being unfair and that I should give Charlie a chance, his ratings at WBCN and WMMR had been good, and he'd worked well at WMMS, a former Metromedia station in Cleveland. I was told he understood that things were different at WNEW and that I would be his adviser as sort of a program director emeritus. I could certainly appeal directly to Mike if I disagreed with any direction Charlie gave.

I naïvely agreed to approach things with an open mind. As I welcomed Charlie to the station, he was very aware of my "drug addict" quote and wanted me nowhere near his programming decisions. He refused any orientation from me, saying that he'd rather learn things on his own. I began to realize that we would be enemies as long as we worked together, and that he was in a position to get me before I could get him.

He was given a gift from the gods weeks after he arrived. WPLJ inexplicably decided to change formats to Top Forty, leaving their three-plus share AOR audience behind. Their research indicated that for the long term, Top Forty had more growth potential. They fired most of their staff and left us with our pick of their experienced and popular jocks, people like Tony Pigg, Pat St. John, and Carol Miller. All three eventually worked at WNEW.

Charlie acted swiftly in his first months. He fired Pete Larkin and installed McEwen in the overnights. I viewed that as a warning shot at me, since he knew that I liked and valued Larkin. He steered the station almost directly to where WPLJ had been musically but with a slightly broader playlist that included select locally popular artists. He hired his wife, Lisa, as music director, rather than rely on Jim Monaghan, who knew the market better. But Jim was another one of "my guys," so he tabbed him as morning show producer. He moved Dave Herman to middays and brought in Dan Carlyle to do late nights. He bumped Fornatale to weekends.

His quick scuttling of Superstars 2 was the right move. Charlie knew radio, and despite my problems with the way he treated people, he understood that WPLJ had just given us their audience and that if we didn't take it, someone would. K-ROCK was about to change from Top Forty to classic rock, a relatively new format that only played rock oldies from the sixties and seventies. It had been purchased by Karmazin's Infinity Group, which was now gobbling up some choice properties. Dan Ingram and Rosko (who had come back from France and worked at several Top Forty and urban stations) were fired as the station charted a different course. They took some former PLJ staffers, but clearly the AOR audience was ours for the taking.

And take it we did. Charlie relentlessly pressured the record labels for everything he could get, and since we were now the only rock outlet in town that played new music, we were gladly given most of what he wanted. Whatever wasn't given, he took. He convinced one of our producers to bribe a recording engineer with drugs to get a test pressing of a new Stones release. Their label had to promise us a boatload of favors when we reluctantly agreed to pull it off the air. When Marty Martinez was dispatched to cover a David Bowie press conference, he was given a roll of OUT OF ORDER yellow tape stolen from the phone company. In the days before cellular technology, reporters would file their stories from pay phones in the lobby of whatever venue the event took place in. Martinez arrived early and taped over all the receivers, so that the other reporters were forced to seek phones in the street, most of which really *were* out of order. Martinez simply pulled the tape off one of the phones, filed a report, and got a big jump on announcing the tour dates.

Kendall's way of handling the consultants was unique and effective as well. Whenever they would come to town, Charlie would make sure they were set up with a nonstop parade of hookers and cocaine. They stayed in their hotels and missed scheduled meetings at the station. Upon leaving, the grateful consultants would report that WNEW sounded just fine.

Charlie fired my brother for playing Monty Python's "Sit on My Face." Unfortunately, in a situation like this, Dan had erred big time and I was powerless to defend him. In today's raunchy radio environment, the Python bit sounds tame, but at that time the obvious spoof on oral sex was in questionable taste for a station like WNEW. We had a female sales and promotions manager, and Kakoyiannis was very uptight about anything that might be construed as degrading to women. But essentially, these things could be dealt with in ways other than dismissal. There were suspensions, even fines that could be levied. In retrospect, it came down to the fact that Charlie didn't like Dan on the air. He thought he tried too hard to be funny and wasn't, always pushing for something that wasn't there. And he'd committed the cardinal sin of being my brother and my hire. The only plea was one for mercy but Charlie wasn't merciful in those days. After a nine-month exile, Dan-o would eventually be rehired by Charlie, who marveled at how he'd improved in so short a time.

Charlie yelled at people, forgot promises and commitments, and generally was hard to work for. But whether it was WPLJ's abandoning the fray or Charlie's innate programming skills, our ratings soared from the midtwos to a four share. My morning numbers went up as well, and we did even better when Charlie removed McEwen from overnights and made him my sidekick. With Jim Monaghan producing, McEwen and I piled up some great numbers. The station even did a television commercial for us with me as Sonny Crockett and McEwen as Rico Tubbs, based on the *Miami Vice* satires we did. We did our show from many different local clubs with live music, the most memorable of which was pressed in a record— Elvis Costello's rendition of "My Funny Valentine."

Things were sweet for a while and our ratings made us impervious to Charlie's pressure. I still wasn't getting along with him but we'd declared an uneasy truce, since it seemed we both needed each other. And I had to admit that although I didn't like his tactics, they did work for the betterment of the station. He updated WNEW's remote capacity with wireless mics and transmitters and we covered every concert as if we owned them.

We got what we hoped would be a much-needed boost due to the impatience of Doubleday, the company that owned WAPP. After a solid start with 103 days of commercial-free music, they faded quickly and after two years changed formats, on October 5, 1984. Their defection gave us another ratings uptick and we sailed to a 4.3. K-ROCK had yet to become a factor, although they hired Jay Thomas, a talented disc jockey turned actor turned disc jockey to do mornings. Jay had been very successful some years before at 99X, the Top Forty successor to WOR-FM.

Charlie Kendall was responsible for a major innovation in his use of technology. For years, most stations, including WNEW, used a card system. Each song was given a grid card that the jocks had to initial whenever they played the record. The music director had to scrutinize the cards and discern patterns to see if jocks were cheating by playing only their favorites and ignoring the rest. This resulted in a lot of paperwork for both parties, and the system could easily be abused.

Computers were just beginning to be used to program stations. The knee-jerk reaction is that this represents a bad trend, and certainly given the direction radio has taken in the last decade there is justification for that viewpoint. But the computer saves the jocks and programmers a lot of work by replacing the card system and the resultant paperwork with a mouse click. Charlie junked the cards and replaced them with a program called "Selector." Despite some initial bugs, Selector works at most radio stations where the music director simply feeds songs into it, and the computer spits them out at random. The music could then be perfectly balanced according to the factors the PD views as important.

But Charlie knew that WNEW was still different and that a computer-
ized list of scattered rock hits was not what the jocks and audience expected
of the station. So he contacted the system's programmers and instructed
them on how to build some flexibility into the system. What they invented
together was "DJ Select," and it may go down as Kendall's most important
contribution to the medium.

DJ Select allowed the jocks to delve into any category so that segues
could be made and sets designed intelligently. One merely had to click on
a song that didn't mesh well with the others and the whole list of available
tunes in that category would be at the jock's disposal. Songs that had been
played too recently or were played at the same time a couple of days earlier
were eliminated. The program director set the rules, and rather than sift
through hundreds of cards in different bins to avoid conflicts, a jock had a
dozen choices at his fingertips, all cleared for airplay. The music director
could simply print out the changes the jocks had made and there was instantly a permanent record of what was played. Instead of hastily scrawled
music sheets, the jocks just clicked on the replacement songs and they
were automatically entered neatly into the system. The DJs could thus
have maximum flexibility, without the capacity to cheat easily.

This was a system that Charlie wisely pioneered, and it seemed to en-
capsulate the best of both worlds. I commended his innovations and his respect for the jocks' freedom to program their own music, knowing that this
system tangibly achieved what Harrison and I had dreamed of at WLIR.
But forces over all our heads conspired to upset the roll we were on. Suddenly, our four-plus share and morning revenues weren't good enough,
even though they represented new heights for the station.

Group president Carl Brazell could certainly be cast as the greedy one
here but he was under great stress due to another surprise development—
Kluge sold him Metromedia. The old man was reenergized when he foresaw the rise of cellular-telephone technology and needed to liquidate his
radio assets to fully fund his new endeavor. Rather than take on the lengthy
process of finding a buyer and awaiting FCC approval, he hit upon the idea
to sell to his own employees. He offered the whole chain to Brazell and his
group of general managers for the fair market value, at least in his eyes, of
$285 million. He even agreed to intercede with the investment bankers at
Morgan Stanley to leverage the deal. Although the GMs were men of
means, most of the money would have to be borrowed. He gave Brazell
forty-eight hours to answer before withdrawing the offer. After gaining no

sleep throughout the entire period in his efforts to forge the coalition, Brazell agreed to Kluge's terms.

The new company was called Metropolitan Broadcasting (the original name Kluge had started with) and they assumed huge debt from the outset of their venture. Doomed from the start, stations had to increase revenues almost twofold just to stay in business. Immediately, plans were laid to spin off some of the chain to keep the others afloat.

The ripple effect was felt in Los Angeles, where Michael Harrison was told at KMET that KIIS and Rick Dees were now his target, not the vanquished KLOS and KROQ. Although still owned by Malrite, the venerable WMMS in Cleveland also heeded the siren's call for bigger profits and turned to Top Forty, although they played almost exclusively singles from rock bands in an amalgam they called Rock Forty. They were the role model for what Brazell envisioned for KMET, as the Cleveland rocker broadened their appeal even further and reached sixteen shares. They had become such a habit in the market that people who didn't even listen would cite them in Arbitron diaries because they were so hip to listen to. Much of what drove them to change was that AOR gurus had declared that artists like Prince were inappropriate for rock stations, which Kid Leo and his gang considered racist.

Despite the increasing corporate pressure, Mark McEwen and I still felt safe in the mornings throughout 1985. We blew Jay Thomas out in short order, and he was replaced by a weird guy who most considered a failed afternoon jock at WNBC. He had been fired when his superiors objected to a sketch that he did on the air about having sex with barnyard animals. His name was Howard Stern.

Where the Streets Have No Name

A CONTEST WAS STAGED in 1984 in cooperation with *Radio and Records*. A collective of record companies were its sponsors, and it was brilliantly conceived and executed. The setup was simple: It was open to program directors across the country and each week, they'd be asked to evaluate a certain number of records. They were to rate the records based on their final chart potential—would this song be a top twenty, top ten, number one, or miss the charts entirely? At the end of the year, the results would be tabulated and the winner would be given a grand prize, which turned out to be a red Mercedes-Benz convertible (ironically, like the one Mel Karmazin got when he joined Infinity).

What a masterstroke for the record labels! Here was a legal inducement to get program directors to listen to their new releases. In order to win the car, the programmers would have to carefully evaluate each song for its hit potential. Unspoken was the fact that if one were to pick a record to succeed, they would naturally champion the song on their own airwaves in an attempt to help it up the charts. *Radio and Records* profited, not only raising their already high profile with the labels, but making themselves must reading for the PDs, who naturally wanted to check their progress.

And of course, most program directors fancy themselves to be great judges of talent. Their calls on which records should be played and which should be avoided are a large factor in determining the success of their radio stations. To win or place highly in such a competition would raise one's stock in the industry, and possibly lead to a better job in a larger market. At worst, it might convince a recalcitrant general manager of their value. And who wouldn't want to tool around in a red Mercedes?

The winner of the contest, as it turned out.

Mark Chernoff, a short, slender man with sandy brown hair and a mustache, was programming WDHA in Dover, New Jersey. He had grown up a radio devotee, loving WABC, and then worshiping WNEW-FM. But he was also a scholar of the entire medium, aware of what WPLJ, WMCA, WNBC, and all the other major stations were doing. Like most programmers, he started out doing DJ work at a small station, eventually working his way up to WDHA. Like WLIR, it was a respected suburban station—its signal blanketed the middle and northern portion of New Jersey, but failed to reach Manhattan. Record promoters would visit a couple of times a month, and saw WDHA as a starter station for their new acts. If they couldn't get a record played at WNEW-FM, they could work the suburbans—generate some sales and requests, and hopefully get noticed in the big city. Smart programmers in the large markets would key on certain smaller stations for guidance when the call was close. It was almost like the chain of progression in baseball—first you succeed in Class A ball, then AA, AAA, and finally, if the talent is there, you get to the majors.

One always had to be wary of stations that were too malleable to record company inducements. Heavy airplay may accompany a promotion, based on a large schedule of advertising and free concerts that may have nothing to do with a record's potential. No smaller-market programmer was immune to such enticements, because revenue is so critical, but Chernoff was able to maintain his reputation for integrity despite those pressures. WDHA was considered a good bellwether because of its proximity to New York and Chernoff's acumen at selecting hits.

And now he had proven it. *Radio and Records* called him with months left in the contest to inform him that he'd won. He was so far ahead of the competition that no one else could possibly catch him in the remaining weeks. Chernoff, with children to put through college, eschewed the convertible for a trust fund to help pay for their education. This was not your typical radio dude.

Chernoff was able to strike a balance between his dedication to an all-consuming business and his devotion to his family. He was active in his community and supportive of his sons' Little League, coaching their teams when most others would be attending record company parties. He was as immune to hype as one could be in this business, and his discipline paid off when WNEW-FM needed a music director.

Charlie Kendall had been served notice that his wife could not stay in the position. Aside from the nepotism issue, the two represented a power block that alarmed Mike Kakoyiannis. So when the word went out that WNEW was looking, Chernoff applied, speaking first with Kendall and then going through the Muni ritual. Mark had met Scottso at a convention some months earlier, and the two had spent time together, sharing common tastes in music. Muni also appreciated Chernoff's total lack of artifice in a business filled with phonies constantly striving to advance their own causes. But leaving the interview with Muni, Mark felt that WNEW wasn't really interested in him, having spent most of it listening to Scott regale him with stories. Sound familiar?

Weeks passed and Chernoff hadn't heard from Kendall. Through friends in the business, he discovered that the candidate list had been narrowed to two, and that he was one of the survivors. His friend Jim Del Balzo of CBS Records suggested Chernoff call Kendall to thank him for the interview and to ask if he needed anything more from him. It was possible that Charlie hadn't decided yet, or had and was postponing it.

Mark agreed to make the call, feeling despondent about not getting the job, but hoping to plant his foot in the door for future consideration. Upon reaching Kendall, the program director cut him off as he began to thank him for his time.

"Great, man," Kendall said. "When can you start?"

Kendall had thought he'd already informed Chernoff that he'd gotten the job and was wondering why he hadn't heard from him. Chernoff maintains that he never received any such call. However, he wasn't about to argue the point and quickly gave notice to WDHA. Mark would later play a huge role in the further ascension and eventual undoing of WNEW-FM.

Meanwhile, at around this same time in Los Angeles, Mike Harrison was having his meeting with Lee Abrams on how to fix KMET so that they could beat Rick Dees and give the struggling Metropolitan a chance to stay afloat. There was no rancor between the two but that meeting convinced Harrison that his time at KMET as program director was over. Abrams couldn't refute Harrison's logical arguments in favor of his own music mix. They went back and forth into the night, and Abrams wound up getting sick. Harrison literally had to carry him back to his hotel room. It was the beginning of the end for KMET.

The next day, Michael informed Bloom that he was resigning as PD and wanted only to continue as a talk show host. He offered the station his counsel, but knew that he wasn't going to be needed. He suggested that Bloom resign as well, before the deluge, which he now saw as inevitable.

Bloom was outraged. He said that Harrison was deserting him by not sticking it out as program director. Since Harrison had made a commitment to travel to Australia for two weeks to consult a broadcast group there, he suggested they declare a truce and revisit the situation upon his return. By the time Michael landed back in the States, Bloom had hardened his position. Not only was Harrison out as PD, but he was taking away the talk show as well. He didn't want anyone that disloyal around the radio station. Bloom didn't even deliver the bad news in person; he chose to send the message through his secretary. Thus Michael's ten-year involvement with KMET ended on a destructive and spiteful note.

Although I sympathized with my friend's struggles on the West Coast, I had my own problems to deal with. My relationship with Charlie Kendall wasn't improving. I decided to clear the air with him once and for all, trying to improve our communication difficulties. I sat in his office and explained that neither myself nor McEwen responded well to verbal abuse, and that if he could learn to stop yelling and screaming at us, we shared enough common ground to work together. I said that the tirades only caused us to tune him out, and that a different tact would serve him better in making his points.

His response was worse than I could have anticipated. "You've got a lot of nerve telling me how I should conduct my business," he said calmly. "I'm the boss, you work for me. If there's any adjustments to be made, you have to adjust to me. Not the other way around."

I mumbled something about both of us working on the problem, but he wasn't having any of it. Mark and I knew that he wasn't thrilled with our morning show. I was his declared enemy from the start, and Mark was my sidekick. But I'd also misinterpreted my friendship with McEwen. My overall impression was that we got along very well and were friends above and beyond work. I had driven him out to New Jersey in search of a house. We ate meals together, played golf together, socialized outside of work frequently. We unburdened our respective romantic troubles on each other— he about his estranged wife and their attempts to reunite, and me about a volatile relationship I was having with my fiancée. It wasn't a complete bed of roses—we did disagree about show content on occasion, but I thought that was a normal occurrence when two people spend a lot of time creating a project together.

Later I found out that McEwen suspected me of being a closet bigot. I was hurt, since I'd hired the man after WAPP had dismissed him and had accepted him as an equal when I was doing the show by myself. Somewhere down the line, I had started to refer to him as the Dusky Moor, a quote from Shakespeare's *Othello*. I thought that the appellation was a harmless acknowledgment of his dark, dashing image. It was Kendall who told me that Mark found it insensitive, and that it spoke of my disregard for his feelings.

When I confronted Mark about it, he admitted that he had told Charlie about how it had bothered him. He also resented his role in our *Miami Vice* parodies and thought that they had become stale. More resentments came out and as I listened I began to believe that perhaps I was insensitive. It was like breaking up with a lover you've unconsciously taken for granted, where you're read chapter and verse all the things you'd done wrong since you met. You had admitted your transgressions and thought that they'd been forgiven and forgotten. But then there are dozens of other slights and offenses that you weren't even conscious of, minor incidents that had been laughed off when they occurred.

It comes down to trust. I felt that I could trust McEwen, but obviously he didn't feel likewise. If I had a beef with him, I'd tell him and it was quickly forgotten. For whatever reason, he held it all inside until it was too late. After that, our chemistry was never the same. I was guarded when I teased him on the air for fear that he would take my jibes seriously, and he protected his turf as funny man by insisting on more autonomy to do bits on his own. I was merely to serve as his straight man. Our respective romantic difficulties didn't help. I was totally devastated when I had to call off my wedding six weeks prior to the scheduled date, and he was experiencing the daily ups and downs of a reconciliation.

In any team situation, especially if it involves only two people, success and failure can be equally dangerous traps. When you are successful, you tend to paper over differences, which can then grow until they get out of hand. When things aren't going well, small differences can be magnified to the point where they become insurmountable obstacles. Friends constantly whisper in your ear that you would be better off without the other guy dragging you down, and your ego tells you that they're right. You tend to look for solutions outside yourself, when a hard look in the mirror might reveal the source of your problems. We had our good moments, but the numbers were shifting inexorably in Howard Stern's favor. Looking back, I don't think that anything Mark and I could have done would have changed that.

Our last best chance came when John McGhann, a former director of NBC's *The Source,* agreed to produce our show. McGhann was just what the doctor ordered, a cheerleader who could boost our sagging spirits. He was constantly nudging us in the right direction, lavishing praise when we succeeded and offering encouragement when we fell short. His infectious enthusiasm even made Charlie believe that the show might work after all. But John wanted to be an actor, and after a couple of months of working with us, he left for Los Angeles. He was able to score some nice guest shots on television, including a role on *L.A. Law,* before his death at a much-too-early age.

After John left, Charlie felt the show went downhill. I didn't believe that, but when Stern's numbers passed ours in the summer ratings book of 1986, they decided to pull the plug. When we got off the air one Friday in mid-October, Mike Kakoyiannis's secretary told us we were both wanted in his office.

That walk down the corridor was the longest I've ever taken. It felt like we were on Death Row, about to be executed and powerless to earn a reprieve.

"Are we going to be fired?" Mark asked as he turned to me, incredulously.

"I don't know. Sure feels like it, though, doesn't it?"

By our downcast looks upon entering his office, Mike knew we had already figured it all out and there was little that he could offer to ease our pain.

"Fellas," he began. "What can I say? You've just done your last show. I know you guys tried hard, but the results just weren't there. Stern has to be stopped, and his momentum is getting to be too much. I'm sorry. You know I like you both personally, but this is business."

Mike hinted that there might be an opportunity for me somewhere else soon, but he wasn't specific. He went on about severance issues, but we were too stunned to absorb his words. Neither one of us had much to say. We asked about who would be doing the show and he replied that Charlie would be handling it on an interim basis until they found a replacement. Our newswoman, Lisa Glasberg (now Lisa G), would be kept on for now.

Mark and I went out to breakfast and lamented our fate, second-guessing every decision we'd made in the two years we worked together. The fact that we weren't being replaced by some hotshot from another market made it even worse. It was like being told that "you guys are so bad we've got to get rid of you now even though there is no Plan B." We didn't blame each other, though, and I felt that whatever the fates had in store, Mark and I had buried our differences and would still be friends. I was wrong about that. At first we talked regularly, but over the years my phone calls to him went unreturned until I finally stopped trying.

He was hired by CBS television to be the jolly weatherman on their new network morning show, even though his weather background consisted of reading ten-second reports off the wire. Al Roker was the obvious role model, but Mark's comedy experience and friendly persona were a natural for morning television. I wasn't quite sure what I wanted to do, until Kakoyiannis approached me about producing a sports show for WNEW-AM. As it turned out, I wound up hosting *The Sports Connection* on that station, which led to my current career path. But as events would curiously transpire, my next air work was on WNEW-FM.

McEwen and I had no idea that Charlie Kendall himself was on thin ice. His drinking and cocaine use had gotten worse as his unhappiness at WNEW grew, and it caused mood swings that made him difficult to work with. He had resigned time and again in battles with Kakoyiannis about control. Mike had resisted moving Dave Herman to middays, and was now battling Charlie on his plan to return him to mornings to succeed Mark and me.

Mike felt the need to be in complete control of what went over the air. He told Charlie that as a rookie general manager, he'd made the mistake of not riding herd closely enough on me when I was program director, and he wasn't about to make the same error. He also felt that Charlie could be a bit of a loose cannon, and needed to be reined in at times to save him from himself. Mike had a tight relationship with our promotions director, Rose Polidoro, and if Rose wanted a campaign on the air over Charlie's objections, Rose generally won out. Mike had also usurped Charlie's authority by hiring Carol Miller without Kendall's knowledge or approval. It was presented as a fait accompli and Charlie had to bite his tongue and live with it. He was forced to fire Meg Griffin and replace her with Carol. Jeff Pollack would soon replace Abrams as consultant and his advice about retooling the station by firing everyone was reaching some of the proper ears within the company.

Finally, not two weeks after we'd been sacked, Kendall's frustrations built to the point where he'd had enough. He typed a lengthy, strongly worded memo to his bosses, detailing his unhappiness with Mike's constant undermining of his authority. He spelled out the conditions under which he would stay on, and stated unequivocally that if those conditions weren't met, he would resign immediately.

Before submitting the memo to Kakoyiannis, he showed it to Muni. Scott perused it and said, "Why don't you just put a gun to your head now, Fats. It'll be less messy."

He showed it to his production manager, who also urged him to withhold the memo. But his wife knew the toll the constant grief was causing her husband and favored the power play. She was convinced that Charlie was in the right and that Mike would cave in to his demands. Kendall agreed, and never seriously considered the possibility that he was overplaying his hand. So Charlie submitted his Magna Carta and within minutes was called in Kakoyiannis's office.

"Charlie, I'm going to pretend this never happened. I'm going to tear this memo up. Now let's sit down like men and reach some kind of understanding. I don't want to lose you, but I can't accept this." This showed progress for Mike, who had reacted impulsively to inflammatory memos in the past.

Buoyed by his wife's support and his own sense of righteousness, Kendall believed that if he stood firm, Mike would have to agree to his ultimatum. "No, Mike," he said defiantly. "The memo stands."

Two days later, Kakoyiannis sent for him again and accepted his resignation. Mark Chernoff was elevated to program director. Dave Herman returned to do mornings, but was unable to stop the Howard Stern onslaught. Chernoff came to see me in my *Sports Connection* office, shortly after he'd gotten the job of his dreams.

"I didn't agree with Charlie's decision to fire you guys," he said. "I'm not sure this would have been the morning show I would have gone with, but I thought you deserved more time. In any case, it's too late now, but I think you're a good jock and I want to keep you active here. Can you work next Saturday afternoon? I'm stuck. I really need you."

Barely a month after I was fired, I was back on the air, albeit as the lowliest fill-in man, instead of a popular and highly paid morning cohost. But under Chernoff's more gentle guidance, the station rose to new heights, achieving a high-water mark of 4.4 in the 12+ share. Mark continued Charlie's format but with a lighter touch, loosening the musical restrictions just a bit and adding songs that he knew had been popular in New York before Charlie's arrival. He softened the sound by taking a little of the harder-edge songs out of the rotation, on the belief that they encouraged teens at the expense of our older audience. He wasn't the pushover some expected him to be, showing surprising toughness when the station's interests were involved. He solidified what was to become the golden era for WNEW-FM, in terms of ratings and revenue. But a series of business transactions having nothing to do with good radio pushed him into the waiting arms of the competition—and Mel Karmazin.

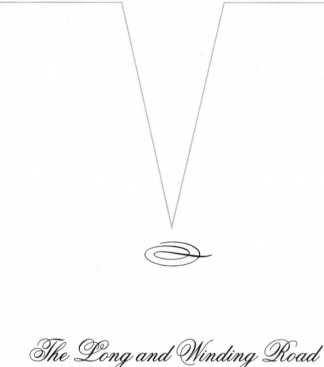

The Long and Winding Road

Ironically, the seeds for WNEW-FM's ultimate destruction were sown as it reached the height of its ratings popularity. It took years for the vine to finally wither and yield no more fruit, but for KMET, the end came with shocking suddenness.

George Harris, Charlie Kendall's successor at WMMR in Philadelphia, was brought in to fix KMET after Harrison resigned and lasted only a few months. There was no chemistry among Harris, Howard Bloom, and Lee Abrams. Frank Cody was next and was out within a year. Larry Bruce was last in the string. Barely a year from the time Harrison departed, the station's ratings sank back to a one share and they flipped formats, becoming "The Wave," a smooth-jazz station. One of the first triple-Z jazz outlets, they changed their call letters to KTWV and hired Harrison's *Goodphone* assistant Christine Brodie to program it, where she remains to this day. It has been a modest success, but never achieved the ratings it had in the early eighties.

Harrison moved back to the East Coast and bought his own talk station in Springfield, Massachusetts. He did the morning show, served as general manager, sales manager, and almost everything else. Caught in the crossfire after the changeover at KMET, Howard Bloom was dismissed.

Metropolitan Radio, as many had predicted, was a fool's errand. Carl Brazell had known that he faced an uphill climb, but believed that he and his other general managers were up to the task. Was it altruism, sentimentality, or shrewd business acumen that had caused John Kluge to sell his life's work to Brazell and company?

It was probably a combination of the three. He undoubtedly wanted the company he had formed to remain in good hands, staying true to the principles that had guided him in amassing an enormous personal fortune. This was not the prime consideration, however. By giving his general managers financing and only forty-eight hours to respond to his offer, he executed a cagey business deal. He left radio and television completely for the nascent cellular-technology business. I don't have to tell you how that worked out.

These were the go-go eighties. It was a time when you could buy a home for three hundred thousand, live in it for a year, and sell it for four hundred. Wall Street was creating new millionaires daily. No one saw an end even remotely in sight. So when the numbers at Metropolitan didn't add up—when you leveraged $285 million with the only hopes of payback coming if your gross doubled in two years—it wasn't blocked by more conservative heads. The financiers at Morgan Stanley figured that if Brazell and company couldn't hack it, they'd sell at a profit to someone who could.

One by one, Metropolitan spun off stations until only three remained—WMMR, KMET, and WNEW-FM. By then, they were grateful to find an angel to bail them out of their fiscal condition, and that company was Legacy, which was investing heavily in what Karmazin famously called "oceanfront properties." In New York, that meant WNEW-FM, a stable AOR with an impeccable reputation and solid management in place. Ratings had jumped to a 4.4 share under Chernoff as the competition struggled to find an identity. But whereas Brazell was a veteran radio man who profited by the sale after an honest attempt to run the group, the owners of Legacy had a track record of buying and holding short term, and then selling at an immense profit.

This hadn't been possible in the past. With Reagan's policy of deregu-lation, the FCC had relaxed its rules on station ownership. Previously, the government viewed broadcasting as a public trust and wanted stability. When a license was applied for, they sought proof of sufficient capital. They wanted to know that their licensees would operate their businesses for at least three years in a responsible manner in the public interest. But now broadcasting was looked upon as just another business, with the sta-tions a mere commodity. If leveraged buyouts and hostile takeovers worked for Gordon Gekko, it was good enough for radio. The bankers were in charge and FCC approval was merely of the rubber-stamp variety. As long as Wall Street ratified the deal, the FCC was assuaged and gave transactions only a perfunctory look.

It was at around this time that Kid Leo decided to leave WMMS in Cleveland after a sixteen-year run. Malrite had a national program director, and every decision Leo made was being questioned, down to the level of what singles they decided to add. There were so many layers of corporate management that radio just wasn't fun anymore for this child of free form who loved music. He resigned to take a position with CBS Records that al-lowed him to work directly with artists.

Mark Chernoff initially wasn't too concerned about new ownership. The intelligent thing to do would have been to leave well enough alone. With ratings and profits at an all-time high, why upset the big apple cart? But Legacy wanted instant results so that their bottom line would look good to potential suitors. That meant using their own people rather than Metropoli-tan's and their hastily made decisions started a snowball rolling that would turn into an unstoppable avalanche.

The first ghastly move was to bring in a general manager from Rochester's WCMF named Pete Coughlin. Under his leadership, the sta-tion in upstate New York had shares in the mid-teens and dominated the AOR market. This was impressive unless one looked further and discov-ered that when Coughlin had taken over the station, it had numbers in the mid-twenties. He had spent his childhood in the metropolitan area, so it was assumed he understood the market. This assumption allows that when a ten-year-old leaves New York for the hinterlands, he takes with him a complete understanding of the media in the tristate area. Sound business reasoning, to be sure. Immediately upon joining WNEW-FM, he wanted to tear the place apart.

Actually, he planned to wreak havoc well before he started. Although the Legacy takeover wouldn't actually take place until after the first of the year in 1989, Coughlin called Chernoff and asked him to brunch before the holidays. At the meal, he made it clear to the young programmer that WNEW's current ratings were unacceptable, despite the fact they were at an all-time high. Chernoff gently tried to tell him that New York City wasn't Rochester and that rock stations could never aspire to double-digit numbers. Coughlin took this as defeatist talk. He then proceeded to tell Chernoff that every jock on the station was either too old or too weak to continue, and that he wanted to replace the entire air staff. The music needed extensive pruning as well. And if Mark was unwilling to go along with his directives, he'd be looking for a job along with the rest of the staff.

The brunch had a dampening effect on the holiday season for Chernoff. There was no way he would be able to work with this man in the long run, but he held out the slight hope that someone higher up at the new company would see Coughlin's agenda as destructive. But at around that time, Legacy co-owner Carl Hirsch visited the station and it fell to Mark to show him around. While touring the offices, Hirsch asked Chernoff about how he felt about dealing with consultants. Treading lightly with his soon-to-be boss, he said that the program director should be the ultimate authority for what went over the air, but that a consultant's input could be helpful in certain areas. Hirsch then asked about specific people and Chernoff was either mildly critical or noncommittal. Then the name Jeff Pollack came up.

"There's a guy who's really out of touch," Chernoff began, and then detailed his negative feelings about Pollack's history of slash-and-burn tactics at stations he had consulted.

"That's too bad," replied Hirsch, who then went on to tell Mark how close he was with Pollack, how they'd been neighbors in California.

It soon became clear who was pulling the strings. Coughlin had been Pollack's recommendation—a weak man he could manipulate. All of Coughlin's critical comments about the air staff and the music were the same ones he'd heard from Pollack in one form or another over the years. Trouble ahead, trouble behind.

Muni was an obvious target. Approaching sixty, he didn't fit the stereotype of the young, hip AOR jock. His health had improved since he'd given up drinking, and his voice was still the most distinctive New York had ever heard.

A quick story about the power of Muni's pipes. I had built a house on the shore in Toms River, New Jersey, and invited Scott over to watch some football. I'd adopted a golden retriever named Lindsay several months before, but although she was generally well behaved, she had one vexing habit—she wouldn't come when called. She had broken loose from her leash several times, and finding her was an annoying hour-long exercise of cat and mouse until we could trick her into coming close enough to be captured. Dog treats, cajoling, stern warnings—nothing seemed to work when she wanted to play her games. She once got free and swam out to chase some ducks, almost drowning when she realized that she was too far out in the bay for her exhausted legs to power her back ashore. Luckily, a friend and I borrowed a paddle boat and rescued her before she went under.

During halftime of one of the football games, Muni excused himself to go out for a smoke, the one vice he continues to cosset. He asked if he could take the dog with him as he strolled along the shore. As they began their walk, Lindsay saw a squirrel and tugged at the leash, easily breaking Muni's light grasp. She took off in hot pursuit, but Scottso immediately yelled, "Dog! Stop!"

The disobedient and startled Lindsay halted in her tracks and waited, shoulders bowed, until Muni reattached the leash. We've tried the same approach many times thereafter, but it doesn't work, even when we imitate Scott's throaty growl.

Muni's numbers were solid, but afternoon AOR jocks in other markets had stronger ones. Plus, Muni was still the most powerful man at the station and a potential roadblock to any changes Legacy wished to make.

The apparent disregard for Muni highlights a problem that managers have made for decades and continue to make. When coming into a station, it is common for a new program director or general manager to listen to the current air staff and evaluate them based strictly on what they sound like at that given moment. But so much of a jock's popularity is based on a vast reservoir of goodwill built up over years. In Muni's case, some listeners went back with him to WABC in the early sixties. His Beatles connections still held a warm place in their hearts. Those who knew him only from WNEW recalled his classic interviews with Elton John, the Who, the Grateful Dead, et cetera. Most saw him as an avuncular presence who had experienced musical times considered almost mythological. Muni had attained larger-than-life status and reverence. His name was instantly recognizable and identifiable with the station, To many, he *was* WNEW-FM.

Objectively, were there other jocks who did better interviews? Almost everyone did, but most didn't have the respect of the rock community that Muni garnered, so he could still score exclusives where others couldn't. His long-term relationship with artists allowed him a kinship with many of them that no one else had. While they were both still drinking, Muni conducted his most notorious interview with Elton John. Elton liked to play DJ and, with his encyclopedic musical knowledge and keen sense of humor, probably would have been a good one. Scott would let him take over the show on occasion and, this time, John was reading a live commercial for the Pink Pussycat Boutique, a shop that sold sexual paraphernalia. WNEW's sales department had a difficult time convincing the emporium's owners that it was possible to craft a commercial that could sell their products and yet remain appropriate for airing at a time when the FCC's restrictions on salacious material were much more vigorously enforced than they are today. The carefully worded live copy intimated much about the sensual pleasures awaiting the customers of the Greenwich Village shop, but was couched in vague terms with harmless double entendres to please the station's legal division. In bold letters on the top of the page was a clear instruction: "Read exactly as written, NO AD-LIBBING!!!!"

This presented a challenge for Elton John, who was riding a crest of popularity, with record sales in the millions and sold-out concerts throughout America. If he had thought at all about the worst-case scenario, what could happen? Would his old friend Scott Muni ban him from the station? Refuse to play his records? Certainly such a penalty might affect his sales to a minimal degree, but the ensuing publicity could only enhance his naughty reputation. John had recently declared his bisexuality in a *Rolling Stone* interview, so what did he have to lose?

"Do you like to rim your boyfriend?"

Pete Larkin, WNEW-FM's production director at the time, immediately stopped leafing through a pile of discarded albums in the music library and bolted for the on-air studio, incredulous at what he'd heard through his radio speakers. Through the double layer of soundproof glass, he saw Elton John, obviously feeling no pain from the effects of his champagne of choice, Dom Pérignon. He'd toted three magnums with him on his annual visit to the Scott Muni show, and was now deeply denting the second bottle as he spoke into the guest mic.

"Or do you just like to eat pussy?"

Larkin sprinted to the professional model TEAC reel-to-reel tape machine that was chronicling the events of the day's broadcast. He tore off a sliver of paper to insert into the ten-inch rolling reels to mark the spot of the infraction, knowing that he'd be called upon many times to document what Elton had said.

"So if you're the world's biggest faggot, or you just like to, you know, fuck, visit the Pink Pussycat Boutique. And now here's my latest record."

Muni had turned purple at this point, restraining the impulse to burst out laughing. WNEW-FM's license survived the incident.

The annual Elton John visits changed in tone after Muni gave up drinking. Elton confided that he had gone through a twelve-step program as well and now whenever they meet, John whispers into Muni's ear, "Sober for ten years now, Scott. One day at a time." When Elton told him that he was getting married, Muni exclaimed, "C'mon, Elton. You? We both know you're not serious."

No smiles were exchanged as Elton told him that his mother had insisted that he marry to have a child and continue the family name. "In that case, I'll have to explain some things to you," Muni replied. "That thing you do doesn't produce kids. Do you want me to tell you how it's done?" With that, the former Reg Dwight burst into laughter. How many other jocks in the world could deal with Elton John in that manner?

He had also forged a deep and lasting friendship with Bill Graham, probably the foremost concert promoter in the history of rock. In addition, he managed bands like the Grateful Dead, Van Morrison, Santana, Jefferson Airplane, and countless others. His loyalty and respect for Muni resulted in the station garnering many exclusives on artists he represented or shows he promoted. At one time, when the local promoter's share of the WNEW Christmas concert threatened to slash the money that UCP would receive to almost nothing, Muni called Graham on the West Coast. Bill offered to fly in and promote the show for free, and even tried to talk the artist into a smaller expense allowance. Tragically, Bill Graham's life was cut short in a helicopter accident a few weeks later.

Although from completely different backgrounds, Muni and Graham shared a no-nonsense sensibility when it came to dealing with artistic temperaments. Once, when Van Morrison played the Bottom Line, Muni went backstage minutes before the scheduled live broadcast. He arrived to see Graham emerge from Morrison's dressing room, disheveled and bloodied. "The little bastard threw a chair at me and we went at it," said Graham. "He'll do your broadcast, but it'll have to start a few minutes late." Morrison proceeded to do a flawless set, showcasing his virtuoso skills on sax and vocals. Three nights later on that same tour, Morrison walked off the stage at the Academy of Music after playing only a few numbers and canceled the rest of the remaining dates.

Graham could be equally forceful with his audiences if the situation warranted it. Once, when Jefferson Starship played a free WNEW concert in Central Park, the city police threatened to shut it down if the inebriated concertgoers wouldn't stop climbing the surrounding trees. Muni was dispatched to go onstage between songs. "Please stop climbing the trees or we'll have to stop the music," Muni pleaded. His entreaties fell on deaf ears, so after the next song, Graham grabbed the microphone.

"Get your fucking asses out of the trees, you bunch of shitheads." Within seconds, the woods were cleared and the show continued.

During a performance at the Fillmore East, a man dressed in a fireman's uniform leaped onto the stage from the audience pit and grabbed the mic. Graham, thinking he was a prankster from the crowd, wrestled it away and dragged the offender offstage. He was about to issue a savage beating when the man screamed, "Bill! The deli next door is burning to the ground. We've got to evacuate the theater." The alarm was real, and Graham calmly cleared the hall.

Perhaps that's how Muni learned that sweetness and gentle persuasion don't always work in the rock world. At the Capitol Theater in New Jersey, Lynyrd Skynyrd was scheduled to do a live radiocast when Ronnie Van Zandt objected. "I ain't going on some radio station. Not in the mood tonight. The hell with that. I ain't going on 'til they go off."

When Muni was informed that the band was backing out of their commitment, he burst into the backstage dressing room. On the table was a large bottle of Jack Daniels that Van Zandt had already put a good-sized dent in. Muni grabbed the bottle, took a long swig, and then waved it at the reluctant singer.

"Listen, you little cocksucker, you may not think you're going on the radio but I guarantee you, once you start to play, you *are* going to be on our air. And there ain't nothing you're gonna do about it. Right?" He took another pull of Jack, wiped his mouth with his sleeve, and strode, John Wayne–like, out of the room. The concert broadcast was brilliant.

Of course, there were times when the artists struck back. In their wild younger days, the Grateful Dead's dressing rooms were virtual pharmacies— a complete assortment of drugs were proudly displayed for all to indulge. Although Muni liked his scotch and would down an occasional Heineken, drugs were outside his realm. He knew of several bad experiences that had happened to friends and his older brother, so Scott was afraid of anything harder than an occasional toke of marijuana when it was passed. The Dead weren't content to let things be when he continually turned down their offers of acid. They wanted to expand his consciousness, but Muni steadfastly resisted, despite their persistent advocacy. Finally, at one of their later concerts, they seemed to have given in. One of their roadies ushered Muni directly to the beer cooler and offered him a bottle, popping it open for him with a loud *swoosh*. Old Scottso chugged a few swallows, but upon sensing its bitter aftertaste, he realized he'd been dosed. He put it down immediately, but the damage was done. Led onstage, he quickly introduced the band, then ran out of the hall and hailed a cab. Arriving home just as his world started to spin, he had the presence of mind to lock all the doors and windows so "I didn't do that flying bit. It was a rough night, but I survived. But I remember putting the bottle down and when I came offstage, it was gone. Some stagehand must have had a hell of a night."

Graham's artists always seemed to be playing tricks on Muni, some of which he didn't mind. Once, while interviewing Grace Slick of Jefferson Airplane, Scott paused during the questioning to read a live spot. While he was in the middle of a serious commercial read, Slick climbed atop the desk housing the console and lifted her skirt over her head. Muni glanced up and beheld that her morning ritual did not include donning panties. An unnerved and distracted Muni was unable to finish reading, so he merely issued his trademark grunt and started the next record.

Like Graham, he always believed in giving struggling new artists a break. When the Allman Brothers complained to Bill that they wanted to play by themselves with no opening act, Graham insisted that they have not one, but two acts before them. "How do you think these bands get started?" he'd ask. "How did *you* get started?" Muni shared that philosophy and fought to have new music on the station, even when classic rock seemed to be the way to go.

Was he as hip with new music as some others? Most of the new artists who met him were surprised at his overall grasp of their material and his sense of historical context. Did he have the more energetic, up-tempo approach that afternoon drive jocks now boasted? No, but he didn't put you to sleep either. Did he work hard? Not especially, but what did he really need to work hard at?

If you were to weigh his value simply on tangible items, there might be a hundred jocks better than Scottso. Indeed, if you were starting a station in Kansas, you probably wouldn't hire him. But his intangibles in New York far overwhelmed the competition. His contacts in the business gave WNEW an advantage on new releases or with prestigious bands for concerts or interviews. And his father-confessor role with the air staff helped tame many a budding border dispute.

Artists would often confess their problems to Muni as well. Pete Townshend first publicly revealed his tinnitus in a lengthy talk with Scott when he spoke eloquently of how he struggled to survive in a rock band, given his hearing loss. Townshend was so detailed when discussing the Who that Muni often teased him that he was going to ask a question and then go out for a cigarette while Pete crafted a long-winded answer. All the members of the band were frequent guests on the show; in fact, Keith Moon once arrived almost an hour before the rest were due and therefore had the microphone to himself for an extended period. He revealed that Daltrey, Townshend, and Entwistle were constantly lecturing him about his weight and drug and alcohol consumption. He admitted that he was worried as well, since he feared that if he didn't curtail his wastrel habits, he was going to die. Barely a month after the interview his fears were tragically realized.

Even some of Scott's quirks were positive factors—his ridiculous antics with producer Tom Tracy were a morale builder, helping to lighten the mood at the station when the pressure escalated. Muni and Tammy would often start their act in a closed elevator, with Tracy calling Scott a peckerwood motherf—r and threatening to carve him up with a knife. Muni would answer back with racial slurs and the terrified occupants of the lift would exit before they reached their floors to avoid these obvious madmen. All of the constant back and forth was in jest. In fact, when one general manager told Muni he planned to fire Tracy, Muni suggested that he turn in his own resignation first, since he would be canned shortly thereafter. Although he laughed it off, a week later at a company function, while Muni and the man spoke to George Duncan, Scott brought up the proposed firing in a mirthful manner. "Hey George, what would happen if our friend here fired Tom Tracy?"

"I'd fire him before I'd let him do that," Duncan said, with a straight face. Needless to say, Tammy kept his job.

Muni and Tracy also had pet names for staff members, all of whom Tracy pegged as latent, or in some cases, active homosexuals. Marty Martinez became "Martina," Dan Carlyle was immediately tagged "Danielle." I was "Rochelle." Scott would needle Tracy with things like, "You people have your own towns. Dobb's Ferry. Harper's Ferry. And your own Christmas carols: Don we now our gay apparel." The two men were completely at ease with their differences, and their loose-lipped trash talking provided needed comic relief through some tough times. Muni's steady hand on the tiller had kept the station on course, when many others had drifted into oblivion.

Ironically, the one interview Muni wanted more than any other was denied him. Dennis had his John Lennon and I my Bruce Springsteen, but for Muni the Holy Grail would be an interview with Bob Dylan. When Scott started at WNEW in 1967, the very first record he played was Dylan's "Like a Rolling Stone." The reluctant troubadour just didn't visit radio stations, and the only rare audiences he granted were on his turf—on his terms. Aside from the 1978 visit backstage at Nassau Coliseum, the only times he sat down with radio people were with Dave Herman in July of 1981 in England, and several years later with my brother Dan-o at Dylan's West Coast home. Herman was displeased with the results because Bob played his acoustic guitar during the entire chat and didn't reveal much of anything. Later, Dave speculated that the canny singer had affected this so that the tape could not be edited cleanly and distort the exact meaning of his words, such as they were.

My brother was equally frustrated. He traveled three thousand miles to see the man and was met with vague monosyllabic answers. He felt that Dylan never warmed to him, and went home disappointed in his inability to draw the legend out. But years later, when CBS promotion man Jim Del Balzo brought a group from the station backstage at the Beacon Theater to meet the star, Dylan's ears perked up at the mention of the station. "WNEW?" he exclaimed. "Yeah, that cat from your station came out to see me. I heard that show. He was cool. Great. Best interview I ever did. Want some whiskey?" He proffered a bottle of Jack Daniel's.

Dan-o didn't feel vindicated by the praise and still pines for a second shot. But Muni has yet to get his first recorded conversation with the man, perhaps because Scott rarely travels to do an interview, preferring the subject be brought to him. Even though his son, Mason Munoz, worked for CBS Records and accompanied Bob on tours, he couldn't convince him to pop up and pay his dad a visit. And the only time Dylan did go to a radio station, it was under such bizarre circumstances that few of his fans were aware that it happened.

WKTU was a disco station that never would dream of playing a Dylan record. They were doing a charity radiothon with their star jock, a man using the moniker "Paco." For a brief period, his was the highest-rated show in town, as he spoke in a deep rumble reminiscent of Ricardo Montalban, thrilling the Studio 54 crowd. Paco was friendly with Arthur Baker, a producer of disco records who was enjoying some popularity with rock artists who wanted to freshen their sound with the new rhythms. He remixed Springsteen's "Cover Me" and "Dancing in the Dark," largely to the consternation of Bruce's fan base. But now he was working with Dylan in an attempt to make the folk rocker more commercially acceptable. When his Latino buddy Paco called asking for some artist help for the radiothon, Baker promptly squired Dylan up to KTU. CBS Records launched a massive cover-up to hide the event from Muni, who would have gone ballistic had he found out. That's how much the music community respected and feared Scottso.

But all Pete Coughlin saw was a gray-haired old man who had outlived his usefulness. In Chernoff, he saw a wimp who thought he knew more about radio than Jeff Pollack. And Pollack, pulling Coughlin's strings, saw Muni as an obstacle to the changes he intended for WNEW—changes that would come swiftly if he had anything to do with it.

In his first couple of days at the station, Coughlin lost any chance he had with the staff over one incident. Word of the story spread like fire on a gas-soaked cross. Muni was on the air, playing a Chuck Berry song, when the new general manager summoned Chernoff to his office after hearing the opening riffs.

"Why are we playing this nigger music?" Coughlin demanded to know.

Chernoff couldn't believe what he'd just heard and asked his boss to repeat the question. He did so without hesitation, and Chernoff, still reeling, asked that he convey his feelings to Scott Muni directly. Mark retrieved Scottso and marched him back into the office. Coughlin asked the question again, without rephrasing.

Muni and Chernoff looked hopelessly at each other. Scott merely said, "You keep stepping in shit, don't you? Do you realize what would happen to us if what you just said became public? You can't be serious." He turned on his heel and headed back to the studio.

"I feel like some Motown, Fats," he told his engineer upon arriving. "Pull out some Supremes, Temptations, and Four Tops." Those groups comprised the next few sets on the air.

Mark was left awkwardly alone with Coughlin. "By the way," he ventured. "How do you feel about us playing Jimi Hendrix?"

"No problem with that," Coughlin answered. "Why should there be?"

"Well, he is black."

"He is?"

After that incident, any hopes Chernoff had about remaining at the station under the new regime were dashed. His dream job of programming the station he'd loved as a child and working with his boyhood heroes were destroyed.

He contacted Tom Chuisano, the former WNEW sales manager who had defected to Infinity to head Karmazin's K-ROCK. They had lunch but Chuisano, although impressed by Chernoff's intelligence and résumé, already had a program director and didn't see an immediate change coming. He did suggest that Chernoff talk to Karmazin, and arranged a meeting.

Mel sympathized with Mark over what was happening at WNEW— sad on one level that his training ground had fallen into the hands of fools, but happy on another that it created an opening for K-ROCK to win the rock wars in New York. He told Chernoff that Ken Stevens at WJFK in Washington was looking for a program director and that although he gave his general managers autonomy in running their operations, he thought that Mark would be a good fit in D.C.

Chernoff went home with a heavy heart and discussed the situation with his wife, Sally. He had grown up in New Jersey and established deep roots. Sally taught school there, and the children were all involved in community activities. Yet there was nothing for him in New York; it was only a matter of time before he'd be fired at WNEW. His contract ran out in mid-February, mere weeks away. There was nothing for him at K-ROCK, and there were no other rock stations in the market. Out of options, he reluctantly called Karmazin and told him he'd be interested in talking to Stevens.

He liked the man immediately upon meeting him. He had opinions on what he wanted the station to do, but was open to Chernoff's superior knowledge of programming. Their outlook was similar in how they would achieve their goals, and as the meeting ended, Chernoff knew he'd have the job, if he wanted it.

After more soul searching he decided to accept the offer, but only on his terms. He wanted to work Monday through Thursday in Washington, he told Stevens. He needed to spend the extended weekend with his family in New Jersey. While in Washington, he'd work day and night, for however long it took for him to get the job done. Upon the completion of the school year, his wife and family would move down to join him and he'd assume more normal hours. And the announcement would have to be held off until he finalized things at WNEW. Stevens agreed, and now all Mark had to do was execute the bittersweet task of informing Legacy.

He didn't have to wait long. Coughlin told him that he and the owners wanted to meet with him at a local restaurant Tuesday evening after work. Classic setup, he thought. Do it away from the station, in the evening in a public place, to avoid a disruptive scene. But rather than stomp out of a crowded eatery, Chernoff short-circuited their plans and started the discussion before they could leave the offices. Sure enough, the owners began with expressions of doubt mixed with sympathy—that unfortunately things weren't working out and that maybe Mark wasn't suited for what they wanted to do.

"That's great," he interrupted them, "because I've already accepted another job."

It was their turn to be stunned, or at least act that way. This was the ultimate act of disloyalty and it confirmed their feelings that Mark wasn't a company man. *I quit, you're fired.*

So Chernoff went to work for Ken Stevens at WJFK, and despite the uncomfortable family situation, he liked the people he was working with and found Stevens to be a fair-minded boss. Sally had come down during a break and they'd found a house they liked in the planned community of Reston, Virginia. They signed a contract to buy it and put their house in New Jersey on the market.

But fate intervened. Suddenly, there was a job at K-ROCK. Pat Evans, one of the few female program directors in the country, had grown tired of being humiliated by Howard Stern, on and off the air. She also wasn't happy with the high-pressure atmosphere in New York, with Infinity's corporate headquarters lodged in the same building as the station. She resigned, eventually accepting a position at the more laid-back KFOG in San

Francisco. Chernoff interviewed with Chuisano again and was offered the job. Stevens was completely understanding of Mark's desire to go home, and luckily Mark was able to extricate himself from the Reston house and withdraw his New Jersey residence from the market.

Coughlin lasted at WNEW-FM two months longer than Mark had. His crude comments in the presence of clients soon convinced Legacy that the man was an embarrassment, in too far over his head. He was shown the door after less than ninety days in the position. Shortly thereafter, at a manager's meeting when the change was announced, Jeff Pollack passed by Muni and sang softly into his ear, "Scottie got his way-a" in a childish tease. Muni grabbed the slender consultant and swore that if he ever taunted him again, it would be his last act on earth. Scott had repeatedly tried to bail Coughlin out of jams that his loose mouth had gotten him into, and was deathly afraid that if any of his indiscretions were made public, the station would suffer irreparable harm. It wasn't just politics with Scott; it was his life. Pollack seemed to see it all as a big game, a power struggle.

But major damage was already done. Chernoff sadly realized that had he been able to hang in sixty days longer, he likely could have remained at WNEW-FM. He's convinced that had things broken that way, he'd still be there today, and the station would be playing rock and thriving. Now he was working for the enemy and although not a vengeful man, he knew all the station's strengths, many of which he'd propagated, and he also knew their weaknesses.

Chernoff's replacement at WNEW was Ted Utz, whose history in radio is unlike almost any other, in that he'd done things in reverse. The typical path is disc jockey to programmer to general manager, then in a few cases, to ownership. But Ted Utz, who graduated Syracuse University a year ahead of my brother Dan in the mid-seventies, decided that upstate New York needed an AOR station and organized a group of friends and investors to seek a license. Staked with eight thousand dollars of his own money, Ted petitioned the FCC and performed all the tests and applications necessary for approval. He even managed to get college credits for his labors, and learned a great deal more in his practical pursuits than he had in school. While he was doing this, he worked part-time at WRNW in Westchester County, New York, along with my brother, Meg Griffin, and a big, nerdy, skinny Howard Stern. After completing the rigorous requirements the FCC mandated for ownership back then, WAQX Syracuse was born, and immediately started pulling big numbers in a market starved for rock. His success was noted by Lee Abrams, who invited him to program a similar station in Albany, New York. Although WAQX was a labor of love, Ted's 25 percent share afforded him little control and he yearned to break free and to be his own boss. So in a strange turn of events, he accepted Abrams's offer, and achieved similar success in Albany, then Providence and Dallas before following Charlie Kendall and George Harris at WMMR in Philadelphia.

A tall, craggily handsome man whose bearing belies his youth, the always elegantly dressed Utz was able to build on WMMR's already positive numbers, especially strengthening John DiBella's morning show for the inevitable assault by Howard Stern in syndication. Although the Stern juggernaut did surpass WMMR in the morning, it took longer to do so in Philadelphia than it had in any other major market. So Utz already had an impressive management résumé when he hit New York, and continued to burnish his star in the country's largest marketplace.

Utz had been promoted by Legacy to be in charge of regional AOR programming because of his successful stint as program director at WMMR. He'd become their at-large troubleshooter, bailing out stations in Detroit and Los Angeles. Initially brought in at WNEW to mediate disputes between the programming staff and Coughlin, Utz soon gleaned that the rifts ran much deeper than that. The sales staff had turned on their boss as well, and Ted reported to his superiors that the situation was irreparable. Given his ownership experience in Syracuse, Utz was handed the reins, originally as a temporary replacement for Coughlin. But his stellar revenue performance (increasing billing by 15 percent the first year) gave the station stability, and he ascended to the general manager's post on a more permanent basis. With a veteran sales staff in place, Utz could concentrate on the programming, which still bore Kendall's signature with Chernoff's variations. There was a little tinkering to do, but he inherited a generally solid situation from his predecessor.

After only a few months, another buyer was entering the picture. Legacy was looking to expand their holdings, and made inquiries about buying Group W from the powerful Westinghouse Company. However, Westinghouse was looking to acquire radio properties, not sell them. Legacy was thus convinced to peddle their stations for a tidy profit. WNEW-FM was under new ownership once more, the third owner in just over a year.

Group W had experience in the New York market with the successful all-news WINS. Despite this, they also pressured Utz to achieve even higher 12+ shares, especially during morning drive.

But Stern's massive numbers in the morning were now affecting mid-days as well, since he often stayed on the air at K-ROCK until eleven-thirty. At WNEW, Coughlin had insisted on firing Ray White from 10 A.M. to 2 P.M. and replacing him with Pat St. John. The disruption gave Chernoff an opening and he figured that if he could strengthen the rest of that time slot, and then bolster afternoon drive, K-ROCK could become more than just a one-man station dominated by Stern.

Pete Fornatale was now just doing part-time duty at WNEW-FM for not a lot of money. As his contract expired, Chernoff lured him over to K-ROCK, ostensibly to do weekends. But the master plan was to slide him back into his old midmorning slot, as an engaging follow-up to Stern. Since the program often lasted less than three hours and Stern left him with gargantuan numbers, the offer was appealing to Fornatale. K-ROCK began to win the midday battle.

It was during this period that I almost made the switch to K-ROCK. Working without a contract, I had nothing to tie me to the old place but heritage. I was working quite a bit as a sports-talk host at WFAN, a job I landed shortly after *The Sports Connection* was canceled. I knew my aspirations lay there. Many of the jocks I'd worked with over the years at WNEW were gone, and management was changing on a regular basis. There was little discretion in music selection—everything was laid out on the computer and DJ Select had been temporarily eliminated so you couldn't change anything you found objectionable. There wasn't room for creative segues anymore, and sets tied together by musical strings were virtually impossible to do. Utz was a generally nice man, who had gone to school with my brother, but he had left me hanging to save his own skin once, so my trust in his protection was shallow.

It happened during an all-day charity event Bill Graham was producing from San Francisco that continued during my Sunday afternoon shift. It featured Jefferson Starship, Santana, and Boz Scaggs, all classic Bay Area artists that Graham had given their start. Journey would be headlining, playing with Steve Perry again after a long hiatus, which was a big deal in AOR land. The concert producers called to tell me that under no circumstances was I to broadcast any of the Journey set. They hadn't played together in a while and were worried that if they indeed did reunite more permanently, they might be harmed by a sloppy performance. I called Utz and asked him how he wanted it handled.

He said to go ahead and run the Journey concert. After all, once we had, what could they do—send us a nasty letter? Following instructions, I aired their set, informing the audience that we had an exclusive—the reformation of one of the decade's premier rock bands.

That Monday I received an angry phone call from Columbia Records, threatening me with legal action for putting the concert on. They had spoken to Utz first and he had told them that I'd made the decision on my own, and that any repercussions from it should come my way. Bill Graham was furious and was demanding my head from Muni. Since he and Graham had been friends for over twenty years, Scott read me the riot act for betraying his buddy. I explained that I had been instructed by Utz to run the broadcast. Muni said that he'd try to calm down everyone involved and charged into Ted's office.

That was the last I heard of the matter. After the storm subsided, I went back to work the following weekend as if nothing had happened. No lasting harm had been done—I was angry that my boss had used me as a scapegoat, but I felt powerless to react. Utz later explained that there was nothing anyone would do to punish me if I had made the call independently, but that the station could have been on the hook for damages if he took responsibility. Also, it might strain relations with an important record label, which could compromise us on exclusives. The harm to my reputation for integrity apparently wasn't considered important.

I was very open to Chernoff's overtures. I figured that since Fornatale's defection, Group W would be wary of losing their heritage position in the market by further attrition. So I had numerous conversations with Mark about a role at K-ROCK, but none of the offers he made exceeded my current salary at WNEW by enough to make me think seriously of jumping ship. My projected role at K-ROCK would essentially remain the same as it was at WNEW: weekends and fill-ins.

By this time, the decision would strictly be based on money. As much as I liked working for Mark, my contact with management was so limited that it made little difference. I still could play new music at WNEW; K-ROCK was strictly rock oldies. My future seemed to be in sports talk anyway, so DJ work just amounted to a way to subsidize that. It was sad, but since the experience of being fired and no longer enjoying the freedom to program my own music, it had become just another job.

Utz had gotten wind of my discussions with Chernoff and called me. I confirmed that I was seriously considering making the move. What would it take to keep me, he wanted to know. I gave him a number and he said he'd get back to me. Weeks went by and I didn't hear from him. Meanwhile, Mark was upping his offers slightly and pressuring me for a decision. Finally, I called Utz with an ultimatum: I gave him a figure that topped Mark's final offer by ten thousand dollars and said that if I didn't have an answer by the close of business the next day, I would leave.

I was uneasy with the strategy. I felt like a traitor to the station that had given me a start in New York radio and nurtured me through some hard times. But Chernoff kept my FM career alive by continuing to ask me to do fill-ins while I was working on *The Sports Connection*. I owed him a debt of gratitude for that. But I wasn't sure about what working with Stern would mean either. All in all, I hoped Utz would accept my terms and keep the status quo.

Thankfully, he did. In all, I'd gotten a 25 percent raise, which made life very comfortable. I wasn't making the kind of money I'd made doing mornings, but my weekdays were free—most of my shifts on WNEW-FM and WFAN were concentrated in the forty-eight-hour weekend period. I could envision riding out the rest of my career that way, under the radar of management.

Chernoff's next move brought in Mark Volman and Howard Kaylan to do afternoons. The pair had recorded under the name "The Phlorescent Leech and Eddie," but were better known as the main force behind the band the Turtles, who'd enjoyed several hit records in the late sixties, most notably "Happy Together." They were quick-witted and very entertaining when being interviewed in their musician days, so Chernoff had the inspiration to use them as occasional fill-ins, where they performed well. But the ability to be entertaining during a short guest stint and to fill four hours daily was a gulf they were unable to bridge. They talked a great deal, often pointlessly, and Muni frequently cleaned their clock with his minimalist approach.

At WNEW, Utz had enough personal dominion to hold off the massive changes that Legacy had originally wanted, and was able to keep Pollack's influence at bay. He had brought in Dave Logan from KFOG in San Francisco to be his hands-on program director, with Ted calling the major shots. During this period, no jock was fired although there was unrest and dissatisfaction among the staff with what they perceived to be a tight music policy. A clandestine meeting was called by Scott Muni and held at my brother Dan's apartment, at which the staff openly revolted against the way the station was being run. Some recall the meeting as a vote of no confidence for Utz, but the outcome was that Dave Logan was fired as program director two days later. Opinions differ on why this happened. The majority felt that Logan was not diplomatic enough with the staff. Each member had their idiosyncrasies, especially Muni, and had to be delicately handled. Each was thought to be more valuable than any program director, and thus they had to be cajoled into performing as opposed to being ordered. Logan admits that upon taking the job initially, he had much to learn about what made the station special, in addition to holding off the consultants who wanted to fire the whole staff. He wasn't well versed in the music that was popular in New York but not on the West Coast, where he'd spent the majority of his time in programming. An example of that was when Muni was playing Squeeze's "If I Didn't Love You" one afternoon. As the song is about to close, the band repeats: "If I . . . if I . . . didn't . . . didn't . . . love you . . . love you, love you." Logan came bursting into the studio screaming that the record was stuck. That incident served to illustrate to the staff that Dave didn't know his music, although Squeeze was a band whose popularity was confined to pockets along the East Coast and he couldn't be expected to be familiar with all their work.

He was also placed in the impossible situation, like I was years before, of creating order out of chaos without being given the necessary tools and authority to do so. If Muni disagreed with a Logan directive, he could always appeal to Utz and the chances are that Logan would be overturned. In a good cop–bad cop scenario, Utz could play the benefactor, coming down on the side of freedom, while Logan was given the dirty work, the task of cleaning up sloppy mechanics or correcting programming transgressions.

There is an alternative view that Utz used Logan as a scapegoat, fearing that he was in danger of being replaced by Group W as general manager. He took over the programming chores himself so that he would have a job when the reins were handed to his successor. In any case, Logan was the unfortunate victim of circumstance.

Mark Chernoff wasn't finished raiding. Vin Scelsa was back in radio after his sabbatical following the formatting fallout in 1981, and was doing a Sunday morning show at K-ROCK. But the big prize was still out there. Dave Herman was unhappy with Ted Utz at WNEW, despite the fact that Utz had resisted Legacy's order to replace Herman in the mornings immediately. Ted urged patience, insisting that Dave's ratings would improve if he could implement some formatics, like he had done with John Di-Bella's *Morning Zoo* in Philadelphia. Dave was uncomfortable with the changes Ted was suggesting and felt underappreciated. They had had a particularly ugly incident in Berlin (of all places) that created more bad blood.

Part of Utz's strategy to build the morning show was to promote Herman through high-profile events. One of these was a trip to Russia immediately after Boris Yeltsin took over the presidency. Ted traveled to Moscow with the morning-show staff and personally supervised all the details. The struggling new economy had yet to emerge from chaos, and hotels and food were a problem as the citizenry shook loose the bonds of communism. But being there at that historic time raised the show's profile and brought revenue into the station as they were able to obtain a premium sponsorship from Absolut vodka. The next big promotional trip took place a year later as Pink Floyd celebrated the demolition of the Berlin Wall. Ted brought along his new girlfriend, and rather than mother-hen the whole operation he left the minutiae to Logan and the show's producers while he took in the sights. But Dave and Ted were never on the same page as far as arrangements, formatics, or anything else about the trip. Whether it was Ted's lack of attention, or Dave's expectations of more deferential treatment, tensions mounted between them as the week continued. It finally exploded in the lobby of a Berlin hotel as Herman tried to attack the larger, younger, and more athletic Utz with his fists. No one was injured, but starting a fistfight with the boss is not a recommended way to win points within an organization that isn't labeled WWF.

So when Dave's contract was scheduled to expire later that year, Utz wasn't too eager to respond to his agent's request for more money. The personal dislike between the two men was a palpable presence at the station. Utz knew that there was nothing anyone could do to beat Stern in the morning. People who wanted music and a friendly, familiar voice found that in Dave, but Stern had become a must-listen to anyone wanting outrageous entertainment. No one could beat him on his own terms—Stern stretched the T&A envelope as far as it could be pushed. The best anyone could hope for on an AOR station was a ratings share in the mid-three range, which underperformed the rest of the day by as much as a full point. More talk—humor or information—only drove listeners away. Only a music-intensive program with impeccable formatics could even hope to hold the ratings steady.

Dave's initial posture was for a 33 percent raise and a three-year guarantee to do mornings. Utz brought the proposal to his superiors at Group W and they rejected it out of hand. They proposed a slight decrease in pay, with an incentive package that, if achieved, could bring Herman into the monetary ballpark he sought to play in. They would only offer a one-year assurance of mornings, however.

Group W wanted to make this the final offer, but Ted convinced them to go along with a one-year extension for mornings at Dave's current salary, something in the $300,000 range. He believed this to be a fair tender and felt it would be accepted in the end, but was prepared to go in another direction if Dave balked. Ted believed that any veteran New York jock with the respect of the audience could pull the same numbers that Dave had. There was no chance of hitting a home run by bringing in a shock jock from outside, and any attempts to shake the current formula would only alienate the audience.

To Ted, this limited Dave's value to the station. So in the final days of the negotiations, when Dave's agent advised him that Herman would not work past the end date on his contract, Utz took this as an idle threat. Who would hire him to do mornings for more money? Utz played hardball, and although the contract was set to expire the following Friday, Ted took a scheduled vacation to the Caribbean beginning that Wednesday.

Word had gotten out to Karmazin that negotiations were not going well. Much like any other business, it is considered tampering to discuss an offer with another station's talent while he is still under contract. But it happens, like when Cousin Brucie jumped from WABC to WNBC, and as long as the contact goes undetected, it's hard to prove and few lawsuits are ever filed. But Karmazin believed in playing by the rules, so he waited until after Herman's final show to officially call Dave's agent, Don Buchwald. He said that if Dave wasn't on the air Monday morning, he'd assume the contract had expired and he'd be free to forward an offer from K-ROCK. With Ted out of town until the end of the following week, there was no one to deal with at WNEW.

Monday morning I was rudely awakened at a quarter to six by overnight man Ken Dashow. He'd rung Dave for his traditional wake-up call and had been told that Herman was not coming in. He'd informed the station—no contract, no work, and he meant it. There was also no Utz, and since I was the guy who did Dave's show in his absence—would I come in and do it? I hastily dressed and hurried into the city.

Mel Karmazin awoke that morning to my voice instead of Dave's and correctly assumed that a contract had not been signed. He and Buchwald met, and an offer was extended for afternoons at K-ROCK. The money was actually less than WNEW was talking about, but the term was a guaranteed three years. Mornings were out of the question because of Stern. Herman still wasn't sure. He'd done mornings on and off for twenty years at WNEW. Afternoons against his old friend Muni weren't an appealing prospect, but the security was tempting and he wasn't even sure that he was wanted at the old place anymore. He called Muni and explained his dilemma, but how could Scott know if the offer from Mel was real or just a gambit to raise the stakes? Money was still solely the general manager's province, and there was no general manager to be found, although Ted was available by phone if the crisis dictated.

The next day, Mel upped the offer slightly but added this proviso: The contract must be agreed upon by the close of the business day or it was off the table. Dave was torn by his loyalty to Muni and the call letters and his distaste for Utz. He also realized that mornings against Stern would be a chronic losing proposition. Pacing the floor of his apartment like a madman, he vacillated from one position to the other. Minutes before the deadline he called Buchwald, who advised him to accept Karmazin's offer. A bird in the hand and so on.

Karmazin was playing the game with the acquiescence of Chernoff and Chuisano. He could have forced the issue with them, but didn't want to strip them of their independence. Both agreed that Dave would be a welcome addition in the afternoon but gulped when they saw the size of the offer. Even though the salary and terms were generous, Mel argued, they paled at what the station could expect to take in if it could become competitive with Muni in the afternoons. One thing Karmazin never hesitated to do was to "overpay" for what he considered to be "oceanfront property." His track record shows that if there is an acquisition that he projects will benefit his interests, he'll pay whatever it takes instead of lose the deal so that he can be known as a tough negotiator.

Buchwald called to accept the offer, and now all that remained was to negotiate away the noncompete clauses from Dave's prior contract with Group W. Noncompete clauses mean simply that upon the termination of a contract, a jock could not work for a direct competitor for a specified period, generally 90 to 180 days. These clauses have been struck down by the courts almost every time they are challenged, but stations continue to place them in contracts in the hope that they'll discourage valued talent from abdicating for greener pastures. In Dave's case, it took thirty days before he could join the staff of K-ROCK.

For me, it was another opportunity to be thrust back into the spotlight.

Believing as he did that mornings were limited at WNEW-FM by market forces already in place, Utz allowed me to work until a permanent replacement was found. When the morning ratings actually increased under my watch (I was making less than a third of what they had paid Dave), Group W saw this as win-win for their station and I was handed the job permanently. (Well, as permanently as any job in radio is.) However, within two rating periods, afternoons were highly competitive between Herman and Muni. My morning increases had not come at Stern's expense, so Chernoff saw the deal as win-win for him.

The Legacy–Group W transfer and its resulting disruptions had now seen Chernoff, Herman, and Fornatale cross over to the competition, seriously weakening WNEW's depth. And like a football team that loses its stars to age and free agency, the effects might not be immediately visible on the scoreboard. But the core of quality players erodes until the intangibles that differentiate the winners from the losers deteriorate, so slowly as to go almost unnoticed. And by the time anyone does notice, it's too late.

Despite those problems, the Ted Utz era, from 1989 to 1992, saw the ratings and revenues reach record heights. Cash flow increased by 15, 12, and 15 percent under Utz's leadership, and ratings maintained a consistent level approaching 4.0 12+. In the key twenty-five- to fifty-four-year-old demographic, WNEW thrived in all the day parts, and combined with the heritage image the station still enjoyed, Madison Avenue subsidized it heavily. The lineup was solid—I was doing mornings with Ken Dashow as sidekick, Pat St. John in the middays, Muni in the afternoon, and Carol Miller, my brother Dan, Jim Monaghan, and Marty Martinez at night. All the jocks had come to terms with the music, and since we had DJ Select back again on the computer, our hands weren't completely tied. The station sounded consistent all day, and was still the place to go for new music. Despite K-ROCK's 12+ victories, they were largely Pyrrhic since most of the advantage came as a result of Stern's posting double digits in the morning. As Infinity was later to learn, the prime Stern listeners were the type who didn't want classic rock during the rest of the day, but were into the emerging grunge movement from Seattle and all it entailed.

But despite the success it was having, Group W was uneasy with the situation at WNEW. Ted's mentor and champion, Mike Craven, resigned in December of 1991, and Utz lost a valuable protector within the company. Ted had also garnered the reputation of being somewhat of a lax boss. He would often take long weekends in the Hamptons, or leave the office early and come in late. He had inherited a crack staff, not just with programming but on the sales and promotional end as well. He'd delegated a great deal of authority to them. Whether this happened because Ted was becoming complacent or because he understood how things worked, it was absolutely the right approach at that point in time. As lords of their own realms, the department heads thrived on the autonomy and produced better results than they would have if a Simon Legree had monitored their every move.

But in most corporate environments, control is a key word and the heads of Group W wanted Ted Utz present at the station and riding herd on the troops. The Herman defection was handled poorly in the press, as Dave gave a number of interviews singling out Utz as a negative factor, and saying that WNEW succeeded in spite of, not because of, his leadership. Ted responded in *Newsday* by calling Dave a cancer that was threatening to spread throughout the station if it wasn't stricken. It was bad public relations and might have been an element in Ted's dismissal.

By late December in 1991, Utz was told his contract would not be renewed and that a new general manager was coming in. He was free to seek other employment within the company, and could even stay on as program director if his new boss was amenable.

Ted called Mel Karmazin and shortly thereafter, the two were having lunch. Mel was close to Dave Herman, so it's possible that he had no interest in Ted, having heard Dave's horror stories about the man. But Mel, during that period of his surging career, still had time for exploratory meetings.

Always on top of the data, Karmazin congratulated Utz on his fiscal management of WNEW-FM. He confided to him that it was always a station he had wanted to own. "What a franchise," he said. "You've got a great air staff, a solid position in the market. A top-notch sales crew. Revenues are great. We're all going to get hurt by this recession, but you're in a better spot than most to ride it out. I'd give my eyeteeth for that property."

The lunch ended as Karmazin told Utz he admired the job he'd done, but that Infinity was fully staffed with programmers and general managers and that Mel was loyal to those who had come up through the ranks with him. No job offer was forthcoming, but the two parted amicably.

Ted realized that if he was to stay in New York, programming WNEW might be his best hope. The incoming general manager was a man known to him; in fact, he'd literally saved the man's life that summer.

Group W was hosting managers' meetings in a tropical location, and most of the time was spent enjoying the sun and frolicking. A group of higher-ups had rented Jet Skis and were engaging in daredevil stunts in the crystal-clear waters. The Detroit general manager couldn't swim, but was a fun-loving guy who liked to take chances. While going a bit too fast, he fell off the Jet Ski as he banked sharply and flailed about in the water. Sensing his colleague was in trouble, Utz, a powerful swimmer, dove in and pulled the man to safety.

That should count for something. So with some little trepidation, he welcomed Kevin Smith to his former position.

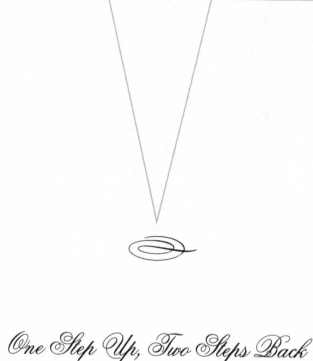

One Step Up, Two Steps Back

KEVIN SMITH WAS A product of St. John's University in Queens, New York, and was, as a failed New York football coach was described, "a dese, dems, and dose guy."

He wore his Bronx accent proudly and actually used it as a tool to baffle his adversaries. Kevin liked to be underestimated in business, which takes great cunning and native intelligence, not to mention a lack of ego. A nice-looking man in his mid-forties, you could envision him on the sidelines as a Catholic university hoops coach, exhorting his team to victory. He was a huge Los Angeles Lakers and Dallas Cowboys fan, strange choices for a native Bronxite, as these were teams most New Yorkers loved to hate.

Despite his place of birth, Smith's radio sensibilities were fostered in Detroit, a market vastly different from New York, although many great jocks hail from the Motor City. Detroit is a hard-rock town, like Los Angeles and to some extent Boston. New York tends to like British music and more cerebral material. Its rock roots are firmly planted on the Jersey shore with Springsteen. Unfortunately, Kevin's midwestern experience caused him to be the architect overseeing the collapse of WNEW-FM.

He was an incredibly sweet man with a very good heart who saw past cutthroat corporate sensibilities and was genuinely concerned about people. He told me that his master plan was to put in five more years, become fully vested in his pension plan, and then retire by age fifty to play golf and dabble in whatever he chose. He'd saved his money carefully, and was looking forward to living modestly without all the corporate crap.

When I first met him, I took to him instantly. He exuded a mischievous charm and he liked the fact that I could talk sports with him, something he found rare in the realm of FM jocks. He'd take me out to breakfast after the show and say, "I want to bond with my morning guy." We got along very well, even after our business interests failed to coincide.

Like Karmazin, he took the tack that as general manager he knew nothing about programming. But all the while, he believed that he knew more about the big picture than those he appointed to lead. He was under a mandate from Group W to fix the morning show, even though our ratings were solid and revenue was constantly improving. Ken Dashow and I were meeting on a weekly basis with Utz, our sessions usually lasting two or more hours. We'd review tapes of bits we'd done, and Ted was encouraging and supportive, with occasional nudges toward adjusting this or that. In all, we were pleased about what we were doing—enjoying working together along with our sports guy, Bob Papa. But we were severely limited in what we were allowed to do, and that wound up killing our chances for greater numbers.

Our first limitation was that we were not allowed any sexual humor. We were told to stay away since Howard Stern was the master of that game and we couldn't win if we played on his field. We didn't envision spanking naked lesbians on our show, but tying our hands in this area eliminated a huge wealth of material. We talked sports but were told to keep it brief, since if we went too far, we'd alienate our female listeners. Besides, sports were for young males, and Howard had them locked up anyway. Most of our talk had to center on music.

This is typical of narrow-minded AOR thinking. Focus groups tell you that people listening to AOR radio are mainly doing so to hear music.

Duh! But by the nineties, how many AOR artists were doing things that anyone cared about? Was it compelling to hear that Van Halen was in the studio working on some new tracks, or that Mick Jagger might be doing a solo project next year? The music culture on that level was dead—only the new music scene in Seattle had any real excitement going for it, and their demos skewed younger and we were advised away from it.

One of our best features was taken away from us either by cowardly corporate attorneys or a crafty Kevin Smith, blaming them for his own squeamishness. The bit was named "the wake-up call," and many morning shows across the country employ a similar gag. We'd solicit mail from listeners who wanted to play a practical joke. In their letters, they'd explain a sticky situation that a friend or loved one was in. Perhaps it was a tenant-landlord dispute. Kenny would call, disguising his voice with any of a number of accents at his command. He'd pretend to be the landlord and explain that he was painting the apartment that day and that everything would be left out on the street until he'd finished. The listener would naturally come unglued at the prospect. Ken would goad him on before finally revealing that it was a wake-up call from WNEW-FM. The calls were taped in advance, so they could be edited or excised entirely if they weren't funny. But one morning, Smith showed us a corporate memo forbidding such calls unless the prankee was informed that the call was being taped for broadcast before beginning. That obviously would ruin the joke. We pointed out that other stations were doing the same bit with impunity, and that we always asked permission to air the tape afterward, in case it might prove too embarrassing or lead to some real trouble. Plus we were careful to avoid incriminating situations like unpaid parking tickets or back taxes due the IRS. Sorry, we were instructed, the consent must be obtained prior to taping. There went our funniest routine.

So what was left? Very little. We felt like we were going up against nuclear missiles with squirt guns. I thought that Ken and I were a pleasant listen and that our music was on target, but that if we were to achieve double-digit numbers, we'd have to completely let loose and do a typically trashy morning show. Even if we did that well, it would take years to put even a dent in Stern's loyal following. And there was always the danger of losing our existing 3.8 share by chasing away listeners who enjoyed some good music, headline-style news, weather and sports, and a laugh or two.

Ted felt that if we stayed the course and sharpened our act, we'd get to a four share and make a lot of money for Group W. But Kevin Smith wanted to go for the gusto. He took Ken and me to breakfast one morning, and we listened to him describe his vision for the morning show. It directly contradicted everything Ted had been telling us. Utz joined us later and we presented him with our dilemma—Kevin wants more talk, you want the talk segments in bite-size pieces with emphasis on music. Which is it to be?

Ted started to answer and Kevin cut him off. It was clear that they weren't on the same page, and by the way Smith hustled us out of the diner, it was also clear he didn't want us listening to Utz. We were now going to have to choose loyalties and there was actually little choice. Ted was probably on the way out; Smith was the new boss and it was apparent that any program director he picked would be a puppet executing *his* game plan. If we were to survive, we'd better follow our general manager, even if he was leading us down the wrong path.

Unfortunately, what it came down to was that Kevin Smith was a proactive guy with ambitious plans for the station at a time when it needed a Ted Utz to gently guide it through its charted course. It would never be the number one station in New York with the top-rated morning show. If Group W could just accept that, WNEW would make a lot of money for them. But sucked in by the fool's gold of big numbers in other markets, they assumed that something was wrong with the station. No one seemed to understand that New York was not a predominately rock and roll town. The ethnic makeup of the area and its history all mitigated against rock being a mainstream format like it had been in places like Detroit and Philadelphia. To quote Clint Eastwood, "A man's got to know his limitations."

But the capitalist quest for more, more, more killed the goose that laid the golden egg. Ted and Kevin increasingly clashed on programming, and the final straw was a free concert we sponsored on the beach in Asbury Park, New Jersey. We'd been doing these shows for years, with artists like the Asbury Jukes, the Hooters, and Brian Setzer. Traditionally held on Memorial Day weekend, they often drew a hundred thousand people for a day of sun and rock and roll. The whole staff came down for the weekend, but Ted got there late and left early, sunning himself with his shirt off while his department heads handled the jumbled scene. Backstage at a rock show is always controlled chaos, and minor problems erupt by the minute. It was nothing we couldn't handle, but Kevin Smith seemed appalled by Ted's apparent lack of concern. Right after that weekend, he announced that Ted would be leaving the position to pursue other opportunities. Perhaps the die had already been cast, but Asbury seemed to crystallize all that separated the two men.

Although it was Utz's Waterloo, Asbury Park was one of our best promotions. Others were not so successful. At a U2 concert in the New Jersey Meadowlands, we tied in with the Virgin Atlantic Lightship to do a typical radio contest, asking listeners to make up banners with the station's call letters, the airline logo, and the band's name. The blimp would fly over the concert grounds, spot the biggest and best banners from the air, and then radio down to a ground crew who would reward the winning entries. The airship only had room for the pilot and one passenger, and Marty Martinez was selected to take the flight and judge the contest. Marty was never a big fan of flying, and in the hour prior to the trip downed a six-pack of beer and a couple of large sodas. While aloft he asked the pilot where the facilities were.

"You mean you didn't bring an engineer's cup?" the pilot asked.

"What the hell is an engineer's cup?"

The pilot explained that since the blimp had no bathroom, male fliers were told to bring along a plastic bottle in which to relieve themselves. Since Martinez had no cup and a powerful need to expel all this liquid, he asked what the alternatives were. The pilot explained that although it was frowned upon, fliers in such a dire predicament had to lean out of the cupola and do their business over the side. As Martinez unzipped his fly, the pilot bade him wait and said that because of wind currents, he would have to use the opposite side of the cab lest he drench them both with a wet surprise. As he maneuvered the blimp around, he nodded to go ahead to Martinez, who proceeded to empty his bladder of seventy-two ounces of beer and thirty-two ounces of Coke on the concertgoers below, who were anxiously looking skyward in hopes of winning the contest.

Unfortunately, this act symbolizes how the station treated its listeners in its waning years. I hate death scenes in movies and want them to be over fast. So forgive me if I spare you some of the gory details of the endgame. Pat St. John became program director. Smith had casually tossed the position my way, but taking it would mean giving up my sports-talk career and I wasn't about to do that. And even though I had been extended a two-year contract to do mornings, I knew deep down it wasn't going to work under our self-imposed handicaps. I like to think that maybe I could have changed the course the station took if I'd accepted the PD job, but who knows?

Pat's reign was a complete catastrophe. He immediately expanded our playlist to include a lot of stuff he'd liked in Detroit that simply had no history in New York. We lost our musical focus and consistency. Our morning jabbering eroded our ratings, and I was told by the end of the year that my stint in AM drive would be over soon. I accepted the inevitable and went back to emphasizing music. My last morning ratings book that spring was the highest since the Mark McEwen era. I went back to weekends, fillins, and WFAN.

My replacement was Pat "Paraquat" Kelley, an agreeable sort who'd been Cynthia Fox's hippie morning-show sidekick at KMET. He told everyone he thought he was being hired to reprise the role he'd played in Los Angeles and was shocked to discover that he was supposed to be the main host. In truth, he'd sold management a bill of goods with his considerable powers of persuasion and they never actually heard a tape of his work. What were they thinking? His musical knowledge was extremely limited and he knew nothing about New York. He did a directionless talky program and his ratings declined within two books to half of what they had been when I left. He was fired after seven months.

The overall ratings were now spinning downward at an alarming rate. Pat St. John took over the morning show, Dennis Elsas returned to full-time work in the middays, and Ted Edwards was hired to replace Pat as PD. I took a liking to Edwards initially, but he proved to be another disadvantageous choice. In July of 1995, he changed the format of the station to some kind of alternative mishmash, while retaining all the full-time jocks at Smith's behest. When the first monthly trends showed that we'd lost a third of our audience, he panicked and restored half of the classic rock library. Now we were pleasing nobody and the numbers reflected that.

After the switch, I had lunch with Edwards. He started by saying that at the meeting when the format change was announced, everyone had clapped and said "it was about time," except me. He wanted to know why.

I took a risk and decided to be honest. "Ted," I told him, "I've been here for twenty-five years. I've done mornings. I've been program director. I've done overnights. I've played every kind of music from Mozart to Nirvana. I'm not programming the station anymore, and I'm sure you're not interested in my second guesses on all the mistakes that have been made.

You've done research. You think you know the market and what's out there for us. I'll support whatever decisions you make. I just work here. I don't know if this alternative idea will work. Maybe it will. And I'll sell it on the air like a professional, and I'll do whatever it takes to make it work. But I can't be a phony about this like the rest of the staff."

"Now wait a minute," he interrupted. "The rest of the staff is genuinely enthused about this. They're going into this with great excitement and they believe it will work. They've told me so."

"Look, Ted. I like you. But I've known all these people for a long time. If you told them you were going to play Lithuanian folk songs and polka music, they'd tell you how brilliant you were. Look through their bullshit. As long as they have jobs, they'll tell you whatever you want to hear."

"I can't believe that."

"Believe what you like. But judge it by what you hear coming out of the speakers, not what they tell you to your face. And trust me, I'm not going around sowing dissension. But they all tell me privately that they have their doubts. Whatever. You've got to get performance out of them. That's all that counts."

"I expect you to be enthused. If you can't be, then I don't know if you should be on the team."

"That's your call. Like I said, on the air, I'll give you what you want. I do think a lot of this music is really good and I'll be supportive publicly, despite my misgivings."

After the lunch, I had very ambivalent feelings. I felt liberated by finally telling Edwards the unvarnished truth about what I thought. But the truth wasn't so pleasant for me to face. I basically was repeating, "What's the figure? Frank Sinatra, Frank Zappa. What's the figure?" It was a far cry from my first days at the station when I passionately believed in everything I said and played. But if I had no say in the music, how could I be expected to feel passionately about all of it? That's an impossible task, and we all were faking it now. It was a gold-lined coffin. The money was still good, and there was always the hope that someday, the right person would return to make the station work again. But I also realized that my little dialogue with Edwards could mean the end of my days at WNEW-FM. I think Kevin Smith talked him out of canning me and saved my job. Two weeks later, I was demoted to weekend overnights.

Whether the alternative format ever had a chance with the old AOR jocks will never be known. They never gave it a real chance before retreating. At around this time, WBCN was faced with the same dilemma. Oedipus was still program director, but WBCN had straddled the line between classic and alternative too long. When the alternative trend started in the early nineties, he tried to play it both ways. A competitor, WZLX, came in and instantly branded themselves as "classic rock." And ZLX's timing proved fortuitous as Michael Harrison had just sold his AM news/talk station and was available to come in and program. Another station declared themselves the alternative headquarters in Boston, and for the first time in a decade, WBCN was squeezed on both sides and started to leak oil. Ratings began to erode and Karmazin pressured Oedipus to stake out a clear direction. In his view, they'd blown their chance to grab the classic-rock mantle and needed an easily identifiable handle.

Harrison imported his old friend Alan Colmes, late of WNBC in New York, to do mornings at ZLX and Colmes's brand of quirky humor initially didn't play well in New England. Harrison was convinced that he could build the show into a major force if given time, but the owners were pressuring him to make a change. Michael had been at WZLX less than a year when he finally admitted to himself that he just couldn't work in a corporate environment. He couldn't stand the politics and backstabbing that detracted from the pursuit of his larger goals. Tired of the grind, he resigned rather than fire his friend. He had foreseen the talk-radio revolution and quickly slid back into publishing industry info with a new magazine called *Talkers*. He was finally his own boss again, but in the meantime had established WZLX as *the* classic rock station.

As it turned out, WBCN had gotten on the alternative bandwagon early enough, and had now built some credibility, not to mention a familiarity with that music. They slowly converted to what is known as "active" rock. This encompassed the few classic bands that retained fans among the younger audience (like Led Zeppelin) while concentrating on new and harder-edged alternative and metal. Gradually, they began to replace some of their more traditional jocks with younger ones who had grown up with grunge and heavy metal. In the meantime, the FCC relaxed its rules on station ownership and Infinity was able to increase their holdings. Impressed with the success of the classic-rock WZLX, Karmazin simply bought it.

Laquidara was still doing mornings on WBCN and was a legitimate fan of the new music, playing quite a bit of it on his show. Since Charles still had good ratings, Boston was the only Infinity-owned FM station in a major market that didn't feature Howard Stern in the morning. His program was tape-delayed and played at night. But this chafed at Stern's ego so Tony Berendini, the station manager, approached Laquidara with a choice. Karmazin wanted Stern on WBCN in the morning and, as they were flipping to be completely alternative anyway, would Charles consider taking his show, lock, stock, and big mattress, to WZLX? Although he'd remained young and adventurous in his musical tastes, his audience hadn't and most of them had already migrated to the classic rocker.

He was being asked to make the move voluntarily, but Laquidara knew that if he didn't accept he would be fired with his first down ratings book. He agreed to go to WZLX where he replaced George Taylor Morris, a WLIR alum, as the new/old morning man.

But unlike WBCN, WNEW now had no heritage morning show. WNEW's testing also showed that no one knew much about alternative bands in New York because they weren't played by the rock stations in the market, and only by the Top Forties when they had hits. Boston was obviously a different kettle of fish. But the vagaries of the New York market offered WNEW another chance for survival, possibly its last. The failure to seize that opportunity resulted in the long slow fade that killed it forever.

Get Back (to Where We Once Belonged)

MARK CHERNOFF LEFT K-ROCK in March of 1993 to become the program director of WFAN. A lifelong sports fan and experienced at dealing with big-time morning shows and big-time egos because of his work with Stern, Mark was brought in to handle Don Imus and Mike and the Mad Dog, the highly rated afternoon team. WFAN was the highest billing station in the country, and it was a step up from K-ROCK. Besides, Mel wanted the move and Mark was always apprehensive of contravening Karmazin's requests.

So K-ROCK now was under new programming management and, like WBCN, it found alternative music to be the panacea to keeping Howard Stern's listeners with the station after the star signed off. In January of 1996, K-ROCK fired Pete Fornatale, Dave Herman, and the rest of the staff in favor of a bunch of fresh young jocks raised on alternative music.

WNEW was handed the classic-rock franchise on a silver platter. This time I did make my feelings known directly to Kevin Smith: Junk this half alternative–half classic format and go classic all the way. Alternative people will flock to K-ROCK—they're playing it all the time with more credible jocks than we have. Classic fans are disenfranchised. Welcome them home! Buy TV time to let the world know! Classic Rock Lives at WNEW! Bring back Dave and Pete in some capacity. Seize the moment!

Instead, WNEW added a few more classic-rock cuts, which sounded ridiculous played next to Silverchair. Jocks were told not to use the term "classic," since it tested negative with the audience. Ratings did rise slightly, but not enough to significantly reverse the trend downward. We'd blown the perfect opportunity to score a solid three share, which by this point was all anyone could hope for in such a confused and fragmented market-place. Instead we wallowed at 1.3, and Ted Edwards was fired that spring. Instead of 1996 being a pathway back to glory, it was a transitional year for WNEW-FM and a lost opportunity.

After Ted Edwards was released, there was no program director for several months. Kevin Smith told all of us that he didn't want to make an-other mistake, so he was going to take his time and find the right guy. So we drifted through the late spring, half classic, half alternative until Kevin found his man: a genial, heavyset fellow named Steve Young.

Steve had been a programmer in Seattle and was well respected within the industry. For his first couple of months, he acted intelligently—he lis-tened and evaluated. The luckless Kevin Smith had finally done the right thing, but he'd done it at the wrong time. As Young patiently stayed the course while formulating his plan, he was preempted as another station, WAXQ, picked up the classic-rock banner.

By November, Young's scheme was complete—his was going to be a hybrid active-rock station, playing some new music while still rooted in the classics—in essence, what WNEW had done in its golden years. The lineup would be juggled, Muni's role downplayed, some of the younger jocks elevated. The specifics aren't important now.

The reason that the plan never saw the light of day was more of the corporate maneuvering that had bedeviled the station over the last decade. As mentioned previously, the FCC had dramatically raised the number of radio stations that could be held by one group, and Karmazin was looking to expand Infinity with more "oceanfront property." His pitch was to buy as many of the CBS/Group W stations as he could, but like the Legacy inquiries into the same group years earlier, he came away with much more than he had anticipated. Why not merge completely, Westinghouse ventured? Fine, said Karmazin, as long as I control the radio properties. Agreed, said Michael Jordan, CEO. Upon hearing the news, office pools were formed betting on when Mel would rule the entire company.

So Mel was given stock (worth some $250 million in the newly merged corporation) and control of dozens of radio stations, including the one closest to his heart—WNEW-FM, the place where he had spent several formative years. Shortly before the acquisition officially was to take place, Karmazin got word of the Young-Smith plan. He lined up a meeting with the principles, but first made a call to his informal adviser on rock radio, Mark Chernoff. Mark was actively programming WFAN and had expanded its success, but he retained his curiosity about WNEW and K-ROCK, continuing his lifelong interest in the New York rock scene. He was always available with an opinion for Karmazin if he requested one.

"Mark," Mel asked. "What would you do if you had control of WNEW-FM?"

Chernoff didn't have to think very long before responding, "Classic rock with classic jocks." He then outlined a plan that would bring back the old lineup of Herman, Fornatale, Muni, Elsas, Miller, and Jim Monaghan playing the same songs that had worked for them at K-ROCK and earlier at WNEW. He'd season the mix with special weekends, concert tapes, live studio performances—all the elements that had made the station unique. Then, as listeners began to catch on that their favorites were back, he'd widen the playlist and begin to expose new artists that fit the classic mold.

"Thanks," said Mel. "Just asking."

Armed with Chernoff's advice, he took a meeting with Smith and Young, at which they outlined their plan. Karmazin listened patiently, asking pointed questions at times, until the presentation was finished. He then challenged them both to explain why this would work and why Chernoff's ideas wouldn't, without attributing them directly to Mark.

With Karmazin, you must passionately sell any foray into uncharted territory with great conviction. Young and Smith, perhaps intimidated by the man's reputation, found themselves hedging, suggesting compromise strategies before their ideas were actually rejected. Sensing a halfhearted commitment on their part, he pressed them with tougher questions and instead of vehemently defending their position, they backed off further. If this was the best they could do, he wasn't buying into it. It is possible that his mind was made up before the meeting.

After further conversations with Chernoff, he presented them with another option—execute Mark's plan with Young at the helm. Steve responded that he hadn't accepted the programming job to be someone else's puppet with no authority to act independently. He would rather resign. Karmazin immediately accepted the resignation without argument. Young, his pride fully intact, returned to Seattle until WAXQ called him back to New York several months later. Kevin Smith, by this point, had more serious concerns.

His wife had become extremely ill, and her long-term prognosis was not good. They'd been together since college, and although he put up a brave front, the knowledge that she could be taken from him at any moment was eating him up inside. He'd put in his required time to become vested in the company's pension plan. Although he still wanted to save WNEW, his wife's comfort in what would be her final months was paramount. He had a young daughter whose care was now falling to him. He agreed to Mel's terms, to wit: Chernoff would program WNEW part-time while still handling WFAN and report directly to Mel, bypassing the traditional general manager's role. Kevin's responsibilities would be limited to his sales expertise, which was considerable.

In January of 1997, the new/old format took effect. At that point, the station's 12+ rating had sunk to a 1.1. Under Chernoff, with the new/old lineup, the number rose steadily until by the end of the year, it had increased to a 1.9, outdistancing the neophyte WAXQ during every period. But things weren't happening fast enough, and Mark was confronted with a choice: Leave WFAN to become full-time general manager for WNEW, with the freedom to hire a program director of his own choosing to carry on the format, or return to WFAN. Kevin Smith, whose wife had died a few months earlier, was taking early retirement and moving to Florida to play golf and try to make some sense of the hand he'd been dealt.

It was a hard decision, but Mark had always loved programming and didn't covet the responsibility of managing a sales and promotions staff. He pleaded to be allowed to continue in both jobs, but by this time, Mel had given up much of his supervision of the radio division to Dann Mason, a holdover from Group W. Karmazin controlled not just CBS radio but television as well, and was soon to take the helm of the entire CBS/Infinity

Corporation, eventually merging it with Viacom. He had bigger fish to fry than just one station, even though it did hold a special place in his heart. Besides, some members of the WFAN staff needed constant babysitting, and had complained to Mel that Chernoff wasn't at their beck and call. Reluctantly, Mark gave up the WNEW job to concentrate full-time on WFAN.

Scott Herman, the GM of WINS, conveniently located on the next floor of WNEW's building, was appointed general manager of WNEW and was told preemptively that his operations/program director would be Garry Wall.

I consider this man to be the most enigmatic program director that I ever worked with. For most of his twenty-one-month reign, the staff tried to figure out what he wanted for the station. We couldn't, and the conclusion we were led to was that he couldn't either. There were two alternatives:

1) He had no knowledge or appreciation for the heritage of the radio station and planned all along for it to become an extreme FM talk station. He was convinced that he could make his reputation by arising Phoenix-like from the ashes of a failed rock station with this hot new format. Any moves he made while it was a rock station were intended for purposes of self-immolation, so that by the time he switched formats, no one would care.

2) He came into the job with no agenda, willing to take it wherever the research indicated it should go. Unfortunately, his radio skills were so unformed that he lacked the ability to discover a clear path and the will to follow it.

I favor the latter alternative. It seems that after years of hiring managers who were afraid to tamper with the staff due to personal reverence of their legend, Wall was brought in to inspect the place as an alien from another planet would. Indeed, some members of the staff, perplexed by his unblinking demeanor, called him "Metal Boy." With no preconceived notions, no agenda, all he brought to the table was a willingness to try anything that struck his fancy. To say that he thought outside the box would be like saying Ted Kaczynski had some unconventional theories about democratic government. Basically, the plan was to disregard history and start fresh. Jocks were shuttled in and out like chess pieces, with no regard for their humanity or personal security.

This might work if you were a certified genius who could do things in a completely new fashion that would revolutionize the medium, but for all his apparent intelligence, Wall's radio acumen was sorely lacking. Here are two examples that illustrate the problem. At the first meeting he held with the staff, Wall was asked what the station should be called. Should it be WNEW, WNEW-FM, or NEW? Should the slogan be "Where Rock Lives," "Classic Rock and Classic Jocks," or "New York's Rock Station"?

At various times in our history, we had been known by these appellations, and more. "Whatever," he replied, "it's not important."

Given the fact that we'd all become complete sycophants just trying to keep our jobs by then, no one challenged this assertion. But you learn in Radio 101—no, make that Life 101—that what you call yourself has an enormous part in establishing your identity and image with others. Indeed, if your name is Ice T Cool J, one's expectations would not be that of a Harvard-educated member of the literati, just as John Beresford Tipton III might not fit your conception of a migrant laborer. This, of course, amounts to prejudice, but it's a fact of life.

At that initial meeting, Wall suggested that we all speak to his secretary and schedule a "getting to know you" meeting with him privately. Good idea. When not in a public setting with peers, some of the staff might open up and give more honest opinions. So I dutifully arranged a meeting. Given my experience with Edwards, I resolved to be a bit more circumspect with the new guy until I got a read on the lay of the land.

As I marched into his office, he sat at a small round table, devoid of clutter, CNBC's stock quotations silently streaming on the television behind him. The Arthurian table seemed a lot more democratic than a big imposing desk, it was more like you were an equal—instead of an underling approaching the almighty boss. Even though I knew that this was corporate window dressing, at least the fact that he embraced it was encouraging. Approaching things with an open mind, I sat down and met Wall's blank gaze.

"So," he started, "what can I do for you?"

"You suggested this meeting," I said. "You wanted to get to know us. Here I am. Do you want to know about my history here for starters?"

"Not really. Why is that relevant?" he answered coldly.

He wasn't making this easy. I perhaps foolishly thought that as senior member of the staff next to Muni in terms of years at the station, my counsel might be of some value. "Well, I just thought that since I've been here twenty-eight years, that—"

"Twenty-eight. Doesn't have the same ring as thirty, does it?"

"I guess not." I tried not to react to what seemed to be a deliberate insult. Maybe he was just trying to be funny. "At any rate, I've done mornings, I've been PD—"

"Well, gee, everyone's been PD here at one time or another, even the janitor from what I hear."

If he wanted to imply that my opinions were as valued as the janitor's, he'd gotten the message across. This was an odd way to get to know a valued employee. Strange, but I was getting another message entirely. *Okay boss, I just clean up here, what do you want me to do?*

Properly humbled, I continued. "All right, Garry. I'm just here to find out what you want us to do. What's the plan?"

"No plan. What do you want to do?"

"I've done every kind of radio there is, from classical to talk. I'm just trying to gather what approach you're looking for. High energy, lots of talk, tight with no talk, whatever?"

"Whatever you're comfortable with. It's up to you. I'll be listening and evaluating every one here from ground zero over the next month. Do whatever you like."

I laughed, perhaps a bit nervously. "Can you tell me what criteria you'll be judging us by?"

"Whatever. If I like what I hear, you'll be here. If I don't, you won't. Simple as that."

I'll try once more, this time in English. "Well, what do *you* like? What are you looking for?"

"Nothing. I'll know it when I hear it."

One more attempt at adulation to keep my job. "Whatever role you see me in, I'm willing to discuss. I'm not here to make waves or challenge you, I just want to execute your ideas the way you want me to and help the station win again."

"Good." He said this casually and dismissively, as if I'd just offered him coffee with cream or without. No acknowledgment that I was pledging unconditional loyalty to the call letters.

This seemed like as good a place as any to end this exercise in mind fuck, so I rose and solicitously said, "Well, I know that you're a busy man with a lot more important things to do. Just let me know if I can help in any way."

"Fine." He didn't arise to shake hands, which was just as well. I walked out feeling that I'd just wasted a four-dollar toll on the George Washington Bridge. Confused, I drove home, wondering at several points if I should turn around and go back and bust him in the mouth. The more I thought about it, the more I was convinced that his plan was not to get to know any of us, because we wouldn't be around long enough. Would a call to Mel be in order? Would he even care? I was calculating my severance, trying to figure if I could survive on just my earnings at WFAN. Obviously, WNEW-FM was not long for this world.

With no direction or leadership, the station pinged back and forth from classic to classic/metal to classic/alternative to alternative/classic to talk. I was doing two weekend shows, and I never knew what I'd be doing from week to week. And if *I* didn't know, what were the listeners to think? Pete Fornatale was bumped from middays to late nights, a time period he'd never done in his thirty years of professional radio. When he didn't quit at the change, he was fired and replaced with someone from a small market in New Hampshire. Dennis Elsas was summarily dismissed and replaced by another unknown in the market. Wall called my brother while he was on summer vacation and told him that he needn't hurry back; he was being replaced. We were being picked off one at a time and we all were looking around at our comrades, wondering who'd be next.

Scott Muni and Dave Herman were fired on November 13, 1998. The afternoon shock jocks that Wall had hired made fun of them both as dinosaurs who should have been extinct twenty years before. They reveled in sleaze as Dave's ex-wife joined them on the air to humiliate him with disparaging remarks about his sexual prowess. The ratings had slid back down to the 1.1 region, with the new morning show at an embarrassing .4. No one knew what they were supposed to be doing.

My last show was on September 12, 1999. I was informed of this after the fact in a telephone call from Wall a few days later. He mentioned that he'd tried to call earlier but couldn't get through. In the terse conversation, Wall alluded to the fact that he planned a big party for all the station's alums on its anniversary, October 30, but it was not to be, like so many of his other plans.

Fortunately, I had gotten wind of the change through the grapevine the previous Friday and I resolved to play whatever I wanted and say good-bye properly to the few listeners who had hung in there over the twenty-eight years I had been at the station. It was the first time since the mid-eighties that I'd had an active hand in programming my own show. It was alternately invigorating and frightening. Like riding a bike, you never forget how to do it, but I had a few close calls when I almost couldn't find a good segue until there were just a few seconds remaining on the previous track. By the end of the four hours, I felt mentally exhausted, but happy. I was able to close an unpleasant chapter of fear and loathing—what WNEW-FM had become all about in its death throes. But by closing out as I started—with total freedom—I was able to appreciate all the great times and wonderful rewards WNEW had given me for almost three decades. My eyes welled up as I listened to my final record, Springsteen's "Racing in the Streets." I closed with a brief farewell, and uttered for the first and last time, "WNEW-FM, Where Rock Lived."

Mercifully, the day after I signed off, September 13, 1999, the station became FM talk at 102.7, not even acknowledging its legendary call letters. But ironically, since I am now covering New York Giants football, my pre- and postgame shows are still heard on the station, sans call letters.

Garry Wall was fired a few weeks later, ostensibly because he had no control over his afternoon team, who had played an immature prank on the White House at a time when CBS was seeking approval of the Viacom merger. The truth is probably that they were looking for an excuse to end his disastrous regime and this latest example of his slipshod management gave them a tangible reason.

The circle was closed with a real tragedy two months later when Kevin Smith passed on. His awful luck followed him to the end. While in Florida playing golf, he'd collapsed near the end of a round. He was brought in for tests, where they discovered a massive brain tumor and an advanced case of lung cancer. They gave him six weeks to live. He was fifty-one years old, and never sick a day in his life until that point.

Photograph

THE EVENT THAT encapsulated thirty-two years of rock radio at WNEW-FM occurred in New York City on the evening of November 3, 1997. The Museum of Television and Radio, on West Fifty-second Street, held a forum, reuniting the surviving members of the staff from the early free-form days.

The museum forum took place during the Chernoff interregnum, when Mark had brought the original jocks back for one last swipe at it. We were almost a year into the venture, and the ratings had risen steadily, although not fast enough for CBS. We were working for Karmazin again, but this time with several layers of management in between. Our fervent hope was that Mel's sentimental attachment to the station and his loyalty to Chernoff would buy us the time we needed to resuscitate the old lady from the damage inflicted upon it by the prior administrations. Although we were cautiously optimistic, an air of finality hung over the evening. Celebrating our thirtieth anniversary as a rock station, we had survived continuously longer than all the rest. WNEW was on borrowed time, but it seemed that it had cheated death before, and might just wink at it again.

Two of the giants responsible for its inception were not present. Alison Steele, after a lengthy bout with cancer, died on September 27, 1995. Since leaving the station in 1979, she had worked at WPIX and WNEW-AM, and started a store called Just Cats on Manhattan's Upper East Side. Chernoff brought her back to rock radio at K-ROCK in the early nineties—the Nightbird flying again on overnights—so that she could be reinstated in her union's health-care plan. Although she was undergoing painful radiation and chemotherapy treatments, she didn't complain publicly and her listeners were shocked upon her demise to hear of how serious her illness had been. She never shared her struggles with the audience, carrying on heroically until the end.

George Duncan had left Metromedia in March of 1986. Although he could see the future of cellular technology, his true love was radio and he'd amassed enough money working for Kluge to be able to buy his own chain of small stations in Florida. On June 10, 1995, he attended a class reunion at Cornell. After a weekend of partying and reminiscing, the alums challenged the current varsity squad to a game of lacrosse, and Duncan plunged right in. At sixty-four years old, the strain was too much for his heart and he died on the field.

On the panel that night were the station's first three program directors: Nat Asch, Scott Muni, and me. Our collective terms encompassed sixteen years. At this time, the station had had three PDs in the previous sixteen months. I had my first opportunity to have an in-person meeting with Rosko, who had a profound influence on my career as a role model and as one who provided me with an opening to join the staff. He had been diagnosed with cancer five years before and appeared small and frail, but his magical voice was as vibrant as ever. Also in attendance was Jonathan Schwartz, about to see another dream broken. WQEW, the station that had picked up the baton of standards from WNEW-AM, was sold to Disney and flipped to all-children's radio, leaving Jonno temporarily out of work. Pete Fornatale and Dennis Elsas were there, along with Dave Herman, all of whom had been restored to their original shifts at 102.7 by Chernoff.

Vin Scelsa, back doing his Sunday night *Idiot's Delight* program on WNEW-FM, shared the stage with Zacherle, whose radio appearances were limited to Halloween specials on WCBS-FM.

The group swapped stories of the good old days, and then took questions from the audience. Those who were still working at the station were asked about their frustrations, dealing with a tight classic-rock format, as they nostalgically recounted a time when they could play and say whatever they wanted. Dave Herman answered directly—it was frustrating but he understood the limitations, given the soaring value of FM franchises and the fact that these highly leveraged broadcast groups needed big returns on their money. Muni replied that it hurt him not to be able to play new music, which he considered the lifeblood of any station.

Fornatale responded by reading a parable, typed onto a piece of white paper that he carefully unfolded from his breast pocket. It seems that at a board meeting, a university chancellor had been visited by an angel of the Lord, who told him that due to his meritorious service, he was being rewarded. The angel offered him a choice—he could have either infinite wisdom, great wealth, or incredible beauty. After a moment's contemplation, he chose infinite wisdom. There was a great commotion of thunder and lightning, followed by a beatific peace, during which the chancellor's head was encased in a faint halo and he sat speechless.

"Say something," cried a colleague.

After a moment's pause, he answered, "I should have taken the money."

There was general laughter and applause in the room, but some quickly stifled nervous chuckles from the panel. To a man, the parable had hit home. We had all started out in progressive radio thinking of ourselves as artists, embracing the heady freedom of creating a radio program from the tools of our imagination, limited only by our own vistas. Now, we were ruled by a benevolent dictator who had grown up listening to us. As radio goes today, it was the best that could be expected. But as we wistfully recounted the past with our exaggerated stories, the facts were clouded by foggy memories—middle age interfered for some, dotage and disease for others. But palpable was the knowledge that most of us had sold out years before. The two proud rebels onstage, Schwartz and Scelsa, had always held firm against the incursion of the money changers. But the rest of us had joylessly accepted the hands we were dealt, awaiting our next paycheck. We never had the economic freedom to be defiant, and were robbed of our spirit as a result. We rationalized that we still were well paid for jobs that required no heavy lifting. It wasn't a dishonorable fashion in which to slouch toward retirement. We dimly hung on to the hope that somehow, if we held out long enough, the circle of fools controlling our fate would spin in our favor once more.

In many ways, I think the panel got more of a kick out of the evening than the audience of three hundred or so who packed the museum's auditorium. There were some uneasy moments onstage—as Rosko sang the praises of Howard Stern, some of the others held their nose in contempt. But old feuds were put aside; even Jonathan Schwartz and Rosko embraced, and we generally comported ourselves as gentlemen. There was mild disagreement when I disputed Dave Herman's contention that the glory days were gone for good. Sadness too, as Nat Asch began the proceeding by eulogizing Duncan and Steele, our two fallen comrades. In a lighter vein, he admitted that his several attempts to oust Steele in the early days were misguided, but proudly boasted that he'd also had to fire Sally Jessy Raphael, and that he'd fire her again today.

No one had the self-destructive instinct to address the present-day troubles with radio, especially those who were still working. Rosko had learned the hard way that venting your emotions in public is not the best way to survive in a business increasingly made incestuous through consolidation. He was working at K-ROCK in the early eighties, when it was trying to be a Top Forty station, perhaps a reflection of the old WABC. They had brought back Dan Ingram and some of the other great jocks of the past. After suffering less than spectacular ratings, the station was purchased by Infinity and converted to its classic-rock incarnation. Rosko could have blended in nicely but, in a pique, he expounded on the air about what a beautiful mosaic K-ROCK had been and how a racist named Mel Karmazin had taken it away in favor of a bland, white, suburban-oriented, vanilla rock station. The outburst cost him dearly, and not only the job at K-ROCK. Years later, Rosko was the voice of CBS Sports when Infinity merged with CBS and Mel took over both companies. Rosko's contract wasn't renewed and his lucrative job vanished, causing him to sue the company (unsuccessfully, as Karmazin maintained that he had no hand in the dismissal—believable with all that he had on his plate at the time).

Scelsa challenged Schwartz on a question from the audience. A man wanted to know how Jonno viewed his eight-year foray into progressive radio, when all along he had been a lover of his father's standards, playing them on the radio exclusively over the last two decades. Schwartz replied that he quickly embraced rock music, and loved the freedom that Asch and Duncan had given him to craft his own program. "We spoke Russian and they didn't," was how he put it, meaning that the jocks had some idea of what they were doing, but management didn't.

Scelsa reminded everyone that Schwartz had said on his last show in May of 1976, "Frankly, I never liked the Doors, and it gives me great pleasure to know that I'll never have to play them again."

An upbraided Jonno retorted that there were many other groups he did like. He also confessed to having learned the music by listening to Rosko on the air, and how in the early days he stole albums from Rosko's locker to educate himself. But Bill "Rosko" Mercer maintained that if this was true, it was a case of the blind leading the blind. Most of what *he* learned was from visiting local colleges and listening to the students. In the early days, he and Duncan would travel anywhere they were invited to host similar forums—ostensibly to teach, but in reality to learn.

Ironically, one of those panels was held at Fordham, where it was organized by a young Pete Fornatale, and another at Queens College, by Dennis Elsas. He was impressed and intimidated by the intelligence of Fornatale's probing back then, and it was instrumental in Pete being hired as the station went into its youth movement. Rosko asserted that by listening and giving the audience what it wanted, WNEW struck the right chord at the right time with the young people it was trying to reach.

And here the dichotomy surfaced. When the somewhat older group of Steele, Schwartz, and Rosko learned the music, coming from backgrounds of standards and jazz, they were essentially entertainers trying to learn about their audience. The next wave of Fornatale, Elsas, and myself didn't have to be taught—we *were* the audience. PD Nat Asch saw the first group as a bunch of leaders who shaped popular taste by exposing the new music and gallantly risking failure with their bold choices. In reality, the kids were instructing the adults. The older jocks weren't leading, but following—doing informal research with their potential audience and trying to stay ahead of the curve.

The most peculiar aspect was that the adults ultimately did it better. Their intellect and grasp of larger issues enabled them to distill what they heard and filter it through their experience. They came out with a product that wasn't afraid to be diverting, while our generation was so averse to artifice that we eschewed the standard rules of entertainment and risked being tedious with our earnest approach.

We were students and fans of the music, and brought enthusiasm to the task. But we were devoid of pretense: We had no act. We were defined by the music we played. When one thinks of Rosko, it's his poetry that one remembers, and the same is true of Steele. In Schwartz's case, his story-telling rules the memory. Muni—his voice and larger-than-life persona. With Elsas, Fornatale, and me, it was our music. When we meet listeners today, they fondly remember a new artist that we turned them on to—a Bruce Springsteen or Dire Straits—that they first heard on our shows. Once the liberty to use our curious ears as an instrument was taken away, we had no act—just a modest, intelligent approach that is no longer valued in commercial radio. The early group became legends, we were supporting actors; while vital to the success, we weren't the stars.

Still, our passion for the music served us well. Although Fornatale and Elsas are working only on noncommercial radio today, they had long and illustrious careers at a world-famous station. They were steady performers who always were well liked, if rarely loved. I was fortunate enough to get into talk radio and ride that wave into the present, but my performance ca-reer at WNEW-FM had its share of ups and downs. Schwartz and Steele left with their legends intact.

It's analogous to a modern ball player, who perhaps should retire years before he does to protect his legacy. But the lure of big money and failure to find another vocation cause him to hang on. The new audience sees him only as a washed-up .220 hitter who can never deliver the big blow, never having seen him in his early glory days. When Steele left progressive radio in 1979, she vanished from her rock audience for twelve years before resurfacing in the relative obscurity of K-ROCK's overnight. Even then, her shows could still be viewed as a time capsule, since Chernoff gave her the freedom to program half of her selections. Schwartz became the ulti-mate authority on Sinatra, and his exploits in that field were unheard by most in the rock generation. As the baby boomers aged, however, many of them came to respect the quality of that music and appreciated Jonno's en-cyclopedic knowledge and peerless presentation.

A *New York Times* piece on WNEW-FM written in 1970 but never pub-lished was shown to Fornatale in manuscript form. The author described Muni as the station's heart; Rosko, its soul. Schwartz represented its intellect. Zacherle, eccentricity. Alison Steele was its femininity, and Fornatale, youth. Whereas the others still have the same perceived identity, Pete's has faded away to the inevitable aging process.

But what became of those true pioneers—those who blazed trails in Top Forty or paved the way for the progressive revolution, the main characters in our story? The following is reported in July 2001.

RICK SKLAR MET a tragic end. A devoted runner, he tore an Achilles tendon while jogging. Minor surgery was performed to repair the injury, but Sklar had an adverse reaction to the anesthetic and died on the operating table.

Along with Don Imus and Wolfman Jack, WNBC had an impressive lineup of disc jockeys but always struggled to keep up with WABC. Shares for both stations continued to wilt in the face of FM's challenge, and by May of 1982, it became clear to the entire industry that FM was the place to hear music, and WABC closed down as the preeminent Top Forty station of its time, flipping to a news-talk format. WNBC hung on a little longer, but was sold off by the network in 1988 and was converted to all-sports WFAN.

Even in its current talk incarnation, WABC will still do special weekends as a tribute to the golden days it once enjoyed. Both WNEW-FM and WCBS-FM, who at times could lay claim as its successor, have produced programs honoring the great station. A website devoted to MusicRadio 77, created and managed by Allan Sniffen, has thrived for years, and was an invaluable aid in telling their story.

Radio life goes on for the rest: Bruce Morrow bought and managed several stations of his own before selling at a nice profit. His partner was Legacy's Bob Sillerman. Morrow and Dan Ingram still dabble on weekends at WCBS-FM, the hugely successful oldies station in New York. Muni now hosts a taped one-hour program on WAXQ, and it has that station's highest ratings. He enjoys limited freedom to play what he likes. But it's all for image—they don't want him to do full-time work. Tom Tracy married a respected female judge and lives in South Carolina.

Vin Scelsa still plays whatever he wants, on the noncommercial college station WFUV. Still a stubborn nonconformist, he insists that his contracts state unequivocally that he have total artistic control of his program. As long as management signs off on it, he will remain an oasis of freedom and creativity in a tightly formatted world. He'll never make it a full-time living, as he once briefly did, but with his other resources he doesn't have to. Fornatale and Elsas are also at WFUV (and Dennis has an active voice-over career, like his late hero Bobaloo). Meg Griffin works for Sirius satellite radio, while Dave Logan and Lee Abrams are at rival XM.

Schwartz is heard weekends on WNYC-FM in New York and on XM satellite radio. Although you won't hear much rock on his watch, he still is able to play the great music of past generations and is not ruled by a program director. His writing has given him the economic freedom to be his unique self—he is loved by many.

Zacherle is retired, doing occasional ghoul shows when called upon. He's had a rich, full life, and his tastes remain simple. Living in a rent-controlled apartment, he probably still owns his old VW convertible.

Michael Harrison produced a comprehensive radio special, *The Official History of Rock and Roll*, before he began publishing *Talkers*, his trade magazine serving the talk-radio industry. His influence on the spoken media echoes his pioneering efforts in the early days of AOR. L. David Moorehead died at the age of sixty-two in July 1996, and Howard Bloom had a heart attack and passed on in November 1993. Pat "Paraquat" Kelley sells real estate in California.

Tony Pigg is the announcer for *Live with Regis*. Dave Herman is now program director for eYada, a computer-based talk format on the Internet, bankrolled by the founder of DIR, Bob Meyrowitz. Dave says he now has a better understanding of what I went through in attempting to bring structure to the chaos at WNEW-FM. Marty Martinez works with him there.

Tom Donahue died in 1975; his widow, Raechel, produces documentaries for PBS. Sam Bellamy is a paralegal in Southern California. Charles Laquidara retired after doing mornings at WZLX and currently lives in Hawaii. Maxanne Sartori works for a record label.

Jeff Pollack consults for the Hollywood film industry and assembles soundtracks. Ted Utz was a television general manager in Santa Barbara, California, before returning to New York as an executive for SFX, the radio-station owners and concert promoters. Charlie Kendall went on to do programming in Florida and South Carolina, bought stations in Mississippi, including the one he started on at age fourteen, and was the macho voice of over sixty AOR stations. He hosted the syndicated *Metal Shop* for years. He is a pioneer in computer-based radio and his interests in new media expand daily. He's been sober since 1993, and now is the nicest guy in the world. My brother Dan-o works with him at Click Radio. Jim Monaghan does part-time at WDHA.

Mark Chernoff is still at WFAN, dealing with Don Imus and Mike and the Mad Dog on a daily basis. He still listens extensively to music radio and has his finger on its dying pulse. Mike Kakoyiannis recently sold his interests in a group of country stations. John Reiger sold WLIR after clearing his debt and now lives comfortably on the eastern end of Long Island. Ted Webb works in public service in Nassau County.

Mel Karmazin is arguably the most powerful man in broadcasting. We all speculate that he bankrolled the forum at the museum as a final tribute, knowing that the end was near and that he could no longer justify the continuance of WNEW as a rock station, despite his nostalgic feelings toward it. We may never know. There's a very good chance that if this story has interested you, you are working for him in some manner, however indirect.

In August of 2000, Bill "Rosko" Mercer finally succumbed to the cancer he had bravely battled for so many years. In an obituary, one of his colleagues recalled Rosko telling him that as a boy, he had read an article by Albert Einstein and actually called the great man to discuss it. The world would be a much richer place if a transcription of that conversation existed. I often think of him and draw inspiration from his work.

With the coming of satellite radio, featuring hundreds of new frequencies and specialized formats with limited or no commercial loads, free form may yet again arise from the ashes to fly higher than it has ever flown before. And the prospect heartens all my colleagues from the golden days of FM, hoping for one last shot at glory, dreaming that they might have a hand in introducing their almost forgotten art form to a new generation.

But whatever any of us do for the rest of our lives, we will always hold a special place in our soul for 102.7 WNEW-FM, the one station that broke all the rules and got away with it longer than anyone else. May it rest in peace, love, and understanding.

INDEX

ABOUT THE AUTHOR

RICHARD NEER started in radio while attending Adelphi University and pioneered progressive radio on Long Island after graduation. In 1971, he joined the staff of WNEW-FM and worked there as a disc jockey and programmer for over twenty-eight years. In 1986, he became a sports talk-show host at WNEW-AM. He moved to WFAN in July of 1988, where he is currently a weekend personality and pre- and postgame host for New York Giants football. He is the sports editor for *Talkers* magazine and appears regularly on various syndicated radio and television shows. He lives in New Jersey with his wife, Vicky, and their willful golden retriever, Lindsay.